Debating God's Existence

Believers and Skeptics in Friendly Conversation

Edited by

ANDREW DRINKARD

William B. Eerdmans Publishing Company
Grand Rapids, Michigan

Wm. B. Eerdmans Publishing Co.
2006 44th Street SE, Grand Rapids, MI 49508
www.eerdmans.com

Published 2026
Printed in the United States of America

32 31 30 29 28 27 26 1 2 3 4 5 6 7

ISBN 978-0-8028-8558-6

Library of Congress Cataloging-in-Publication Data

Names: Drinkard, Andrew, 1986– editor
Title: Debating God's existence : believers and skeptics in friendly conversation / Andrew Drinkard, ed.
Description: Grand Rapids, Michigan : William B. Eerdmans Publishing Company, [2026] | Includes bibliographical references and index. | Summary: "In this edited volume of essays, theists and nontheists engage in constructive conversation about the existence of God"—Provided by publisher.
Identifiers: LCCN 2025032999 | ISBN 9780802885586 paperback | ISBN 9781467470179 epub
Subjects: LCSH: Theism | Atheism | God—Proof
Classification: LCC BD555 .D63 2026
LC record available at https://lccn.loc.gov/2025032999

Quotations of Scripture marked ESV are from the English Standard Version. Quotations of Scripture marked HCSB are from the Holman Christian Standard Bible. Quotations of Scripture marked KJV are from the King James Version. Quotations of Scripture marked NASB are from the New American Standard Bible. Quotations of Scripture marked NIV are from the New International Version. Quotations of Scripture marked NKJV are from the New King James Version. Quotations of Scripture marked NRSV are from the New Revised Standard Version.

Contents

Foreword

The Road to Theism

Paul Copan

In the Anglo-American world in the 1950s, God-talk was considered gibberish by many academics and philosophers in particular. There was no significant theistic representation in the guild of philosophy. It seemed that theistic philosophers were the outliers. There was some movement in Oxford with C. S. Lewis's establishment of the Socratic Club in 1941, which he presided over until 1954. In 1948 Christian philosophers at Oxford (the "Metaphysicals") had begun to meet. In 1957 Basil Mitchell of Oriel College wrote an important edited book, *Faith and Logic*, that offered pushback on academic assaults against belief in God. Tucked into this time period was the 1947 BBC debate between Christian philosopher Frederick Copleston and atheist philosopher Bertrand Russell.

In 1967 the *Encyclopedia of Philosophy* was published. Atheist philosopher Paul Edwards was the editor, and he sought to revive the vision of the French Enlightenment *philosophes*—primarily articulated in the anti-religious vision of Denis Diderot and Jean le Rond d'Alembert's *Encyclopédie ou dictionnaire raisonné des sciences, des arts et des métiers*. Edwards's atheistic "ideological commitment" drove this twentieth-century project.[1] Yet, that same year, the Christian philosopher Alvin Plantinga's *God and Other Minds: A Study of the Rational Justification of Belief in God* appeared. Among other things, it offered a bold salvo against the prevailing logical positivism of that era, exposing it as self-referentially self-refuting and incoherent. In the next decade, he—along with William Alston, Robert Adams, Nicholas Wolterstorff, and other Christian philosophers—founded the Society of Christian Philosophers, and its journal *Faith and Philosophy* would be launched in 1984. The influence of

1. Paul Edwards, introduction to *Encyclopedia of Philosophy*, ed. Paul Edwards (Macmillan, 1967), 1:xi.

Christian philosophy was growing. This is evidenced by two new encyclopedia projects that rose to prominence in the next decade: the online *Stanford Encyclopedia of Philosophy* (1995) and the *Routledge Encyclopedia of Philosophy* edited by Edward Craig (1998). Both encyclopedias were noticeably more sympathetic to theism, and many contributors were Christians.

Between these two projects, a supplement to Paul Edwards's *Encyclopedia* appeared in 1996. This volume was not edited by Edwards himself, and he was dismayed by its more theistic and "religious" turn—evidence of a shifting of the tide. Edwards claimed that this supplementary volume "did not meet the standards of the original work and should not be considered an authoritative addition to the *Encyclopedia*."[2]

In 1997, on the fiftieth anniversary of the Copleston-Russell debate, Christian philosopher William Lane Craig debated the world's leading atheist philosopher at that time, Antony Flew.[3] The organizer of the debate, which was held in Madison, Wisconsin, was Stan Wallace, a fellow doctoral student at Marquette University. He shared with me follow-up correspondence between himself and Antony Flew, who wrote Stan to inform him of his growing realization that the case for God from science was persuasive to him, namely, the beginning of the universe, the fine-tuning of the universe, the emergence of first-life, and the complexity of biological life. He would later write about this once he officially became a believer in God.[4]

The following year, another professional Christian philosophical society emerged—the Evangelical Philosophical Society—with its journal *Philosophia Christi*, the first issue of which was published in 1999. William Lane Craig stepped into the presidency, and I was nominated vice president. The philosophical landscape continued to shift. The late atheist philosopher Quentin Smith (Western Michigan University) lamented in 2001 that naturalistic philosophy was now being thoroughly challenged. For Smith,

> the secularization of mainstream academia began to quickly unravel upon the publication of Plantinga's influential book on realist theism, *God and*

2. Paul Edwards, "Statement by Paul Edwards Concerning the Supplementary Volume of the Encyclopedia of Philosophy," *Inquiry* 41, no. 1 (1998): 123–24, https://doi.org/10.1080/002017498321968.

3. See Stan Wallace, ed., *Does God Exist? The Craig-Flew Debate* (Routledge, 2003).

4. Antony Flew and Roy Abraham Varghese, *There Is a God: How the World's Most Notorious Atheist Changed His Mind* (HarperOne, 2008). See also Gary Habermas and Antony Flew, "My Pilgrimage from Atheism to Theism," *Philosophia Christi* 6, no. 2 (2004): 197–211, https://doi.org/10.5840/pc20046224.

> *Other Minds*, in 1967. It became apparent to the philosophical profession that this book displayed that realist theists were not outmatched by naturalists in terms of the most valued standards of analytic philosophy: conceptual precision, rigor of argumentation, technical erudition, and an in-depth defense of an original world-view. This book, followed seven years later by Plantinga's even more impressive book, *The Nature of Necessity*, made it manifest that a realist theist was writing at the highest qualitative level of analytic philosophy, on the same playing field as Carnap, Russell, Moore, Grünbaum, and other naturalists. Realist theists, who hitherto had segregated their academic lives from their private lives, increasingly came to believe (and came to be increasingly accepted or respected for believing) that arguing for realist theism in scholarly publications could no longer be justifiably regarded as engaging in an "academically unrespectable" scholarly pursuit.
>
> Naturalists passively watched as realist versions of theism . . . began to sweep through the philosophical community, until today perhaps one-quarter or one-third of philosophy professors are theists, with most being orthodox Christians. . . . In philosophy, it became, almost overnight, academically respectable to argue for theism, making philosophy a favored field of entry for the most intelligent and talented theists entering academia today. . . . God is not "dead" in academia; he returned to life in the late 1960s and is now alive and well in his last academic stronghold, philosophy departments.[5]

Smith also noted how respected mainstream academic publishers were continuing to produce distinguished works that were thoroughly theistic and often distinctively Christian in orientation.

To illustrate, I offer some perspective from my own experience. In April 2000, fellow Christian philosophers William Lane Craig, Douglas Geivett, and I spoke in various cities in Sweden. We met with pastors and Christian academics, who told us that it was virtually impossible to do a doctoral dissertation on theism or arguments for God's existence. When I returned to Sweden in 2014, I met again with church leaders and academics, who told me that it was now quite acceptable in Sweden to do a dissertation on some aspect of theism or natural theology. The influence of theistic philosophy, alongside the philosophy of religion in general, was spreading.

5. Quentin Smith, "The Metaphilosophy of Naturalism," *Philo* 4, no. 2 (2001): 195–215, https://doi.org/10.5840/philo20014216. Note: the one-quarter to one-third is an overstatement, but this captures the surge of theistic input.

In October 2002, William Lane Craig, David K. Clark (another Christian philosopher), and I were in Moscow. While visiting there, we gave lectures at various universities. I spoke at, among other places, Moscow State University. Before my talk there, I was told about, and while on site would strongly feel, the lingering Communistic atheistic ideology still hanging heavily in the air. The professor in whose class I spoke was quite antagonistic to belief in God, and this seemed to be the standard post-Communism attitude in the academy. Fast forward to 2024. Moscow philosopher Evgeniy Loginov invited me to participate in the book project *The Existence of God? Contemporary Positions and Approaches* (officially published in Russian in early 2025).[6]

On January 6, 2025, Evgeniy sent me an email. He mentioned that from 2016 to 2024, he and his colleagues at the Moscow Center for Consciousness Studies conducted a large-scale survey of philosophers to explore their views on proofs of God's existence, which culminated in his book project. The survey results indicated that the "Russian philosophical community was found to be significantly more theistic than its English-speaking counterpart"—46 percent in 2015 and 44.7 percent in 2024. Sixty percent of their correspondents considered arguments for and against God's existence as rational arguments. Ninety percent of analytic philosophers surveyed denied "that Kant's critique of theoretical proofs of God's existence destroyed rational theology." Interestingly, the ontological argument "was the most popular argument for theism in our survey."

The philosophical landscape has significantly changed, even though naturalism remains the dominant worldview in the academy today.

God, Debate, and Collegiality

When I was living in upstate New York in the early 1990s, I was organizing a series of debates for William Lane Craig. I contacted Paul Edwards, whom I mentioned above, to see if he would be willing to debate Craig. Edwards, who had recently retired from his teaching position at Brooklyn College, declined the invitation because of health concerns, but he expressed great respect for Craig's work on the Kalām cosmological argument, and he invited Craig and me to visit him in his Manhattan apartment, which we did in October 1993. We had a very cordial conversation over a glass of wine. Edwards shared openly

6. The Russian title is *Существование Бога? Современные позиции и подходы*, ed. Evgeniy Loginov (Umozrenie, 2025). Available at https://umozrenie.com/?product=existence-of-god.

how atheism was liberating for him. And he confessed that whenever he felt shackled by the weight of theistic arguments, he would reread Bertrand Russell's *Why I Am Not a Christian* to free him up, though, oddly, Russell's essay is widely agreed to be fairly sophomoric, as Craig pointed out. Even so, the night was filled with good cheer and graciousness and engaging discussion.

I also mentioned atheist philosopher Quentin Smith earlier. In 2007 fellow Christian philosopher Chad Meister and I coedited a book entitled *Philosophy of Religion: Classic and Contemporary Issues*. We invited Smith to write an essay for the book, which he gladly did. He was so cordial and easy to work with, and he even wrote to our Wiley-Blackwell project editor Jeff Dean, telling him that he considered the final product to be "fabulous" and he "thanked [his] lucky stars" that two trained philosophers (Chad and I) copyedited his chapter rather than in-house copyeditors. He was so pleased that the entire editing process went so smoothly.[7]

One of the privileges of editing books has been the opportunity to work with philosophers whose beliefs cross the spectrum of religious beliefs, ranging from pluralist John Hick and rabbi Jacob Neusner to Hindu Arvind Sharma and religious naturalist Donald Crosby. And though I am a theist, I've been grateful for friendly and collegial engagement with philosophers who have denied belief in God—Michael Ruse, Bede Rundle, Kai Nielsen, Richard Gale, Graham Oppy, and (as mentioned) Quentin Smith.[8]

So it is in this warm spirit of engagement and friendship that I have enthusiastically agreed to write a foreword to this book. The remarkable ascendancy of philosophical defenses of belief in God and the more level playing field with naturalists and other secularists, as Quentin Smith noted, is certainly illustrated within this present book.

The Debate Before Us

I first heard of Dan Barker in the 1990s. I became acquainted with his 1992 book *Losing Faith in Faith*, which tells the story of his deconversion after having been a pastor and songwriter. I have since read interviews with Dan and seen some of his debates (I didn't realize till recently that he has engaged in 140 debates with theists—an impressive achievement!). By his own admission, he is not a professional philosopher or scientist, and I do have questions about

7. Jeff Dean, email message to author, May 20, 2008.

8. See Chad V. Meister and Paul Copan, eds., *The Routledge Companion to Philosophy of Religion*, 2nd ed. (Routledge, 2012).

what he accepts or rejects as evidence for belief in God or the Christian faith.[9] But Dan is certainly eloquent, tenacious, and dogged in challenging belief in God. And I appreciate what he expresses in this present volume: "I think the most important thing we can do is listen to each other. If we are not learning, we are not growing. The trick is to balance confidence with humility. I am pretty sure of myself, but if I am wrong, I need to know it."

I have appreciated Adam Lloyd Johnson's work on God and morality—an area in which I have done a good deal of work. For example, his 2020 edited book *A Debate on God and Morality: What Is the Best Account of Objective Moral Values and Duties?* engages with leading philosophers such as William Lane Craig, J. P. Moreland, and Erik Wielenberg. His more recent 2023 work *Divine Love Theory: How the Trinity Is the Source and Foundation of Morality* presses to the point of a robustly personalized source of objective morality, namely, the tripersonal, loving God of the Christian faith. I am heartened that Dan Barker could engage with a worthy representative of theism.

Finally, I am grateful for Andrew Drinkard's invitation to contribute a foreword to this book. Andrew has been my master's student in the Philosophy of Religion program at Palm Beach Atlantic University. He has a keen philosophical mind, a good heart, and a gracious spirit. It is fitting that he would be editor of a book such as this. Even so, for Andrew to have enlisted such a stellar lineup of contributors to comment on the debate and make their own particular case for or against God (or somewhere in between) is quite a remarkable feat.

I am pleased to endorse robust debate and the cordial dialogue that pervade the chapters of this book. Though the viewpoints presented here stand in strong opposition to one another—though others offer more nuanced positions—this book serves as a model for mutual respect and principled engagement.

Paul Copan
Pledger Family Chair of Philosophy and Ethics
Palm Beach Atlantic University
Ides of March, 2025

9. See Justin W. Bass's commentary on his 2015 debate with Dan Barker, "Fact Checking Dan Barker: From Our Recent Debate June 6, 2015," Daniel B. Wallace (Blog), posted on August 1, 2015, https://tinyurl.com/32z72c8n.

1

Disagreeing Well

An Introduction to the Big Questions

Dolores G. Morris

There are an awful lot of books about the existence of God. It would be reasonable to ask whether the world really needs another one. I would not be writing this chapter were I not inclined to answer that question in the affirmative. I believe that this book is important, that it is uniquely valuable. To that end, I set two overarching goals for this chapter. I aim to show the reader *why* she ought to read this book, and *how* best to approach the material. I am convinced that this collection of essays is timely, insightful, and important. Like all philosophical essays, it should be read with care and charity. The careful reader will find much of worth here—even while she also finds, almost certainly, much with which she will disagree.

Origins and Aims

The idea for this collection arose out of a debate held in Orlando, Florida in 2022. There, at a conference hosted by the Florida Humanist Association, Dan Barker and Adam Lloyd Johnson met to debate the question: Does God exist? Dan Barker is a former pastor, now an atheist, who serves as copresident of the Freedom from Religion Foundation. Adam Lloyd Johnson is a Christian theologian who is the founder and president of Convincing Proof. The philosophical and theological disagreements between the two are extensive. It may surprise readers to learn that the tenor between them was largely one of kindness and respect. Dan praised Adam as "a great guy. He's articulate, he's intelligent, he's gentle." Adam, too, began his contributions by expressing gratitude for having found "a community where atheists and theists work together . . . listen to each other, and deal with the best arguments for and against God." Despite their disagreements, each came prepared to debate the issues rather than attack the character, integrity, or intelligence of the other. As all discussions should be, this was an exercise in rigorous thinking and in charitable listening.

Notably, the debate itself was the result of a friendship founded on precisely this kind of rational discourse. Andy Searles is the pastor of an Orlando church. David Williamson is cofounder of an Orlando chapter of the Central Florida Freethought Community. Somehow, in the face of these clearly disparate biographical facts, the two became friends. More than that, they became conversation partners. Andy spoke on the benefits of their friendship in his opening comments: "There's something that happens within the relationship that puts down all the noise from the outside and allows us to understand—and I'm a better person of faith because of the challenges that David offers me." David responded by noting that the shared ground between them was the impetus for hosting the debate. He urged those in the audience to adopt the attitude central to their friendship: "With that spirit in mind . . . discovering overlapping values and learning about the common ground that we have . . . with that spirit we invite you to listen and participate today." We have, then, two pairs of people with a single trait shared among them: they disagree with each other about something they hold dear, and they do so without disparaging one another.

It is with disappointment, but without surprise, that I note that *commenters on the internet* have failed to take heed. At the time of my writing, the top comment on the YouTube video of this debate says: "It's hard to comprehend that this is still a debatable issue in 2022."[1] From there, things deteriorate. The religious training of children is equated with child abuse; atheism and skepticism are dismissed as empty bluffing. The people behind the usernames seem to be trapped in what Alan Jacobs calls *refutation mode*. As he rightly notes, "In refutation mode, there is no thinking."[2]

The dismissive tone of the comment section contrasts starkly with the epistemic humility displayed by Dan Barker, Adam Lloyd Johnson, Andy Searles, and David Williamson. On the other hand, it is exactly in accord with much of what is found on social media. There, it is altogether too common to find Christians accusing atheists of "just wanting to sin," or atheists decrying belief

1. "Debate: Does God Exist? Dan Barker vs. Adam Lloyd Johnson," posted March 25, 2022, by Convincing Proof, YouTube, 1:36:31, https://www.youtube.com/watch?v=H32WynQMkeo&t=3s. This live debate was held March 5, 2022, in Orlando, Florida, at the biennial conference of the Florida Humanist Association.

2. Alan Jacobs, *How to Think: A Guide for the Perplexed* (Profile, 2017), 18.

in a "sky daddy." If we are to believe the internet discourse, then theism is nothing more than irrational wish-fulfillment and atheism can be dismissed as amoral egoism. Neither is in very good shape from the perspective of the online critics.

This brings me to the first reason why I'm convinced this anthology is important. The chapters in this book are intended to bridge two worlds: the *academy* and the *internet*. As a result, and by design, the contributors bridge these worlds as well, albeit in different ways. Some work as professors, others as intellectually rigorous laymen with a large platform. Some—like Joshua Rasmussen and Philip Goff—work with one foot on each side of this divide, publishing both academic and popular texts while maintaining a broad online presence. Others primarily devote their efforts to one world or the other, like Joe Folley and Robin Collins. Even so, they do so in a way that remains both academically rigorous and reasonably accessible. Not all of the authors included here have a PhD in philosophy (most do). Even so, all have educated themselves on the literature relevant to their topic. They are uninterested in echo chambers; they are committed to rational dialogue.

We need more of this. We need more careful thinkers who are willing to speak to a broader, wider audience. We need more online influencers who are able to give careful and reasoned arguments for their positions. One goal of this anthology is to advance this project on both fronts—to bring good philosophical reasoning about God to a larger, more diverse audience.

Values and Virtues

In pursuit of this aim, this volume is, likewise, an attempt to foreground some central intellectual virtues. I have already remarked upon the significance and scarcity of careful and rational public dialogue about God. In truth, the problem generalizes; it is not limited to discussions about religious belief. The greater the personal significance a topic holds, the harder it is for people with strong convictions to entertain doubts, consider objections, or listen carefully to those with a contrary view. It is difficult to be invested in something without thereby becoming defensive. It is, in contrast, relatively easy to surround oneself with like-minded thinkers and to disregard—or outright dismiss—the concerns of those who believe otherwise. Those who work to overcome this tendency do so, in part, by cultivating intellectual virtues.

In *The Excellent Mind*, Nathan L. King defines intellectual virtues as "the character traits of excellent thinkers, where such thinking extends not just to our *getting* truth, knowledge, and understanding, but also to our *keeping* and *sharing* them."[3] They are, in short, the kinds of habits and behaviors that foster careful thinking. One such virtue is *epistemic humility*, which I previously attributed to the hosts and participants of the debate that culminated in this book. Epistemic humility is exactly what it sounds like: humility with respect to one's knowledge. There is, of course, much more that could be said. Untangling the virtue of humility takes work. The limits of what one can know and what it means to have knowledge—these things are far from settled. Rather than work toward a more comprehensive definition, I think this virtue, like most virtues, is best shown by exemplification.

My favorite illustration of epistemic humility comes from an interview that philosopher Michael Ruse gave with *The Guardian* in 2009. Ruse was an atheist. He was not an agnostic; he believed that God does not exist. Even so, in this interview, he freely acknowledged that he could be wrong. More significantly, he expressed discomfort with what he perceived to be an *absence* of epistemic humility and intellectual charity in the popular work of the "New Atheist" movement. In an interview entitled "Dawkins et al Bring Us into Disrepute," he explained: "I don't have faith. I really don't. Rowan Williams does as do many of my fellow philosophers like Alvin Plantinga (a Protestant) and Ernan McMullin (a Catholic). I think they are wrong; they think I am wrong. But they are not stupid or bad or whatever. If I needed advice about everyday matters, I would turn without hesitation to these men. . . . I don't think I am wrong, but the worth and integrity of so many believers makes me modest in my unbelief."[4] Ruse was not alone to lament the lack of epistemic virtue among these atheistic figures. On the contrary, so common was the charge that there is an entire chapter of a book devoted to these accusations.[5]

To be clear, my purpose here is not to pile on the New Atheists. Instead, I want to emphasize that these criticisms were often lodged *by fellow atheists*. Where online discourse tends toward tribalism, careful philosophical thinking ought to work against the instinctual pull to affirm those with whom you agree and scorn those on the other side. Ruse reveals this good habit in the passage above, casually affirming that his theistic peers are "not stupid or bad

3. Nathan L. King, *The Excellent Mind: Intellectual Virtues for Everyday Life* (Oxford University Press, 2021), 4.

4. This interview appeared in the November 2, 2009, issue. See https://tinyurl.com/w3u32c9r.

5. Ian James Kidd, "Epistemic Vices in Public Debate: The Case of 'New Atheism,'" in *New Atheism: Critical Perspectives and Contemporary Debates*, ed. Christopher R. Cotter, Philip Andrew Quadrio, and Jonathan Tuckett, Sophia Studies in Cross-Cultural Philosophy of Traditions and Cultures 21 (Springer, 2017).

or whatever." Now, *not stupid* is faint praise indeed! Taken in context, Ruse's flippant language clearly refers to the kind of extreme disdain exemplified by those who lack epistemic humility. We can, as Ruse shows, *disagree* without thereby finding each other *stupid* or *bad* or . . . whatever.

The authors of the essays in this book are like Ruse in this way. They exercise *epistemic humility*. This is not to say they do so perfectly. (Nobody ever does.) Even so, these authors see the value in tempering their certainty, at least with respect to some of what they affirm. They take care not to overstate their case; they remain open to correction, objections, and new ideas. This is not a prerequisite for philosophical disagreement, but it is, and should be, a common consequence. After all, it is absolutely a prerequisite for philosophical *dialogue*.

Anonymous internet philosophers and theologians are a lot like armchair quarterbacks. It is altogether too easy to criticize something from a distance. It is especially easy to do so when criticism is the entirety of your contribution, when you are not the least bit invested in *doing* the thing you believe is being badly done. In contrast, those who have devoted time and energy to thinking carefully about the issues involved tend not to be so prone to hubris or disdain. The authors featured in this book were chosen, in part, because they are willing to do the work that tends to yield epistemic humility.

Rational Disagreement

Humility is one aspect of careful, rational disagreement, but it is not the whole of it. A nearby, related virtue is that of intellectual *charity*. To be epistemically humble is to acknowledge the limits of one's own knowledge. When I admit that my confidence in certain firmly held beliefs may not rise to the level of certainty or grant that I cannot prove some of I what I take to be true, I am demonstrating epistemic humility. In contrast, being charitable requires me to consider *your* beliefs in a certain light. Epistemic humility and intellectual charity often go hand in hand, but they are importantly different virtues. Crudely stated, the former applies to how we think about our own beliefs, and the latter applies to how we think about the beliefs and arguments of others. Indeed, in *The Excellent Mind*, King describes the principle of charity as an "*Intellectual Golden Rule*: In intellectual activities, do to others as you would have done to you."[6]

By rejecting tribalistic impulses, striving for epistemic humility, and working to practice intellectual charity, we promote and encourage charitable

6. King, *Excellent Mind*, 241.

disagreement. Because charitable disagreement is so central to the aims of this project, it is worth unpacking. In the first place, charitable disagreement must be, most obviously, *charitable*. The authors in this text work to exemplify this virtue. They share a commitment to careful, well-reasoned dialogue. They treat each other with respect. They are willing to listen to, engage with, and even learn from one another. Consider one brief example from the opening paragraph of David Baggett's chapter on the Moral Argument. Commending the tone of the debate, Baggett writes: "There were moments when Barker's passion came through, but he seemed to direct his ire at certain views he disagreed with rather than at Johnson. Friendly discourse on vexed questions is, as Johnson said a few times, something of a lost art nowadays, so this was a refreshing exercise, and both debaters are to be commended. In the same spirit, although I will launch criticisms of views I think are misguided or arguments I think weak, none of my attacks are of those holding or advancing them." In the face of significantly contradictory positions, charity asks us to resist the urge to dismiss, minimize, or otherwise disparage our intellectual opponent. Instead, charity requires us to listen carefully, to put in a good-faith effort to understand, and to consider the strongest version of the position being proposed, not the weakest.

In the second place, and just as significantly, charitable disagreement really does involve a difference of positions. Dan Barker and Adam Lloyd Johnson disagree about the existence of God; the hosts of their debate, David and Andy, do as well. Like these men, the contributors to this volume affirm substantially disparate claims about fundamental reality. Although some of the contributors to this anthology are agnostic about the existence of God, others hold their view with confidence—whether that view be theism or atheism. Even those who remain uncertain about the existence of God may, nevertheless, hold very strong views about some particular feature of reality. As a result, they might firmly reject a conception of God that is (just as firmly) endorsed by a fellow contributor.

To state the matter plainly: it is not possible for all of the authors in this volume to be correct. If atheism is true, then no God exists; this must, of necessity, rule out the existence of the Christian God affirmed by many of the contributors. Likewise, if the God of Christianity really does exist, then the atheists are wrong. There is no mutually amenable middle ground available, no worldview that could serve as a compromise between these positions. These authors hold contradictory views about matters of great significance.

The significance of this disagreement is not merely metaphysical. The existence or nonexistence of God is, for most or all of the authors in this anthology, *personally* significant. It matters whether or not God exists. It matters for our ontology, for our conceptions of morality, and for our identity. When two people disagree about what happened to the Library of Alexandria, they can "agree to disagree" and move on. Very little hangs on what happened to the Library of Alexandria.[7] When two people disagree about the existence of God, the philosophical repercussions are likely to be extensive. It is, therefore, all the more admirable, and all the more important, that the authors of this book practice and promote charitable disagreement.

Recognizing Complexity

I have claimed that the epistemic virtues of humility and charity are more common among academic philosophers and other educated, professional practitioners than they are in most casual online discourse. There are exceptions, and my claim is not about *perfection*, but as a general rule the difference is notable. We are now in a position to ask why that might be. Why, when the professionals practice humility and charity, are the casual amateurs more likely to be overconfident and contemptuous? I think the reason is fairly straightforward, and it takes us back to the armchair quarterback: most of the things that matter turn out to be more complicated than they first appear.

The same is true with respect to theism and atheism. It is easy to discard the idea of God when you have not yet come to see how many other things have their foundation in a theistic worldview. It is easy to dismiss skepticism about God when you have not yet come to see the difficulty of reconciling theism with certain indisputable features of reality. At first glance, it may seem that affirming theism or atheism is the *end* of the process of inquiring about God. On the contrary, for the careful thinker it is only the beginning.

In a particularly illustrative passage from *Existentialism Is a Humanism* Jean-Paul Sartre called upon his atheistic peers to exert *greater consistency* in just this way: "Towards 1880, when the French professors endeavored to formulate a secular morality, they said something like this: God is a useless and costly hypothesis, so we will do without it . . . nothing will be changed if God does not exist; we shall rediscover the same norms of honesty, progress and humanity, and we shall have disposed of God as an out-of-date hypothesis

7. This is not to say that people don't have strong opinions on the matter. One of the most passionate (and entertaining) arguments I have been a party to centered upon rival explanations of the Library's demise. Even so, the disagreement, even unresolved, had no lasting impact. At the end of the day, it just *does not matter* to us. It makes no difference to who we are, what we are, or why we are here.

which will die away quietly of itself. The existentialist, on the contrary, finds it extremely embarrassing that God does not exist, for there disappears with Him all possibility of finding values in an intelligible heaven."[8] To be clear, my claim is not that Sartre was correct about the moral implications of atheism. In fact, in chapter 12 David Enoch defends the compatibility of atheism and an objective moral framework. Instead, what this passage so clearly illustrates is the necessity of thinking carefully about ontological commitments. If morality is conceived of in a way that requires the existence of God, then rejecting the existence of God will require a reconceiving of morality. Sartre's claim was not that morality required a Creator God; his point was rather that morality required *some* basis, and removing God as that basis would have philosophical consequences. Atheistic morality, he thought, would have to be something more than theistic morality minus God. There was *work* to be done.

It seems to me that we have seen a growing recognition of, and increase in attention to, these kinds of concerns over the last several decades. On the theistic side, Christianity in the West has been confronted with two trends: the "New Atheist" movement and the rise of *deconstruction*. In many ways, the two are very different. The New Atheists aimed to expose *the truth*; deconstruction, at least on some construals, encourages believers to think more broadly about what *truth* even means. More notably, the former is an endeavor aimed at atheism while the latter, often, is not. On the contrary, so prevalent is this process that Russell Moore wrote in *Christianity Today*: "I think the case could be made that all of American evangelical Christianity is deconstructing—at least in some sense of the word."[9] Whether or not Moore is correct, this much is clear: a growing number of Christians are thinking, speaking, and writing about the process of disentangling and reevaluating their beliefs about God, people, and the church.

I will not attempt to unpack the many and diverse ways of understanding deconstruction, nor will I engage with the arguments given by the New Atheists.[10] Instead, I want to note one feature held in common by the arguments of New Atheism and the push toward deconstruction: each takes as its starting point the basic claim that Christians have, of late, been insufficiently reflective about their faith. Each challenges believers to work through complex questions about what they believe, why they believe it, and what else follows from those

8. Jean-Paul Sartre, *Existentialism Is a Humanism*, trans. Carol Macomber (Yale University Press, 2007).

9. Russell Moore, "The Most Dangerous Forms of Deconstruction," *Christianity Today*, February 9, 2022, https://tinyurl.com/4tcbe4mc.

10. For that, see Dolores G. Morris, *Believing Philosophy: A Guide to Becoming a Christian Philosopher* (Zondervan Academic, 2021).

beliefs. To varying degrees, Christian responses to new atheism and to the deconstructionist movement have often been shaped by the recognition that religious belief is *more complicated* than they thought.

At the same time, a growing number of atheistic or agnostic figures have come to the same conclusion about their own position. Many have shared their experiences not as *conversion* stories but as acknowledgments of the complexity of our world.[11] There are, in their view, societal costs to rejecting theism. Some of those costs are associated with rejection of Christianity in particular. Tom Holland's *Dominion* is, perhaps, the most obvious example. With the subtitle "How the Christian Revolution Remade the World," a prospective reader might mistakenly conclude that Holland is a Christian.[12] He is not. He remains an atheist. The driving idea behind *Dominion* is not that the theological claims of Christianity are true—that God exists and that Jesus was God incarnate. Instead, his claim is that Christian theology is inextricable, or at least difficult to disentangle, from a great deal of Western culture. As Holland described it in a roundtable discussion hosted by Stanford's Hoover Institution: "I realized that essentially I, my friends, the country, the civilization I live in, is actually not really the heir of Greece or Rome at all. It's been profoundly and utterly shaped by Christianity to the degree that I would say . . . we are all of us, in a sense, goldfish swimming in Christian waters."[13] Holland is not alone. Douglas Murray and Jordan Peterson are two of the more famous (if controversial) advocates of what Murray calls "Christian atheism."

Of course, it scarcely needs stating that "Christian atheism" is not theism. In becoming convinced that Christianity has had a positive shaping effect on our culture, neither Holland nor Murray nor Peterson has come to believe that God *exists*. They are, in a sense, analogous to the Christians who *deconstruct* rather than the ones who *deconvert*. What, if anything, do these groups have in common—the converts, the deconverts, the Christian atheists, and the deconstructors? Maybe this: they came to believe that things were more complicated than they initially took them to be.

11. There are, of course, also conversion stories. In his recent book, Justin Brierley discusses this all in greater detail. See Justin Brierley, *The Surprising Rebirth of Belief in God: Why New Atheism Grew Old and Secular Thinkers Are Considering Christianity Again* (Tyndale Elevate, 2023).

12. Interestingly enough, this subtitle was used only in the US edition. The British title was *Dominion: The Making of the Western Mind.*

13. "Does God Exist? A Conversation with Tom Holland, Stephen Meyer, and Douglas Murray," posted January 10, 2023, by Hoover Institution, YouTube, 1:07:29, https://www.youtube.com/watch?v=02u54a1FL28. This interview by Peter Robinson took place October 17, 2022,

These are the features that make this book worth reading. The book is a conversation. It stems from a debate on a topic that is philosophically, personally, and societally significant. This debate, in turn, grew out of a friendship founded on careful disagreement. It is an exercise in and an example of charitable disagreement.

Go and Do Likewise

If the authors of these chapters are willing to extend intellectual charity to one another, if they make some effort to maintain epistemic humility, then readers of this book should work to do the same. Read slowly, read carefully, and read with an eye toward understanding. Resist the urge to enter *refutation mode.*[14] Instead, work to develop what Kathleen Fitzpatrick calls "generous thinking."[15] It may help to think of this, as Nathan King does, as a species of the Golden Rule: read the work of others as you would have someone read your own work. Read the arguments you oppose as you would have your opponents read the arguments you support. Put in a good-faith effort to understand what is being said, how it is being defended, and what the implications of these claims may be. Expect to find something of worth, even if you do not expect to be ultimately persuaded. Practice epistemic humility; read with intellectual charity.

This is not always as easy as it sounds. Nor is it always clear exactly what it requires. We might ask: *How* charitable? Are there limits to what epistemic humility requires? Just how *open* does the reader's mind need to be? These are difficult questions. I am inclined to believe that the intellectual virtues are, as Aristotle took them to be, best construed as a mean between extremes. Indeed, King locates *virtuous* open-mindedness somewhere between the vicious extremes of being *close-minded* and being rationally *indiscriminate.*[16] I think this is right. There are epistemic costs to closing your mind to further inquiry; there are epistemic costs as well to closing your mind to rational scrutiny. Charitable reading, then, cannot mean unreflective acceptance of all that is read. There must be more to it than that. There is virtue, too, in some degree of *steadfastness.*

14. Jacobs, *How to Think*, 18.

15. Kathleen Fitzpatrick, *Generous Thinking: A Radical Approach to Saving the University* (Johns Hopkins University Press, 2021).

16. King, *Excellent Mind*, 210.

Looking to Literature for an Analogy

As I have said, I am inclined to believe that virtue is more clearly seen through exemplification than it is through stipulation or definition. To that end, I want to close with an extended analogy that will, I hope, go some lengths toward demonstrating what the kind of reading I am advocating for looks like in practice. In 2020 Alan Jacobs published *Breaking Bread with the Dead: A Reader's Guide to a More Tranquil Mind*. In this book, Jacobs acknowledges the challenges that come with reading "old" books. Many of the "great works" of literature are also landmines of subtle (or overt) racism, xenophobia, misogyny, and all manner of what we would now consider cultural insensitivities. Even so, Jacobs maintains, *we should read them*. What better way to encounter these differences than in a format so easily controlled? As he writes, "There are many wonderful things about books, but among the most wonderful is that you can close them when you need to, when they become a little too strange, too disturbing. It's like being able to quit someone's table instantaneously but without causing trouble or offense."[17] I want to suggest that the same is true for reading challenging philosophical writing about something that matters deeply to you. Jacobs writes that "to encounter texts from the past is a relatively nonthreatening, and yet potentially enormously rewarding, way to practice encountering difference."[18] The same holds for differences that span worldviews rather than historical eras.

Not everybody agrees with Jacobs. There are those who favor a stronger stance, rejecting work from the past for failing to meet our present-day standards. Although I fall mostly on the side of Jacobs, my goal in this chapter is not to defend that position with respect to ancient texts. Instead, I am interested in the way that this view can serve as an analogy for careful philosophical reading. It is not a perfect analogy, but I believe it may be of some use. Very broadly stated, there seems to be at least some difference between (for example) encountering racist attitudes in historical literature and encountering them in contemporary writings. We might put the difference this way: in both cases the racism is *wrong*; in both cases we find it offensive. In the former case, in contrast to the latter, we can tell a better story about *how* they arrived at those wrong beliefs.

17. Alan Jacobs, *Breaking Bread with the Dead: A Reader's Guide to a More Tranquil Mind* (Penguin, 2020), 34.

18. Jacobs, *Breaking Bread*, 36.

When we "break bread with the dead," we read the words of a person whose cultural context is different from our own, sometimes to a radical extent. A wealthy white woman born on a southern plantation in 1900 is likely to have formed some racist beliefs. Should she write a novel—say, *Gone with the Wind*—we should not be surprised to find evidence of those beliefs and resultant attitudes. The sociohistorical context of the author's life gives us a framework to make sense of this offensive content. Crucially, this is not to say that this framework *justifies* those beliefs. Jacobs writes:

> Many times over the years I have read, or heard, people encouraging readers of old books to set aside their modern assumptions in order to enter into the world of the old text. I think this is bad advice. Does anyone really think that women reading Shakespeare's *The Taming of the Shrew* should "set aside" their belief that women are not here to be "tamed" by masterful men? Should we ask them to consider whether Petruchio's point of view might not be right after all? No: but what we need to do is keep all our values in play, not just some of them.[19]

This is what I want to advise for readers of this volume. When reading these chapters—and *especially* when reading the chapters whose conclusions you oppose—*keep all* of your values in play.

What does this mean? In the context of literature, Jacobs encourages us to maintain our "modern assumptions" but also to resist the temptation to ignore anything of value in an imperfect text. Here, Jacobs introduces the work of Patrocinio Schweickart. In her essay "Reading Ourselves: Toward a Feminist Theory of Reading," Schweickart asks how a feminist reader, fiercely opposed to patriarchal structures, should respond to a text that reveals itself to be deeply patriarchal. Jacobs explores the options: "You might do several things. You might set the book down before it affects you any further. Schweickart does not recommend this. You might, alternatively, become more deeply drawn into the thought-world of the book and increasingly assume its masculine point of view—Schweickart calls this being 'immasculated,' being immersed in masculinity, and she does not recommend this either. Instead, she suggests, you should look for what she calls a 'utopian moment'—a moment when something deeply and beautifully human emerges from that swamp of patriarchal ideology."[20] This is what it means to read with *all* of our values

19. Jacobs, *Breaking Bread*, 44.
20. Jacobs, *Breaking Bread*, 82.

in play. In a sense, it is to read with what Nathan King would describe as a *virtuously* open mind.

The careful reader, in this scenario, does not need to fully accept the framework being given by the author. Indeed, she can reject it as false; she can even reject it as harmful. At the same time, the *truly* careful reader will remember that good things can be found in problematic places. As Jacobs concludes, "You don't silence the part of you that sees the problems with the book, its errors, its moral malformations; neither do you silence the part of you that responds so warmly to that 'utopian moment.'"[21]

The Analogy Applied

Philosophical writing is rather unlike historical works of great literature. Even so, I submit that we have much to learn from Jacobs and from Schweickart on this matter. In unpacking the analogy, I want to articulate two main pieces of advice. First, we should read that which we find challenging. Second, we should "keep all our values in play" while doing so. This means, in part, that we should be open and even *expect* to find something of real value in works that we oppose.

In the first place, remember that Jacobs wrote that "to encounter texts from the past is a relatively nonthreatening, and yet potentially enormously rewarding, way to practice encountering difference."[22] Likewise, I say, for philosophical and religious difference. Some readers may look askance at the very idea of a philosophical argument being perceived as *threatening*. I am sympathetic to this attitude but increasingly convinced that it represents a simplistic, naive conception of actual human thinkers. We are social creatures; we are, as James K. Smith likes to say, something more than "brains on sticks."[23] At the same time, we are also capable of logical deductions and rational inference. When we encounter philosophical difference on a matter of great significance, we would be right to ask whether there might be some risk of unwanted rational consequences.

Suppose that you are reading this book as a committed atheist. It is likely that there is some story behind your atheism. Maybe you were raised to be skeptical of the religious or supernatural; maybe you were raised in a religiously devout home. In the latter case, perhaps you have suffered some

21. Jacobs, *Breaking Bread*, 82.

22. Jacobs, *Breaking Bread*, 36.

23. James K. A. Smith, *You Are What You Love: The Spiritual Power of Habit* (Baker, 2016).

significant relational consequences for your beliefs. I do not mean to say that these possibilities exhaust the range of options. Not at all. What I do mean is that your atheistic commitments are a part of a much larger framework, and that framework contains not only rational commitments but also some very human experiences. An atheistic reader who finds herself compelled by an argument for theism may perceive some degree of threat in that argument. After all, should she find herself completely persuaded and thereby *converted*, there may be social consequences in addition to the purely rational ones.

Precisely the same is true for the reader who is a committed theist. Most philosophical theists are practitioners of some particular religion. In this volume, the theistic contributors are Christians. At least many of the theistic readers are likely to be as well. For these readers, a powerful argument for atheism will have philosophical, religious, and social consequences, too—sometimes to the point of genuine disruption. Even the agnostic reader is (ordinarily) agnostic *for a reason*. An atheistic or agnostic reader who is compelled toward theism may, as a result, be further compelled to consider Christianity, Judaism, Islam, or a non-Abrahamic religion. A religiously active Christian reader who becomes convinced of atheism may, as a result, be compelled to seek an alternative source of community, ritual, or structure. In short, even a purely rational deduction about the existence of God has the potential to bring wide-ranging consequences. The person who knows this—who is, perhaps, even *wary* of this—is guilty of little more than a reasonable degree of self-awareness.

This is the first sense in which I find wisdom and guidance in the words of Jacobs. Insofar as these arguments pose some threat, however minimal, what better way to encounter that difference than through slow, careful reading? This is especially noteworthy in the age of social media. Online discourse is fast and (often) sloppy. Claims are made, but there is little time or space for a serious defense or engagement. By the time you've thought through the position under discussion, the online world is onto the next thing. This is not a process that tends toward depth. On the contrary, it favors a superficial treatment of rhetorically powerful claims. Again, there are exceptions here. Even so, the format of an article, book, or even podcast is far better suited to substantial reflection than is social media. Finally, as Jacobs notes, you can always put the book down and take a break.

The second way in which his advice applies to the reading of philosophy is this: even when we read *critically*, we ought to remain *open to insight*. A feminist reader may find truth and beauty in an otherwise offensive piece of fiction; a Christian reader may find truth and beauty in an argument for a conclusion she rejects. More than that, she may find insight *into* her own beliefs about God. Consider an example from my own life pertaining to the problem of divine hiddenness. In 2015 Erik J. Wielenberg published a paper entitled "Skeptical Theism and the Parent–Child Analogy."[24] In it, he argued that the Christian claim that God is *like a parent* ultimately undermines the evidence for the existence of the Christian God. No loving parent, Wielenberg claims, would ever allow a particular kind of harm that we find in this world: hiddenness in the midst of great suffering. Thus, Wielenberg gives an argument not merely against theism but against Christian theism in particular.

I have argued that Wielenberg's argument fails as an argument against the existence of the Christian God.[25] I have also written that it is an important and insightful argument; Christian theists would do well to read and reflect upon Wielenberg's work here.[26] Here is why: Wielenberg notes that the Christian God, if he exists, "permit[s] His children to experience apparently gratuitous suffering and abandonment when He could avoid doing so."[27] I think he is right. I think this is significant. To be clear, the claim is not that such suffering *is* gratuitous. Nor do I believe that God *actually* abandons his children. Wielenberg's claim is about the human experience, about how things *seem to us*. It isn't merely that I think Wielenberg is correct about this. I think there is more evidence than he suggests. I think the strongest evidence is to be found in the Jewish and Christian scriptures. The Abrahamic God allows his children to *feel* that they have been abandoned in the midst of suffering. The book of Psalms alone would suffice to make this point; the last words of Christ on the cross would as well.

Here is my point: as a Christian theist I have gained significant insight into my own beliefs through an atheistic philosopher's argument against the existence of the Christian God. This insight is not an endpoint but rather a beginning. Much of what I hope to work on over the next several years stems from a reconsideration of the hiddenness of God—what it tells us about divine

24. Erik Wielenberg, "The Parent–Child Analogy and the Limits of Skeptical Theism," *International Journal for Philosophy of Religion* 78, no. 3 (2015): 301–14, https://doi.org/10.1007/s11153-015-9533-2.

25. Dolores G. Morris, "Sleep Training, Day Care, and Swim Lessons: Skeptical Theism and the Parent–Child Analogy," *Faith and Philosophy* 40, no. 1 (2023): 24–42, https://doi.org/10.37977/faithphil.2023.40.1.2.

26. Morris, "Sleep Training," 24–42; Dolores G. Morris, "Toward a Theology of Tension: A Response to Dru Johnson," *Philosophia Christi* 26, no. 2 (2024): 247–65, https://doi.org/10.5840/pc202426220.

27. Wielenberg, "Parent–Child Analogy," 307.

providence, human expectations, and religious experience. Very briefly stated, I am convinced that the Christian and Jewish scriptures tell us to expect some degree of divine hiddenness. If this is so, then a Christian or Jewish philosopher ought to take that into consideration when reflecting on arguments *from* hiddenness. This requires a reconfiguration of sorts; it requires further reflection. I am glad to have read Wielenberg's work. I am better for it.

Conclusion

We have much to learn from one another. We can only do so if we take each other's work seriously. This means, in the first place, actually reading the arguments for an opposing view. It means reading them slowly, carefully, and with charity and humility. It means striving for *generous thinking* and actively resisting *refutation mode*. It means reading and then rereading, and then reading again. This does not mean reading without any prior opinions. It does not require us to set aside our deeply held convictions. If we hold them on the basis of good reasons, those reasons remain relevant even in the face of new arguments. What it does require is that we stay open to new insight—even, and perhaps especially, in places where we least expect to find it.

2

Does God Exist?

A Debate

Dan Barker and Adam Lloyd Johnson

The contents of this chapter are based on a debate between Adam Lloyd Johnson and Dan Barker that took place in March 2022 in Orlando, Florida, at the biannual Freethought Florida Conference (FREEFLO). David Williamson served as moderator. The dialogue has been edited for clarity.

Opening Remarks

ADAM LLOYD JOHNSON: I'm thankful for the opportunity to have this debate where we can provide an example of how to disagree on something very serious, but in a respectful way. It seems like this is something our culture has forgotten how to do. My aim is to engage with people I disagree with in a friendly way, not to combat them as an enemy but more to appeal to them as a friend and to truly listen. For example, I frequently interact with atheist philosopher Erik Wielenberg. Though we disagree and write against each other's positions, we respect each other, and I would say have become friends over the years. We go out to eat, speak at conferences together, and we even wrote a book together. I brought him to the University of Nebraska, where he had a public debate. He even wrote an endorsement for my book *Divine Love Theory* that went on the back cover, even though the book is mostly arguing against his atheistic moral theory.

In this debate I'm arguing for mere theism—that there is a God. So, I'm not going to be arguing for Christianity or the Bible specifically. I am only arguing that there is a Supreme Being.

First though, let me describe my journey regarding belief in God. I grew up in rural Nebraska where almost everybody seemed to believe in God, though nobody ever talked about him. When I grew up and went to university, I wondered if the most educated people there would all be atheists, and that maybe it was just us rural farmers that believed in God. Though I did have some professors who were atheists, I also had some professors who were theists. On the first day of astronomy, Dr. Gaskell, after he explained his academic credentials, told us that the most important thing he had found in his research is Jesus Christ. For philosophy, I had world-famous philosopher Robert Audi, who's well known in the field of epistemology and moral intuitionism. He's been president of the American Philosophical Association and president of the Society of Christian Philosophers.

My college experience helped me realize that there are very intellectual educated people who believe in God and many intellectual educated people who don't believe in God. I knew even in college that it's not a good reason to believe in something just because there are some smart people who also believe it, so I wanted to dive into this topic. I really wanted to understand why different people believed in God and why others didn't. At first, all I could find was material at the popular level, which is mostly on the internet today. Basically, it was garbage. Bad arguments made for God and bad arguments against God. It was mostly atheists and theists just making fun of each other, attacking character instead of arguments and not really listening to each other while making overly bold and confident claims, building strawmen, or rattling off a hundred things just to make their opponent look silly instead of dealing with their best arguments.

Thankfully though, as I continued researching and thinking about this, I eventually found a community where atheists and theists work together, listen to each other, and deal with the best arguments for and against God instead of making fun of the worst ones. I was so thankful to find a community like that, and as you might have guessed, the community I'm talking about is the field of philosophy of religion and the philosophy of religion departments at universities around the world. I wanted to be a part of this community, so I worked on my PhD in philosophy of religion and enjoyed studying the best arguments for and against the existence of God. Now I'd like to share why I believe that there is a God.

One of the things I'm fascinated by is that many different thinkers around the world throughout history have independently concluded that there is a God. Of course they use different names for their idea of a Supreme Being (Theos, El, Ahura Mazda, etc.), but their descriptions of such a being are remarkably similar. For example, many of these thinkers throughout history around the world describe this Supreme Being as spaceless, timeless, immaterial, powerful, the creator of everything, intelligent, and the source of morality.

It's not a coincidence that many thinkers came to these similar conclusions because they arrived at them through similar thought processes, that is, by observing and reflecting upon the world around them. These similar thought processes I'm talking about are three types of theistic arguments that arrive at similar conclusions about what this Supreme Being is like—first-cause arguments, design arguments, and moral arguments.

In the book *Does God Exist? A History of Answers to the Question*, W. David Beck documents how these arguments can be found around the world and throughout history by different thinkers. For example, Plato argued for a divine being "from the order of the motion of the stars, and of all things under the dominion of the mind which ordered the universe" (*Laws* 966e). He concluded there's a "best soul" who is the "maker and father of all" and the "King" who ordered the primordial chaos into the rational cosmos we observe today (893b–899c). Similarly, Aristotle argued that there's a first unmoved mover; a living, intelligent, immaterial, eternal, and supremely good being who is the source of order and the cosmos (*Physics*, book 8; *Metaphysics*, book 12).

This isn't limited to just Western thinkers either. Eastern philosophers throughout history have made similar arguments. In his book *A Handful of Flowers of Logic* (I love that title) the Hindu thinker Udayana gives eight arguments for the existence of God, four of which are first-cause arguments. More recently, Gandhi published several articles arguing for the existence of God using first-cause, design, and moral arguments. He wrote, for example, that "there is an orderliness in the Universe, there is an unalterable law. . . . That law then which governs all of life is God. Law and Lawgiver are one."[1]

Now I'll briefly provide some contemporary versions of these arguments. One resource that I often recommend that provides more of the scientific details behind these arguments is *Modern Physics and Ancient Faith* by Stephen Barr, a physics professor at the University of Delaware. The first argument I'm going to cover is a contemporary and basic version of the first-cause argument.

1. Whatever has a beginning must have a cause.
2. The universe had a beginning.
3. Therefore, the universe had a cause.

1. Mohandas Karamchand Gandhi, "God Is," *Young India* 10, no. 41 (1928): 340.

A contemporary advocate of this argument is Dr. Robert Koons, a philosophy professor at the University of Texas. His chapter in the annual *Oxford Studies in the Philosophy of Religion* will be helpful if you want to dig deeper into this argument.[2] I'm just giving the simple, bare-bones version here.

You might notice that this argument doesn't conclude with the existence of God; it just concludes that the universe had a cause. Why do people think this cause is God? Many thinkers have concluded that the best explanation for this cause is some sort of a Supreme Being through abductive reasoning, that is, an inference to the best explanation. That's how we often think through things. Something happens, and so we look for an explanation. We think through lots of possibilities of what could be the explanation or the cause, but what's the *best* explanation of it? That's the sort of abductive reasoning that I'll be using. For example, since the universe itself is space, time, and matter, those things didn't exist until the universe began. Therefore, it's reasonable to conclude that this cause, which existed prior to space, time, and matter, is spaceless, timeless, and immaterial. Also, it's reasonable to conclude that this cause is very powerful since it brought the universe into existence.

Moving on, here's a basic version of the design argument. Sometimes it's called the fine-tuning argument.

1. We've only ever seen design come from an intelligent mind.
2. The universe has evidence of design (this is that fine-tuning aspect and why it's sometimes called that).
3. Therefore, the universe was designed by an intelligent mind.

A contemporary proponent of design arguments is Francis Collins. Collins is a geneticist who earned his PhD in physical chemistry from Yale and led the project that mapped out our human genome. He was awarded the National Medal of Science and appointed Director of the National Institutes of Health by President Barack Obama. I often recommend his book *The Language of God: A Scientist Presents Evidence for Belief*.

Many atheists, including Christopher Hitchens, agree that this fine-tuning argument is the strongest argument for God. In the documentary film *Collision*, Hitchens says that "at some point, certainly, we are all asked which is the best argument you come up against from the other side. I think every one of us picks the fine-tuning one as the most intriguing. . . . That one degree . . .

2. Robert Koons, "Epistemological Foundations for the Cosmological Argument," *Oxford Studies in Philosophy of Religion* 1 (2008): 105–33.

one hair different, then nothing. . . . You have to spend time thinking about it, working on it. It's not a trivial argument. We all say that."[3] Premise 1 is based on the empirical observation that we've never seen design come from any other source except from an intelligent mind. So when we see elements of design in the universe, it's reasonable to conclude that it came from some sort of intelligent mind analogous to ours. From this argument, many have concluded that this first cause is also intelligent.

The third and final argument is the one that I specialize in: the moral argument for God. Here's a basic version.

1. There are objective moral truths independent of our minds.
2. The existence of God is the best explanation for how there could be objective moral truths.
3. Therefore, God exists.

A contemporary proponent of this argument was Robert Adams. He was a philosophy professor at Oxford, Yale, Rutgers, and UCLA. Like Plato, Adams argued that God is the best explanation of objective morality in the sense that God provides the ultimate moral standard, a moral yardstick if you will, such that we can measure the goodness of other things by comparing them to God. If they resemble God in a morally pertinent sense, then they are good.

For premise 1, consider these two beliefs of mine: "green is my favorite color" and "2 + 2 = 4." Now, what if a mad scientist put something in our drinking water or gave us pills so that we all woke up tomorrow believing that blue was our favorite color and that 2 + 2 = 5. Would my new belief that blue is my favorite color be true? It would because a belief like that is dependent on my own mind. Green used to be my favorite color, but now it's blue because of what that mad scientist did. My favorite color is a belief that's dependent on my mind. But what about the belief 2 + 2 = 5? The mad scientist also gave me a pill to think this, but would that make it true? If all of us tomorrow believed that 2 + 2 = 5, would that make it true? The answer is no. And the reason is because 2 + 2 = 4 is an objective, mathematical truth that exists in a sense beyond our minds.

Similarly, ask yourself a question about this third statement: "It's wrong to abuse women." Is that statement more like "my favorite color is green" or is it more like "2 + 2 = 4"? In other words, if somebody gave all of us a pill and

3. Darren Doane, director, *Collision* (LEVEL4, 2009). The quote from Hitchens occurs at time stamp 1:24:20.

we woke up tomorrow morning thinking that it was morally okay to abuse women, would that make it morally okay to abuse women? I would say no. I think we would agree that seems to be more like the mathematical truth—it's objectively wrong to abuse women no matter what people think. It's a truth that's independent of our minds and what we think. It's objectively true that women should not be abused. There are some moral truths that seem to be more like mathematical truths in that they're objectively true independent of our minds. More and more atheist philosophers are agreeing there are objective moral truths. Atheist philosopher David Enoch wrote that when he first defended this in 2003, "I claimed the great philosophical advantage of being in the ridiculed minority," but this view is "making an impressive comeback."[4] Stephen Finlay has also stated that he "classifies this as the now dominant view."[5]

For premise 2, I agree with atheists like Nietzsche, Sartre, Russell, and Dawkins that if there is no God then there is no objective good or evil that exists beyond what we think. Since objective moral truth is part of reality, many conclude this "first cause," that is, God, is also the best explanation for where this morality comes from. And so the moral argument concludes that there is a God.

In conclusion, thinkers throughout history have independently developed similar arguments as they observed the world and concluded that the best explanation for what we see is the existence of a supreme being.

DAN BARKER: Many people already know my story. I was a preacher; a true believing preacher. I believed in God. I preached for nineteen years, and I changed my mind. I like to say that I didn't throw out the baby with the bathwater. I threw the bathwater out and I found out there's no baby there. I was one of those preachers you would not have wanted to sit next to on a bus. I was so sure Jesus was coming soon, that the Bible is reliable, that God is real. I got the goosebumps. I got the feelings. But more than that, I had what I thought was the rock truth of the reliability of scripture. I did change my mind, and if anyone wants to know more of my story, they can read it in my book *Godless*.

4. David Enoch, *Taking Morality Seriously: A Defense of Robust Realism* (Oxford University Press, 2011), 6.

5. Stephen Finlay, "Normativity, Necessity, and Tense: A Recipe for Homebaked Normativity," in *Oxford Studies in Metaethics*, ed. Russ Shafer-Landau (Oxford University Press, 2010), 57.

From my point of view, this debate is easy because the atheist has nothing to prove. Atheism is simply the absence of theism. So I don't have to get up here and give a bunch of talking points to prove that there is no God.

The first time my wife Annie Laurie and I visited Iceland, we saw that it is really a beautiful country. Just gorgeous scenery. We were driving along this road, and there was a place where the road was going straight and then veered in a semicircle before going straight again, as if it was avoiding something. The driver told us it was in fact avoiding something; it was avoiding elves. There are people in Iceland who still believe in elves, and the government accommodated this belief by diverting the highway so that it wouldn't disturb where some people thought these elves actually lived, according to the history. I thought, well that's cute. This is local culture. I mean, it's a free country. People can believe what they want. If someone wants to believe in elves, fine. What would you call an elf believer? An Elvist?

What if one of them says, "But it's true, Dan. You have to believe in the elves"?

I would say, "Well that's fine for you. You can believe that."

And then the Elvist says, "But I have good reason for believing in these elves. I really do."

"Well, that's okay. You can have your belief. That's fine with me."

"But *you* need to believe it," the Elvist replies, "because the Ancient Elf, thousands of years ago, was killed. And then he came back to life, and if you don't believe in him, you're going to be punished."

And then I'm thinking, well, that is maybe not so cute anymore. "But that's *your* belief, right?" I might respond, "Give me some reason why. Are there really elves there where the highway bends?" What if the Elvist were then to turn to me and say with folded arms, "No. You have to prove that there are no elves."

Is that the way to argue? Who has the burden of proof? The burden of proof beyond any reasonable doubt—even Adam admits there's reasonable doubt because he's met many of the philosophers of religion who have reasonable doubt about the existence of the Great Elf—is on the theist. All I must do today is demonstrate that he, as sincere and smart as he is, has failed to make a case beyond a reasonable doubt.

Most atheists will say in general not that God has been *disproved*, but that God is *unproved*. We also say that we are open to changing our mind. I would love to know if there are really elves. I would love to know if there is really a god. That would be an amazing thing to know. So, bring it on; let's hear what you have here.

Atheism is simply the absence of theism. Although there is a subset of what one might call hard atheists who say they believe or know there's no God, most of us atheists and agnostics simply lack a belief. I think this is based on generally six lacks or absences:

1. The lack of a coherent definition
2. The lack of good evidence
3. The lack of good argument
4. The lack of agreement among believers
5. The lack of a good reply to the problem of evil
6. The lack of a need to believe

The first lack is the absence of a coherent definition of a God. Some have defined God as "A timeless, immaterial, spaceless being." What does that mean? What's the coherency? We know what a being is; a being is an agency that occupies space and time. A being can be measured. It can be weighed. We know what beings are. How can you take that word *being* and then apply it to something that's *non*being? "To be" means to exist in space and time, and yet you're defining this creature as a spaceless, timeless, space-time thing. That's not coherent.

There are a lot of other reasons why the definitions of different gods, and there are many different definitions, fall flat. We can't even debate their existence because we don't even know what we're talking about. It would be like arguing for the existence of a married bachelor. Should we have a debate for a married bachelor? No, you don't even get off the ground.

There are many mutually incompatible properties in these definitions of these gods that have been proposed, and some of them cancel each other out, especially the so-called omni-gods. A lot of these omni-words cancel each other out. The Christian God is traditionally defined as a being who is personal, omniscient, omnipotent, and omnibenevolent. Yet those characteristics cannot coexist logically. It's like the married bachelor.

My favorite one is what I call FANG: the free-will argument for the nonexistence of God. If God is a person who has free will, he's a personal being who can make choices. (Regardless of what you think about humans, we're all debating about whether humans have free will or not. Atheists, theologians, philosophers, and scientists disagree about whether we humans have free will, and we can have that debate some other time, but certainly most theists believe that God himself does have free will.) But in order to have free will, you have to have options. You have to have a period of uncertainty where you haven't chosen strawberry or vanilla yet, or chocolate. You have to have a period of uncertainty during which you can make your decision. But if God knows the future, including his own future, he has no period of uncertainty. There is no phase where he's able to exercise a decision because he knows what he is going to do in the future. If you know the future, you cannot have free will.

That doesn't mean there's not some other kind of God that could be modeled by tinkering with definitions, and theologians have tried different ways of doing that. And of course, many of these definitions are not falsifiable. What is it that would actually prove your God hypothesis to be false? We rarely hear anyone give an example of a statement, which if true, would make that original hypothesis false.

The second lack, which I think is the biggest one, is the lack of evidence. The Elvist might say, "Well yeah, I have evidence. There are stories about elves. There are songs and books and sagas about elves. Have you ever eaten a box of Lucky Charms? There's a leprechaun on the front. There are pictures of elves."

And I would say, "Well, okay, that's evidence. But is that *good* evidence?" It's more evidence of culture and myth-making; more evidence of human wishful thinking to explain the world. But think about this: if there really were *good* evidence for a God, by now someone should have won the Nobel Prize for pointing that out. Any scientist in the world would jump at that, wouldn't they? If there was solid evidence of the existence of a hitherto unknown force in the cosmos, then someone should have found it, and they haven't yet. So, that's an absence.

I'm not saying this disproves God. But it's a lack. It's an absence of God. In fact, "Exhibit 1" in this plank is this debate right now. If God exists, why are we *arguing* for him? If God exists, why are we *debating* his existence? Why are we falling back on words and abductive reasoning? If there's a God, he seems pretty puny, doesn't he? Does he need philosophers to come up with arguments for his existence? This doesn't disprove the arguments, but it does show that this being is kind of hiding himself. And if he really is going to all this trouble to hide himself, what business do you have to try to expose him? He's doing a good job of hiding himself. So this debate itself is an argument for the lack of evidence.

The third lack is an absence of good argument. During my rebuttal, I'll talk about the three major points that Adam brought up. The design argument is kind of like the guy who's so surprised about how they got all those rivers to flow right along the state borders. How did they do that? Look at that! It must have been a massive feat of engineering and public expense. Well, there needs to be a word for this. It's like when your premise is backward, when you think that the state borders came first, and the rivers came later. Vic Stenger, who wrote the book *The Fallacy of Fine Tuning*, was an astrophysicist. Stenger said, "The universe is not fine-tuned for us. We are fine-tuned for the universe."[6]

Yet, there's a fallacy that happens in the making of your premise that somehow this design is evidenced when it's a backward, kind of inside-out thinking. I think we need a new word to describe this type of argument. We have deductive logic, which is pretty powerful for formulating hypotheses that lead to solid conclusions. We have inductive logic, which despite being weaker than deductive logic, is still pretty good for generating some premises. We have what Adam called abductive logic, which really is just a fancy word for your "best guess." And that's okay. When you're trying to solve a crime, you're looking for a prime suspect. (Actually, prime suspects are people who do exist.) But I think we need another kind of word called "postductive logic."[7] It's kind of like the post hoc fallacy. You know, the rooster crows every morning, and the sun comes up—wow, powerful rooster! Of course, we all see the illogic of that. Well, Adam is making the same mistakes when he's talking about the fine-tuning argument. He's assuming a certain temporal causality here, even with the so-called formation of the big bang, by admitting that space and time came into existence at the big bang and yet saying something must have come prior. How can you describe prior to time? Time is a dimension. What is higher than height? What is wider than width? It's dimensions that we're talking about, and yet Adam seems to be talking about them as if they were things, as if time could somehow exist "outside of time," which is not a coherent concept.

There are other problems with some of these arguments. Most of them fall into what we would call "god of the gaps." We can't explain something like the appearance of fine-tuning? So then God seems to be—conveniently the God that I was raised with—the right answer to plug that gap. But we know through history that science has been plugging those gaps all along. What caused the thunder? They didn't know. It must have been some agency, some big being called Zeus or Thor or something up there. Well, now we *do* know something about electricity and about the weather. That gap is closed. It was open for a while, and people were free to plug it with their god. There are some gaps that exist in science right now. We admit it. There are many unanswered questions.

6. Victor Stenger, *The Fallacy of Fine-Tuning: Why the Universe Is Not Designed for Us* (Prometheus, 2011), 23.

7. While "postductive logic" is the term Dan used during the debate, he now uses the term "contraductive logic."

Why is the cosmological constant so razor-thin perfect in our universe right now? Why is it so close to zero? Could it have been some other number?

And then, of course, the fourth lack is the lack of agreement. Theists—people who believe in God—don't agree with each other about the nature or moral principles of this God. They argue with each other. Adam mentioned morality, and yet if you take any moral issue of the world right now that we're struggling with—whether it be gay marriage or abortion rights or the war or gun control or dozens of other important issues—you'll find good Bible-believing, church-going Christians on both sides of those issues. The Bible is not a clear moral guide.

The final absence is the lack of a need for a god. (I'll come back to the problem of evil in a moment.) Millions of good people—*tens of millions* of good people in this country and hundreds of millions of good people in the world—live happy, meaningful, productive, moral, and purposeful lives without believing in a God. We march in the same marches with believers as well. In the real world, we know how to live a moral life through the intention of avoiding harm in the real world. There are no objective moral values; that's an oxymoron. I'll talk about that later during my rebuttal.

So based on that, it is justifiable—it's not proof, but it is justifiable—not to hold a belief in a god.

Rebuttals

DAN BARKER: I would like to start with fine-tuning. Fine-tuning assumes the facts of physics, in which if there *is* fine-tuning, it's "we" who are being fine-tuned by natural selection to survive in this universe. If there *is* fine-tuning, then it's assuming the facts of an old universe. And that assumes the truth of evolution. Because that's how we got where we are through the chemical processes and through carbon and stars and all of that.

I would like to ask Adam for a better definition of a god. Not just some spaceless and timeless being. You know, in the Old Testament, God had a body. He had a face. He had hands. Moses was told not to look at his face. "Thou shalt see my back parts: but my face shall not be seen" (Exod. 33:23, KJV). But what was Moses actually looking at? While he was looking at the backside, was there something physical there? Of course, modern Christians have sort of turned God into an immaterial thing, whereas in ancient times they believed that God was an actual being. There's a book out called *God: An Anatomy* by biblical scholar Francesca Stavrakopoulou who points that out.[8] So, please give us a better definition of what this being is, not just some "best guess."

Moreover, if there's a God, why would he need to fine-tune anything? It looks like God has stumbled onto this scene where there's all this randomness, and he goes, "Oh, I'm going to have to tune this. I'm going to have to tune that. And pretty soon, I'm going to make it so that human beings, which are the most special thing in the universe, can exist." Victor Stenger, whom I talked about earlier, pointed out that, yes, it is true that if you did turn this one dial by the smallest amount, then life would not be permitted. But he showed that there's more than one dial. You could adjust this constant, but then if you adjust this other one in a corresponding way, like riding a bicycle you could stay in balance. There are many other ways that life-permitting universes could exist without being in this exact universe. It may be different from ours, and it may evolve through natural selection in a different way. Stenger didn't say there's just one numerator to the probabilities. If you take these huge numbers scientists give concerning the probability of one of these constants being off, it assumes that the numerator is just one. And so, if you're going to make an argument from abductive reasoning for the existence of something that we don't know about that you're going to propose as a prime suspect, then why can't I use the same abductive reasoning to say that this justifies the hypothesis of a multiverse? There may be ways to confirm a multiverse, but right now (without confirmation), if we can use the same reasoning, we could argue the following illustration.

You're convicted of a horrible crime. You're blindfolded. You're tied to a stake, and you're being told that you're going to be executed by one hundred expert shooters. And you hear, "Ready, aim, fire!" You hear the crack of one hundred rifles. But nothing hit you. You're still alive! Do you just say, "I guess I was lucky"? That calls out for some kind of explanation, doesn't it? Did a wind come along and deflect the bullets? Did they actually all miss at the same time? You could think of a number of "prime suspects," or a number of possibilities for what the best explanation is. "Well, maybe they all like me, and they missed on purpose." That would be one explanation that's more like a theistic explanation. But what if you took off your blindfold and looked around and you learned that there were 101 prisoners being executed that day? None of the shooters missed! You happen to be that one out of 101 standing there saying, "I'm here!" Is it luck? Well, yeah. So, if that number in the numerator is higher than the number in the denominator, when you're calculating your probabilities, then you have a near certainty.

8. Francesca Stavrakopoulou, *God: An Anatomy* (Knopf, 2022).

In fact, how do you know that the numerator is not orders of magnitude larger than that? It doesn't even have to be some weird kind of multiverse. It could just be different pockets within our own cosmos where the laws are slightly different, in which case, any observer obviously is going to exist in a universe that permits observers to exist (this is sometimes called the weak anthropic principle). That's just pretty clear. Fine-tuning would look the same in the universe with a god as it looks without a god, so it doesn't get you anywhere.

As for the moral argument, there are no objective moral values. That's an oxymoron. That's wrong because a value is a function of a brain. It's a concept. To be objective is to exist independent of a brain, so how can you have a value as a part of the brain exist outside of the brain as an objective thing? What you're doing is reifying the concept of moral values. You're turning that into a thing that somehow exists objectively. I will say, and I think most atheists will say, that although objective moral values do not exist, most of our moral values can be objectively verified, just like you can objectively verify that 2 + 2 = 4 by getting two apples and another two apples and putting them together. So, we have values that we choose not because they come from outside the universe, but because of the way in which we bump into each other in *this* natural biological world where harm often occurs. These values exist in our mind, and to say that they are objective outside of the mind is to beg the question. You're assuming some realm or transcendent entity that's above and beyond spacetime, above and beyond nature. You're assuming some distinct Platonic realm where these things exist. You quoted Plato earlier, and yet most of my atheist friends refuse to reify concepts into things. We just treat a concept as what it is—part of a functioning mind. That would be like asking, "What happens to the soul when the body dies?" Well, couldn't we also ask, "What happens to digestion when the stomach dies? Where does the digestion go? Does it live in another realm somewhere? Why is it that when I walk across the stage, my digestion follows my stomach?" The brain is also a bodily organ. It's functioning and it has things that we call values. It's a higher level. It would be more like an emergent thing (not even a property) we describe as the values that we use to get through life, and it only works in a functioning mind. If I walk across this stage, isn't it weird that my "soul" is following my cranium? What's tethering it? Obviously it's wrong to think of a soul (or a digestion, or a functioning, or a label for something that's working) as a thing that needs to be explained in some way. We explain it only when the organism is functioning.

Morality simply boils down to the intention to act with the minimal amount of harm in the real world. That's what we mean by morality. If you're going to judge religion as good or bad, what are you using to judge it with? Real-world stuff. Does it harm women? Does it encourage slavery? You're using actual physical things to measure objectively whether these values you have are worth holding onto. If they're not, then you discard these values, and they no longer exist in a real or imagined world.

I think you can boil down morality to one word, and that's the word *harm*. I know there are other philosophers who might disagree with me, as there are other ways of articulating a moral philosophy. Whatever harm is—you can probably make a list of a hundred things that you would say are harmful—it's natural. It's material. Even psychological harm is natural because it's harming a living organism. If you are acting with the intention of minimizing real harm in the real world, you are acting morally because that's what we mean by morality. I would invite you to define the word "morality" before you use the word. Is it following God's rules? Or is morality using your mind to see if there is some real-world objective basis for these conclusions that you have in your mind?

The moral principle doesn't get us anywhere in this debate.

The fine-tuning argument might give us a suspect, an imaginary suspect, but it doesn't get us anywhere. It doesn't get to the elves under the ground. It just gives you permission to consider that there might be some suspect out there who would answer your questions.

The cosmological argument, I think, begs the question, because when you use that phrase "everything that begins to exist," you're arbitrarily dividing reality into two groups: things that do begin to exist and things that don't begin to exist. Where did you get that from? Where did you get the idea that there would be things that *don't* start to exist, so that we could even make the phrase "things that *do* begin to exist"? We have no concept or knowledge of things that do not begin to exist, and if you think that's what God is, then you are importing your conclusion into your premise, which is called begging the question. The Kalām argument, for many other reasons, begs the question and compares apples and oranges. It doesn't get us any closer to any real evidence for a real God.

ADAM LLOYD JOHNSON: Let me respond to the many good issues that Dan has brought up. I agree that God of the gaps arguments are poor arguments, and we all must be careful to avoid them. It's a mistake when we have a gap in our knowledge to say that it must be God. Some theists have made that mistake, and a lot of things that people used to think were caused by God we've now learned have natural explanations. However, that doesn't mean that everything has a natural cause. It's also a mistake when we have a gap in our knowledge to say that there must be a natural cause. That would be a "natural cause of the gaps." No, what we need to do is evaluate each situation and try to figure out what's the best explanation for what we're seeing and its observable effects. That's what these arguments for God are that I described earlier. They start with things we observe or experience—the beginning of the universe, design, morality—and then through abductive reasoning conclude that God is the best explanation. Dan seems to dismiss any argument for God as a God of the gaps argument, and so I would like to hear from him an argument for God that he wouldn't consider a God of the gaps argument. In terms of fine-tuning, let me just for the sake of time recommend one resource. It's a relatively new book written by Luke Barnes, who earned his PhD from Cambridge, called *A Fortunate Universe: Life in A Finely Tuned Cosmos*. This science is very engaging; if you like science, this is great stuff to dive into.

As for the hiddenness of God, I agree at times that God feels hidden. Sometimes I wish there were more evidence for God. Obviously the more evidence the better. But I think there is a lot of good evidence for God and good reasons to believe in God, such as the arguments I presented. These arguments start with evidence, the effects we see, and then propose God is the best explanation for the cause of these things. And there might be good reasons why God doesn't give us more evidence. For example, God might know (I'm speculating here) that if he revealed himself more it wouldn't make any difference. Those who reject him with this amount of evidence might very well also reject him even if they had more evidence. I've heard Dan say on many occasions that he would reject God even if he revealed himself very obviously and directly. If that's true, then why would God give Dan more evidence?

As for immateriality, I don't see any good reason to think that immaterial things can't exist. A good case can be made that there are immaterial things that exist outside of space and time like abstract objects, mathematical truths, and the truths of logic. Many atheists, as I've noted, claim moral truths exist outside of space and time, so the idea of an immaterial being that exists outside of space and time is not incoherent. Many atheist philosophers, like John Searle, David Chalmers, and Jaegwon Kim, claim that our minds are immaterial, that is, our consciousness. They're based on our physical brains, yes, but the consciousness our brains produce is immaterial. So, when we see the effects that our immaterial human minds can generate, like the beautiful music that Dan produces and designs with his mind, I think it's an analogous step when we see that sort of design in the universe and attribute that to a designer—possibly an immaterial mind just like Dan's immaterial mind designs beautiful music. When we see this universe, beautifully fine-tuned for life, it seems reasonable to conclude that something analogous to our minds produced it, because we've never seen design come from any other source than an intelligent mind. I don't see why we should think that immaterial things can't produce physical effects. My mind is immaterial, and it produces effects in the physical world. My mind moves my body to pick something up. Dan's immaterial mind creates beautiful music. Things can be created by sheer thought, and I'm just proposing that God can create a physical universe with sheer thought like we can create music. We might not know exactly how the immaterial interacts with the physical, but I don't see why it couldn't.

Of course we don't see God directly, as Dan pointed out, but we see effects that point to God. There's a lot of things that we don't see directly, but we infer their existence by seeing their effects. For example, we don't observe historical events directly, but we infer what happened in history from the effects and the evidence that's left behind. So, if there is an immaterial being like God, we would imagine that there would be evidence, such as a contingent universe that's finely tuned for life.

I'm glad Dan brought up the idea of a multiverse; there's a lot of rich literature on the subject. It seems a bit of a stretch, in an attempt to dismiss the idea of one unobservable being who designed the universe, to propose an infinite number of unobservable universes. One intelligent, powerful being seems to be a much more plausible explanation than an infinite number of universes. First, I think there's more evidence for God than there is for a multiverse. But even if there is a multiverse, it still would require a first cause unless we're willing to accept an actual infinite regress of causes. A multiverse would still seem to require fine-tuning in that there'd be some sort of universe factory that itself would seem to require fine-tuning in order to produce fine-tuned universes. The worst problem, though, with the multiverse explanation (or multiverse objection) is that it proves too much. It's like a multiverse of the gaps argument. You can explain anything away with a multiverse objection. For example, let's say, hypothetically, that every single day the clouds formed a message all around the world in different languages that says, "Here I am, I am God, believe that I exist." Well, if that happened, with the multiverse objection we could just say that if there was an infinite number of universes, then certainly everything that could happen must happen in one of those universes, and we just happen to be in the universe where that happens. The multiverse objection is just too strong. It would dismiss any sort of potential evidence for God or anything like that, so I think the multiverse objection just accomplishes too much.

The last thing I want to touch on is this issue of morality. I hope you understand that I'm not claiming that atheists can't be moral people. They can. I'm not claiming that atheists can't know morality. No, they can know moral truth. That's not my argument at all. The argument that I'm making is more metaphysical or metaethical, if you will. That is, there are these objective moral truths like there are objective mathematical truths. But where do these truths come from? What's the best explanation of how there can be objective moral truths? There are numerous theories out there. Some of the atheists that I interact with propose Platonic ideas or brute ethical facts of the universe that are just out there in a Platonic sense. I disagree with that; I think God is the better explanation. In my book *Divine Love Theory* I argue that the Trinity is the best explanation of objective moral truth and compare that with the leading atheistic theory of objective morality.

Questions and Answers

DAVID WILLIAMSON:[9] This question is for Dan: If free will is an illusion, then how can we condemn the actions of those who do bad things?

DAN BARKER: My position is that free will is an illusion and we live in a deterministic universe. But illusions can be good things. Depth perception is an illusion, but it's very useful to help us navigate the world that we're in, even though your two eyes are merging into one three-dimensional object. I think free will is an illusion that helps us navigate the moral landscape that we're in. Of course, we morally judge the rightness or wrongness of behavior on the outcome. I'm a consequentialist; I think everyone must be consequentialist. Look at the consequences overall. If we overall are intending to end up with less harm in the real world, then regardless whether we have free will or not, our minds still make judgments, even if they are deterministic, because we're making deterministic judgments about moral actions. So, I think free will isn't even relevant to whether we can still justify our moral actions, because that's how we survive.

ADAM LLOYD JOHNSON: I'm a big believer in free will—libertarian free will. My friend Tim Stratton has a similar ministry to mine called FreeThinking Ministries, and he's taken that idea, arguing that theism is the best explanation for how we could have free will. Without free will, it would be difficult to even

9. At this point in the debate, the moderator invited audience members to ask questions.

make a case that we can trust our own beliefs. He has an argument called the Free Thinking Argument in which he argues for God from the fact that we have free will.

DW: Question for Adam: Why would you assume that God is good?

ALJ: Well, I might not make that assumption if I'm starting at ground zero. There's a sense in which none of us start at ground zero, since we're all born into a culture or family and grow up with certain ideas. But all of us come to a certain age where we reflect on those ideas we've been taught by our culture, family, or church. We start to reflect and think: Is what I've been taught actually true? That was my process, and I'm sure it was similar for many people. So part of my journey was to explore these things, thinking, "I've been taught my whole life that there is this God, but what's the evidence? What are the reasons that some educated people believe this?" And that's what took me down this path of philosophy of religion. As for knowing if God is good, I think I would make the argument that God is good in this way. First, I acknowledge morality and moral truth seem to be an integral part of this reality. I, and many atheists, try to make a case that there are objective moral truths. If there are objective moral truths, if that's part of our reality, then you must think, well, how could that be? How could there be objective moral truths that don't change even when we change our minds? If we all changed our mind and thought it was okay to rape women tomorrow, would that make rape right? No, that seems to be objective moral truth. So, when you think through what's the best explanation of that, this idea combined from other arguments for God, it makes sense that if God is the source of this universe, then he would also be the source of morality. And if something is the source of morality, then you could infer like Plato did that this being would be the Ultimate Good. God is the good and everything else is measured according to that. That's how I would work into that, drawing on a lot of the philosophy of Robert Adams and John Hare at Yale.

DB: Rape is bad because it's harmful, and harm is something we can measure. That's what we mean by good: we're avoiding that harm. And that's measurable; we can see it. We don't need an edict. And if you're talking about the God of the Bible—I know *you* are talking about mere theism—the God of the Bible is supremely immoral and harmful and ugly. He's genocidal, he's infanticidal, he's pestilential, he's angry, he's jealous. If you read the words of the Bible itself—and I know you're a Christian theist, so you tend to love that being—he actually took credit for raping women (Jer. 13:15–26). He actually said you should be happy to dash babies against the stones (Ps. 137:9). So, if we're talking about morality, let's judge it in the objective world. Look at the actions and words of that being you claim to worship, and then you tell me that that is a good God. Not because he says he is, or because you have an argument, but because of his actions and his words. I never did say that if I met God I would reject him. I said I would reject his morality. If I met God, I would have to accept it, but it doesn't mean I have to worship him. I could tell him, "You created a hell, then you go to hell. You're the one who's the criminal here." I can say that, can't I? And don't I have the freedom to make the moral judgment about the character of a being that I read about in a book? He is not a moral being, and he's not a good God—if you're talking about the Christian God. Maybe you have a different God that you worship.

DW: I appreciate the passion there, and I understand that it's hard to let arguments stand, and when you're having long form conversation versus short form conversation you can see how different that is. Dan, can nothing create something?

DB: Well, some scientists say yes, and some say no. But before that question is even a coherent question, before you can assume that the word nothing is a "thing" that would or would not have the potential to create or do something, you must define what you mean by "nothing." The word nothing means "no thing," and "no thing" is the absence of a thing. So, before you can have nothing you have to have something. You must have a thing that you negate. The whole concept of nothing and nothingness doesn't seem like a coherent thing, but we do have some scientific examples. We would say a vacuum is completely empty, and yet right now, out of emptiness, because of quantum potential there are occasional particles that come into existence. Matter and antimatter cancel each other out, but occasionally one of them escapes, maybe at the event horizon of a black hole. And voilà, in an absolutely empty vacuum sometimes something does come from nothing.

ALJ: I don't have anything on nothingness, but I would like to say one thing about the Bible. As Dan said, this debate is about the existence of God, not Christianity or the Bible. So all I'm defending is that there is a God, a Supreme Being. Now, the concerns that Dan raises might cause me to question the Bible or, more likely, whether Dan is interpreting the Bible correctly. But either way, they don't cause me to doubt God's existence. Because my belief in God is based on the arguments I presented, not the Bible.

DW: Question for Adam: If God has a plan, isn't it disrespectful to pray for him to change it?

ALJ: Well, as I said before, I'm a big believer in libertarian free will, so I think we do have free will.

DW: Can you first declare that this is not libertarianism politically, for those who don't maybe know.

ALJ: There are different versions of free will. Compatibilist free will is one version. But I would be one who affirms libertarian free will, and that has nothing to do with politics. In a nutshell, some people think of libertarian free will as just being able to choose the opposite or being able to choose otherwise. If I could choose an apple or an orange, then I have libertarian free will. A better definition of libertarian free will is that you are the cause of your choices. So if you have libertarian free will, then you're a causal agent. You are the ultimate cause of your choices. I also affirm a theological position referred to as Molinism. Molinism understands how God and human free will do not contradict. God can still be in control of the universe even though we make libertarian free will decisions. This would be part of how I would explain prayer in that God can incorporate our prayers into his plan through that process of our free choices.

I also wanted to mention something that Dan was talking about with God and free will. I don't think that omniscience and free will contradict. It's important to remember that libertarian free will isn't necessarily being able to choose otherwise; rather it's being the ultimate cause of your choices. As long as the person, or in this case God, is the ultimate source of his choices, then the choices are free, even if it was known ahead of time. Knowing something is different than causing it, just like knowing something about the past. My knowledge that Joe Biden chose to run for president doesn't cause Biden to run for president or make that decision. No, his choice to run in the past causes my knowledge of it. Similarly, God knowing something about the future, let's say that Alexandria Ocasio-Cortez will run for president someday, doesn't cause her to make that choice. It's her future choice that causes God to know that ahead of time, but her decision is still free in the sense that she is the cause of that choice. That's how I understand our free will and God's omniscience work together.

DB: Even the strictest determinists will say that we are the cause of our choices. If you need a justice system or a moral system where a criminal is on trial for committing some horrible crime, you don't go back to the big bang or to some primal mover. You go to the nexus, to the organism itself. According to your definition, a computer program is the source of the cause of the actions that it makes. So that's a totally different debate. But I just wanted to say that if God knows the future, then *his* hands are tied. He cannot do otherwise than what *he's* chosen, so according to what I think most of us would judge to be a personal being who can make decisions, that kind of being cannot make decisions. Because it's like a computer program that's already been scripted in advance.

DW: This is a question for Adam and Dan: What would change your mind?

ALJ: I do think that all of our beliefs, and this is something that I agree with Dan on, should be based on good reasons and evidence. I am not one of those folks who affirm or promote any sort of blind faith, like believing something because it works or believing something because it makes you feel good. I want to know what is true and what corresponds to reality, so I think all of our beliefs should be based on good reasons and evidence. Now, can we prove something with absolute certainty? I agree with Dan and think the answer to that is no outside maybe a few mathematical principles. All of our beliefs have an element of uncertainty in them, so we need to do the best we can based on study, research, reasons, and evidence to base our beliefs on good reasons and evidence. Bottom line: I would change my belief if I encountered what I considered to be good reasons and evidence that there is no God.

DB: God is supposedly omniscient. He knows what's going to happen tomorrow. The God of the Bible also promises that he will answer your prayers, and whatever you request, he will do. He says it many, many times in the Bible; "Whatsoever you shall ask for in prayer believing you shall receive" (Matt. 21:22; see also Matt. 7:7–11; 18:19; John 14:13–14; 15:7; 16:23–24; 1 John 3:22). You're asking me what I would accept as proof. So, if you were to ask God to tell you what's going to happen tomorrow, and God would tell you, "Adam, I want you to tell Dan that tomorrow at 12:14 p.m., a meteorite from the south-southwest weighing 4.2 pounds is going to hit the earth. It is going to go through his Navajo rug upstairs and end up six inches below the basement floor. It's going to be composed of 1 percent iridium and 8 percent iron," and so on. If God told you to tell me that that's going to happen, and then it *did* happen tomorrow, I would take that as very strong evidence. There would be some uncertainty there, of course, but I would say, "Whoa, the Bible is true: you can ask for anything! God *does* know the future." All of you can think of other examples of things that would change your mind. I would be happy to change my mind. If it's true, it's true, right? I don't know if I would *worship* that being, from what I know of his scriptures—that I am actually interpreting correctly, by the way. And who couldn't interpret it correctly? I mean, really? This all-caring, all-knowing, omniscient, all-powerful God wrote a book of so much importance to the human race that we can't understand it without experts explaining to us the true context?

ALJ: Well, that meteorite might just happen to occur in the one universe that we're in though.

DB: Yeah. But I would still raise the probability very high. I wouldn't put it to 100 percent, but I think I would be convinced, especially if you told me that in advance. I would probably say, "Yeah, you got something there, Adam."

ALJ: But if there's a multiverse with infinite universes where everything eventually happens somewhere, we might just happen to be in the universe where that meteorite happens.

DB: But I'm not arguing for a multiverse. I said at the outset that if we're going to play your abductive reasoning game, then I could play the same abductive reasoning to come up with the multiverse, which seems as likely as a prime mover.

Closing Remarks

DAN BARKER: I like Adam. He's smart, he's educated, he's articulate, and from what I know about him he's a good man. I think we could be friends, maybe. Unless you believe in hell. If you actually believe there's a real hell where I'm going to be tortured forever because of my choice, and you're going to be rewarded in heaven, then I don't think we would ever be *best* friends. I think people should be judged by their actions, no matter what they say—if they want to believe in elves or in Allah, fine; it's a free world. Most Christians and most theists are good people just by human nature. Just like most atheists and agnostics, we're basically good people, with a few fringe people on the edges that are causing a lot of problems, which occurs in every group. There are some bad Christians and there are some bad atheists in the world, so my criticisms of theism are not directed at you, Adam, and I think you understand that.

You mentioned the prime mover or cause outside of the big bang. You said this being must be incredibly powerful. But power is work over time. Power is a physical, natural thing. How can an immaterial being, who doesn't exist in space and time, have power? You would only say he's *all*-powerful if you're comparing it to something else, like creating a puny universe. Saying God is powerful doesn't mean anything at all, so you're smuggling concepts into your premises that don't belong there.

I do think moral truths can be objectively justified. I wouldn't say it in the way some philosophers say that objective moral truths exist, because they don't. The brain is a functioning organism. The mind is a function of that organism, and when the brain dies the mind is gone. You're talking about the word *mind*, but a mind isn't a thing. You're committing that reification mistake, that there are *things* in the universe that need some justification. But these are just labels for the way things function. Just like digestion or circulation of the heart. "When the body dies, where does the circulation go?" We don't ask that question; it's a dumb question. And it's the same thing with minds: "When the body dies, where does the mind or the soul go?" That's a dumb question. It's only a biological organism that has a physical, material, functioning brain that produces what we would label as a mind, and for you to take that and then jump to something transcendent is a huge category mistake.

I guess I would just ask, in light of the six lacks or absences I gave, did Adam connect the dots? Did he do a good enough job filling those gaps? I don't think he did. I'm still not convinced. I'd be open to being convinced, but for now, for this reason, I am not. And we didn't even get to talk about the problem of evil did we? Maybe in another debate we could do that.

ADAM LLOYD JOHNSON: I want to thank Dan for having this conversation with me. We recognize that most people don't change their mind in these sorts of debates. But I think they can be helpful as an introduction for a lot of folks to these topics, so that they can dive down into a deeper understanding with books, YouTube videos, and conversations. I hope that we've modeled how people can disagree vehemently on important issues while being friendly. I think many would agree with me that this seems to have been lost in our culture right now. So, let's shut Facebook off, let's shut Twitter off, and instead go out for coffee and have these conversations face-to-face. Let's be aware that we're going to disagree but still love each other in the midst of that.

In this debate I've argued for mere theism, namely, that there is a God, a Supreme Being. The question isn't about whether we like God; many times I don't like God. The question is not about whether we agree with God; sometimes I don't agree with what God does. This debate isn't about whether we fully understand God. One of the things that Dan mentioned is that theists disagree with each other. Well, of course we do. It just means we don't fully understand God yet. Scientists disagree with each other about their scientific theories all the time. It doesn't mean their theory isn't true; it's just that they haven't got it all figured out yet. They're still working on it. So, the fact that theists disagree among themselves makes no difference as to whether God exists. The key issue is: Is there a God? All I've argued is that there is a Supreme Being who actually exists. I'm not making an emotional appeal; I'm not condemning you; I'm not using rhetoric to try to sway you; I've simply tried to provide good reasons and evidence to believe that there is a God. I'm not claiming I can do this with absolute certainty as we've talked about, but there's nothing we can prove with absolute certainty except maybe some basic mathematical principles. As finite beings we're left, which is sometimes frustrating, trying to figure out the truth as best we can based on deductive, inductive, and abductive reasoning. I agree with Dan that we should base our beliefs on good reasons and evidence, and there are good reasons and evidence to believe in God. I acknowledge there are some good arguments against God too. We didn't get a chance to talk about the problem of evil, and we could talk more about the hiddenness of God. But at the end of the day, when I compare arguments against God with the arguments for God (the beginning of the universe, the design of the universe, and these objective moral truths) it seems to me that the most reasonable explanation is that there is a God who created and designed the universe, and who is the source of objective moral truth.

3

Expanding on the Debate

Additional Points and Arguments for Theism

Adam Lloyd Johnson

I had a wonderful time at the 2022 FREEFLO conference organized by the Florida Humanist Association. Everyone I interacted with there was respectful and friendly. I especially have fond memories of some interesting conversations I had that weekend with those who seemed open to the idea that God does exist. Dan was a great interlocutor, and though I very much enjoyed my debate with him, I wish we had more time that night to delve deeper into the topics we discussed and to address additional issues. Thankfully this book allows us to do just that. In this chapter I'll provide more details concerning topics we discussed in the debate and address other important issues we didn't have time to cover.

Why Believe the Christian Description of God Is Correct?

In light of the debate's time constraints and the audience profile (I'd guess 90 to 95 percent were atheists), I chose to argue only for mere theism—that there is a God. That's why I didn't present my overall case for Christianity but instead only argued that there is a Supreme Being. As I noted in the debate, many different thinkers around the world throughout history have independently concluded there is a Supreme Being. Many of them have described this being in similar ways, for example, as spaceless, timeless, immaterial, powerful, the creator of everything, intelligent, and the source of morality. Though many of them came to these conclusions independently, we can see the thought processes that led them there were similar in the sense that their thinking culminated in similar first cause, design, and moral arguments as they observed and reflected on the world around them.

Even though these thinkers, and the people groups they belonged to, came to similar conclusions about this Supreme Being's basic attributes, there were also some differences in their descriptions. Consider for example the differences between how today's two most popular theistic belief systems, Christianity and Islam, describe God. While they agree on God's basic attributes, they disagree over various details concerning what God is like. So how do we know whose description of God is correct? Dan actually helped answer this question in the debate!

In order to know whose description of God is correct, it'd sure be nice if God himself would just tell us what he's like. And of course that's exactly what most theistic groups claim, namely, that they have some sort of communication from God in which he explains in more detail what he's like. For example, Christians claim the Bible is from God, whereas Muslims claim the Quran is from God. Since obviously not everything that claims to be a message from God really is, how do we know what truly is a message from God? This is where Dan provided some helpful advice.

In the debate Dan said that if I claimed to have a message from God that included information about the future (he proposed predicting a meteorite would hit his house) and later what I predicted actually came true, then he'd consider that to be very strong evidence for God. In other words, Dan would consider this to be strong evidence that the message I claimed to be from God truly was from him. What Dan described is what I often refer to as the "miracle test." Because there are so many fakes (people who claim to have a message from God but know they're lying) and mistakes (people who think they have a message from God but really don't), I'm very skeptical about anything that claims to be a message from God. But if someone claims to have a message from God and can perform impressive miracles (such as predicting the future as Dan described), then this greatly raises my confidence that the message really is from God, because only God can perform miracles or give someone the ability to do them. Dan's not alone in this; many thinkers throughout history have been proponents of this miracle test. For example, John Locke, one of the most influential Enlightenment thinkers, argued in his work *A Discourse of Miracles* that because miracles contain a hallmark of the divine they are crucial in establishing whether or not something is really a message from God.[1]

Think about it this way—imagine two people came up to you on the sidewalk and claimed to have a message from intelligent beings from another planet. I'm sure you'd be highly skeptical of such a claim, and rightly so considering all the fakes and mistakes out there. But let's say one of them also claims

1. See also book 4, Chapter 19 ("Of Enthusiasm") in John Locke's *Essay Concerning Human Understanding*.

to have technology from these aliens and then uses it to raise up a semitruck three hundred feet above the ground, spin it around, and gently set it back down. I'm sure that would greatly increase your confidence that they really did have a message from extraterrestrials! Of course, as Dan mentioned, this sort of test isn't foolproof because we might be getting tricked somehow by a skilled illusionist. But if several people investigate it thoroughly and conclude it's legit, it seems reasonable, as Dan noted, to consider this to be very strong (although not absolute) convincing proof. Though the miracle test is the strongest way we have to verify whether a message is truly from God, it can be combined with several other tests (e.g., the moral test, consistency test, etc.) to raise our confidence even further that a particular message is from God.

Though there are several good reasons to conclude Jesus's message, as described in the New Testament, is from God, his miracles and resurrection are the strongest reasons. Because we have so many early, independent, corroborating, and extensive historical sources that describe Jesus's miracles and resurrection, I and many others are convinced Jesus's message is from God.[2] Antony Flew, one of the most famous atheists of the twentieth century, admitted that "the evidence for the resurrection [of Jesus] is better than for claimed miracles in any other religion. It's outstandingly different in quality and quantity."[3] As for the specific miracle Dan mentioned—predicting the future—I'm most impressed by the prophecy in Daniel 9 that predicted several hundred years in advance when the Messiah would arrive. Jesus of Nazareth fulfilled this Old Testament messianic prophecy and many more.[4]

Even though I believe there is a Supreme Being because of first cause, design, and moral arguments for God, this "miracle test" is what convinces me that Jesus's message really is from God and thus his description of God (i.e., the Christian description as found in the New Testament) is correct. How did Jesus describe God and what was his primary message? In brief, Jesus described God as a Trinity, as one being but three persons: Father, Son, and Spirit. He also explained that we humans were created by God for the purpose of expanding the

2. To consider the historical evidence for Jesus's resurrection in particular, I suggest the highly renowned work by N. T. Wright, who was a professor at the University of St. Andrews and Senior Research Fellow at the University of Oxford. See N. T. Wright, *The Resurrection of the Son of God*, vol. 3 of *Christian Origins and the Question of God* (Fortress, 2003).

3. Antony Flew and Gary Habermas, *Did the Resurrection Happen? A Conversation with Gary Habermas and Antony Flew*, ed. David Baggett (InterVarsity, 2009), 85.

4. For a thorough evaluation of these prophecies see Herbert W. Bateman IV, Darrell L. Bock, and Gordon H. Johnston, *Jesus the Messiah: Tracing the Promises, Expectations, and Coming of Israel's King* (Kregel Academic, 2012).

loving fellowship of the Trinity. The very meaning of your life is to enjoy loving relationships with God and with others. Love is the foundation of ultimate reality, since it's intrinsic to the relationships between the divine persons of the Trinity. The problem is that our moral failures have broken our relationship with God and, for many of us, broken our relationships with other people.

Thankfully though, God still loves us. That's why he orchestrated a way for our moral failures to be forgiven and for us to be reconciled back to a right relationship with the God who created us and loves us. One of the members of the Trinity, Jesus, God the Son, took on human nature and lived as one of us, giving us a perfect moral example of how humans should live. Though innocent, he died on a cross to take the punishment we deserve for our moral failures. Jesus warned us not to trust in our own efforts to fix our relationship with God; it's impossible to earn our way back into a right relationship with God because our moral failures are just too great. He promised that if you'd trust in him and what he did for you on the cross instead of trusting in what you yourself could do, you'd be forgiven for your moral failures, reconciled back to God, and welcomed into heaven to love God and love others for all eternity. Jesus summarized all of this in the most famous verse from the New Testament: "For God so loved the world that He gave His only begotten Son, that whoever believes in Him should not perish but have everlasting life" (John 3:16).[5]

The Relationship Between Faith and Reason

In the debate I said I agree with Dan that all our beliefs should be based on good reasons and evidence. Since people are often surprised when they hear me say that, I'd like to elaborate further here on the relationship between faith and reason. Some try to dismiss or belittle my belief in God by claiming it's just a matter of faith. While I agree my belief in God does involve faith, I don't

5. Note that Jesus's message is radically different from Dan's mischaracterization of it when he said we'd be punished if we don't believe in the ancient elf that came back to life. While we all deserve God's punishment for our moral failures, Jesus took that punishment on our behalf on the cross. Jesus's message from God was that if we trust in what he did for us, then we'd be forgiven and thus escape the punishment we deserve for our moral failures. In other words, our justly deserved punishment from God is based on our moral failures (our selfishness, greed, hatred, etc.), not our lack of belief. However, according to the New Testament trusting in what Jesus did for you on the cross is the means through which you can be forgiven of these moral failures and reconciled back to God. It'd be similar to a situation where I had terminal cancer, someone invented a cure for cancer, and I decided not to take the cure; my death would be caused by the cancer, not my decision to refuse the cure.

think it should be belittled for that reason because all my beliefs, as well as all of everyone else's beliefs, involve faith to some degree. Many non-Christians, and even some Christians, tend to think some beliefs, like our scientific beliefs, are proven facts based on evidence while other types of beliefs, like our religious beliefs, are mere faith based on wishful thinking. But this is a gross misunderstanding of how human beliefs work.

This misunderstanding has been pointed out most helpfully by well-known scientists Michael Polanyi and John Polkinghorne.[6] These two thinkers have been the most well-known proponents of the epistemological position called critical realism, which I also affirm. Critical realists maintain there's nothing we can know for sure with absolute certainty, except possibly a few mathematical principles. We need to do the best we can through study and research to base our beliefs on good reasons and evidence while recognizing it's always possible we could be wrong. Since all our beliefs have an element of uncertainty in them, all our beliefs, including our scientific beliefs, involve trust (i.e., faith).

So what is faith? Keep in mind that the same word can be used to mean different things. Just think about all the different ways we use the word *bark*. Similarly, the word *faith* can be used to mean radically different concepts. Sometimes it's used to mean an irrational, blind leap of wishful thinking. Indiana Jones famously illustrated such a blind leap of faith at the end of *Indiana Jones and the Last Crusade* when he steps out over what seemed like a bottomless pit with no good reason to think he'd survive. That type of faith is the opposite of reason, that is, it's negatively correlated with reason—having more reasons and evidence for something decreases your need for such blind faith.

However, the term *faith* can also be used to mean a rational decision to trust someone, or believe something, based on good reasons and evidence. That's why I often use the terms *blind faith* and *rational faith* to differentiate between these two ways of using the word *faith*. As an example, consider that my faith (rational trust) in my wife has grown over our twenty-nine years of marriage as I've gotten to know her better because I've discovered more reasons and evidence to trust her. This sort of faith (rational trust) is not the opposite of reason but is positively correlated with reason—having more reasons and evidence for

6. Michael Polanyi, *Personal Knowledge: Towards a Post-Critical Philosophy* (University of Chicago Press, 1958), 12; John C. Polkinghorne, *The Polkinghorne Reader: Science, Faith, and the Search for Meaning*, ed. Thomas Jay Oord (Templeton, 2010). For a good introduction to the epistemological position called critical realism, which was promoted by these two scientists, see Esther L. Meek, *Longing to Know* (Brazos, 2003).

something actually increases your faith (rational trust). This sort of rational trust will always be a part of our marriage relationship though, because neither of us is omniscient. If we were omniscient and knew everything past, present, and future, then we wouldn't have to trust each other because we'd just know the other person completely and with absolute certainty. In other words, because there will always be an element of uncertainty due to our finite knowledge, our relationship will always involve this rational trust. However, it's important to note that faith and uncertainty are not the same thing; faith is the decision to trust someone or believe something based on good reasons and evidence when we have a degree of uncertainty, and all of our beliefs have some degree of uncertainty. As for God, I believe he exists based on good reasons and evidence, even though I can't prove that with absolute certainty. Critical realists like Polanyi, Polkinghorne, and myself argue that all of our beliefs work this way—our scientific beliefs, philosophical beliefs, religious beliefs, and so forth.

For this reason I've always found it odd to strictly label our various beliefs into different categories. Take my beliefs about abortion: Are those moral, scientific, political, or religious beliefs? I have no desire to categorize these beliefs, but others may if they like. The way I understand it is that I have certain beliefs about reality, in this case abortion, and those beliefs are either true or false. I'd say the same thing about all of my beliefs, including my belief that there is a God and that the Bible is from God. You may call those religious beliefs if you'd like, but as I understand it they're simply beliefs about reality that are either true or false.

This was driven home to me in a humorous way several years ago when I asked a local coffee shop if I could hang up a poster on their public bulletin board advertising an upcoming debate about the existence of God. The barista said they wouldn't allow this because their policy was not to hang up any religious material in their store. I explained that since both debaters had a PhD in philosophy, were both philosophy professors, and that the debate was taking place at a large public state university that this material wasn't religious but philosophical. As a result they allowed me to hang up the poster on their bulletin board! This is just one episode that reminded me how silly it can be to categorize our beliefs. Instead of using labels to dismiss certain beliefs we disagree with ("That's just your religious belief!") or to try and silence people advocating for their beliefs ("Don't try to push your religious beliefs on others!"), let's just admit we all have and advocate for beliefs about reality we think are true but that could be wrong.

Last, I want to acknowledge that some Christians, particularly those who've been influenced by postmodern philosophy through thinkers like Søren

Kierkegaard, do think of faith as the opposite of reason, as a blind leap of faith. But most Christians throughout history, as well as the New Testament, have maintained that faith is simply trusting something on the basis of good reasons and evidence. I trust (i.e., put my faith in) my wife on the basis of good reasons and evidence she's a trustworthy person. Similarly, I trust (i.e., put my faith in) Christ based on good reasons and evidence that he is the Messiah. Just like my trust in my wife has grown as I've seen more evidence of her character, my trust in Christ has grown as I've learned more reasons and evidence that Christianity is true.

Christianity and Science

Dan often says that the question of God's existence is a scientific question. However, this depends on how the terms *scientific* and *science* are being used. For example, if the term *science* is being used, as it often is today, to refer specifically to only natural science (that is, the search for natural causes), then obviously the existence of God isn't a scientific question because theists propose God is outside of nature. But if we're using the term *science* in the older, more traditional sense of knowledge in general (in traditional English even theology used to be called a science), and we're open to the idea that there could be nonnatural causes, then in this sense it is scientific to observe effects we see around us and try to figure out what's the best explanation for them, even if that explanation ends up being beyond nature. And when we observe that the universe had a beginning sometime in the finite past and that it has strong indications of being fine-tuned (i.e., designed for life), it seems to many of us the best explanation for these things is the existence of a God that exists beyond nature.

Science, and I'm referring specifically to natural science here, is a great way to know things about reality, but it's not the only way to know things. Even the idea that we can only know things via science can't be settled via science. Besides science, we can also know things through intuition, historical investigation, deductive logic, and some would argue we have some sort of *a priori* knowledge built into us to begin with. For further discussion on this issue from someone who thinks very much like me on this issue, see the writings of the well-known scientist and critical realist I mentioned above—John Polkinghorne.[7]

7. Polkinghorne, *Polkinghorne Reader*.

Did God Command Genocide in the Old Testament?

In the debate Dan brought up concerns about some verses in the Old Testament where God seems to do or approve immoral actions, such as commanding the Israelites to destroy the Canaanites. Since our debate was about the existence of God, not Christianity or the Bible, I responded by explaining all I was defending was the position that there is a God. The concerns Dan raised might cause someone to question if those sections of the Bible are accurate or really from God (though I noted they should question more whether Dan is interpreting those verses correctly), but they have no bearing on whether or not God exists. My belief that there's a God is not primarily based on the Bible but on first cause, design, and moral arguments.

It's also important to keep in mind that the primary question isn't whether we like God, agree with everything God does, or understand why God does what he does. There are times when I don't like God, agree with God, or understand God! Regardless, the primary question is: Does God exist? I believe there are good reasons and evidence to believe he does. However, since I also believe the Bible is from him and accurately records what he's done and said, I can honestly say there have been times where I've struggled with these verses in the Old Testament. How could, and why would, a morally perfect God do such things? Below is a brief summary of the conclusions I've come to as I've wrestled through these issues myself.

First, some of these situations in the Old Testament are merely descriptive; it's not approving what happened but merely describing what took place. For example, regarding the verse in which Dan claimed God said we should be happy when babies are dashed against the stones (Ps. 137:9), it should be noted that the Israelite author here is being held captive in Babylon after the Babylonians had enslaved, raped, and killed his family. It's in that context he wrote this psalm to explain that the Babylonians would soon suffer a similar fate that they had afflicted on others. In other words, the enemy of the Babylonians would soon defeat them and do the same things to them that they did to the Israelites, including dashing their (Babylonian) babies against stones. This was a cry of outrage from a distraught writer, not a command to commit such actions.

As for the sections where God commands the Israelites to destroy certain people groups such as the Canaanites, there are several things to keep in mind. First, scholars who specialize in ancient Hebrew have pointed out that it was a common literary practice at the time to use hyperbolic or exaggerated language to describe such events.[8] There's even evidence of this within the text. For example, in one verse the Israelites are told to completely destroy all the Canaanites, but the very next verse tells them not to intermarry with them so they don't get caught up in their evil practices such as child sacrifice (Deut. 7:1–3). Since they obviously couldn't intermarry with them if they were completely destroyed, it's reasonable to conclude the Hebrew word *herem* that we translate into English as "utterly destroyed" was only hyperbole. Some scholars even say the Hebrew word *herem* should be translated into English as "removal from use," because it was a way of saying a group should be "militarily defeated."[9] In other words, it didn't literally mean everyone in the nation was to be killed, only the ones who stayed to try to fight. These scholars argue this was a methodical process that gave people a chance to surrender and walk away, which would be similar to when our Allied troops tried to defeat the Nazis—the Nazis were given a chance to surrender, but those that resisted were fought and defeated.

Second, at certain times it's appropriate to harm people to prevent them from causing greater harm to others. The Allied troops were justified in causing the Nazis a lot of harm in order to stop them from harming others. Similarly, some of these ancient people groups were causing horrendous harm to others via human sacrifice and rape, and thus God would be justified in commanding the Israelites to stop such atrocities. If God does exist, and there's solid evidence to believe he does, then he's the judge of the universe and has a right to command people to punish evil, even up to and including capital punishment.

Third, these situations can't be called genocide because they weren't about attacking the Canaanites due to their ethnicity. No, this was punishment for their evil. Don't forget that, according to the Old Testament, God also punished the Israelites for their evil just as much as he punished the Canaanites and other ethnicities (2 Kings 17). In addition, when any ethnicity turned away from their evil, whether they be Israelites or other people groups such as the Ninevites in the book of Jonah, God mercifully withdrew the punishment he was about to bring upon them.

Fourth, we should interpret difficult verses in light of clearer verses. In many different ways the Bible communicates that God promotes love, humility,

8. William J. Webb and Gordan K. Oeste, *Bloody, Brutal, and Barbaric? Wrestling with Troubling War Texts* (IVP Academic, 2019), 136–230.

9. William J. Webb and Gordan K. Oeste, "Bloody, Brutal, and Barbaric? Online Appendixes," IVP Press, 2019, 33–34, https://tinyurl.com/5ccfu3da.

forgiveness, and care for others regardless of their ethnicity. For example, God told the Israelites that "when a foreigner lives with you in your land, you must not oppress him. You must regard the foreigner who lives with you as the native-born among you. You are to love him as yourself, for you were foreigners in the land of Egypt. I am Yahweh your God" (Lev. 19:33–34, HCSB). Treating foreigners in this way might seem normal today, but at the time this was quite a radical idea. Verses like these need to be taken into account when we struggle through these difficult Old Testament situations. For example, let's say you knew your departed grandmother for a long time and from that experience, and the testimony of many others, you have all sorts of evidence she was a kind, generous, and loving person. How would you react if someone told you that some fifty years ago she did something that seemed, at least on the surface, horrendous, such as hitting a child? You wouldn't immediately conclude she was some cruel wicked person. Yes, you'd look into it and try to understand what happened. Did she really do such a thing? Did the person who told you about it misunderstand or misinterpret the situation? Could she have been justified somehow if, say, she was trying to protect another child in the moment? Certainly you'd want to evaluate the situation as best you could, but even if you couldn't figure out all the details and motivations for sure, based on all the other information you know about her being kind and loving, you wouldn't conclude she must have been a cruel, wicked person. Similarly, because we know so much about God's kindness and love, both through his actions and what the Bible says about him, we shouldn't jump to conclusions when we're faced with a few difficult verses, even if we can't figure out all the details and motivations.

If you'd like to dive deeper into this issue and other difficult Old Testament situations, I encourage you to check out the books on these topics by Paul Copan.[10]

The Problem of Evil

Even though Dan didn't bring up the problem of evil in the debate, I want to address it here because many think it's the strongest argument against the existence of God. This argument is often summarized as follows:

10. Paul Copan and Matt Flannagan, *Did God Really Command Genocide? Coming to Terms with the Justice of God* (Baker, 2014), 1. Paul Copan, *Is God a Moral Monster? Making Sense of the Old Testament God* (Baker, 2011), 2. Paul Copan, *Is God a Vindictive Bully?* (Baker Academic, 2022).

1. There is a vast amount of evil (some would include suffering here) in our world.
2. If an all-good, all-powerful God did exist, he wouldn't allow this vast amount of evil.
3. Therefore, we should conclude God doesn't exist.

Note that this is only an argument against the existence of an all-good, all-powerful God. Some theists reject premise 2 because they believe God isn't all-powerful. An example of such a theist is former atheist philosopher Philip Goff, one of the contributors to this book, who converted to Christianity in 2024.[11] However, most theists affirm God is all-good and all-powerful, and therefore they've developed various responses to this argument.

Such theists often argue that evil doesn't prove there's no God, only that we might not know why God allows evil. In addition, they've proposed various reasons why God might allow evil. The most common is that God allows it in order to bring about some greater good or prevent a worse evil. This reason has been developed into various "greater good theodicies," which represent the most popular type of response to the problem of evil. Consider that even at a human level we sometimes allow and even cause pain or suffering (such as allowing a surgeon to cut our child) because we know it will bring about a greater benefit or rescue them from a greater harm. However, because I think there are a few problems with greater good theodicies, I've developed a different response I call a divine love theodicy, which I'll summarize below.[12]

Sometimes we think God could've created any set of circumstances we can imagine. People often refer to these different sets of circumstances as possible worlds but I prefer the term *timelines*. Each timeline includes everything that would happen from the beginning of the universe through eternity future. We could use the term *imaginable timelines* to refer to all the timelines we (or God) could imagine, which would be a large number indeed. For example, we can easily imagine a timeline where no one freely chooses to do evil, but it may be

11. You can watch Goff's interview on Capturing Christianity where he first announced his conversion at https://www.youtube.com/watch?v=vM_Thg165O8. See also Goff, "Is the Universe a Conscious Mind?," *Aeon*, February 8, 2018, https://tinyurl.com/bdzdh2sm; Goff, "Christianity and a God of Limited Power," *Philip Goff* (website), accessed November 3, 2025, https://tinyurl.com/e5pbu2r5.

12. My divine love theodicy is based on aspects of previous theodicies I've found compelling combined with ideas from my divine love theory. For a full account of my divine love theory, see Adam Lloyd Johnson, *Divine Love Theory: How the Trinity Is the Source and Foundation of Morality* (Kregel Academic, 2023).

the case that this timeline could never actually happen. In other words, it very well could be that not all imaginable timelines are actually viable.

Why would some timelines not be viable? If God is all-powerful, surely he could've created a timeline almost like this one but with less evil, right? Maybe not. It might be the case that God imposed constraints on himself that limited the number of timelines he could choose from. For example, he may have decided to create human beings with free will and constrain himself from forcing them to do what he wanted because that would violate their free will. Why would God impose this sort of constraint on himself? One possible reason is that free will is required to experience the greatest good, that is, loving relationships with God and with others (this includes relationships in this life and the eternal afterlife).[13] Since love requires free will, if God forced us to love, then that wouldn't be real love; we'd just be puppets doing what God forced us to do. Nobody wants to be in a relationship with someone who's forced to love them.

If God chose to constrain himself from forcing us to do what he wants, then this would have limited the timelines from which he had to choose. For example, let's say it's the case that I'd never freely choose to wear blue shorts under any circumstances in which God would place me. If that were true then even though we could imagine timelines where I'd freely choose to wear blue shorts, none of those timelines would actually be viable, since I'd never freely choose to do that and therefore God could not choose any of those timelines. Of course, God could force me to choose to wear blue shorts, but if he decided not to violate our free will, then those timelines where I freely chose them wouldn't be available for God to choose from (i.e., they wouldn't be viable).[14]

It might be the case that in every timeline in which God gives us free will, some, possibly all, will always choose to do evil. If this were true, then even though we could imagine a timeline where no one freely chooses to do evil, such a timeline wouldn't be viable. Keep in mind that the number of viable timelines are a smaller subset of the larger number of imaginable timelines. If

13. Theists have often described the greatest good we can experience as some sort of union, fellowship, communion, or friendship with God. Elsewhere I've argued that loving relationships with God and others are the very purpose and meaning of life; see Johnson, *Divine Love Theory*, 56–57, 154–57.

14. As a sidenote, readers familiar with the literature on this topic will notice that what I'm calling imaginable timelines and viable timelines have historically been called possible worlds and feasible worlds, respectively. I'm using these different terms because they better communicate the ideas I'm trying to explain, are easier for people to understand, and I figure that folks who are more familiar with the older terms should be able to easily follow along.

this was the scenario that God faced, then he would've had to choose between these three options:

1. Create no humans.
2. Create a timeline with human puppets that look like they're enjoying loving relationships and that never choose to do evil, but really God is just pulling their strings and forcing them to do these things and thus there wouldn't be any real love.
3. Create a timeline with human beings who have free will so that there would be true loving relationships, knowing that some, possibly all, would sometimes use their freedom to do evil.

It's reasonable to think God would choose the third option because even though he knew it would involve some evil, he also knew there would be real loving relationships, the value of which outweighs the evil.

Now even though God imposed on himself the constraint of not interfering with people's free will, he could still orchestrate various circumstances to minimize evil and suffering. Therefore, within this third option there'd be many different ways God could allow things to play out by, for example, placing people in different circumstances. But keep in mind that the number of viable timelines would be limited because God constrains himself from violating people's free will. Therefore, he couldn't eliminate all the suffering our evil choices would cause merely by adjusting circumstances. But couldn't he still orchestrate circumstances to minimize the evil and suffering people experience? Maybe that's exactly what God did. Maybe out of all the viable timelines within option three, he chose this timeline we're experiencing because this one had the least amount of evil.

Additionally, it might be that if God prevented any specific evil in this timeline, that'd somehow lead to worse evil or suffering later on. But couldn't God just step in and prevent that later evil or suffering then too? Well, it might be that if God removed the consequences of our evil choices, then overall we'd make many more evil choices. In other words, lowering the consequences of our evil choices might result overall in us making many more evil choices. Since evil choices themselves are intrinsically bad regardless of their consequences, it might be better overall to have many less evil choices but those choices result in serious consequential suffering than it would be to have many more evil choices that result in little to no consequential suffering.

Or, maybe minimizing evil wasn't God's only goal. Maybe God had other goals in mind as well such as, for example, to maximize the greatest good—loving relationships with God and with others in this life and the afterlife. If that was the case then, after evaluating every viable timeline, God chose the one that maximizes the quality and quantity of loving relationships for a given amount of evil. That might be the timeline we're living through—we could be experiencing the best viable timeline, the one that maximizes loving relationships for a given amount of evil.

We might think God could lower the amount of evil while keeping the quantity and quality of loving relationships the same. But that's impossible for us to know given our finite knowledge; we just can't fathom all the ripple effects, either in this life or the next, that'd come from adjusting various circumstances. It's reasonable to think that changing the circumstances to adjust the amount of evil would have ripple effects that'd eventually affect the overall quantity or quality of loving relationships. If this were the case, then God could've chosen another option that resulted in less evil and suffering. But this would come at a cost: to sacrifice either the quantity or quality of what loving relationships were possible. We might think that the benefit of increasing loving relationships isn't worth the cost of the extra evil that might be entailed. But again, as finite beings it's extremely difficult for us to do that sort of moral tradeoff calculation. We tend to overestimate the cost of evil and suffering, especially when we're in the midst of it. But if God is all-good and all-knowing, then he'd know exactly how to calculate the best tradeoff and how to maximize the quantity and quality of loving relationships for a given amount of evil. In game theory terminology, this timeline would be called a Pareto optimal scenario.

Since this discussion is so conceptual, it might be helpful to walk through a specific hypothetical example to consider the process of how God may have chosen the particular timeline we're experiencing. Though it'd be difficult to quantify, for the sake of thinking this through let's assume we can measure the amount of evil in a timeline on a scale of 0 to 100, with 0 being the least amount of evil and 100 being the most. Let's assume we can also measure the quality and quantity of loving relationships of a timeline on a similar scale of 0 to 100.

Of all the many imaginable timelines, consider timeline 42, where loving relationships are at maximum level of 100 and evil is at the minimum level of 0. Clearly timeline 42 would be preferable to the timeline we're experiencing, but let's say this timeline, while it's imaginable, is not viable because if God gave us free will, there are just no circumstances in which we'd all make such free choices that would result in these levels. To keep things manageable in this illustration, let's suppose, because God constrained himself from violating our free will, there were just a few timelines that were actually viable from which God could choose. Consider then these six timelines:

Timeline	Imaginable	Viable	Loving Relationships	Evil
4	Yes	Yes	30	4
8	Yes	Yes	77	21
15	Yes	Yes	98	94
16	Yes	Yes	64	18
23	Yes	No	77	20
42	Yes	No	100	0
All other timelines	Yes	No		

Presumably there were many more viable timelines God could've chosen from, but I'll be able to illustrate the type of constraints God might have faced by limiting the list to just these.

Let's say God chose timeline 8 with loving relationships at level 77 and evil at level 21. This seems reasonable considering the other viable options he had to choose from. We and God could certainly imagine a timeline such as 23, in which God orchestrated the circumstances (which would include him stepping into history at times to prevent some evil) such that there'd be slightly less evil (level 20 instead of 21), and yet loving relationships would stay at level 77. However, let's say that this timeline wasn't viable because changing these circumstances would cause ripple effects (I'm mostly thinking here of changes to our free will choices in response to these changed circumstances) that would lower the level of loving relationships.

God may have considered timeline 15, since it would have a much higher level of loving relationships (98 instead of 77). But it seems reasonable he wouldn't choose that option because it also drastically increases the level of evil from level 21 to 94. Similarly, God may have decided against timeline 4 because even though evil would drop from level 21 to 4, loving relationships would drop from level 77 to 30.

God could've chosen a timeline, say timeline 16, in which he orchestrated the circumstances such that the level of evil would be lowered from level 21 to 18. But let's say that because the ripple effects of these changes would lower the loving relationships from level 77 to 64, God would choose not to actualize this timeline.

In conclusion, I'm not claiming the situation in my divine love theodicy is exactly what happened, though I'm confident what I've described above, or something close to it, is what took place. But even if I'm wrong, the purpose of proposing this is to show there are plausible explanations for why God might allow evil. We're justified to conclude God has reasons for allowing evil and suffering, even if we don't know for sure what those reasons are.

Don't get me wrong, when I think about the evil and suffering in the world and in my own life, I can understand why people wrestle with this issue. Because the suffering due to our evil choices is very real and can be utterly devastating, I sympathize with those who struggle to believe in God because of it. Like many, I've experienced terrible evil and suffering myself. In fact, I got some troubling personal news a few weeks before our debate in 2022 that cut me to my core and almost caused me to cancel the debate. I talked with Dan and the debate organizer about it, and they were supportive and encouraging. In such times I wonder why God would allow this pain and why he wouldn't rescue me from it. There've been times when I've felt God didn't care or might not even exist. But when my emotions settle down and I consider the situation more broadly, I conclude there are two reasons the problem of evil shouldn't lead us to conclude there's no God. First, there are so many good reasons to believe there is a God, such as fine-tuning arguments, first-cause arguments, and moral arguments. Second, even if we don't know precisely why God allows evil, there are several possible, reasonable explanations for why he does.

Is the Idea of God Incoherent?

Sometimes atheists, including Dan, argue that the very idea of God—a necessary eternal being with attributes such as immateriality, omniscience, omnipotence, and omnibenevolence—is incoherent or illogical. I agree with the basic reasoning here, namely, that if something is illogical then that's a good reason to conclude it's not true. But I disagree with the assertion that the idea of God is illogical. Within the field of philosophy of religion this issue is sometimes called the coherence of theism.[15]

First, I'd like to address Dan's comment in the debate that theists don't agree with each other about God's attributes, that is, what God is like. The fact that theists disagree about some aspects of what God is like shouldn't cause us to conclude God doesn't exist. It's similar to the fact that people disagree about exactly how to define life but that certainly shouldn't cause us to conclude life doesn't exist. It's the same with God. Just because there's disagreement on exactly what God is like is a poor reason to conclude there is no God.

15. For a classic work on this topic see Richard Swinburne, *The Coherence of Theism*, 2nd ed. (Oxford University Press, 2016).

When scientists disagree with each other about a scientific theory, does that mean the theory isn't true? No, it just means they don't have it all figured out yet. It's the same with God. The situation between theists and scientists is also similar in the sense that most scientists agree on certain basic scientific truths but disagree over secondary issues they're still trying to figure out. Similarly, most theists agree on certain basic truths about God but disagree over secondary issues they're still trying to figure out. That's why I find the following popular meme a bit silly: "There have been 5,000 different beliefs about God throughout history; what makes you think yours is correct?" First, though there are some differences, the beliefs about what God is like around the world throughout history have been quite similar. They might have a different name or use a different term to refer to their idea of a Supreme Being, but their descriptions of a Supreme Being are remarkably similar. In addition, the same meme could be said of beliefs about the sun, moral issues, and political positions among others. Since there have been so many different beliefs about these topics, what makes you think your beliefs about them are correct? Even naturalism (the idea that all that exists is the natural, material universe) is just one belief system among many. Should that fact cause naturalists to doubt that naturalism is correct? Surely not.

One of the most common ideas shared by theists concerning what God is like, from Aristotle to contemporary Christians, is that God has various omni- (some say infinite) attributes such as omniscience, omnipotence, and omnibenevolence. Atheists have argued the idea that some of God's attributes are infinite is incoherent, and in the debate Dan claimed these omni- characteristics can't coexist logically. But it's unclear why we should think either of these assertions is correct. It's true philosophers and mathematicians have convincingly argued an actual infinite series can't exist in reality.[16] However, when theists say some of God's attributes are *infinite*, they're using the term qualitatively, not quantitatively, in order to describe his perfections. Most theists also maintain God is *simple*, as opposed to being composite, in the sense that he's not made up of quantitative parts, be they physical or nonphysical. In other words, they're not saying there are some sort of infinite quantitative parts in God. They're merely saying some of God's qualities, such as his knowledge and power, are unlimited. He knows everything that can possibly be known and has the power to do everything that logically can be done.[17]

16. For example, check out the grand hotel paradox by David Hilbert, one of the most influential mathematicians of the twentieth century. George Gamow described this paradox in *One, Two, Three . . . Infinity: Facts and Speculations of Science* (Viking, 1947), 17–21.

17. Theists often qualify God's omnipotence like this as a way to explain they're not

Now I'll address Dan's concerns about two of these omni- attributes: omnipotence and omniscience. First, in the debate Dan argued it was incoherent for me to propose that an immaterial God is incredibly powerful because power is physical, natural, and defined as work over time. While we sometimes use the term *power* to mean work over time, there are many other ways the term can be used. In this context I was using *power* simply to mean the ability to do something. And I don't see any good reason to think only natural (i.e., material) things have power. Certainly that's what naturalists believe, but that's because they maintain only material things exist, something which has to be argued for, not merely assumed. However, even within a naturalist's belief system there's at least one example of an immaterial object that has the ability to do things—a mind. It's perfectly coherent to say Albert Einstein had a powerful mind because what we mean is that his immaterial mind had the ability to do great things. It's similarly coherent to propose, even if the proposal ends up being false, that there's an immaterial mind analogous to human minds that's so incredibly powerful it can create the universe, which is material, out of nothing.

When it comes to omniscience, Dan argued the idea of God is incoherent if it includes the proposals that God is omniscient and has free will because these attributes logically contradict each other. He called this argument FANG (the free-will argument for the nonexistence of God) but such an argument, even if successful, wouldn't conclude there's no God, only that God can't have both omniscience and free will. However, since I believe God has both of these attributes I'll argue here that they don't contradict each other.

Much has been written about the assertion that if God knew the future then we humans couldn't have free will. For example, some have argued that if God knows what we'll choose in the future, say that I'll buy a Toyota Camry tomorrow, then when that time comes I'll have to make that choice. I won't be able to choose otherwise because then God would've been wrong. And if free will is defined as the ability to choose otherwise, then I don't have free will. In response, I'd first point out that it's been convincingly argued by solid philosophers that it's problematic to define free will as the ability to choose otherwise, though many think of free will in those terms.[18] Instead I, along with many others, maintain that free will is best understood in terms

claiming God can do illogical or contradictory things, such as creating a married bachelor or creating a rock so big he can't lift it.

18. John Martin Fischer et al., *Four Views on Free Will*, ed. Ernest Sosa, Great Debates in Philosophy (Blackwell, 2007), 15.

of *sourcehood*, a position sometimes called causal agent libertarian free will.[19] This position maintains that, for example, I, the person Adam Lloyd Johnson, am the ultimate cause of my choices. Regardless of how it's precisely defined, the basic idea of free will is the ability to make choices that are free in the sense that they're not caused by any prior conditions. This is the opposite of determinism, which is affirmed by Dan, that maintains our choices are not free because they're determinatively caused by some sort of prior conditions (brain chemistry, prior events in life, laws of nature, God, etc.).[20]

As long as we're talking about free will as the ability to make choices that aren't determined by any prior conditions, then whether we define free will as the ability to do otherwise or the ability to cause our own choices, God's knowledge of our future choices wouldn't negate our free will. The reason for this is that God's knowledge of our future choices doesn't cause or determine our future choices. It's actually just the opposite—it's our future choices that cause God's foreknowledge of them. In other words, just like our knowledge of other people's past choices doesn't cause those choices (those past choices are what cause our knowledge of them), God's knowledge of our future choices doesn't cause those choices (those future choices are what cause God's foreknowledge of them). If I choose instead to buy a Jeep Wrangler tomorrow, then that's what God would foreknow about the future. I'm the ultimate cause of my future choices, and those choices are the cause of God's foreknowledge of those future choices. If our choices aren't determined by any prior conditions, then those choices are free even if they're known by God ahead of time. The key point to remember here is that foreknowledge does not equal forecausation.

Similarly, it's *possible* that God's foreknowledge of his own choices wouldn't negate his free will because his foreknowledge of his future choices would be caused by his future choices, not vice versa. In that scenario his choices would still be free in the sense that they're not determinatively caused by any prior conditions. I'm merely saying this is *possible* because we don't know exactly

19. Eleonore Stump, "Moral Responsibility Without Alternative Possibilities," in *Moral Responsibility and Alternative Possibilities: Essays on the Importance of Alternative Possibilities*, ed. David Widerker and Michael McKenna (Ashgate, 2006), 152.

20. In the debate Dan said free will is an illusion and that we live in a deterministic universe. Dan also said even the strictest determinists say we are the cause of our choices. This is a peculiar remark and may indicate Dan is unfamiliar with the philosophical discussion about free will because determinism is nearly always used to mean just the opposite: our choices are caused (i.e., determined) by other things besides us, namely, some sort of prior conditions.

how God's choices and knowledge work.[21] Even if this scenario I've presented concerning God's knowledge and choices is merely *possible* but not actual, that would still defeat Dan's FANG argument because it claims it's logically impossible for God to have omniscience and free will—all that's required to defeat a claim of impossibility is a possibility, not an actuality.

Does the Bible Promise God Will Give Us Everything We Pray For?

In the debate Dan mentioned verses in the Bible that seem to say God will give us anything we pray for. Since we obviously don't get everything we pray for, Dan seemed to be implying that the Bible is wrong about this, or maybe that prayer itself is nonsensical. I'm honestly surprised that Dan is confused about basic communication. When my wife tells me she'll buy me anything I want for my birthday, she doesn't have to take the time to qualify her statement with dozens of stipulations, conditions, and limitations because I know what she means. For example, I know she has in mind things that are reasonably priced, generally good for me, and within her ability to get. That's why I wouldn't ask her for a Ferrari, radioactive waste, or the planet Mars. Similarly, God didn't have to spell out all the stipulations, conditions, and limitations on such promises about prayer because it's obvious what he means, given what we know about him from the rest of the Bible. God is not a genie in a bottle; he's not going to give us everything we ask for, and thank God for that!

21. Many theists have concluded God's choices and knowledge work such that he chooses and knows all things at once, not sequentially. Such theists still talk about God's thoughts and decisions sequentially but understand that to be talking about God in human terms, much like when we say God has a strong arm. They maintain God's thoughts and choices may be logically sequential but not chronologically sequential. They hold God's knowledge and decision making is analogous to ours but not exactly like it. They admit we don't fully understand how God's knowledge and choices work, but just because we don't understand something fully doesn't mean it's incoherent.

4

Expanding on the Debate

Additional Points and Arguments for Atheism

Dan Barker

I have done 141 formal public debates since 1985, but this one stood out, and not just because Adam is one of the most genuinely friendly and respectful opponents I've had. Our debate resulted not only in this book but in a new book of my own. During my opening statement, after hearing Adam mention abductive reasoning, a thought popped into my head. You can see that I ad-libbed and proposed *postductive* as a response to *abductive*. I was trying to verbalize how I think Adam got some things backward. The audience did not seem impressed, nor should they have been. *Postduction* is the wrong word. I should have chosen a prefix that means not "after" but "inverted" to express the fallacy I was struggling to articulate. Two and a half years later, my book *Contraduction* was published. Contraduction is a hidden fallacy that inverts reality. I will talk about it below.

I am not a professional philosopher or scientist. But it doesn't take much expertise to notice that the experts, especially theologians, disagree with each other. So why not think for ourselves? I have never challenged anyone to a debate, but I keep getting invited to debates. I am learning as I go, correcting mistakes and adjusting arguments. I think anyone who cares about truth can learn to reason like a scientist—open to rethinking opinions.

The most important thing we can do is listen to each other. If we are not learning, we are not growing. The trick is to balance confidence with humility. I am pretty sure of myself, but if I am wrong, I need to know it. I believe people like Adam are sincere and open, as I was during my own ministry, and I truly want to understand his thinking, admiring his intelligence and respecting his humanity if not always his conclusions. That is how a fruitful debate can occur.

It was a short debate. We never did get to the problem of evil. I write about that—or the "problem of suffering," as many are calling it—in my article "Supernatural Evil" in *God and Horrendous Suffering*.[1]

This chapter applies only to comments made during the debate itself. In my concluding thoughts, I will reply to what Adam has written since then and to the other contributors, none of which I have read yet.

Authority

It can be useful to quote authorities to support a point. But notice that Adam sometimes used authority simply to say: look how many people agree with me. He stated, for example, "Many different thinkers around the world throughout history have independently concluded that there is a God," and "More and more atheist philosophers are agreeing there are objective moral truths." He mentioned scholars but did not always quote their relevant thoughts. Those authors might indeed have remarkable insights. And they might not. But merely mentioning them without content leans toward argument from authority.

Everything said during a debate should be available for inspection during that debate. A debate is not a college lecture with textbooks. When I mentioned the astrophysicist Victor Stenger, I quoted his relevant remark, a remark that became available for examination *during that debate*. I could have listed many thinkers who agree with me, but truth is not determined by vote.[2] If your argument is good, it doesn't matter if everybody or nobody agrees with you.

Adam is not unfair. He acknowledged "there are very intellectual educated people who believe in God, and many intellectual educated people who don't."

Evidence

I was surprised that Adam came to a debate called "Does God Exist?" (notice the capital G) and then argued only for "mere theism." What is that? Are we to offer it mere worship? Theism is not a god; it is a belief system. Mere theism could lead us to Brahman, Vishnu, Amun-Ra, Baal, Zeus, Thor, Kokopelli

1. Dan Barker, "Supernatural Evil," in *God and Horrendous Suffering*, ed. John Loftus (GCRR, 2021), 88–117.

2. A jury does vote on the reasonableness of the evidence, but a jury does not produce truth. A jury produces a verdict, which legally stands for the truth. Verdicts have sometimes been wrong.

or thousands of other deities. Or to Kishelëmukong, the creator god of my Lenape tribe who dreamed our world into existence. Adam believes in the personal God of Christianity and claims to have convincing proof, yet he avoided talking about the Lord he worships. "I'm not going to be arguing for Christianity or the Bible specifically," he said, "only that there is a Supreme Being." Why not? The God he praises is said to perform miracles and utter prophecy. He reportedly intervenes in the natural world with signs and wonders.[3] He promises to answer prayer and move mountains.[4] Why didn't Adam lead with the resurrection of Jesus or fulfilled prophecy? Or evidence of the healings at Međugorje? Since Adam represents the philosophy of religion, I assume that in his field mere anecdotes are not convincing enough to be brought to a serious debate.[5]

I didn't realize I was arguing only for mere atheism that day. But I suppose that is not a bad way to say it. As I mentioned, the atheist has nothing to prove. All I have to show is that Adam failed to prove his case beyond a reasonable doubt.

In place of evidence, Adam offered an abductive suggestion that some of the profound questions of our existence might be answered by plugging those gaps with what some thinkers consider the "best explanation." He candidly admitted his handicap: "Sometimes I wish there were more evidence for God. Obviously the more evidence the better. But I think there is a lot of good evidence for God and good reasons to believe in God, such as the arguments I presented. These arguments start with evidence, the effects we see, and then propose God is the best explanation for the cause of these things." The honesty is admirable, but the argument is backward. Notice that Adam equates effects with evidence. When we look for evidence, we begin with an idea of what it would look like. We don't start with effects. If I suspect my neighbor trespassed on my property, I would not point to a falling leaf or a scurrying chipmunk and say, "There's the evidence!" I would look for a footprint that matches my neighbor's shoe, or their baseball cap in the bushes, or perhaps blood on the nail that scratched someone who climbed over the fence (blood that can be compared with my neighbor's blood). I might examine security footage. I know what my neighbor looks like. If I am surprised to see that a

3. God is a "he," if you believe the Bible. He is called "Father." He said he was Israel's "husband" (Jer. 31:32; Isa. 54:5). He impregnated a woman who gave birth to a son.

4. "All things, whatsoever ye shall ask in prayer, believing, ye shall receive" (Matt. 21:22, KJV). See also Ps. 37:4; Matt. 18:19; Mark 11:22–24; 1 John 3:22.

5. To his credit, although Adam probably claims to have a "personal relationship" with God, he did not offer personal experience as evidence, as some apologists do. He most certainly knows that subjective thoughts and feelings are not objectively testable.

patio chair was knocked over, can I say, "My neighbor did that!"? Not everything is evidence.

So what exactly are we looking for? And why look? How do we know there is a missing God? Doesn't the very search beg the question? What evidence fits God? Using an argument to turn an observation or effect into "evidence" for a hypothetical being is retrograde reasoning. If you are hunting a bear, you don't follow deer tracks. You know what the evidence looks like *before* starting your search. You can't take any unexplained observation and say "I found the bear!"

I do understand what Adam is grasping at. When I was a minister, I found that kind of reasoning to be confirmatory. Of all the potential explanations we can think of, the God I believed in seemed to be the *best* explanation for some of our unexplained (or weakly explained) observations. But I now think that is a backward understanding of evidence.

If God, for example, is powerful (by definition), and we see something in the universe that appears to be the result of power, can we say, "There! That fits my definition"? That's like hearing thunder and saying, "Praise Thor!"

Adam did say God is powerful: "many of these thinkers throughout history around the world describe this Supreme Being as spaceless, timeless, immaterial, powerful, the creator of everything, intelligent, and the source of morality." But what is power? Power is material. It can be measured. Power is work over time, a measure of energy transfer. Work over time requires space, time, and matter. It follows that a "spaceless, timeless, immaterial" being cannot have power.[6] Respecting the scriptures he believes in, if Adam had come to the debate with a talking snake, called down fire from heaven, made the sun stop moving, or performed a verified faith healing, I would have to give him credit for offering evidence of the power of God.[7] Some dispensationalists believe we are living no longer in the age of miracles but in the age of grace, so we should not expect to see signs and wonders any more. But perhaps a better reason for the admitted absence of evidence is that is difficult to see how a powerless being can be the best explanation for powerful effects.

Even if it is, a best explanation is not convincing proof.

6. Power can also be conceived as ability, such as the authority to have your orders carried out, like power of attorney. But this always results in a material effect in the natural world. In mathematics, a power increases a value, such as "the power of ten." But those usages have nothing to do with the power theists attribute to a creator.

7. Adam did make a prophecy that has since been fulfilled. He said (in our 2022 debate): "God knowing something about the future, let's say that Alexandria Ocasio-Cortez will run for president someday. . . ."

Best Explanation

In place of evidence, Adam raised three intriguing arguments: causality, design, and morality. I will respond to those in a moment. First I want to point out what I think is a fatal flaw in his general approach. His arguments all aim at a best explanation: "We think through lots of possibilities of what could be the explanation or the cause, but what's the *best* explanation of it? That's the sort of abductive reasoning that I'll be using." Adam used the phrase "best explanation" a dozen times. However, that approach works only under certain conditions. In order to have a "best" explanation, you need more than one possible explanation, each of which has a probability derived from what we know about the laws of nature. The prime suspect is the hypothesis with the highest probability. A probability is a number. How do we know what those numbers are? To the point, how does Adam know what the probability of a Supreme Being is?

Regarding the fine-tuning argument, there are at least three items in the list: chance, multiverse, and Supreme Being. (There may be more, but the only ones I can think of are too outrageous to be taken seriously).[8] We have a rough idea of the probability of chance as an explanation for why the constants of the universe appear to be finely tuned for life: it is not zero, but it is extremely low. (More about fine-tuning below.) But no matter how microscopic, it *is* a number. That's what allows us to add it to the list, possibly to be rejected.

It is hard to estimate the probability of a multiverse. We know that at least one universe exists. Remember that I am not advocating for a multiverse. But some scientists do. The astrophysicist Victor Stenger emailed me: "The multiverse is predicted by our best existing knowledge. It is in principle observable. As long as it remains plausible it serves to refute any argument that there had to be a creation and that the universe is fine-tuned." But since we have no direct observation yet of multiple universes, the idea remains a hypothesis. In spite of our current ignorance, we *can* say that a multiverse cannot be ruled out. Perhaps we could try Bayesian statistics and start with 0.5 (a 50 percent chance). But we don't know how that number might raise or lower as we gain more information. It could be as low as chance. If it is higher, then a multiverse, with randomly varying constants for each universe, is a more likely explanation than the random chance of just one universe. It raises the numerator. It tosses more rolls of the dice. In any event, since the probability of a multiverse is not zero, it *is* a number, perhaps also to be ultimately rejected.

8. Chaos, for example. There were certainly many gods of chaos in history.

We don't need exact probabilities in order to illustrate the problem Adam faces. Unlike the multiverse, we don't know that at least one god exists. (If we did, we wouldn't be having this debate.) Nevertheless, into the list of possibilities with accompanying probability estimates Adam throws a Supreme Being. So we are forced to ask: What is God's number? (Our debate, remember, was titled "Does God Exist?") How likely is it that such a being exists? With chance and the multiverse, we can make a stab using physics and math. Can we do that with God? Adam can't try Bayesian statistics, like I tried with the multiverse, because there is no physical-law plausibility to a hypothetical supernatural being, but if he does, he will get only the same 0.5, which means the probability of God would be *no worse* than the multiverse. He can't say it is best.

Why should an immaterial being be added to the list of material alternatives? It's apples and oranges. An item that does not have the same characteristics or metrics as the others can't be part of the comparison set. If we ask what fruit has the best taste, we would not add an Apple iPhone to the choices. And if we did, it would fail the test.

If Adam doesn't produce a number, the game is rigged. But let's be charitable and allow that the probability of a Supreme Being might theoretically be non-zero. There are many things we don't yet understand about the cosmos, so perhaps Adam might surprise us and produce a number. But then, how does he know it is not lower than the others?

If Adam replies that the "physics and math" of an immaterial Supreme Being are not merely natural but transcendent, then he has obviated the fine-tuning argument because that argument stems from *natural* physics and math. A scientist, then, might claim (equally ludicrously) that the likelihood of the multiverse also hinges on unknown transcendent properties. And then where are we?

So I ask Adam: If you don't have a numerical probability of the existence of God, how can you compare it with the other choices? From what he said in the debate, I gather he will respond that although we can't pick an actual number, logic raises the odds. His arguments are not merely abductive. They are also deductive.

Kalām Cosmological Argument

Adam's first argument is often called the Kalām cosmological argument. Here's how he phrased it:

1. Whatever has a beginning must have a cause.
2. The universe had a beginning.
3. Therefore, the universe had a cause.

Early Islamic scholars argued that there had to be a beginning to everything because if there were an infinite series of preceding events, we never could have traversed it to arrive at "now." Since we *have* arrived at "now," the past must be finite. Modern thinkers have combined this idea with current big bang cosmology to argue that our universe must have had a beginning.[9]

But what is a beginning? There seems to be no consensus among scientists and philosophers about the nature of time—presentism, eternalism, A-theory, and B-theory offer different interpretations, each generally questioning our subjective experience. In my book *Contraduction*, I argue that whatever time is, it doesn't flow. Time is a dimension, and dimensions are not things.[10] They are concepts. Since *begin* is a temporal word, and since we don't all agree on what *time* even means, I don't think we can speak with certainty about the "beginning" of the universe. We certainly can't talk coherently about the "beginning of time." It would be like asking "What is the beginning of height?"

In the chapter "Cosmological Kalamity" in my book *Godless*, I raise three objections to the argument. I summarize them and add two more here.[11]

The Kalām argument is self-refuting. If an actual infinity cannot be a part of reality, then God, if he is actually infinite, cannot be a part of reality. He exists only as a concept. Responding to this by claiming that God exists "outside of time" (whatever that might mean) is irrelevant. If God is a personal being, then his thoughts are orderly, in or out of time. Before he said "Let there be light," he had to decide to say it. The deciding did not logically occur *subsequent* to the acting. God (if he exists) could not have said, "Look! I created a universe! Now I will decide to do it." In anyone's mind, there are antecedent thoughts, and those thoughts stretch back as a chain of events or connected progression of preceding thoughts. By the logic of Kalām, if God's antecedent thoughts are infinite, then he never could have traversed them. He never could have said "Let there be light." But if he *did*, then his antecedent thoughts are not infinite, and he must therefore have had a "first thought." Some try to get around this by claiming that there is a difference between actual infinities, potential mathematical infinities, and the conceptual infinities of the nature of God, but that is just theology. (Numbers are concepts, so it follows by that defense that God is a concept.) In any event, this does not address the question of antecedent thoughts in an *actual* mind. If God exists, like the universe, he

9. Including William Lane Craig, *The Kalām Cosmological Argument* (Macmillan, 1979).
10. Dan Barker, *Contraduction* (Hypatia, 2024).
11. See Dan Barker, *Godless: How an Evangelical Preacher Became One of America's Leading Atheists* (Ulysses, 2008).

must have had a beginning. If this is not true, then the Kalām reasoning is irrelevant to the debate.

The Kalām argument begs the question. The curious phrase "Everything that begins to exist" looks artificial. Outside of apologetics, does anyone actually say that? It arbitrarily divides reality into two sets: things that begin to exist (BE), and things that do not (NBE). But the existence of something that does not begin to exist is the very thing theists are trying to prove. Bringing the conclusion into the premise is circular reasoning. We can't use the BE-NBE dichotomy in a premise if NBE has not first been shown to exist. Have we ever observed anything like that? If, for example, I speak the phrase "things that exist" in an argument, I am separating reality into two groups, implying that things that *don't* exist actually do in some way. But how can something that does not exist thereby exist?[12] That is an equivocation: existence in conception means something entirely different from existence in actuality. Likewise, why say "things that begin to exist" unless I believe that things that *don't* begin to exist actually exist? NBE seems to be pulling a rabbit out of a hat.

But let's proceed. Assuming that NBE is a meaningful set, what elements would belong in it besides a supernatural being? If God is the only item accommodated by NBE, then the Kalām reduces to:

1. Everything except God has a cause.
2. The universe is not God.
3. Therefore, the universe has a cause.

That's a tautology, not an argument. In order to avoid begging the question, NBE must accommodate more than one element, even if it contains only one. In addition to a personal supernatural cause, NBE must also allow (if not contain) more items, including something like an impersonal natural cause, and *those* elements must be examined (and possibly eliminated) before jumping to any conclusion about the nature of the cause of the universe. I know that the question of the nature of the cause is beyond the scope of the Kalām (which argues only for "a cause"), but since Adam is using the argument in a "Does God Exist?" debate, the circular reasoning is relevant. And this leads to the next objection.

The Kalām argument is artificially precise. Another clue that the Kalām might be begging the question is in the disguised monotheism of the first

12. If you think this analogy is strained—it might be, because no analogy is perfect—then ignore it. The argument doesn't need it. An analogy can sometimes be useful as an illustration, but never as an argument in itself.

premise: "Everything that begins to exist has *a* cause," that is, a single cause.[13] In reality, things that begin to exist have multiple causes. I can't think of an instance of something that begins to exist that has only one cause. Maybe Adam can, but that would be an exception, not proving that *everything* that begins to exist has a cause.

By the way, did you notice how Adam subtly altered the wording of the Kalām argument? The Kalām cosmological argument says "Everything that begins to exist has a cause," but Adam changed it to "Whatever has a beginning *must* have a cause." The Kalām argument's premise is simply an observation. Adam's premise shifts from observation to interpretation and imposes necessity, which fits nicely with intention, and with theism. Since most things (probably all things) that begin to exist have multiple causes, it is curious that the Kalām argument limits itself to "a cause." I think we can say that in most cases there is a single *proximate* cause out of the array of causes, some more distant in time than others. But even in that proximate sense, "a cause" does not mean "a single cause." It means "one out of many causes."

The house my wife and I live in was built in 1937. The parts existed, but the house did not "begin to exist" until . . . when, exactly? When the owner signed the contract with the builders? When the first shovel started digging the foundation? When the last brush stroke painted the exterior? Our house sits on a smaller lot that was subdivided off a property that had a local store above which the owners lived. When one of their daughters got married, they built her a house next to theirs. Did that house "begin to exist" in their minds when she got married? Or did it when she got engaged? Or did it when she was born? Was it when the house was assigned an address or appeared on the tax rolls? The property that was parceled to accommodate our house sits between the store (now an apartment building) and a path leading to a tunnel cutting through the berm that raises the railroad tracks (now a bike path). That underpass was created in the late 1800s by a farmer needing to lead his cows to the field on the other side of the tracks. If it had been cut twenty feet to the northeast, there would not have been room for our house. Was the farmer the cause of our house? His decision was certainly not a proximate cause—he was not thinking about our house—but it was certainly *a* cause of the beginning of our house, which would not exist otherwise.

13. There is no agreement among scientists or philosophers about what "cause" means. At the microscopic level, it seems to be a meaningless word. But at the macroscopic level, where entropy occurs, I think of it roughly as "if A had not happened, then B would not have happened," with A being the cause(s) and B the effect(s).

To be accurate, the Kalām argument should say:

1. Everything that begins to exist has an array of causes.
2. The universe began to exist.
3. Therefore the universe had an array of causes.

That fits nicely with the multiverse hypothesis, and maybe with polytheism. I suppose the Kalām argument might be salvaged by phrasing it in the passive voice:

1. Everything that begins to exist was caused to exist.
2. The universe began to exist.
3. Therefore, the universe was caused to exist.

That makes more sense, but leaves the door open for multiple causes. It doesn't subtly and artificially nudge us toward the monotheistic belief of "a cause" being "a single creator."

The Kalām argument is a category error. Let's notice a logical error that can occur in any argument that mentions "the universe." Look at it again:

1. Everything that begins to exist has a cause.
2. The universe began to exist.
3. Therefore, the universe has a cause.

That is a category error because you can't take a relationship within the universe (such as "Everything that begins to exist has a cause") and then apply that finding to the universe as a whole, as if "the universe" (the set of all things) were itself an object that inherits the relationships of its elements.[14] It jumps up a logical level to create a meaningless conclusion.

In *Contraduction*, I ask: "If all the members of an orchestra play in harmony with each other, does that mean that that orchestra is in harmony with all other orchestras? Since the elements in the set of even numbers are separated from

14. Properties, as opposed to relationships, might indeed sometimes be applied to the set as a whole. If each team member wears green, we can say it is a green team. If each instrument is making music, we can say the orchestra is making music. But relationships within the group, such as "a team of brothers," do not apply to the team as a whole. We would not conclude that that team is a brother to other teams.

their immediate neighbors by a distance of two, does that mean the set of even numbers is separated from the set of odd numbers by a distance of two? What could that possibly mean?"[15]

Since a water molecule is not wet, does that mean water is not wet? Even if a set might sometimes be described by the properties of its elements, the cause of an effect is not a property. It is relational: the cause of an effect in the universe is other objects or effects within the universe. The universe may indeed have had a beginning, but you can't get to its cause—you can't even say it has a cause—solely by bootstrapping from observations within the universe itself.

In his famous 1948 BBC radio debate with Frederick Copleston, Bertrand Russell responded to the causality argument: "I can illustrate what seems to me your fallacy. Every man who exists has a mother, and it seems to me your argument is that therefore the human race must have a mother, but obviously the human race hasn't a mother—that's a different logical sphere."

The Kalām argument backfires. If its reasoning is valid, the Kalām argument supports a multiverse. Let's use the same logic, continuing to respect the Kalām argument reasoning about a beginning, to produce this syllogism:

1. Everything that begins to exist is gravitationally attracted to other things.
2. The universe began to exist.
3. Therefore, the universe is gravitationally attracted to other things.

What are those "other things" to which the universe is gravitationally attracted? They have to be outside the universe. Ignoring the category error (since the argument begins by observing things *within* the universe) and moving the relationship up a level, it would have to conclude that "universes are attracted to other universes." Or to universe-like things. If sound, this logic proves there is a multiverse.

A multiverse is theoretically testable. A few scientists have proposed that the irregular clumping of matter in the early universe, as observed in the cosmic background radiation, can best be explained as the result of being gravitationally attracted by something outside the early universe.[16] This is not the prevailing consensus, but it is not implausible. If true, it would be indirect

15. Barker, *Contraduction*, 67–68.
16. Such as the astrophysicists R. A. Sunyaev and Y. B. Zel'dovich.

evidence of a multiverse—or at least that there is material outside the universe, as the Kalām gravitational argument suggests.

Adam, of course, will reply that even if true, this just kicks the can down the road. Instead of asking for the cause of the mere universe, we would now ask for the cause of the multiverse. That's a good point, but regardless of how we might respond, we have to agree that a multiverse kills the fine-tuning argument. You can argue Kalām or you can argue fine-tuning, but you can't argue both.

Fine-Tuning

Adam said that Christopher Hitchens concluded, "The fine-tuning argument is the strongest argument for God." He made this claim using the following Hitchens quote: "At some point, certainly, we are all asked which is the best argument you come up against from the other side. I think every one of us picks the fine-tuning one as the most intriguing. . . . That one degree . . . one hair different, then nothing. . . . You have to spend time thinking about it, working on it. It's not a trivial argument. We all say that." Notice that Hitchens said "best" and "intriguing," not "strongest," as if the argument had strength. To enhance this subtle shift in meaning, Adam edited the quote by deleting (in his final ellipsis) Hitchens's conclusion: "it doesn't prove design, doesn't prove a designer."[17] Hitchens did not think fine-tuning was a *strong* argument, only that it is not trivial.

"How surprising it is," wrote the agnostic physicist Steven Weinberg, "that the laws of nature and the initial conditions of the universe should allow for the existence of beings who could observe it. Life as we know it would be impossible if any one of several physical quantities had slightly different values."[18] The theistic geneticist Francis S. Collins concurs: "The existence of the universe as we know it rests upon a knife-edge of improbability."[19] The best way to explain this exquisite balance, Adam asserts, is to suggest that there was an intelligent designer who tuned it all so that human life could emerge.

17. Darren Doane, director, "Fine-Tuning Argument," *Collision*, directed by Darren Doane, featuring Christopher Hitchens and Douglas Wilson (LEVEL4, 2009). The quote from Hitchens occurs at time stamp 1:24:20.

18. Steven Weinberg, "Life in the Universe," *Scientific American Magazine* 271, no. 4 (1994): 45, https://doi.org/10.1038/scientificamerican1094-44.

19. Francis S. Collins, *The Language of God: A Scientist Presents Evidence for Belief* (Free Press, 2006), 73.

The fine-tuning argument is a design argument, which is usually stated like this:

1. We have never observed design without a designer.
2. The universe shows evidence of design;
3. Therefore, the universe was made by a designer.

As noted above, any argument that mentions "the universe" is vulnerable to category error, and in this case that should take the reasoning off the table. But let's proceed as if it were not a mistake to apply evidence of design *within* the universe to "the universe" as a whole. There are other problems.

Notice that the argument derives from what we *don't* observe: "We have never observed design without a designer." If we are permitted to induce a conclusion (rather than a premise) from what we do *not* observe, then we could just as well say:

1. We have never observed an effect without a natural cause.
2. The universe appears to be an effect.
3. Therefore the universe had a natural cause.

Or, back to the design argument, we could say:

1. We have never observed a designer who has not evolved.
2. The universe appears to have had a designer.
3. Therefore, the universe was made by a designer who evolved.

I doubt Adam would be comfortable with those conclusions, even though they follow the same logic as his design argument.

Is it true that we have never seen evidence of design apart from a designer? What does Adam mean by *design*? Is a snowflake designed? Are rubies designed? Are the neat parallel ridges on a sand dune designed? Does anyone think a group of elves comes out in the night to rearrange grains of sand or molecules with tiny fingers? Of course not. We can explain the orderliness by the laws of nature—molecular attraction, wind, hydraulics, friction, gravity, and what not. If this is design, then the first premise is false.

Perhaps by *design* Adam means not just natural orderliness but determined complexity, like bird nests, chipmunk burrows, ant hills, and beaver dams. But do wasps and spiders analyze blueprints before constructing their hives and webs? Or can we account for this "design" by the impersonal survival process of natural selection that resulted in the evolution of animal features and instincts? If so, we have design without a designer, and the first premise is again false.

So by *design*, Adam must mean something else. It can't be simple orderliness or evolved complexity. He must mean something like the intelligently designed functional complexity of human machines or architecture. If that is what he means, then the first premise reduces to the tautology: we have never observed things designed by intelligence that were not designed by intelligence. And that begs the question. It smuggles intelligence into the premise that is aimed at concluding intelligence.

As noted above, the fine-tuning argument is based on probability. But in order to arrive at a probability, we need numbers. Increase the numerator and the likelihood rises. Increase the denominator and it drops. How do we know what those numbers are?

As I clarified during the debate, I am not arguing that a multiverse *does* explain the appearance of fine-tuning, only that it could. If there are many universes, this increases the likelihood. I gave the example where you remove the blindfold to learn that there were 101 prisoners being executed by 100 sharpshooters. You were the one lucky prisoner, at least, who was not shot. The odds of being killed changed from 100/1 to 100/101. That is less than 100 percent. Each prisoner had about a 99 percent chance of being killed. At least one of them would survive.

Assuming that the cosmic constants must remain extremely close to their observed values in order for life to exist, multiplying the probabilities of survival of all twenty or so parameters results in a monstrously huge denominator. Let's say it is something like 10^{60} or even larger. (Now there's a power. The power to shrink!) Let's call that huge denominator LN (large number). Assuming there is only one universe in which those values might vary, we have a minuscule survival probability of 1/LN. That is not zero, but it is small enough to be virtually impossible. That is the essence of the fine-tuning argument.

But what if our universe is not the only prisoner being shot at? If there are two universes, the likelihood of survival doubles (approximately) to 2/LN. As the numerator increases, so does the likelihood. There might be LN universes or LN^2 universes, meaning it would be highly improbable for *no* life to exist anywhere.

If Adam were to outright deny the possibility of multiple universes, wouldn't he be limiting God? Couldn't a Supreme Being create more than one universe? Maybe God rolled the dice until it came out right or used a shotgun approach knowing it would hit something. However, we have to agree that the multiverse, for now, is only a hypothesis. "We should apply the rules of science and skepticism to the multiverse hypothesis as vigorously as we would any other," writes Michael Shermer in *The Believing Brain.*[20]

Adam makes what appears to be an excellent point that a multiverse might prove too much. In any one of the random collection of universes, it would be impossible to distinguish between coincidence and miracle, he suggests. Suppose every time it thunders we hear a voice saying "Allah is Great" in Arabic, or every time driftwood settles on the beaches of Goa it spells "Ganesha is Lord" in Marathi. I would not say we just happen to live in one of those universes where strange things like that always happen. I would ask why. If there *were* a god, how could they prove that their supernatural signs are not just random happenings? That's a good question, but I would reply that this is another category error. The randomness Adam is referring to would happen *among* the universes, not *within* them. Once a random universe begins, the laws of *that* universe must be thereafter constant. That's why they are called constants. Any universe in which observers exist must provide an environment where life evolved by uniform natural processes. Deviation is not possible—that's why we call them *laws* of nature—otherwise life could not have emerged. A miracle is a deviation of the laws of nature (in any universe), so if we did see supernatural signs, I would not flippantly pretend it was random luck. I would be in awe. I would take such evidence seriously. I also remind Adam that within *this* universe, we have no such evidence.

Although the multiverse, like God, is unproved, it can have value in an argument. I can say to Adam: If you are going to posit a "best guess" of an intelligent designer to explain the appearance of fine-tuning, then I can respond with a "best guess" of a multiverse. If the multiverse hypothesis proves too much, the designer hypothesis proves too little. Like matter and antimatter, or imaginary numbers in an equation, they cancel out. Someday, if the multiverse or the intelligent designer is confirmed by observation, *then* we can ask if either one is the best explanation for the appearance of fine-tuning.

It turns out that we don't need the multiverse. In his book *The Fallacy of Fine-Tuning*, Victor Stenger shows that even if there is only one universe, the probability of *some* kind of life is higher than what Adam might believe.[21] If the parameters are like dials on a machine, and you adjust more than one at a

20. Michael Shermer, *The Believing Brain: From Ghosts and Gods to Politics and Conspiracies—How We Construct Beliefs and Reinforce Them as Truths* (Times, 2011), 327.

21. Victor Stenger, *The Fallacy of Fine-Tuning: Why the Universe Is Not Designed for Us* (Prometheus, 2011).

time in different directions, you can keep the entire system on a knife edge to be life-permitting in *some* form. Terrestrial life is not the only possibility. Like riding a bicycle, you can stay in balance with small corrections. If the river had flowed differently, we would have a different border.[22]

Even keeping our current values, there is wiggle room. The physicist Lawrence Krauss explains that some constants are not so "fine-tuned" after all: "It is true that if the cosmological constant were much larger than it is, then life as we know it on earth would have been impossible; but if the energy of empty space were far smaller, even if zero, then galaxies would still be forming today, the universe proving even *more* conducive to life in the long run. . . . A cosmological constant set to zero would have been a far better bet for a good designer."[23]

If the universe *was* fine-tuned for life, why is most of it so hostile to life? "The universe is trying to kill us," astrophysicist Neil DeGrasse Tyson has often said. Outside the niche in which an organism evolves—such as the thin membrane of our atmosphere or oceans—nature is lethal. Even within the niche, it is precarious. The universe seems to be elegantly fine-tuned for death.

The phrase "fine-tuning" is teleological. It assumes life is the goal. But that is a human-centric attitude. Universes can exist just fine without us. There are billions of planets where life has not appeared. Are those failures? There could be many universes without life. Are they miscarriages because *we* are not in them?

When looking at the constants of nature, why would the word *tuning* even come to mind? Does Adam believe the creator happened upon a primordial soup of variables and began adjusting them until everything came into focus for wonderful humans to exist? The word *tuning* begs the question. It implies a "tuner" at the beginning of the argument. That inserts intelligence into the premise aimed at concluding intelligence. Asking "If there's no God, who pops up the next Kleenex?" forces the answer to be a "who."

During my opening statement I used the illustration of rivers flowing along borders.[24] That is a contraduction. It is backward thinking because the rivers came first. Another example of contraduction is the sunrise. The sun does not rise; *we* rise. (Lives were lost trying to correct that contraduction. Thinkers like Bruno and Galileo were killed and persecuted by the church for such heresy.)

22. Sometimes rivers do flow differently. Carter Lake in Iowa used to be on the east side of the Missouri River, but after the river changed course, it is now inside the state of Nebraska.

23. Lawrence M. Krauss, "Cosmology Without Design," *Inference* 5, no. 3 (2020): 3, https://doi.org/10.37282/991819.20.34.

24. And notice that when rivers veer from the borders, they head straight to the major cities.

Contraduction is a reversal of order. Have you ever been sitting in a train that is not moving when the train next to you starts to move and you briefly think it is *you* who are moving? You got it backward. You interpreted reality from *your* point of view. The fine-tuning argument is like that. That's why I quoted Stenger during the debate: "The universe was not fine-tuned for us. We were fine-tuned for the universe."[25]

By the way, if there is an intelligent designer, its mind would also appear to be balanced on a knife blade of perfection. Does Adam imagine God asking, "How did my amazing mind become so fine-tuned?" If the creator does not have to ask that question, why do we? (In either case, the answer would be evolution.)

And what about other celestial beings? Adam probably believes God created angels, which are presumably alive. Do those creatures need to dwell in an environment that was fine-tuned for *their* existence? If not, how can they live? If spiritual life, like material life, requires a fine-tuned environment, then wouldn't the spiritual Supreme Being itself be dependent on those same parameters? If you think angels, spirits, and demons are living beings, then you don't believe it is necessary to tune anything in order to be alive.

Setting aside the hypotheses of a supernatural world or a natural multiverse, even if they cancel out, still leaves questions. But the problem now shifts from cosmic to local. Instead of asking about the probability that the universe would be fine-tuned for *us*, we can ask about the probability that some kind of life would be fine-tuned to fit *this* universe. Flip it around: we are looking not for an intelligent designer but an intelligent observer. Not all rivers flow along borders, and not all planets can potentially support life. There are actually more planets than stars in the universe. There are hundreds of millions of planets in our galaxy alone that could potentially support life.[26] Since there are billions of galaxies, there must be bazillions of planets around stars at a distance where liquid water can exist. It is not a stretch to think how gazillions of molecules in Earth's early oceans and lakes bombarded by kazillions of photons over more than a billion years resulted in a simple replicator. One is all that is needed to get the evolutionary process started.

25. Stenger, *Fallacy of Fine-Tuning*, 23.

26. Astronomer Kelsey Johnson writes: "When you consider the sheer number of Earth-like planets orbiting at Earth-like distances around the Sun-like stars—just in our galaxy alone—our sense of importance gets knocked down a notch. Observations from the Kepler mission indicate that in the Milky Way, there are roughly 11 billion of these Earth-like analogs. . . . Be wary of assuming yours is the only example and not part of a much larger ensemble." See *Into the Unknown: The Quest to Understand the Mysteries of the Cosmos* (Basic Books, 2024), 327–28.

As I said in the debate, the fine-tuning argument assumes evolution. Most Christians accept the fact of evolution. Many theists, including most Hindus and many Muslims, are comfortable with natural selection. I assume that Adam, like many thoughtful theists, does not see evolution as a threat to his faith. Because, if you are a believer, who are you to dictate to God how he must have created life? The nonintuitive wonder of natural selection might be precisely what the free and unpredictable actions of a creative deity might look like. (Of course, the brutality of predation and extinction questions the morality of someone who would set up such a cruel system.)

Morality

Adam's specialty is the moral argument. Here is how he phrased it:

1. There are objective moral truths independent of our minds.
2. The existence of God is the best explanation for how there could be objective moral truths.
3. Therefore, God exists.

Both of those premises are questionable. Adam himself abandoned one of them during the debate.

As I said in the debate, the first premise is an oxymoron. What exactly is an objective moral truth? Truth is not a thing. Truth is the degree with which a statement corresponds with reality. The only thing that can be true or false is a statement or, as philosophers like to say it, a proposition. Propositions are produced and understood by minds and spoken or represented in language. If all life in the universe were to disappear but this book remained, the statements on these pages would be mere ink patterns. The "truth" or "value" of these statements would no longer exist because there would be no minds to decipher and interpret them.[27] When Adam talks about "objective moral truth," he commits the fallacy of reification—he turns a statement into a thing. Since a moral value or truth is a concept understood by a functioning mind, and since to be objective means to exist independently of the mind, how can there be an objective moral truth? That is like a married bachelor or a deafening silence.

If objective moral truths exist, what are they? Are the statements "It is morally wrong to eat meat" or "homosexuality is an abomination" or "don't

27. We could say that *if* minds existed that could decipher the symbols, those truths and values would have meaning. We can say the same thing about the proposition "2 + 2 = 4," which is not an objective entity but a statement that can be objectively verified.

boil a goat in its mother's milk" objective truths?[28] If they are, shouldn't they apply to *all* animals? All biological organisms are subject to the same natural laws, like gravity, Newton's laws of motion, and so on. If the statement "it is morally wrong to kill for personal gain" is an objective moral truth, then are lions and eagles murderers? If not, the argument looks like special pleading. Adam uses the analogy of 2 + 2 = 4, which is true independent of humanity, but then compares that to morality, which is true *only* for humans. He is comparing apples and oranges.

And if there are objective moral truths, why do theists (even mere theists) not agree what they are? As I said in the debate, take any moral issue society is struggling with right now—the death penalty, gun control, birth control, abortion, women's rights, LGBTQ rights, doctor-assisted suicide, COVID restrictions, human-caused climate change, and so on—and you will find good Bible-believing church-goers falling on both sides. Where exactly is the "objective moral truth" Adam is talking about? (I discuss this further later.)

But as I also said, it is wrong to imagine atheists have no basis for moral values. I don't speak for all atheists, but although there is no such thing as an objective moral truth that exists outside the mind, we *can* say that there are moral values that can be objectively justified by reference to the real world outside the mind. So if by "objective" we mean not "objectively existing" but "objectively justified," then perhaps we can say atheists have "objective moral values," but that is an entirely different animal from what Adam is picturing. It's not transcendent.

The Golden Rule appears to transcend history and culture. But what does *transcend* mean? The word has different usages. In one usage, for example, the supernatural world supposedly *transcends* the natural world as an objective realm above the mundane. But in another usage, while I am playing the piano, for example, music theory *transcends* the notes I am playing as a conceptual framework above and beyond the scales and chords.[29] Does this mean there is an actual realm of music theory above the physical world? Since moral principles like the Golden Rule appear to "transcend" humanity, we sometimes hear the claim by theists that since there is a moral law, there must be a moral lawgiver above and beyond the natural world. That is an equivocation.

C. S. Lewis proposed that since humans almost universally agree that there are deeds we ought to do or not do, we are acknowledging that we are governed

28. This is one of the laws inscribed on the stone tablets of the Ten Commandments given by God to Moses on Mount Sinai in Exod. 34:26: "And he wrote on the tablets the words of the covenant—the Ten Commandments" (Exod. 34:28). See also Exod. 23:19 and Deut. 14:21.

29. By the way, I'm happy Adam said I create "beautiful music."

by something outside of nature: "Consequently, this Rule of Right and Wrong, or Law of Human Nature, or whatever you call it, must somehow or other be a real thing. . . . It begins to look as if we shall have to admit that there is more than one kind of reality; that, in this particular case, there is something above and beyond the ordinary facts of men's behaviour, and yet quite definitely real—a real law, which none of us made, but which we find pressing on us."[30] Lewis suggested that there is "a Power behind the facts, a Director, a Guide" who created the "Moral Law which He has put into our minds." But that reasoning only makes sense if you swap one usage of *transcend* (or "behind") for another. Lewis appears to be engaging in equivocal reasoning, claiming that a law is a "real thing." It would be equally ludicrous to capitalize "Music Theory" or "Mathematics" or "Art" in order to raise their status to a spooky level "beyond" or "behind" nature.

And this leads to the problem with Adam's second premise. How does he connect the dots? Since moral values reside *within* nature (in our physical brains), we can't say that God (a supposedly transcendent being) is the "best explanation" for them. How could it be better than a natural explanation? As I said during the debate (and in my book *Mere Morality*), morality can be summed up in one word: harm. If you are acting with the intention of minimizing overall harm, you are acting morally. And harm, whatever it is, is natural. The consequences of our actions can be judged by reference to the real world, not by something "behind" it. This corrects a contraduction: it is bottom-up, not top-down. A principle, not a law.

Adam agrees with me on this point. At the end of the debate, he said: "I would affirm and agree with you that our consequences and seeing what causes harm is a good epistemological tool for us in knowing right and wrong." Since Adam knows that there exists at least one natural moral philosophy with objectively justified values, he can't maintain that a hypothetical supernatural being is the best explanation. An immediately accessible natural explanation *must* be better than an inaccessible supernatural explanation. Bottom-up consequences are measurable; top-down commands are not. With a natural moral philosophy, I can say that the reason an action is something we ought not to do is that it causes unnecessary harm. With God the reason is behind a curtain: "Because I said so."

And where does "ought" come from? Why *should* we be moral? It comes from nowhere. Ought is simply half of a conditional statement: *if* we want less harm, *then* we ought to act in ways to minimize it.

30. C. S. Lewis, "Mere Christianity," in *The C. S. Lewis Signature Classics* (HarperOne, 2017), 27.

Immaterial Minds

Adam compared the idea of immaterial minds to the existence of numbers. But numbers are not things. They are concepts. By that analogy, God is a concept.

Adam's own design argument logically contradicts immaterial minds. We could say:

1. We have never observed a mind without a brain.
2. God has a mind.
3. Therefore, God has a brain.

A mind is a function of a brain, which is a physical organ. Mind is not a thing. Mind is to brain as digestion is to stomach. Adam tried to infer the existence of immaterial minds by noting he could not see any minds in the audience, but he knew they were out there. Well, he didn't see any digestion either. Can Adam infer the existence of immaterial digestion?

An immaterial mind is an incoherent concept. (More on this later.) Mind doesn't spookily enter an organism from the outside; like digestion, circulation, and metabolism, it is a function of something *inside* a physical organism. When we die, our minds aren't going anywhere.

Hiddenness

Overall, I was impressed with Adam's intelligence and civility. But there was one moment when his toe inched close to the line of *ad hominem*. On the question of the hiddenness of God, he said: "God might know—I'm speculating here—that if he revealed himself more it wouldn't make any difference. Those who reject him with this amount of evidence would also reject him even if they had more evidence. I've heard Dan say on many occasions that he would reject God even if he revealed himself very obviously and directly to Dan. If that's true, then why would God give Dan more evidence?"

Notice that Adam used the word *reject*, as if those of us who are skeptical about the supernatural are closed-mindedly resisting the truth that is so obvious to him. During my debate with Cardinal George Pell, he compared atheists to dogs at a concert: "They hear every sound but have got no understanding of the music." (As a composer, I wonder if Pell truly understood music.) "Seeing they do not see," said Jesus, "and hearing they do not hear, nor do they understand" (Matt. 13:13, NKJV). Well, anybody can say that. If I were to tell Adam that the reason he is a theist is that he is incapable of understanding atheism, he might feel affronted. How does Adam know that it wouldn't make any difference if I had more evidence? What is he suggesting I do in the face of the admitted paucity of evidence? Have faith? It appears he is stepping out of philosophy and into theology. The word *reject* has different usages. Even if an honest refusal to jump to conclusions amounts to a rejection, rejecting God's existence is not the same as rejecting God's moral authority. As I said during the debate, I would certainly accept God's existence if it were proved beyond a reasonable doubt, but that does not mean I would necessarily like the guy. If Adam's mere theism fleshes out to the biblical God, then I would definitely not admire, much less worship, *that* character.[31] If you lose a war against a powerful adversary and have to concede defeat, does that mean you suddenly love and happily worship the tyrant who forced his will upon you? Like anybody else, God, if he exists, would have to earn my respect.

But back to the question. If there is a God, why is he going to so much trouble to hide himself?[32] During the debate, at least, we did not hear a good answer. The philosopher Delos McKown said: "The invisible and the nonexistent look very much alike."[33] I don't know everything, but what does Adam see that I don't see? He seems to be suggesting it is a matter of attitude.

I used to preach that those who reject God have a rebellious spirit. But now I ask: What's wrong with rebellion? The biblical Daniel was a rebel. Martin Luther and John Calvin were rebels. So was George Washington. Thomas Jefferson drafted the defiant Declaration of Independence, rebelling from a sovereign king. We Americans proudly fought a Revolutionary War to break free from the Lord and Master. We applaud the slave Spartacus for defying the authority of Rome. When you read about slave rebellions, whom are you rooting for? I hope not the masters. The rebellious Elizabeth Cady Stanton and Susan B. Anthony and thousands of uppity women bravely challenged the biblically based patriarchal oppression of human rights and freedoms. Much progress has been accomplished by people with a rebellious spirit.

Adam fought a good fight, but I still see no reason to believe in God, so it's moot to ask if I would reject such a being. Before I make that decision, he first has to come out of hiding.

31. See my book *God: The Most Unpleasant Character in All Fiction* (Prometheus, 2023).

32. "Truly you are a God who has been hiding himself" (Isa. 45:15, NIV). "Why do you hide your face?" (Ps. 44:24, NIV).

33. Delos McKown, *The Mythmaker's Magic* (Prometheus, 1993), 39.

5

Theist Responding to the Debate

Is God Hiding from Us?

Andrew Drinkard

The other day while listening to a Christian radio station, I heard a song that said something to the effect of "How can you not see God in every little thing or moment and how can you not feel his love?" I don't think these were good rhetorical questions used by the singer. For many, it is easy to believe that God exists based on their experience in the world, but for many others it's not. Dan Barker said that if God exists, then we shouldn't need to debate about it. The debate itself demonstrates a lack of evidence for God's existence. Why does God seem hidden from us? Doesn't he want us to believe in him? I will answer the question in two parts. First, I think there is good evidence for the existence of God (some of which Adam Lloyd Johnson presented in the debate), so in one sense I don't think God is *fully* hiding from us. Second, I want to provide some good reasons for why God, in another sense, seems hidden from so many.[1]

In this chapter, my aim is to review what a few leading thinkers have said concerning this topic, expand on some of those thoughts, and include my own understanding of the matter. My goal is not to provide some technical argument that entirely defeats the problem of divine hiddenness but rather reflect on what I take to be good reasons for why this problem exists. A cumulative approach will be used to address this, as I believe there are multiple reasons for why God seems hidden. I will also present two different models showing how God interacts with humans to create meaningful relationships. Before I do that, let me briefly explain what the hiddenness argument means and what is meant by the word *hidden*.

1. God's hiddenness isn't only experienced by nonbelievers, but it's also experienced occasionally by those who do believe in him. The Bible is replete with examples of God hiding, e.g., Deut. 32; Micah 3; Ezek. 39; Isa. 8; 30; 45; 51; 54; 57; 59; 64; Jer. 33; Pss. 10; 13; 22; 27; 30; 44; 51; 69; 88–89; 102; 104; 143; Job 13; 34; Matt. 27; Mark 15.

The Hiddenness Argument

The basic argument concerning the hiddenness of God is that if God loves the whole world and wants the world to believe in him and have a meaningful relationship with him, then we should observe more people in different parts of the world believing that God exists. If God is so powerful and loving, then why doesn't he just show up and end this debate? Although a vast majority of the world population believes in God or some deity, the nontheist rightly points out those who do not.[2] This includes atheists who are resistant toward the idea of God, and atheists who are not resistant. The individuals who are closed to the possibility of God's existence are referred to as *resistant* nonbelievers (because they are resisting the idea of God), and the ones who are open to the possibility of God's existence are referred to as *nonresistant* nonbelievers (because they are *not* resisting the idea of God).

The atheist claims that because we see many others not believing in God's existence, this counts as evidence for the nonexistence of God. Some skeptics have gone as far as arguing that God would *never* allow an individual to experience a period of nonbelief at *any* point in their life, because a loving God would want that person to believe in him at *all* points in their life.

The main argument from atheists like philosopher J. L. Schellenberg (a leading proponent of the hiddenness argument) is that if an all-loving God exists, then he will desire a relationship with everyone who is able and willing (i.e.,

2. A Pew Research survey found that "worldwide, more than eight-in-ten people identify with a religious group. A comprehensive demographic study of more than 230 countries and territories conducted by the Pew Research Center's Forum on Religion & Public Life estimates that there are 5.8 billion religiously affiliated adults and children around the globe, representing 84% of the 2010 world population of 6.9 billion." Pew Research Center, "The Global Religious Landscape," December 18, 2012, https://tinyurl.com/3d5pbmub. It is hard to imagine that billions of people could be mistaken in having a true religious experience of some kind, but my aim is not to provide evidence for God's existence in this chapter (albeit I personally do not think religious experience is a form of evidence meant to persuade others that God exists). Rather, my aim is to show that his nonexistence is not more probable based on the lack of religious experiences by many people. Despite this, many people have argued that religious experience is evidentially valuable for theism. Philosopher Helen De Cruz says, "Since the majority of people worldwide not only believe that God(s) exist(s), but are also confident God(s) exist(s), it would seem rational for a theist to see this as further evidence against global atheism. . . . Even if it turns out that religious experience and ordinary sense perception are not closely analogous, religious experience could still be used as evidence against global atheism." See Helen De Cruz, "Evidential Objections to Atheism," in *A Companion to Atheism and Philosophy*, ed. Graham Oppy (Wiley & Sons, 2019), 482–85.

nonresistant). But because there are able and willing people who don't believe in God at some point in time, and Schellenberg says belief is at least necessary to get a relationship started, then this means an all-loving God doesn't exist.[3]

What about the word *hidden*? When we say God is hidden, we simply mean that (1) God has not revealed himself in such a way that allows us to have a constant direct awareness of his presence (or physically detect him since he is a nonphysical being); and (2) many people across the world do not believe he exists. Many individuals claim they've not had a religious experience nor discovered evidence for God strong enough to afford them belief.

However, God's hiddenness does *not* mean that God has left us without adequate evidence for his existence, and it means that others still have the capacity to recognize and experience God's presence with the ability of entering a meaningful relationship with him. This would be a kind of relationship that involves our admiration, obedience, gratitude, trust, correction, and other features of relationship.

So, for God to be open to everyone and not closed, some atheists say, there should never be a time in which an all-loving God permits unbelief, thereby preventing a meaningful relationship from developing, particularly for those nonbelievers who are *not* resistant to the idea.[4] Moreover, many atheists claim the door would never be closed at any point in time preventing Dan from

3. Schellenberg formulates his argument as follows: (1) If God exists, then God is perfectly loving toward persons. (2) If God is perfectly loving, then God will be always open for a personal relationship with persons. (3) If God exists, then for any person, God will be always open to a personal relationship. (4) If for any person, God is open to being in a personal relationship, then it is not the case that any person at any time is in a nonresistant state of nonbelief in relation to God's existence. (5) If God exists, then it is not the case that any nonresistant person at any time will be in a state of nonbelief. (6) There has existed at some point in time at least one person that is a nonresistant nonbeliever. (7) Thus, it is not the case that God exists. For a detailed treatment, see J. L. Schellenberg, "The Hiddenness Argument," *Annals of Philosophy* 69, no. 3 (2021): 65, https://doi.org/10.18290/rf21693-4. I disagree with premises 2–5 and 7 and will seek to offer reasons why these do not entail the nonexistence of God.

4. Note that atheism could still be false even if the hiddenness argument succeeds. It could be that some sort of deistic God exists that is not all-loving but nevertheless created us while maintaining his distance. Although I do not think this is true nor will I defend this position, it is still a possibility that the atheist cannot avoid. Helen De Cruz says, "But it is clear that even a more charitable reading of Schellenberg (2006; 2007) cannot rule out all forms of theism: we may be mistaken about God's love. Instead of a loving deity, it may well be that we are instead faced with a cold, distant God who is nonetheless the creator of everything that is, and who is also omniscient and omnipotent, merely lacking omnibenevolence." See De Cruz, "Evidential Objections to Atheism," 477.

believing in God if he wanted to. God might provide an experience or do something for Dan enabling him to believe so that a meaningful relationship could develop between them.[5]

So why is God hiding, in the sense that many still do not believe that he exists? I think that God can be all-loving despite creating people he knew would not believe in him. There are several different reasons for why God doesn't reveal himself in such a way that permits all capable persons at any given point in time to believe that he exists.

Evaluating the Evidence

The skeptic says that we lack adequate evidence for God's existence, whether that's convincing arguments or miraculous signs; therefore, we can assume that God probably doesn't exist. However, the skeptic should also be cautious not to dismiss what many consider to be good arguments and evidence for God's existence. One shouldn't approach the topic already assuming there is no evidence for God without properly evaluating the data that is serving as evidence provided by theists and agnostics (otherwise, it's question-begging).

Many nonbelievers have evaluated what has been offered as evidence, but they remain unconvinced for whatever reason. Therefore, they think their unbelief is justified. They don't believe in God because they believe God doesn't exist. But why are so many others out there claiming to have religious experiences? Why do billions of people across the world believe in God, including well-informed intelligent people? Many are persuaded by good arguments and evidence for God's existence. Moreover, approximately 51 percent of scientists—those who we are often told are most likely to be atheists—believe in God or a higher power.[6] This undermines the legitimacy of the claims made by many skeptics who say that only naive, irrational, and delusional people believe in God.

5. Thanks to Mike Rea for his feedback and providing me with a helpful distinction here.

6. Pew Research Center, "Religion and Science in the United States," November 5, 2009, https://tinyurl.com/3a57z34n. Also, see Rice University, "First Worldwide Survey of Religion and Science: No, Not All Scientists Are Atheists," *Phys.Org*, December 3, 2015, https://tinyurl.com/bk4ysup6. Elaine Ecklund, founding director of Rice University's Religion and Public Life Program, was the study's lead investigator. The article states, "The study's results challenge longstanding assumptions about the science-faith interface. While it is commonly assumed that most scientists are atheists, the global perspective resulting from the study shows that this is simply not the case. 'More than half of scientists in India, Italy, Taiwan, and Turkey self-identify as religious,' Ecklund said. 'And it's striking that approximately twice as many "convinced atheists" exist in the general population of Hong Kong, for example, (55 percent) compared with the scientific community in this region (26 percent).'"

God has revealed himself through his effects as observed in the world. This is sometimes referred to as *natural theology*, as Adam proposed in the debate. I agree with philosopher Paul Moser when he points out, "If the God who on occasion hides has left adequate available evidence of God's existence, including signals of such evidence, for all people, then theism will be epistemically unscathed by divine hiding."[7]

In other words, just because God seems hidden from some does not mean others cannot know that he exists, nor does it entail a total lack of evidence for his existence. Perhaps the better question is to ask why doesn't God provide *stronger* evidence for his existence? I think the burden of proof is too heavy for the skeptic to use God's hiddenness as robust evidence against God's existence. To make such a claim is to say that God (who I will presume is all-loving and all-good) could not possibly have *any* good reasons for allowing nonbelievers to exist. As part of this cumulative case, I will now offer some reasons why God "hides" from *resistant* nonbelievers (those resisting the idea of God) and *non-resistant* nonbelievers (those not resisting the idea of God). I will then present two models showing how a seemingly hidden God interacts with humans to create meaningful relationships.

Major Resistant Nonbelievers

I believe there are varying degrees of resistance in nonbelievers, so I would like to distinguish between what I call *major* resistant nonbelievers and *minor* resistant nonbelievers. Both types are resisting God, so why doesn't God give them signs so they can believe in him? Wouldn't an all-loving and all-good God want them to believe so they can begin a meaningful relationship? Many of these resisters want to know if God exists. Surely it wouldn't be difficult for an all-powerful God to give them clear signs to take away their unbelief. Dan says he would like to know. Let's start by looking at the major resistant nonbelievers.

First, we must reflect on what God's intentions could be here. What is the point of our existence? Let's suppose that God's primary aim in creating humanity was to make loving relationships with us. For example, the Judeo-Christian God declares that he is love (1 John 4:16), that he loves us (John 3:16), and wants all of us to be with him forever (2 Pet. 3:9; 1 Tim. 2:4).

However, love is the kind of thing that cannot be coerced. Rather, love stems from a positive relationship in which there are someone to love and someone to

7. Paul Moser, "Divine Hiding," in *Divine Hiddenness: New Essays*, ed. Daniel Howard-Snyder and Paul Moser (Cambridge University Press, 2001), 132.

freely reciprocate that love. Simply having knowledge of someone's existence does not entail love or a meaningful relationship. When I first met my wife, I believed that she existed, but I couldn't force her into a meaningful relationship and fall in love with me. She had to freely choose to do so—and thankfully she did!

Similarly, God desires more than mere knowledge of his existence—he desires a meaningful relationship. Even the demons believe that God exists, but they don't want a relationship with him (James 2:19). God's omnipotence means that he can do all *things*, but contradictions are not things. It's a contradiction to say that God could force us to freely love him. It would be like God making triangles with four sides. That cannot be done because it's nonsensical. If God made us love him or always make the right decisions, then we wouldn't really be free.[8] He would have to program us like androids. In Star Wars, C-3PO may be programmed to attend to the needs of R2-D2, but C-3PO doesn't have the emotional intelligence or volitional capacity to freely love R2-D2.

God wants creatures to be the source of their freely choosing him. It would be quite pitiful if the only way God could get people to want him is if he programmed them to do so. If you programmed C-3PO to exhibit actions that resemble love to you, that machine isn't expressing true genuine love. It didn't freely choose to give you anything. Rather, you gave it to yourself by programming it to do so.

Second, what if God did provide extraordinary evidence of his existence? What makes the major resistant atheist think that a miraculous sign provided by God would be enough to convince her of his existence? Many atheists have declared they would attribute such fantastic events to naturalistic phenomena. Suppose God appeared in front of everyone across the globe in an unmistakable way. The atheist might think they're hallucinating. Or maybe some extraterrestrial intelligence used their advanced technology to trick them into believing that their experience was supernatural.

When asked what it would take for atheist biologist Richard Dawkins to believe in God, Dawkins replied, "Well, I used to say it would be very simple. It would be the second coming of Jesus or a great, big, deep, booming, bass Paul Robeson voice saying, 'I am God, and I created.' But I was persuaded . . . that even if there was this booming voice in the second coming in clouds of

8. I am referring to libertarian free will in which creatures are the source of their choices and are not determined in every decision due to the prior conditions and the laws that govern our world. In other words, there are certain circumstances in which humans have the ability to make decisions that have not been causally determined by factors outside of themselves.

glory, the more probable explanation is that it's a hallucination, or a conjuring trick by David Copperfield, or something."[9]

When atheist chemist Peter Atkins was asked what evidence it would take to get him to believe in God, he replied, "I can't think of any . . . if I agreed with some evidence, then it showed that I'd simply gone mad. I don't think there can be any evidence."[10] Dawkins and Atkins are a couple examples of major resistant nonbelievers that would probably not be persuaded by more evidence of God's existence.[11] Atheist philosopher Thomas Nagel said, "I want atheism to be true and am made uneasy by the fact that some of the most intelligent and well-informed people I know are religious believers. It isn't just that I don't believe in God and, naturally, hope that I'm right in my belief. It's that I hope there is no God! I don't want there to be a God; I don't want the universe to be like that."[12]

Many skeptics are already committed to a belief system or interpretation of the world that excludes the existence of God. Therefore, any evidence that has been provided to them by God could be overlooked or interpreted in a way that favors their already established nontheistic position. As the seventeenth-century French philosopher Blaise Pascal said, people almost invariably arrive at their beliefs not on the basis of proof but on the basis of what they find attractive.[13]

But let's suppose God revealed himself in such a way that enabled these major resisters to believe. This still doesn't achieve what God desires because God doesn't desire mere belief. He desires a meaningful relationship. If God revealed himself in an undeniable fashion to these individuals, it does not entail that these major resistant nonbelievers would want a relationship with God.

Dan seems majorly resistant in this sense. He said (in the debate) that if God revealed himself in such a way that enabled him to believe, then Dan

9. Richard Dawkins, "Richard Dawkins in Conversation with Peter Boghossian," Peter Boghossian, posted November 7, 2013, YouTube, 53:12, https://www.youtube.com/watch?v=RoQurwEZmmQ. This interview occurred on October 11, 2013 at Portland State University.

10. Peter Atkins, "Lennox vs Atkins—Can Science Explain Everything? (Official Debate Video)," Premier Unbelievable?, posted February 17, 2019, YouTube, 1:38:58, https://www.youtube.com/watch?v=fSYwCaFkYno. See at the fifty-nine-minute mark. This live debate occurred at Southampton University on January 31, 2019.

11. There is a distinction to be made here. Think of all the things that people believe and say they would do in some given circumstance, but when said circumstance arises, they do something entirely different.

12. Thomas Nagel, *The Last Word* (Oxford University Press, 1997), 130.

13. This is a quote often attributed to Pascal; though possibly paraphrased, it captures a key theme from *Pensées*. Blaise Pascal, *Pensées*, trans. A. J. Krailsheimer (London: Penguin, 1995).

would tell God to go to hell. Dan doesn't want God, and if he knew for certain that God existed, then it would only increase Dan's averseness. I can somewhat relate to Dan in the sense that, if some ancient Greek god like Dionysus (whose character is morally reprehensible in my opinion) appeared to me in an unmistakable fashion, I know that I wouldn't worship him, devote my life to him, or enter a meaningful relationship with him. I would be majorly resistant despite forming a belief that Dionysus existed.

How could God know what these resisters would do? I take the tradition that God is a supreme being of maximal intellect who possesses abilities that we do not, one of these properties or qualities being omniscience. I think that God's knowledge encompasses everything that *could* happen, everything that *would* happen, and everything that *will* happen (or at the very least has an extremely high degree of certainty for what will happen). I also don't think that God wants to push people further away from him. He wants to do the opposite. So, if God knows that if he were to reveal himself to someone permitting them to believe, and yet that person would still choose to reject God and hate him even more, then it doesn't seem clear that God should reveal himself to that individual. In doing so, God could very well cause that person to become even more resistant.

I agree with philosopher Daniel Howard-Snyder when he says, "If God were to reveal himself to them [resistant nonbelievers] in such a way that they came to believe that God exists, they would or would very likely respond inappropriately; they would or would very likely either reject God's self-revelation or believe with anything from indifference to hostility."[14] No matter how much love God displays towards major resisters, that love is not going to be enough to make them want God, or at least want God for the right reasons. That's what it means to be majorly resistant.

Minor Resistant Nonbelievers and Optimal Relationship

Let's now examine what I call minor resistant nonbelievers. These nonbelievers either (1) are resisting God without even realizing it; (2) would resist God if he enabled them to believe; or (3) no longer believe in God but are open to believing again. These nonbelievers *think* they are nonresistant, but they are truly resistant.

14. Daniel Howard-Snyder, "Divine Openness and Creaturely Non-Resistant Non-Belief," in *Hidden Divinity and Religious Belief: New Perspectives*, ed. Adam Green and Eleonore Stump (Cambridge University Press, 2015), 131.

Recall that God wants a meaningful relationship, intending that it becomes optimized for an eternal future with him in heaven. I call this an optimized relationship because it would be the greatest kind of relationship possible. Why? Because an optimal relationship involves the creature freely loving and valuing their creator for the creator's own sake and experiencing him in such a way that permits the creature to be emotionally, mentally, and spiritually fulfilled for all eternity. In other words, in heaven we will have vastly different experiences than we do now permitting us to be wholly satisfied with God forever. However, this kind of relationship appears to be conditional. For example, if Christianity is true, then the Abrahamic God of the Bible has made it clear that he desires humans to recognize their condemnable moral state and unholy status apart from his redemptive plans. While we are on this planet, the Judeo-Christian God expects a lifelong commitment regardless of the struggles that ensue. Why? Because he intends to mold his followers into holy creatures suitable for his future kingdom. This can only be accomplished through God's grace (unmerited favor) and our willingness to participate.

We've established that major resistant nonbelievers are not open to a relationship with God, let alone one that is optimized for eternity with God in heaven, but it's really the same case for these minor nonresistant nonbelievers as well. God knows that if he revealed himself to them, they would get cold feet and end up refusing to enter a relationship.

The minor resister tells us they not only want to believe in God, but they also want a relationship. They think they aren't resisting God right now. They also think they would not resist God if he enabled them to believe at some point in the future. But how could someone be so certain of their psychology to know this? How do they know that part of their self is not resisting, or would resist God if they came to believe?

It's not contentious to admit that humans are notorious for being extremely selfish, prideful, and comfort-driven. Altruism is frequently taught and reinforced within the young minds of children, yet their selfishness is carried over into adult life. People are prideful. When we are confronted with a personal relationship dispute—whether marital, family or friend—we are easily offended and often dig our heels in rather than humble ourselves and extend forgiveness, grace, and mercy.

People crave comfort. It is not a comfortable thing to be rejected, ostracized, or persecuted for what one believes.[15] Many Christians compromise their beliefs in the secular culture to feel accepted by their peers. The Judeo-Christian

15. According to the 2022 World Watch List, one in seven believers globally experience

God calls us to change in uncomfortable ways that include sacrificing our own goods to benefit others, forgiving those who've wronged us, and loving those who hate us.

This also means suppressing many bad desires that others promote as good. Living in such a way that emulates the nature of a holy god is something many are not willing to partake in. It's easier to idolize other things, indulge unsuitable sexual proclivities, maximize hobby time, overprioritize material goods, maintain ultimate autonomy of your life, and have little to no moral or spiritual accountability. Nobody likes being told what to do, that they aren't good enough, and that they need to change for the better—all which Christianity teaches to some extent.

Paul Moser thinks that God desires a similar type of personal knowledge, stating: "We are thus introducing a notion of knowledge foreign to much philosophy and science, on the basis of what would be God's distinctive character and redemptive purpose. . . . Genuine divine love, like a surgeon's sharp healing knife, would cut deep into the receptive human wills, and the corresponding volitional knowledge of this love's personal source would be equally transformative. The open issue, now cognitively relevant, is whether we are willing to undergo divine love's healing surgery. Philosophers rarely ask, perhaps because the potential fallout is too unsettling."[16]

My point is that many minor resisters would reject visiting this great physician for his healing surgery. I believe they would not be willing to undergo the necessary procedure that follows. The cost for optimization is high, and the road to recovery is not so easy. Jesus and the writers of the New Testament made this patently clear. Regrettably, many desire to be the god of their own life. This is why many (not all) former believers have left the faith and abandoned their relationship with God.

God is looking for a serious commitment for an optimized relationship that necessitates a life of change, love, obedience, and sacrificial living. This relationship is designed to last an eternity, and many would not want to be with God for that duration.[17] This certainly does not mean that those in optimal re-

"high levels of persecution," which equals to "more than 360 million Christians." See Open Doors USA, accessed July 11, 2022, https://tinyurl.com/mtsrx827.

16. Paul Moser, *The Elusive God: Reorienting Religious Epistemology* (Cambridge University Press, 2008), 97.

17. See C. S. Lewis, *The Great Divorce* (HarperCollins, 2002); Lewis evokes strong imagery to help the reader form an idea of what heaven might be like for those unsuited for such an environment. Heaven will be a very uncomfortable place for those who do not want God, and many would rather be separated from him (i.e., hell).

lationships will be morally perfect. However, it does mean these individuals will continue striving to stay in their relationship despite stumbling along the way. God may remain hidden from some minor resisters because he knows they will eventually reject his plans for optimization and deny him. And as with any relationship, they are free to enter and leave, as many have over the years.

The minor resister may disagree and retort that they certainly would stay, hence their perceived nonresistance. Nevertheless, just as so many marriages at the altar begin the same way, often those committed hearts grow cold, and they no longer want to be with their first love. Because God knows what each minor resister would or would (likely) do with great certainty in any given circumstance, just as he does with the major resistant nonbeliever, it doesn't seem clear that God must reveal himself to them if they will later decommit, thereby creating an even unhealthier relationship. God wants as many permanent disciples as possible, not temporary believers. Minor resisters have the freedom to enter a relationship; they just wouldn't be willing to or would later decommit.

But what about those minor resisters who *used* to believe in God but then stopped believing? Why would God enable their belief, but not other minor resisters? That's a good question. I really don't know why. Perhaps any world that God creates like this one would contain humans having (1) the freedom to eventually obtain belief due to the available evidence in nature (or evangelistic efforts by Christians); *and* (2) the freedom to abandon their relationship with God.

One might object that God should not have created persons that he knew would deny him. Well, it may be that a world in which everyone merely believes in God is certainly possible, but actualizing or creating such a world in which everyone freely enters and remains in a healthy relationship with God is not.[18] Any world in which God creates free creatures may be a world in which creatures freely reject him.

Recall, it's impossible to force someone to freely do something. If God created a world in which we were all entering a loving relationship with him, then one could argue that we are not truly free because we have been unilaterally encoded with these non-controllable desires. A world of nonfree creatures controlled to love God does not seem as good as a world of free creatures freely

18. For resources on this topic, see Thomas P. Flint, *Divine Providence: The Molinist Account* (Cornell University Press, 1998); William Lane Craig, *The Only Wise God* (Wipf & Stock, 1999); Kirk MacGregor, *Luis de Molina* (Zondervan, 2015); John D. Laing, *Middle Knowledge: Human Freedom in Divine Sovereignty* (Kregel, 2018); Kenneth Keathley, *Salvation and Sovereignty* (B&H, 2010).

choosing a loving relationship with God. Surely we would say the same of our own marriages and relationships!

In fact, one might argue that nonresistant nonbelievers are actually evidence for the existence of God because so many people desire to be with a transcendent higher power. This cries out for an explanation. Why would someone want to believe in an almighty creator if there wasn't some truth behind these desires? It's not like adults are desperately clinging to the idea that Santa Claus or the Easter Bunny exists. Instead, they're hoping that a superior being exists who can provide a type of fulfillment for which their soul or mind seems to yearn.

Overall, I think the majority of nonbelievers fall into the *minor* resistant camp. Thankfully, many minor (and some major) resisters eventually come to believe in God and enter a healthy relationship with him at the appropriate time.[19] They realize that part of themselves was subconsciously resisting God during their prior state of nonbelief, and now they are delighted to be in a loving relationship with their creator.

If God led them to believe at the wrong time, it may have just pushed them further away. Let's also not forget that numerous individuals testify that they used to believe in God, stopped believing and became resistant, but then *came back* to believing in God and now have a relationship with him. What about them? How do we account for this? It seems that God's arms remain open, allowing the deserting nonbeliever to regain belief and return at the right time.

The reason I spent as much time as I did on the resisters is that I believe the vast majority of nonbelievers (if not everyone) is resisting God to some extent. Nevertheless, the most difficult problem concerning divine hiddenness are those who insist they are not resisting God and really do want a relationship with him.

Nonresistant Nonbelievers

Nonresistant nonbelievers claim they are truly ready to enter a relationship with God. These are nonbelievers telling us they truly would believe, enter, and remain in a relationship with God. Why is God hiding from them? They aren't

19. Here are just a *few* notable atheists (in no particular order) who eventually came to believe in God: C. S. Lewis, Mortimer J. Adler, Aleksandr Solzhenitsyn, Michael Reiss, Frank Morrison, Simon Greanleaf, Albert Henry Ross, John Warwick Montgomery, Marvin Olasky, George R. Price, Antony Flew, Allan Sandage, Rodney Stark, Francis Collins, Rosalind Picard, David Wood, Sarah Salviander, Hugh Ross, Sye Garte, Lee Strobel, J. Warner Wallace, Guillaume Bignon, Ayaan Hirsi Ali, and Larry Sanger.

resisting! Does such a person even exist?[20] Atheist J. L. Schellenberg believes an all-loving and personal God would *not* create humans who, at any point in time, are willing to believe and enter a relationship with God, but for whatever reason cannot due to their unbelief.[21] For God to be open means there shouldn't be any nonresistant individuals out there. God would *always* be open to them and thus a healthy relationship would occur. If God is *not* open to these nonbelievers, then this entails that an all-loving God does not exist.[22]

In other words, Schellenberg believes that if God is truly open to nonresistant nonbelievers, then God will make a way for a relationship to exist between them, and that "God sees to it that nothing God does or fails to do puts relationship with God out of reach for finite persons at the time in question."[23] For example, suppose God creates nonbelieving Sally. Let's say that Sally has always wanted to believe in God but couldn't for whatever reason. Sally is considered a nonresistant nonbeliever because she is open to believing in God and wants a healthy relationship with him, but despite her efforts she isn't able.

According to Schellenberg, because Sally exists and there is no healthy relationship between her and God, God is responsible for preventing a healthy relationship from occurring. Hence, this contradicts what a loving God would do. Since Schellenberg believes nonresistant nonbelievers like Sally exist, he views this as evidence for the nonexistence of God. So, how could an all-loving God be closed to nonresistant nonbelievers like Sally?

Let me start by saying that I think we should be hesitant in accepting Schellenberg's understanding of openness. Although I'm certainly sympathetic to

20. For an excellent inductive approach to this topic, see Charity Anderson's work, including "Divine Hiddenness: Defeated Evidence," *Royal Institute of Philosophy Supplement* 81 (2017): 119–32, https://doi.org/10.1017/s1358246117000212; Anderson, "Divine Hiddenness: An Evidential Argument," *Philosophical Perspectives* 35, no. 1 (2021): 5–22, https://doi.org/10.1111/phpe.12149.

21. J. L. Schellenberg, *The Hiddenness Argument: Philosophy's New Challenge to Belief in God* (Oxford University Press, 2015), 60. He says, "If there exists a God who is always open to a personal relationship with any finite person, then no finite person is ever nonresistantly in a state of nonbelief in relation to the proposition that God exists."

22. In this context, Schellenberg views openness to be the following: "If A loves B, then A will be open to this kind of relationship with B, insofar as A is able to accommodate the consequences of such openness, bringing them into conformity with the flourishing of both A and B and of any relationship that might come to exist between them." See J. L. Schellenberg, "John Schellenberg: The Hiddenness Argument and the Contribution of Philosophy (3/5)," Philosophy at the University of Edinburgh, posted August 28, 2017, YouTube, 14:54, https://www.youtube.com/watch?v=3ce7WipX_Ek. See the seven-minute mark.

23. Schellenberg, *Hiddenness Argument*, 41.

his understanding, I don't accept his personal construal of openness about an all-loving, all-knowing God who has a specific purpose in how he operates within the world. There are many theists and nontheists alike who believe that God should act in nearly the same way as human persons when it comes to relationships. Their modern conception of love often portrays a parent whose entire world revolves around their child's happiness. Although I don't think we should look at God this way, I do believe scripture reveals a God who is actively engaged in human affairs and expresses his love in such a way that permits all people to experience it. They may not experience or feel it in the way they desire, but they are still encountering it on a daily basis (more on that in a moment).

Regardless, I don't think it's at all likely, or even possible, that an all-loving God who is perfectly just could create nonbelievers like Sally that *want* to believe in him their entire life but can't because God is closed to them. I highly doubt such persons exist. But if they do, then after they die, perhaps God will only judge them based on the amount of revelation afforded to them by whatever life circumstances he placed them in.[24]

It could be that every nonbeliever in existence truly is resisting God to some degree and that Schellenberg is just wrong. Perhaps every alleged nonresistant nonbeliever is really just a minor resister, as I covered in the last section. Nevertheless, for the sake of argument, I will grant Schellenberg's view that there are some nonresistant nonbelievers, but I will offer reasons why it does not conflict with God's all-loving nature. Let's call these nonbelievers *temporary* nonresistant nonbelievers.

Why must an all-loving God permit these temporary nonbelievers to believe at *any* given point in time? It seems that God could permit them to believe at the *appropriate* time—a time in which God knows their desire for him has reached the appropriate level for entering and maintaining a meaningful relationship that can be optimized for eternity. Hence, their nonbelief is only temporary. A temporary hiding of God that creates doubt of his existence can be used as a greater good in solidifying that relationship once it finally happens. With an eternity in mind, this short span of nonbelief doesn't seem so bad.

24. Note that this is distinct from the issue concerning those who have never heard the gospel, that is, the problem of the unevangelized. Some of the unevangelized believe in God and have responded positively to the evidence provided by God through nature, and they will be judged on the amount of revelation they've received. The nonresistant nonbeliever, on the other hand, has the same available evidence and sometimes stronger forms of revelation yet cannot believe. We can conclude that an omnibenevolent God who is perfectly just would possibly make some arrangement for the nonresistant nonbeliever who has heard the gospel, tried to believe their whole life and enter a positive relationship with God, but for whatever reason cannot (if such an individual exists).

Given the testimonies of numerous former nonbelievers (who now believe in God) regarding their religious experiences, there is simply too much empirical evidence to disregard this option. Our intellectual limitations already preclude our understanding of why the average human performs certain actions, let alone the actions of an all-loving God who knows all things. Because of God's perfectly good nature and omniscience, we can trust his reasons despite not always understanding them.

Maybe some temporary nonresistant nonbelievers, unknown to them, currently want a relationship with God for the wrong reasons. It could be that they only want to use God to benefit themselves. Many people think of God as a good luck charm that is meant to bring them success and prosperity. Others envision God as a magic genie who may grant their wishes. We constantly see people who profess to be Christians declaring that God always wants what is best for you—he wants your business to thrive, your sickness to be cured, your bank account full, and your ever-changing passions to be fulfilled. I think this is a grave mistake and not true. It seems the almighty creator of the cosmos wants us seeking him for the *right* reasons, as this is necessary for the foundation of a healthy and meaningful relationship that can be optimized for eternity.

Regardless, temporary nonresistant nonbelievers will *not* miss the opportunity to enter a relationship with God because God has orchestrated the appropriate time in which they will believe and freely enter that relationship. This has been factored in before he created the world. If they are truly nonresistant, then they will believe and enter a relationship with God at some point before they die. The key point here is to not think that God's relationship with us should closely resemble that of a human parent-child relationship. When the Bible depicts a parent-child relationship, it does so in such a way that exemplifies the primary aspects of a *good* relationship. What constitutes a good relationship? A good and loving relationship consists of things such as sacrifice, provision, comfort, support, trust, faithfulness, correction, and even gifts. God has demonstrated these things: sacrifice through his Son's death; provision from the resources and goods of our planet; comfort during times of adversity; spiritual growth enabling positive character development; continual forgiveness for our disobedience; correction through a sense of guilt for wrongdoings; intellectual and physical gifts, and so on.

I fear that most nonbelievers and believers alike have formed a conception of God which doesn't match the God that exists in reality, or they've attributed certain distorted characteristics to God that he does not possess. Consequently, this modified deity has built-in expectations that often fall short of said individual. I understand the appeal in thinking that God should act in the same way that we do when it comes to relationships, but I don't think that's accurate. I also struggle to see this carry enough force to conclude that a loving and personal God doesn't exist.

Another reason nonresistant nonbelievers might exist is that God has created other spiritual beings or angels with their own free will. And if other spiritual beings possess free will, then it seems that they can freely choose to do harm to others (just as we do). These nonhuman free creatures could be harming humans by somehow frustrating their ability to believe in God. Room doesn't afford me the ability to speculate how this might be the case. Nevertheless, these nonhuman free creatures would be responsible for the existence of nonresistant nonbelievers. And therefore, God is not directly responsible for the existence of nonresistant nonbelievers. One may object and say God is responsible because God knew what these nonhuman creatures would freely do. But this objection takes us back to the same problem as to why human creatures freely do the bad things that we do. That is, God would rather have a world of nonhuman and human creatures capable of freely choosing to do right or wrong rather than a world of nonfree creatures. Hence, if there are evil forces among us that possess free will and hate humanity, then it's not surprising that these deceivers are actively working to persuade or defraud nonresistant individuals into believing that God doesn't exist.

Before moving on, let me just say that one doesn't need absolute certainty that God exists in order to believe in him. Rather, they just need a certain level of probability. A certain level of confidence is enough to justify their belief and relationship with God. We shouldn't think of needing some robust conversion experience like the apostle Paul's. For many, experiencing God is a very gentle and subtle acquaintance. Perhaps some temporary nonbelievers are distracted with other things they find as having greater value that blemish the opportunity to recognize God's presence sooner (but I digress).

Thus far I've offered some reasons for why God remains hidden from different kinds of nonbelievers. Could there be any other reasons why God remains hidden? As part of this cumulative case, let's briefly examine one other consideration for God's hiddenness and how it benefits everyone—believers and nonbelievers alike.

God Hides for Moral Development

Nontheistic philosophers have claimed that God could give us powerful religious experiences and miracles to the point that we couldn't deny his existence. But if this were the case, what would that mean for our moral autonomy? It seems that in our current times God wants to develop our moral character by giving us more opportunity to choose good over evil freely. Because God is hidden, this affords everyone the ability to make moral choices without feeling coerced.

As philosopher Michael J. Murray says, "Thus, in creating the world, God would seek to establish conditions that would permit the existence of such freedom. A variety of such conditions are necessary, but among them is that there not be overwhelmingly powerful incentives present in the environment that consistently coerce or otherwise force creatures to follow a particular course of action."[25]

Here's a brief (and true) story to help illustrate the point. When I was a kid, my mom told me not to eat any cookies before dinner. One day when I got home from school, I was in our house alone waiting for what seemed like hours to eat (it was probably more like thirty minutes). I was tempted to eat some cookies and wrestled with whether I should despite my mom's warnings. Suppose I freely made the right decision on my own and refrained from eating one of those delicious chocolate chip cookies. This seems to be more honorable than if I refrained only because my mom was standing right behind me watching my every move (and yes, to my everlasting shame, I partook of the forbidden cookies).

Similarly, God wants us to make the right decisions without us having the imminent feeling that he's constantly looking over our shoulder. As philosopher Richard Swinburne points out, "But the more uncertainty there is about the existence of God, the more it is possible for us to be naturally good people who still have a free choice between right and wrong. . . . Agnosticism allows the agnostic to make a more serious commitment to the good than he would be able to make if the presence of God were more obvious."[26]

In other words, it's a common occurrence for God to give us the proper distance we need to make our own moral decisions without the added pressure of his immediate presence.[27] It is more noble to do the right thing because of careful reflection and a desire to seek the good rather than doing the right thing because there's an authority figure watching nearby.

25. Michael J. Murray, "Deus Absconditus," in Howard-Snyder and Moser, *Divine Hiddenness*, 63.

26. Richard Swinburne, *The Existence of God*, 2nd ed. (Oxford University Press, 2004), 270–71.

27. God also may be hiding because this lessens the severity of his discipline regarding our immoral conduct. See Travis Dumsday, "Divine Hiddenness as Divine Mercy," *Religious Studies* 48, no. 2 (2012): 183–98.

Divine Hiddenness as Thin and Thick Theism

We have considered several reasons in this cumulative case for why God hides from resistant and nonresistant nonbelievers. Let's now assess two models that explain how a hidden God creates meaningful relationships with us and what kind of knowledge it takes to do this. Maybe there are more people in a positive relationship with God than we realize. However, as Schellenberg is quick to remind us, "One clearly cannot even get started in a personal relationship without *believing that the other party exists.*"[28] The following two models of how God interacts with his creation will help bring greater clarity to this issue.

Let's call the first model *thin theism*. Thin theism says God is a little more distant giving us a weaker or thinner awareness of his existence. On this model, God manages to make a different type of relationship available to us. Thin theism emphasizes the distinction between personal knowledge (knowledge of) and propositional knowledge (knowledge that). In other words, you can have knowledge from your experience of some individual's existence (personal knowledge) without knowing the identity of that individual (propositional knowledge).

Nontheists are concerned by the fact that some people lack *knowledge* of God, and therefore these nonbelievers do not know *that* God exists. But there's more to the story here. As philosopher Eleonore Stump points out, "But what is essential to a loving relationship with another person is not knowledge *that* but knowledge *of* a person. And knowledge of a person can be had without propositional knowledge that that person exists."[29] Thin theism is considered by many philosophers and theologians as being sufficient to place nonbelievers (or those with only partial belief) into a meaningful relationship with God. Let me explain.

You could be encountering God in some fashion without even being aware that it's him. Awareness of a person is not the same as awareness of that person's identity. For example, suppose you are liberal in your political stance and always vote Democrat. You recently move to a new state and neighborhood. One day while taking your dog for a walk, unknown to you (since you don't like following politics), you become friends with a Republican Senator living nearby who also walks her dog around the same time as you. Because this

28. Schellenberg, "Hiddenness Argument," 64.

29. Eleonore Stump, "Theology and the Knowledge of Persons," *Roczniki Filozoficzne* (*Annals of Philosophy*) 69, no. 3 (2021): 17–18, https://tinyurl.com/2s3f7fvx.

Republican knows you are very liberal and hears you mention your political views occasionally during your walks, she decides to conceal her identity. She's afraid she'll scare you away because of who she is and what she does. She likes you and you like her, but she doesn't want to jeopardize this healthy friendship. In this scenario, you have knowledge of this Republican and are in a meaningful relationship without being aware that she is the Republican Senator of your state. So, you have personal knowledge *of* this individual, yet you do not possess propositional knowledge *that* this individual is the Senator. Likewise, thin theism says that nonresistant nonbelievers (if such persons exist) can be aware *of* God and enter a meaningful relationship with him without having knowledge *that* God is the one whom they are aware of.[30]

Stump rightly adds: "So from a person's sincere self-report that he does not believe in an omniscient, omnipotent, perfectly good God, it does not follow that he does not know God in any way or to any degree. And, clearly, knowing God is not a transparent matter. A person can know God through sensing beauty or through second-personal connection of however limited or dreamy a means, without being aware that he has this knowledge of God."[31] Those moments of awe and grandeur that nonbelievers experience when looking at the night sky strewn with diamond-like stars, walking along a beach with a glowing sunset over the water, gazing down from a mountain top over a valley, holding one's newborn, and so on are all beautiful goods that resemble God's nature, which is the Ultimate Good. Those beautiful goods would not merely exist subjectively in the eye of the beholder, but rather exist objectively as real experiences of the good that flowed from and reflect the nature of God himself. Similarly, philosopher Robert Adams proposes that "things are good by virtue of their relation to one supremely good thing, the central relation being a sort of resemblance or imaging."[32] This involves different categories and degrees of goodness. For example, there is a kind of goodness relating to beauty but also a kind of goodness relating to moral actions resembled in qualities belonging

30. This is also known as the *de re* and *de dicto* conscious awareness distinction. You can be consciously aware *of* (*de re*) something without being aware *that* (*de dicto*) it is what you are aware of.

31. Stump, "Theology and Knowledge," 19. She goes on to say, "I am not claiming that it is true that all persons have some knowledge of God; I am claiming only that it takes more than self-reports of atheism to show that it is false." Thus, the atheist cannot show that God is likely not to exist simply because they do not believe they have experienced him.

32. Robert M. Adams, *Finite and Infinite Goods: A Framework for Ethics* (Oxford University Press, 2002), 40. See also Adam Lloyd Johnson, *Divine Love Theory: How the Trinity Is the Source and Foundation of Morality* (Kregel Academic, 2023).

to persons.[33] In other words, in addition to beautiful goods, our personal qualities and actions can also resemble and convey God's goodness.[34]

Let's consider an even more extreme scenario concerning thin theism and the nonresistant nonbeliever. Suppose you receive a bag of groceries at your house during a time when your pantry is nearly empty due to a rough economy and tight budget. You don't think to check with the grocery store to see if it was delivered by mistake or if someone donated it to you. Part of you suspects someone may have gifted it, but you're not entirely sure. You're just thankful to get some food for your hungry family. In this case, you are receiving a benefit while expressing gratitude for what has occurred even though you don't know who gave it. You only partially believe and suspect that a generous giver was involved. Now, suppose there really was a generous giver involved. This anonymous, generous giver enjoys knowing the blessing they bestowed upon you.[35]

In a way, the recipient of the gift has a meaningful relationship with the giver. Likewise, God blesses everyone on earth in various ways and constantly provides for our needs in a habitable planet with water cycles, agriculture, technology, and so on and enjoys seeing our gratitude. Moreover, everyone at some point acknowledges these benefits while expressing gratitude without necessarily knowing who the benefactor is. Thus, there is still a meaningful relationship occurring.

Concerning this scenario, philosophers Ted Poston and Trent Dougherty note, "We all receive some benefits in this life, and if we are ever grateful for them it seems that we are grateful for their source, so to speak. God is in fact the benefactor of all, so whoever expresses gratitude to the benefactor in fact expresses gratitude to God and is to that extent in a relationship with him. This can serve as the basis for a more meaningful relationship later."[36] Daniel Howard-Snyder agrees, saying, "One can be in a reciprocal, positively meaningful relationship with another person without believing that the other person exists, as when, unbeknownst to you, a benefactor has been looking after your interests in various ways."[37]

33. See chapter 1 of Adams, *Finite and Infinite Goods.*

34. See chapter 7 of Linda T. Zagzebski, *Divine Motivation Theory* (Cambridge University Press, 2004).

35. See Ted Poston and Trent Dougherty, "Divine Hiddenness and the Nature of Belief," *Religious Studies* 43, no. 2 (2007): 193, https://doi.org/10.1017/s0034412507008943. Credit to them (they give an example of money being deposited into a bank account).

36. Poston and Dougherty, "Divine Hiddenness," 193.

37. Howard-Snyder, "Divine Openness," 138.

Although this type of divine-human relationship may not be the kind that some theists expect, it surely doesn't discredit theism. Instead, it just better informs our understanding of how God interacts with us, which might not be as intimate as some prefer or had envisioned.[38] Many theists who hold to this sort of thin theism believe we shouldn't think that God strongly and directly engages us as a best friend or human father does. To do so means we have misunderstood how God generally interacts with his creation, and this mischaracterizes how God is portrayed as the Heavenly Father in the Bible.

That is not to say there won't be moments of intimacy and closeness that one experiences throughout their spiritual journey (albeit in a different way than an ordinary human relationship), especially during moments of suffering and pain. But such false expectations for God to commune with us in the same manner as a human parent does can lead one to doubt the imminence or nearness of God.

This form of hiddenness is only short term, as it prepares and grants us access to a greater, more intimate relationship in the future when we can be directly in the presence of God. Therefore, this momentary time of God's hiddenness is justified because of the greater goods that will result in the future.[39] If God revealed too much of himself to us, like the Republican Senator with the Democratic citizen, we would be scared away. The imminent presence of an omnipotent and holy being like God would push away finite and imperfect creatures like humans. Hence, the nonresistant nonbeliever may currently be in a different kind of relationship with God that has the potential to flourish later.

But is this model of thin theism enough to form a conscious meaningful relationship for the nonresistant? Perhaps. Some say it is and others say it's not. Thin theism says God is more distant but still makes relationship available to us. In the debate Adam's position was to argue for a supreme being that could be representative of thin theism. Dan's concerns about God's hiddenness do not seem detrimental to Adam's argument because Adam's position merely seeks to demonstrate that God exists. It does not aim to show that the Christian God must interact with creation in certain ways that we desire.

Nevertheless, many would claim that thin theism can't account for their direct knowledge of God's existence, strong spiritual experiences, and their continuous

38. See Poston and Dougherty, "Divine Hiddenness and the Nature of Belief," 194–95.

39. Some Christians believe this greater good is the all-loving God making an arrangement for non-resisters after they die. Once they meet God face-to-face and are held accountable for their actions on earth, they are given a chance to accept God after receiving a fuller revelation of him.

budding relationship with him. Maybe some people across the world—believers and nonbelievers alike—experience thin theism to some extent, while others experience the second model, which I'll refer to as *thick theism*.

Thick theism entails a God that seems nearer and gives a stronger or thicker awareness of his existence. Thick theism also allows for a more intimate relationship between God and humans. Although the God of thin theism and the God of thick theism are presumably one and the same, it could be that God is experienced in different ways by different people based on the amount of revelation they've received from him. This includes, but is not limited to, other Christians being placed in their life to manifest God's love to them, access to biblical material and churches, the number of times they've been evangelized, divine encounters in dreams, and so on.

Like thin theism, thick theism also entails an all-loving, all-powerful, perfect God who is worthy of full devotion and admiration. Thick theism says this all-loving God has provided a clearer demand for spiritual and moral transformation to those who are willing to humble themselves and submit to his supreme authority. This is so they can become more like him through a life-long process of moral development. Hence, this model is certainly relevant to optimizing a relationship for eternity as previously discussed. A stronger sense of God's existence is given to those that God knows will change their behavior and enter into a meaningful relationship that includes us striving to fully love him, other people, and even our enemies. Thick theism says we should expect this from an all-loving God. However, this doesn't mean the person will be forced to stay in such a relationship.

What do we say to those who have had a veridical or true encounter with the God of thick theism? These people are justified in believing the truthfulness of that encounter similar to how they are justified in believing various sense perceptions about their experience in the world. As Richard Swinburne notes, "How things seem to be (in contingent respects), that is how we seem to perceive them, experience them, or remember them are good grounds for a belief about how things are or were. The more forceful the experience, the stronger the memory, the more probable it is that what we seem to perceive or remember is true—other things being equal."[40]

For example, I could be mistaken about several features concerning the reality of our world. Regardless, my basic belief of my experience is justified and probably true based on my accurate (not infallible) sense perceptions. This is especially true in the absence of some evidence to make me think otherwise.

40. Swinburne, *Existence of God*, 303.

Similarly, if I have a spiritual encounter(s) with God, one in which I have been morally transformed with new desires, an improved mindset aimed towards love, a new relational awareness and so on, then I am justified in believing that I have had a real divine experience.

Making Sense of It All

It's semi-counterintuitive to say this, but I'm somewhat thankful that God is "hidden." Are there times I wish our awareness of his presence was stronger? Absolutely. But there's something special about walking by faith and not by sight so to speak. It's a wonderful thing to experience the gentle nudging of God while detecting his providential guidance throughout the believer's life. The moments of intimacy during the quiet times that we spend with God are very special. Moreover, experiencing God's supportive comfort during periods of adversity is inexplicable and assuaging. This kind of relational framework seems better than one in which God coerces relationships or visibly manifests himself everywhere we go. Many however do not want to invest the time or stay committed to God, much like their current relationships with the individuals they already believe exist and know personally.

And although we may dislike hearing this, as philosopher Mike Rea suggests, God may have "loves and interests that conflict with and take higher priority than promotion of the good for human beings. . . . Perhaps such things are permitted instead for the realization of legitimate and worthwhile divine goods, or perhaps other goods wholly beyond our ken."[41] In other words, just as humans choose their self-interests at times over the interests of others (which is not a detriment to their character), likewise God's self-interests may include his hiddenness, which outweighs our feelings on the matter. Nevertheless, we can trust this perfect being's character despite our limited understanding of how he interacts with our world.

To summarize, I have presented a cumulative case of plausible reasons for why God seems hidden or is partially hidden. The first reason is that many nonbelievers are majorly or minorly resistant at all points in their lives or would not maintain a meaningful relationship with God. The second reason is that temporary nonresistant nonbelievers will come to believe and freely enter a relationship with God at the *appropriate* time. Additionally, both models of thin and thick theism could be true depending on the amount of revelation each capable and willing adult person has received. God has either thin

41. Michael C. Rea, *The Hiddenness of God* (Oxford University Press, 2018), 79–80.

interactions or thick interactions with every believer and nonbeliever at some point. Furthermore, it's a mistake to think that certain aspects of human relationships should look the same as relationships between God and humans.

The hiddenness problem may be inevitable in any world created by God that involves his desire for us to freely know him so that an optimal relationship is possible. This isn't a strike against God's omnipotence because being all-powerful means that you can do all things, but forcing someone to freely love you and enter a healthy relationship is a contradiction, not a thing that can be actualized.[42] Or maybe God is open to a relationship with everyone in a different sense than what Schellenberg has offered.

God loves everybody, including Dan Barker, and desires they freely enter an optimal relationship (one designed for eternity). However, God won't force people to do this because forced love isn't true love. In a different debate, I heard Dan say (as I have many other atheists) that he'd rather be in hell than be with God for an eternity. Sadly, this correlates well with C. S. Lewis's statement: "The doors of hell are locked on the *inside*."[43] Dan used to be a minister for years, but if he doesn't want to be with God, then Dan has the freedom to make that decision.

Fortunately many nonbelievers eventually come to believe in God realizing that parts of themselves truly were resisting him all along. If you are a nonbeliever that thinks you are *not* resistant to the idea of God's existence, then I encourage you to keep fervently seeking him with a humble and open mindset. Eventually you will find him, and it will all be worth it.

42. See Keith Ward, *The Evidence for God: The Case for the Existence of the Spiritual Dimension* (Darton, Longman & Todd, 2014), 45–47.

43. C. S. Lewis, "The Problem of Pain," in *The C. S. Lewis Signature Classics* (HarperOne, 2017), 626.

6

Nontheist Responding to the Debate

Why Is God Hiding from So Many?

Joe Folley

First of all, I want to give a huge thank you to Andrew, who has skillfully covered most of the background for this topic in his chapter. In the spirit of this book being an extended discussion, I'll frame this chapter around Andrew's chapter and respectfully challenge his refutations of the divine hiddenness problem. My ultimate conclusion is not that divine hiddenness is some sort of knock-down objection to the theist hypothesis, but rather that it could form part of the patchwork of arguments that serve as defeasible evidence against the existence of an omnipotent, omniscient, and omnibenevolent God. For the sake of simplicity, I am also going to take his interpretations of the thinkers he has referenced, including Schellenberg, as read.[1]

I also aim to show that the issue of divine hiddenness has more dimensions than is often thought. Divine hiddenness is often presented as an issue about the binary belief in "God." I will call this the "breadthwise problem of divine hiddenness." Alongside this, there is the issue of how deep one's knowledge of God is. If there is a God, and that God has definite properties, then he cannot be the God of Christianity, *and* the one of Islam, *and* Brahma, *and* the many deific beings of Mahayana Buddhism. These have different (and sometimes contradictory) properties, so this raises a further issue for the theist: If God exists, then why has he not revealed himself to believers in enough detail to obviate contentious debate as to his nature? Again, I do not think this is a

1. Before we get started, I also want to acknowledge how helpful Schellenberg's later survey articles on the divine hiddenness problem have been while gathering sources for this chapter. J. L. Schellenberg, "Divine Hiddenness: Part 1 (Recent Work on the Hiddenness Argument)," *Philosophy Compass* 12, no. 4 (2017): e12355, https://doi.org/10.1111/phc3.12355; "Divine Hiddenness: Part 2 (Recent Enlargements of the Discussion)," *Philosophy Compass* 12, no. 4 (2017): e12413, https://doi.org/10.1111/phc3.12413.

knock-down objection to theism, but I think it is an aspect of divine hiddenness that some of the present solutions are not as equipped to solve. I will call this the "depthwise problem of divine hiddenness."

Last, I want to clarify up front that each of the argument threads I start in this chapter will be necessarily incomplete. My aim is not to give a definitive answer but to provide good fodder for the reader's thinking. So if it seems like I have left out a good potential counter to an argument I have given, that is probably because I have.

What Counts as No Longer Hidden?

The first point Andrew raises to solve divine hiddenness is that if you are a theist, or even just open to theism, then you probably do think that there is some evidence for the existence of God, even if on balance this is not enough to convince you. Famously, the atheist writer Christopher Hitchens said that the fine-tuning argument occasionally gave him pause for thought. If you are a theist, then it makes sense to think God has revealed himself to some extent. However, I take it most people would not say that the existence of God is *certain* or even "fully revealed." Unless you subscribe to one of the scholastic arguments for God's existence as *a priori* certain, you probably think that God's existence is at least "partially hidden."[2]

But what exactly do we mean when we say "revealed" or "hidden" or "partially hidden"? I would suggest a working definition might be: "The extent to which it is reasonable to believe in God's existence, or unreasonable to believe in his non-existence." So to a certain set of theists, who think that theological arguments for God's existence are overwhelming, there is no problem of divine hiddenness.

In many ways, Andrew extends this argument when he says that God could never be completely revealed, because if you don't want to believe in him, you simply will not. Even if you saw God, you could still conclude he was a hallucination, of alien origin, or something like that. However, I think this says more about the structure of belief than it does about the issue of God's revelation or lack thereof.

The Duhem-Quine thesis states (among other things) that we can (almost) always adjust a theory to make it accord with observable evidence.[3] Or, in

2. By way of contrast, this view is not held by philosopher Ed Feser, who thinks God can be known with certainty; see Edward Feser, *Aquinas: A Beginner's Guide* (Oneworld, 2009); Feser, *Five Proofs of the Existence of God* (Ignatius, 2017).

3. W. V. O. Quine, "Two Dogmas of Empiricism," *Philosophical Review* 60, no. 1 (1951): section 6, https://doi.org/10.2307/2266637.

other words, the evidence will always underdetermine reality to some extent. A classic set of historical examples for this come from physics.[4] It was observed that the path of Uranus was not in accordance with the predictions of Newtonian mechanics. Eager to hold onto a theory that had so far been successful, the existence of some planet behind it was postulated, known as Neptune. As it turned out, Neptune does exist, its blue hue living up to its oceanic namesake. Subsequently, irregularities were also observed in the orbital path of Mercury. Aha! We have been here before! There must be some planet in between the Sun and Mercury called "Vulcan" that must be throwing off the path. However, Vulcan turns out not to exist. The strange path of Mercury was explained by the general relativity theory rather than by the postulation of further planets. We can imagine a world where we rejected general relativity, and any observations were accounted for in this *ad hoc* manner, repeatedly postulating the existence of further objects to explain any unexplained phenomena.[5] (Put a pin in this thought, as it'll be returning later in the chapter.)

To bring this a bit more down to earth, imagine that I was hiding in your house (bear with me, I am going somewhere with this). There are many different levels of evidence I could give you that I was there. I could leave empty packets of Roast Beef Monster Munch lying around or the odd plate in the sink. You would probably raise an eyebrow at this. "I don't remember leaving that there," you would think, but you would probably not leap to the conclusion that a philosophy nerd with a fondness for quarter-zips was in your attic. To take things up a notch, I could start leaving you notes, saying, "I live with you; submit to Kant or befall a horrible fate," and you would probably take this as firmer evidence that I was in your house, but you could still explain it away by saying that a friend had left it there as a joke. If I walked into your kitchen in my dressing gown, you would probably scream and conclude that I definitely was living in your house. However, if you wanted, you could avoid this belief. You could say that I was a hallucination, and some people might, but it becomes very reasonable to think that I am living in your house at that point. I have gone from totally hidden, to less hidden, to not very hidden, to pretty much totally revealed, and yet you still could *technically* deny I was there.

I would suggest the problem of divine hiddenness emerges if you believe that the evidence for God's existence is further toward the former end of that scale. I think that many theists could accept this premise, but for any that do not, the rest of this chapter is totally unnecessary for you—there is no problem. But the

4. K. Brad Wray, *Resisting Scientific Realism* (Cambridge University Press, 2007).

5. I am sure that more *ad hoc* adjustments would have to be made than simply the postulation of planets, but you get the picture.

mere fact that someone could reject God's existence even if they had incontrovertible evidence that he does exist does not help solve the issue. This is true of any human belief. We only need to accept that God's existence is uncertain enough to allow for reasonable unbelief. It strikes me that God's existence is an indeterminate enough issue that neither belief nor unbelief is totally "unreasonable." I neither agree with Aquinas (himself citing Ps. 14:1) that nonbelievers are "fools" nor with Dawkins's idea that God is a ridiculous superstition.[6]

With that out of the way, I want to move on to looking into Andrew's arguments, which reference the work of J. L. Schellenberg. Andrew highlights three types of nonbelievers: majorly resistant nonbelievers, minorly resistant nonbelievers, and nonresistant nonbelievers.

Resistant Nonbelievers

I want to begin this section by conceding two things. The first is that I think Andrew is right to say there are resistant nonbelievers of both the major and minor variety. The second is that the unbelief of these agents strikes me as *far less problematic* for the existence of an all-loving God than nonresistant nonbelievers. It is entirely plausible that in explicitly rejecting a belief in God, his love is such that he would respect this as our decision and patiently wait for us to lower our defenses and receive his love. However, I want to throw some doubt on the idea that resistant nonbelievers pose *no problem* for the existence of God. This is because I think resistance to belief in God is not separable from the amount of evidence someone thinks there is for God. Through direct intervention, God would not only raise someone's chances of believing in him but also plausibly lower their resistance to him.

One of the main reasons Andrew gives for why an atheist might reject conclusive evidence for God is the demands God gives them. The idea here is that for many of us, self-interest would override our willingness to forge a relationship with God. God might demand us to reevaluate our sexual ethics, give all we have to the poor, or "pick up [our] cross and follow [him]" (Matt. 16:24). We might be loath to do these things and so rebel against God. Following the path of Milton's Satan, we might conclude it is "better to reign in Hell than serve in Heaven."[7] We might also think that there are a lot of people who would

6. Thomas Aquinas, *Summa contra Gentiles*, trans. Anton C. Pegis, 3 vols. (Hanover House, 1955–1957), 3:38; Richard Dawkins, *The God Delusion* (Bantam, 2006), 56 (and, indeed, the title).

7. John Milton, *Paradise Lost*, ed. John Leonard (Penguin Classics, 2003), book 1, line 263.

not rebel against God in the same way Lucifer did, but nonetheless are resistant enough that were God to reveal himself to them, they would slowly drift away from their faith. Not by some grand act of defiance but instead in the same way we often lose touch with friends: life gets in the way.

However, this argument relies on a questionable assumption: that the knowledge of God's existence would not alter someone's willingness to enter into a relationship with him. It is all well and good for someone to say they *would* reject God *if* they knew he existed, but let's stop and think what that entails. It is depriving yourself of the greatest possible connection you could have with another being, and potentially eternal bliss, out of sheer stubbornness. This would be an act of self-destruction whose consequences are infinite and beyond imagining, and yet this is supposedly done out of self-interest.

Andrew touches upon this point later when he asks how the nonbeliever could "be so certain of their psychology . . . that part of their self is not resisting, or would resist God if they came to believe?" But if they are, as Andrew suggests, motivated by self-interest, pride, and comfort, then to reject God in full knowledge of his existence would be totally irrational, given that eternal joy and suffering are on the table. Out of those, only pride might motivate someone to reject God while knowing he exists. At the very least, any minimally rational agent with even a slight whiff of self-interest would strive to have a personal relationship with God in just the way Andrew seems to desire *if they were certain of his existence*. And not just a self-interested agent, but any agent interested in goodness at all, since God is meant to be the source of all goodness, beauty, and truth.[8] Thus, it strikes me as a mistake to treat "resistance to God" and "belief in the evidence for God" as if the first was entirely prior to the latter. If someone had direct revelation for God, it is plausible that their emotional resistance to the "God hypothesis" would lower along with it.

Of course, Andrew does respond to this. He says that while a relationship with God is optimal "the cost for optimization is high, and the road to recovery is not so easy." On this point I would agree. For example, the God of the Old and New Testament makes an awful lot of demands that are pretty difficult to follow. Lest we get bogged down in specifically Christian examples, the commands of Islam are also pretty demanding, and you only need to have a conversation with an Orthodox Jewish person to realize how much faith is run through every aspect of their lives. However, a large part of what makes

8. Thomas Aquinas, *Summa Theologica*, trans. Fathers of the English Dominican Province, 5 vols. (Benziger Brothers, 1911–1925), I, q. 6 and 16.

divine commands so difficult is the uncertainty around God's existence, or at the very least its lack of immediacy. An example might help to illustrate my point. Imagine that I asked you to give up all your possessions for a year and go destitute for that time. In addition, you would get a rather nasty illness. In return, I promised that the rest of your life would be pure happiness. You would achieve anything you desired and have a perfect marriage. That would be a horrible thing to endure, and you would probably hesitate. This hesitation is likely based on doubting the veracity of my promise. If you were truly certain that I was telling the truth, then it would be a much easier decision.

And this is a far less enticing deal than the one offered by God. The Christian God promises an eternity of joy, a kind of joy that we cannot even imagine on this fallen earth. Any sacrifice compared to that is totally trivial. Thus, we could surmise that if God revealed his existence in ways compelling to all except the most epistemically stubborn, he would increase the number of those willing to embrace a relationship with him. Indeed, much of the erring of the Israelites of the Old Testament begins with their doubts (either about God or about his essentially good nature; see e.g., Exod. 14:11–12). And at points, Christ intimates that for the people of the earth that doubt or unbelief is the cause behind sin (e.g., John 16:8–9).

However, moral or emotional concerns are not the only kinds of resistance. Some could also have an "epistemic resistance," where they are so attached to their atheistic worldview that they would struggle to believe in God under almost any circumstance. But, we can make a similar response here to the argument from moral or emotional resistance. It assumes that this epistemic resistance is independent of the evidence they are presented with for God's existence. For example, I would consider myself a minorly resistant nonbeliever in fairies. It is not just that I do not see any evidence for them; I would have a high level of skepticism for almost any evidence presented to me. Nonetheless, if a fairy knocked on my front door tomorrow and sprinkled me with fairy dust, then I would not just believe in fairies, but my *baseline resistance to belief in fairies would go down considerably*. That is, not only would I believe in fairies, but I would be much less likely to renege on that belief in fairies later. Moreover, if I had an ongoing relationship with a fairy, then that would continually provide new evidence that they exist. If we assume that our prospective resistant nonbeliever is at all rational in their belief formation, then their resistance profile would change along with their belief.

If you accept this argument, then it throws into doubt that all resistant nonbelievers would remain steadfast in their ways after some kind of personal revelation. Andrew appears to concede this point, saying that even majorly resistant nonbelievers have converted in the past. Before his conversion Paul was actively persecuting Christians, but after divine revelation he became an apostle. I struggle to think of a more resistant nonbeliever in Christianity than someone actively involved in the punishment of believers, and yet Paul's conversion does not strike me as *psychologically* strange. Are we to believe that all minorly and majorly resistant nonbelievers would remain so in definite knowledge of a particular God's existence? It is true that Paul was already a believer in the God of Judaism, but we can also appeal to conversions of resistant atheists like C. S. Lewis, Antony Flew, or (more recently) Ayaan Hirsi Ali.

There are some definite responses the theist can make here. It could be that God sees a rejection as a defeasible reason to not reveal himself to a resistant person, but that this could be overridden if they were to play a major role in his plan. This is a pretty familiar maneuver within interpersonal relationships. If someone makes it clear they don't like us, we might want to avoid them. But if working with them was essential to our wider goals, then we still might reach out to them. Once we are there, it only makes sense to try to build as close a relationship as possible, for the smooth-running of our working environment. How convinced you are by this response will depend on whether you think this interpersonal analogy transfers comfortably to an omnipotent and omniscient being. For instance, while we often do not know how to present ourselves to appeal to someone's individual sensibilities, a being of supreme intelligence presumably would.

This is partly why I would gently push back on the way "resistance" is framed in this discussion. Evidence not only plausibly changes belief but also resistance to belief. In the theist presentation of the issue, there is the implicit assumption that God could not design his intervention to meet the level of an individual's resistance without undermining that person's agency.

We might ask why God would have any obligation to reach out to those who have any form of resistance to serving him. And this is where, in the spirit of Schellenberg, we can circle back to the idea that this is specifically an "all-loving" God. In scripture this love is often described in paternalistic fashion (e.g., the Lord's Prayer in Matt. 6). So then a question arises: What would a loving father do with a resistant son? Would he sever any relationship with the son? Or would he persist in actively trying to make contact with him and to overcome the son's resistance, not by force but by showing that he is mistaken about his love? Would he not directly encourage his son to abide by his commandments, gently explaining to him that it is in his best interests to do so? If God is not only just but supremely loving, doesn't his failure to persist go against the predictions the "God hypothesis" would make?

Of course, many religious traditions hold that God is reaching out to us at all times (e.g., Augustine, *Confessions* 1.1–3). However, there are two challenges this response faces. The first is a matter of verification: How do we notice this reaching if, as atheists, we are not currently seeing it? And the second is a matter of degree: If the current, subtle actions of God are insufficient to bring someone into the fold, then what would stop God from revealing himself in more direct and explicit ways? If that is what it would take, why has God not done so? If direct spiritual revelation would evaporate the resistance of a minorly (or sometimes even majorly) resistant nonbeliever, then why has God not used this approach? After all, according to numerous "revealed texts," he has done so in the past.

I am not suggesting that there are no answers to this challenge—this is just an introductory chapter. Nonetheless, I do think it frames the atheist position in this debate, and how the problem of divine hiddenness is not just limited to nonresistant nonbelief but is still present in a less serious way among resistant believers. But I do want to explore one of the most popular reasons for explaining why God might not turn to direct revelation, because I think it raises important nuances in the overall debate.

But Wait! Freedom and Morality

A classic response that many theists give to the problem of divine hiddenness is to suggest that God revealing himself to us would undermine our ability to make moral choices in some way. Andrew touches upon this, and it has been argued in different ways by both John Hick and Michael Murray.[9] The argument goes that if God revealed himself, it would be such a strong motivating force that it would strip away all moral agency from us (or our "morally significant freedom"). The threat of heaven and hell would be just too great for us to have meaningful choice anymore. In propositional form, this would be as follows:

1. In order for meaningful moral choice to exist, the choice must not be so obvious that any rational agent would make the same decision.
2. Certainty in God's existence makes any moral choice so obvious that any rational agent would make the same decision (i.e., following God's will).

9. John H. Hick, *Philosophy of Religion*, 4th ed., Foundations of Philosophy Series (Pearson, 1990). Michael J. Murray, "Coercion and the Hiddenness of God," *American Philosophical Quarterly* 30, no. 1 (1993): 34; Murray, "Deus Absconditus," in *Divine Hiddenness: New Essays*, ed. Daniel Howard-Snyder and Paul K. Moser (Cambridge University Press, 2002), 63–66.

3. Therefore, certainty in God's existence is incompatible with meaningful moral choice.

This is what I take Murray to mean when he describes immanent knowledge of God's existence as "coercive."

The first thing I want to note about this argument is that it is in tension with the one about majorly and minorly resistant nonbelievers. If certainty about God's existence deprives someone of meaningful moral choices, because we would just follow God's word, then there cannot be people who would disobey God if they knew he existed. It seems you can either have this argument or the one about those who would knowingly disobey God, but not both. So anyone who thinks that Richard Dawkins or Matt Dilahunty has not had God revealed to him because God knows he would only disobey him cannot use the "moral choice" defense.

However, I would raise a few challenges to this type of theistic argument. My first point is that we do not generally view informing someone of a true statement as coercion. For instance, if you are about to invest money in a stock, and I happened to know that that company has just announced their bankruptcy, we would not say that if I tell you this, then I undermine your ability to make free financial choices. This is despite the fact that any rational investor would no longer choose the stock. Indeed, if we take definitions of free choice that include being informed to pursue the good, then they would, in a sense, have more agency now that they have access to true information.

The obvious response to this is to point to exceptions to this rule. We tend to think that the mugger who lets us know we will be stabbed if we do not give him our wallet does undermine our agency, and indeed Murray uses this "threat" paradigm in his paper on the subject (and the mugging example).[10] But I would suggest that this is different from the case of God revealing himself to us and his role as a divine judge. It is distinct from human-to-human coercion in two important ways:

1. On a theist standpoint, God sending nonbelievers to hell is just, inasmuch as God's will is never unjust.
2. God's will is not normally considered as exactly like a human will, as it is often conceived of as necessary.[11]

10. Murray, "Coercion and Hiddenness," 30.
11. This view is especially prevalent in Thomistic philosophy.

I think either of these suffice to make God informing us directly and unequivocally of the consequences of our sin noncoercive. With regard to the first point, we do not tend to view informing someone of punishment that we deem "just" as being coercive. Very few people would argue that the police should not inform someone of the legal punishment for a crime they are about to commit because that would be coercion. And I do not think this is a peculiarity of any law, because for laws seen as "unjust" we do sometimes call them coercive. Compare the case of the posters in George Orwell's *1984*, which ominously tell Winston Smith, "Big Brother is watching you," to that of the signs at many UK train stations informing people of the legal consequences for physically assaulting members of staff. The first seems coercive whereas the second does not, and I would argue the difference lies in the perceived "justness" of the consequence. Given that any consequence flowing from God's will must be just in a classic theistic worldview, I would argue that giving us certainty of the consequences of disobeying him would not be coercive.

Second, we do not tend to view consequences that cannot be changed as coercive. The mugger does not need to threaten us, and he could remove this threat if he wanted. So the "If you don't give me your money I will stab you" statement is a false binary. It does not say the third option, which is that he could cease his threats. If the consequence did not come from a human agent but instead a rock fall or some other force that cannot "decide otherwise" than to harm us, then we again do not tend to see this as malevolent coercion but instead neutral information. The thing is that we do not really have a close real-world equivalent for the kind of "necessary agency" of something like many conceptions of the theistic God. Someone like Aquinas viewed God and his will as necessary and unchanging.[12] If this is true, then God can no more not send people to hell than rocks can will themselves to not fall on you. It would be against his nature as a perfectly just being. This seems importantly different from coercion. God would not be saying "do this, or else" but would rather be explaining the natural consequences of our actions. Indeed, it seems difficult to argue that having certain knowledge of God's existence would be coercive without making the very relationship God offers coercive, and I do not think most theists would be willing to affirm this. It is not just the knowledge that the mugger is going to stab me if I do not give him my wallet that is coercive; it is also the *fact* that he is going to stab me. The theist faces a dilemma here: either God's offer is coercive, or God undeniably informing us of that offer is not coercive. At the very least, if the offer remains noncoercive while being unambiguously

12. This is a fun implication of his first way, defining God as pure actuality.

informed of its existence remains coercive, there must be some pretty heavy argumentation to back this up. It is also worth noting that we see examples of far more serious intervention in something like the Old Testament than simply telling someone the truth when God is disobeyed (e.g., Jonah 1:17).

So if a theist wants to counter this, the natural next step is to show the following:

1. A relationship with God is noncoercive, while certain knowledge of his existence, and full information about that relationship, is coercive.
2. There is some other means by which certain knowledge of God's existence interferes with our agency.
3. There is some other important aspect of ourselves that would be undermined by certain knowledge of God's existence (e.g., Murray's claim that the development of our moral character might be undermined).[13]

I outline these to show, again, that the debate extends far beyond this chapter. But of course, we are still only within the scope of resistant nonbelievers. Now we can move onto the meat of Schellenberg's challenge and look at *nonresistant* nonbelievers.

Nonresistant Nonbelievers

A large part of the problem of divine hiddenness, as presented by Schellenberg, centers on nonresistant nonbelievers. That is, people who have no real animosity toward God or objection to his existence, but who nonetheless do not believe. This is a pretty commonplace phenomenon when it comes to nontheological beliefs. For instance, not only am I not resistant to believing that there are a million pounds in my bank account, but I am also positively enthusiastic about the idea. However, despite repeated attempts to find evidence for this, it is simply not there. I have a nonresistant lack of belief in my bank account containing a million pounds.

Schellenberg's contention is that there exist people who are open to believing in God and yet have not had his existence revealed to them. A pretty good example of this phenomenon are people who simply did not or do not get the chance to hear whatever variant of theism is being proposed.[14] Take Christi-

13. Murray, "Coercion and Hiddenness," 30–35.

14. J. L. Schellenberg, "The Hiddenness Problem and the Problem of Evil," *Faith and Philosophy* 27, no. 1 (2010): 45–60, https://doi.org/10.5840/faithphil20102713.

anity, for example. For hundreds of years, millions lived and died in complete ignorance of the existence of Jesus Christ or the gospel teachings. It arrived in China only in the seventh century, for instance. If Christianity is true, then for all that time people in China were deprived of a relationship with God through his Son Jesus Christ simply because they had no way of accessing the key religious texts or encountering missionaries. Unless, by some enormous coincidence, everyone in China happened to be resistant to this belief, it becomes a pretty hard square for the Christian to circle. This "demographic" aspect of divine hiddenness has more recently been explored by Stephen Maitzen.[15] Additionally, Jason Marsh has expanded this argument across time, pointing to those who predated *even the concept* of an all-loving God.[16] Surely these "natural nonbelievers" are nonresistant, since the thought of the classic "tri-omni" theistic God could not even enter their awareness. These, in their own ways, establish that categories of nonresistant nonbelievers do or have existed.

Schellenberg also talks of former believers whose faith God has, in effect, allowed to wane away. These people were clearly not resistant to a belief in God, since at one point they had this belief. They might have then become resistant after their deconversion, but that still does not explain why they were allowed to go from believing in God to not believing in him, considering they were definitely nonresistant at some point, and may be more open to a belief in God than many others. (Although this is a contingent empirical claim that would ultimately require verification.)

Another category is one I would consider myself to belong to: lifelong seeker. To lay my own cards on the table, I am by no means a hardline atheist. I was raised Christian, and it was a belief I took a lot of solace, comfort, and meaning in when I was younger. I remember losing my faith and then spending a lot of time trying to get it back. The reason I spend my time researching religious arguments is partly because I desperately want to be convinced. And I have conceded ground in this direction. For example, I was once a materialist, and now I am much more doubtful about this. This is just my anecdotal experience, but the idea of theism is pretty attractive to me. At a philosophical level, I share the intuitions of Tolstoy, the Stoics, and Boethius that a sense of teleological order in the universe is incredibly appealing and comforting.[17]

15. Stephen Maitzen, "Divine Hiddenness and the Demographics of Theism," *Religious Studies* 42 (2006): 179–80, https://doi.org/10.1017/S0034412506008274.

16. Jason Marsh, "Darwin and the Problem of Natural Nonbelief," *The Monist* 96, no. 3 (2013): 355–57, https://doi.org/10.5840/monist201396316.

17. Leo Tolstoy, *A Confession*, trans. Jane Kentish (Penguin, 2008); Epictetus, *Discourses*

And while you can have this without God, God is one surefire way to get it.[18] I consider myself emotionally and dispositionally predisposed to theism. The only reason I am not a theist is that I have not yet found an argument that has convinced me that there is a God. I would cast myself as a nonresistant nonbeliever in this sense. I take the point made by Andrew and by others like C. S. Lewis that those who do not believe may fool themselves into thinking that they are nonresistant.[19] Recently, Paul Macdonald has questioned whether we are justifed in taking nonresistant behavior as evidence for genuine nonresisant nonbelief, given our capacity for self-deception.[20] I may even be one of these myself. But at the same time, I do not think that *every* lifelong seeker of God is hiding some secret resistance to him. It is possible that many are, but are they *all*? Such a claim would require substantial empirical evidence.

There have been some pretty notable responses to the claims of Schellenberg that there are nonresistant nonbelievers and that this is problematic for the existence of God, and I cannot go over them here now. But I do want to acknowledge just a few.

For instance, it may be only right that some of us are denied a relationship with God, because we are unworthy of it. Rendering it in a single sentence makes this response seem less reasonable than it actually is. For example, we have (almost) all committed some evil actions and so are plausibly unworthy of entering into a full relationship with a perfect being. Some of us might be so far gone that God is *rightly* no longer interested in a relationship with us. A version of this response comes from Travis Dumsday.[21] One potential counter to this is that it remains a problem if we want our God to not only be all-loving but also all-forgiving and never giving up on us, as the Christian God is often presented.[22] For example, Acts 10:43 suggests that it is through the act of belief that we are forgiven, and so if there is a level of sin that prevents

and Selected Writings, trans. and ed. Robert Dobbin (Penguin Classics, 2008); Boethius, *The Consolation of Philosophy*, trans. Victor Watts (Penguin Classics, 2000).

18. For instance, one could have this without God through some form of nonagential teleology. Nagel ends up adopting a position a little like this; see Thomas Nagel, *Mind and Cosmos: Why the Materialist Neo-Darwinian Conception of Nature Is Almost Certainly False* (Oxford University Press, 2012).

19. C. S. Lewis, *Mere Christianity* (Bles, 1952).

20. Paul A. Macdonald Jr., "Schellenberg's Noseeum Assumption About Nonresistant Nonbelief," *European Journal for Philosophy of Religion* 13, no. 3 (2021): 139–56.

21. Travis Dumsday, "Divine Hiddenness as Deserved," *Faith and Philosophy* 31, no. 3 (2014): 293–96, https://doi.org/10.5840/faithphil20149217.

22. Julian of Norwich, *Revelations of Divine Love*, trans. Elizabeth Spearing, ed. A. C. Spearing (Penguin Classics, 1998).

us from ever finding God, then that contradicts Matthew 12:31, which states that all sins can be forgiven (save for blasphemy against the Holy Spirit, but we can't go into that rabbit hole now, however alluring the hole and however fluffy the rabbits). A more recent response by Max Baker-Hytch argues that given the demographic problem of divine hiddenness we discussed earlier, this response is untenable as a universal way of explaining divine hiddenness, since it implies that there would be a tight correlation between moral character and belief, both within groups and between them.[23]

Another theistic response is to claim that we can have a relationship with God without knowing about him. This seems most applicable to those who never had the chance to be exposed to whatever you consider to be the "One True Religion." For instance, Karl Rahner argues that there can be "anonymous Christians" who are in relationship with God without realizing it, through their general pursuit of truth and virtue.[24] While Rahner appeals to this idea in a Christian context, there is no reason why other theistic religions could not do the same. Then nonresistant nonbelievers are nonetheless still in a relationship with God, just not a straightforward one. This questions the assumption by Schellenberg that any relationship with God must be a "conscious reciprocal relationship."[25]

Ebrahim Azadegan, drawing from John Calvin and Reformed theology, has argued that we all truly do have a *sensus divinitatis*, but that we lose touch with this via willful sin.[26] This inner sense of God's existence just *is* his extending a hand to us, and by knowingly betraying that sense, through acting against our God-given conscience, we turn away from him. If Azadegan is right, then there are no nonresistant nonbelievers, but only people who do not know the extent of their resistance. A similar argument is given by James Dominic Rooney, but drawing from an Augustinian interpretation of original sin, rather than appealing to the sin of individuals. The idea here is that before the fall, we did have unimpeded intuitive access to God, but original sin has deprived us of this.[27]

23. Max Baker-Hytch, "On Sin-Based Responses to Divine Hiddenness," *Religious Studies* 61, no. 3 (2025): 658–62.

24. Stephen J. Duffy, "Experience of Grace," in *The Cambridge Companion to Karl Rahner*, ed. Declan Marmion and Mary E. Hines (Cambridge University Press, 2005), 53, where he draws on Rahner, "Anonymous Christianity and the Missionary Task of the Church," in *Theological Investigations*, trans. D. Bourke (Darton, Longman & Todd, 1974), 12:161–78.

25. Schellenberg, "Divine Hiddenness: Part 1," 2–3.

26. I don't want to say "voluntary" or "freely chosen" sin here for Calvinist reasons; see Ebrahim Azadegan, "Divine Hiddenness and Human Sin: The Noetic Effect of Sin," *Journal of Reformed Theology* 7 (2013): 78–84, https://doi.org/10.1163/15697312-12341274.

27. James Dominic Rooney, "We Deserve It: An Augustinian Response to Divine

This is just a taste of the kind of responses out there. As Andrew's and my chapters are largely aimed at introducing the topic rather than settling any particular corner of it, I will leave it there. Do be aware that there are other replies to the issue of nonresistant nonbelief, and there are also counterresponses. But I do want to emphasize one thing: if there is even one nonresistant nonbeliever who is denied a relationship with God for unjustified reasons, the problem stands.

However, now I want to move onto the issue of depth in divine hiddenness, and so lend this problem another dimension.

The Depthwise Problem of Divine Hiddenness

As I said at the beginning of this chapter, I believe that we can extend the problem of divine hiddenness beyond that of simple belief in God by also talking about the "depth" or detail of that belief. This is what I will call the "depthwise" problem of divine hiddenness.[28]

At its most basic level, this is already a very familiar idea. Michael Rea opens one of his articles on divine hiddenness by using the example of Mother Theresa, who was profoundly emotionally disturbed that, despite her belief in God, she no longer had deep religious experiences which reassured her of his presence. It is quite emotive stuff. To quote just one passage from it (also used by Rea): "I call, I cling, I want—and there is no One to answer—no One on Whom I can cling—no, No One—Alone."[29]

In his article, Rea treats this as an example of divine hiddenness, but conceptually it is very different compared to the kind of problem we have already discussed. According to Rea, Mother Teresa is a believer. She thinks that God exists, and even if she wavers in this faith, the belief is clearly firm enough to motivate her continued monasticism. This is not divine hiddenness from the standpoint of the unbeliever but from one who already believes. Considering that between 89 and 93 percent of the world's inhabitants are religious (broadly

---

Hiddenness Arguments," *New Blackfriars* 105, no. 6 (2024): 640–43, https://doi.org/10.1017/nbf.2024.52.

28. Although this has been neglected (in my opinion), we see it mentioned briefly in the introduction to J. L. Schellenberg, *Divine Hiddenness and Human Reason* (Cornell University Press, 1993), 4.

29. Michael C. Rea, "Divine Hiddenness, Divine Silence," in *Philosophy of Religion*, ed. Louis P. Pojman (Mayfield, 1987), 266–67, who in turn is quoting Teresa, *Mother Teresa: Come Be My Light; The Private Writings of the Saint of Calcutta*, ed. Brian Kolodiejchuk (Doubleday, 2007), 186–87.

construed) as of 2007, this is arguably even more serious than Schellenberg's divine hiddenness problem.[30]

To revisit Schellenberg's argument, a key premise is that an all-loving God would want some kind of relationship with us, and a prerequisite to such a relationship is that we know he exists. But this is not the *only* prerequisite for such a relationship. We might also suggest that *continued reciprocation* is another prerequisite. We apply this standard to every other relationship between agents. We even have a word for when this is not met—we call it "parasocial." But this is explicitly not the kind of relationship we are often said to have with God. As the English theologian and mystic Julian of Norwich says, "God made us, he loved us, which love was never slaked nor ever shall be."[31]

This is God actively loving us, not us loving God and him not being that fussed either way. Likewise, the characterization of his love as "never slaked" implies it is continually and actively renewed. It comes from the Old English "slacian," meaning "to relax an effort." This is a being continually engaged in the act of loving, and this is in tension not just with the lack of belief found in atheists and agnostics but also the lack of engagement with many who do believe. Of course, Julian of Norwich is of the minority who professed to have had unmistakable encounters with the divine.

A 2023 Pew Research Center poll found that only 48 percent of religious Americans have ever, even once, felt "a sudden or unexpected feeling of connection with something from beyond this world."[32] This is not even an encounter with God, a messenger of God, or anything necessarily detailed or personal but simply any feeling of connection with something beyond. If you refine it to believing that "spirits or spiritual forces exist and they have personally encountered one," the figure drops to 32 percent. Many of these may not be God-related events but instead reported encounters with ghosts or deceased loved ones. Interestingly, the figure for that was higher among those who said

30. Phil Zuckerman, "Atheism: Contemporary Numbers and Patterns," in *The Cambridge Companion to Atheism*, ed. Michael Martin (Cambridge University Press, 2007), 61. On page 61, Zuckerman concludes that between 500 million and 750 million people "currently do not believe in God." Taking that figure and turning it into a percentage of 6.7 billion (the estimated population in 2007), we have 7.3–11.2 percent of the world being atheist. I have rounded the figures and then taken them away from 100 percent to get my figures here. I recognize this is imperfect, but it still illustrates my point. There are far more religious people than nonreligious.

31. Julian of Norwich, *Revelations of Divine Love*, 96.

32. Pew Research Center, "Spirituality Among Americans," December 7, 2023, https://tinyurl.com/3zyrtz76.

they had no religious views in particular (33 percent) than among Catholics (25 percent). And again, these are not encounters with God but just encounters with *anything spiritual or supernatural, however lacking in detail*. Even if we assume that all of these are attempts from God to reach out and maintain his end of his relationship with us, he is still leaving a majority of *religious* Americans without direct encounter with him.

A similar idea has been explored by Yujin Nagasawa specifically to do with the suffering caused by the absence of religious experiences for believers.[33] However, I want to focus here more on its epistemic dimension. I should also emphasize here that there are not many widespread, up-to-date polls on this topic, so it is possible further investigation could overturn this observation.

So this is a separate issue for the theist: Why is it that God not only does not show himself in such a way as to convince nonbelievers but often does not even show himself to believers? If we see the original problem of divine hiddenness as targeting a failure to *initiate* a relationship with people, then we might see this as a failure to *develop* a relationship with those who already believe.

We might also examine the level of *detail* in which we are said to know God. I think it is plausible that to have an optimal relationship with a being, there must be mutual knowledge. To again draw from our own interpersonal relationships, we often consider a relationship's closeness and love to be limited by mutual knowledge. If a friend of mine knew nothing about me, then many people would say there is a constraint on how "close" we truly are. If I truly loved my friend, we would expect a lot of disclosure on my part.

But if we see God as desiring a close relationship with us, then it is not only nonbelievers who pose a problem for this hypothesis but also believers who have not had the nature of God revealed to them in detail. According to Catholic tradition, Augustine was walking along the beach, and a child was attempting to fit the whole ocean into a hole he had dug in the sand. Augustine gently chided the child, saying that there was no way to fit something so vast into something so small. At which point, the child transformed into an angel and likened this to Augustine attempting to comprehend the mystery of the Trinity with his limited human mind. This struggle over God's nature is also found in his difficulty defining God at the onset of his *Confessions*.[34]

33. Yujin Nagasawa, "Silence, Evil and Shusaku Endo," in *Hidden Divinity and Religious Belief: New Perspectives*, ed. Adam Green and Eleonore Stump (Cambridge University Press, 2016), 252–53.

34. See book 1 of Augustine, *Confessions*.

This is not a particularly isolated anecdote either. It is a feature of many monotheistic traditions that God's nature would be largely incomprehensible to us as limited human agents.[35] But then we might ask: Considering we were designed by him and he controls providence itself, why would he not make us more able to understand his nature, if he truly wanted a developed relationship with us?

As it happens, I don't think that *this specific* question poses too much difficulty for the theist. They might point out that our relationship with God is much closer to that of a very young child to his parent than to a friend. At age three it was not for me to grasp what was behind my parents' decisions nor to demand that they explain their inner nature to me. So let's set the bar much lower and say that a developed relationship with God would not require us knowing his nature in detail, but at the very least we are not massively mistaken about him. I take it this premise will be accepted by a larger number of readers, especially if accurate knowledge of God is relevant to salvation.

If we accept this, then the problem of *divergent* religious views comes back in a pretty major way. For example, let's say that Jesus really was the Son of God, one third of the Trinity, and the only means to salvation. Then why would God allow over a billion nonresistant believers, in the form of the world's Muslims, to have this crucial fact hidden from them? They are clearly willing to take God into their hearts, accept his authority over them, and love him, and yet this would conceal the very route to their salvation. On the other hand, if Jesus Christ is not the Son of God but is leading people away from the true Islamic route to Jannah, then why would God allow over a billion other faithful servants, following what they see as the true path to communion with him, to commit this immense act of self-sabotage? It is a bit like a loving parent allowing their child to be completely mistaken about their home address and totally lose their way home and yet never correct the child's innocent mistake. For that matter, why does God allow many conflicting denominations of each religion to exist when they contradict one another on matters of pretty central doctrine? If the Catholic veneration of Mary were heretical, why would God not let them know? Would he not want this belief to be corrected, considering that Catholics would not be doing this to rebel against God but would rather just be innocently mistaken about what he wants from them, and vice versa for Protestants. Brooke Alan Trisel has made a similar argument that God not correcting errors we believe about our ultimate purpose as humans

35. Helen De Cruz, "Divine Hiddenness and the Cognitive Science of Religion," in Green and Stump, *Hidden Divinity and Religious Belief*, 53. See also Job 26:14; Quran 6:103–104.

is evidence for his nonexistence, or that we were not created with a divine purpose in mind.[36]

The problem becomes even more stark when we step outside the Abrahamic religions and consider fundamentally different faiths. For instance, there are 1.2 billion Hindus in the world, and only a minority are nontheistic. And yet the "mainstream" (as much as such a thing could be said to exist) belief about the afterlife is one of reincarnation, which is incompatible with the Abrahamic idea of the afterlife.[37] If there is a personal God who would want to have a relationship with us, why would he not clear up this misunderstanding, which is depriving one or both of these groups from further developing that relationship?

I envision a few potential responses to this point. The first is to argue a sort of extreme theological syncretism. That is, to say that all of these religions are getting at the same fundamental spiritual truth but through different angles, like everyone feeling their way through the same dark room, starting in different corners. Indeed, in *Nostra Aetate* Pope Paul VI declared the following regarding non-Christian religions: "The Catholic Church rejects nothing that is true and holy in these religions. She regards with sincere reverence those ways of conduct and of life, those precepts and teachings which, though differing in many aspects from the ones she holds and sets forth, nonetheless often reflect a ray of that Truth which enlightens all men" (though I also want to be clear—Paul VI is not a syncretist).[38] However, to respond to my critique here, we would need a far more serious kind of syncretism. We would not just have to say that all religions have truth in them, but that all are either equally true or very close in truth to one another. Anything else would mean God is conferring extreme preference based on geographic location, and this raises its own theological issues if we perceive God as desiring a personal relationship with *each and every one of us.*

The second potential response is to repeat the claims about resistant nonbelief, but this time about those from other faiths than one's own. For example, a Catholic might say that a Protestant or a Muslim has their heart closed in some way to the true faith. Considering both the history between these groups and the way dialogue sometimes occurs online, this is a fair observation. If

36. Brooke Alan Trisel, "God's Silence as an Epistemological Concern," *Philosophical Forum* 43, no. 4 (2012): 383–85, 391–93, https://doi.org/10.1111/j.1467-9191.2012.00433.x.

37. Though eventually breaking free of this cycle.

38. "Nostra Aetate: Declaration on the Relation of the Church to Non-Christian Religions," accessed April 27, 2025, https://tinyurl.com/56nuh6vv.

you think that Christopher Hitchens versus William Lane Craig was heated, you haven't seen a Catholic and a Calvinist arguing about apostolic succession via an Instagram reel. But to reiterate my earlier point, this animosity is based upon disagreement in doctrine or theology. Most Protestants would not reject a direct revelation from God in order to keep to their Protestantism, nor do I think that if most Christians of any denomination had an unmistakable divine message that Islam was true and good they would reject that faith. I am sure there would be some exceptions, but we would need to account for *every single person* in order for this to no longer be a problem for the theist.

Finally, I want to look at what may be the strongest response to the problem of divine hiddenness (in either form), but also demonstrate why it is perhaps the least convincing for an atheist.

Belief Formation, Trade-Offs, and Probability

I want to revisit something I said at the beginning of the chapter about the relative strengths of different beliefs. I argued that if you are willing to add enough *ad hoc* clauses to something, you can maintain most beliefs even in the face of overwhelming evidence. However, this is just an extreme form of a very helpful and reasonable process in belief formation: the way we manage trade-offs between conflicting beliefs.

First, I'll illustrate this with an example, and then we will get into the nuts and bolts of things. Imagine you believe that you have two hands. However, you wake up one morning unable to feel one of those hands. The lights are off and you are unable to check visually that it is still there. You immediately panic because not being able to feel your hand is evidence that it has disappeared or been cut off in the night. However, you quickly relax. Your belief that you have both hands is pretty strongly held, so the fact you cannot currently feel one of them does not destroy that belief. Instead, you quickly come up with a hypothesis that you still have hands, but that something happened in the night that means one is now numb—perhaps you rolled over onto it in the night, cutting off blood flow. This isn't actually a hypothetical; it happened to me the other night. But my point is that we would not necessarily consider this irrational. There was some evidence that my hand no longer existed, but because of the strength of the prior belief that my hand did exist, that belief remains undefeated, and we come up with a hypothesis to resolve the tension. If you are mathematically inclined, you can put this in Bayesian terms, though I will avoid any technicality here.

In his chapter, Andrew appeals to the idea that God may have good reason to keep himself hidden from some people, even if we cannot know it right now.

A similar argument is sometimes given for the problem of evil. God is allowing evil to happen for the sake of some greater good, even if we do not yet know what that good is. We might appeal to the trusty parental metaphor to make this more concrete. A parent might have very good reason to not let their child know where a family gun is kept, for instance, or the combination to a safe. This is because it is in the child's best interests not to know these things. It could be that God has some reason like this for concealing himself from many of us. Perhaps, like Andrew said, it would confer upon us far more responsibility for any transgressions we might then make of God's word, and he wants to spare us this extra sin. Or perhaps there just is some reason, but we do not currently know what it is. A similar point has been made by Justin McBrayer and Philip Swenson, who say we ought to be skeptical of our own ability to know God's reasons for acting as he does.[39] After all, if he does exist, he is so much greater than us. Interestingly, they use this to critique both the problem of divine hiddenness and responses to it.

These arguments are often waved away as "just dodging the question." And to be fair, it is easy to view them that way from the outside. But if we pay attention to the process of resolving discrepancies between different beliefs, the theist response here can be entirely rational, if unpersuasive to the atheist.

Imagine that you are a theist because of Aquinas's first way. You accept each of its premises and its conclusion that God exists. Let's also say that you are very confident in each of these premises and thus equally confident in the conclusion. Then you would have a very high degree of confidence that God exists. Then let's also say that you accept that the problem of divine hiddenness remains a genuine problem for believers, and so think it constitutes positive evidence against the existence of God. However, you are significantly less confident in this than in your belief in Aquinas's first way. In this case it would be rational to remain a theist despite the problem of divine hiddenness and to posit some hypothesis that would reconcile divine hiddenness with the existence of God. Then it makes perfect sense to say that God must have a reason for remaining hidden to so many people and for not openly revealing himself to you in a detailed and personal way. This is not a cop-out, but the most reasonable way to resolve the tension in their beliefs, considering the prior strength of those beliefs. It is hypothesizing the existence of Neptune.

This is one reason why, despite thinking there is no knock-down solution to the problem of divine hiddenness, I also do not think it is necessarily a

39. Justin P. McBrayer and Philip Swenson, "Scepticism About the Argument from Divine Hiddenness," *Religious Studies* 48, no. 2 (2012): 148, https://doi.org/10.1017/s003441251100014x.

major problem for the theist. It is only when used in conjunction with other arguments—such as the problem of evil, critiques of the veracity of scripture, and responses to the positive case *for* God—that a case for atheism is built.

However, I do think the debate inadvertently helps shed light on areas of philosophy of religion that are often swept to the side. The first is that it considers potential nonrational reasons for belief and nonbelief. The whole discussion about resistance to beliefs is not only helpful for atheists to consider whether they truly are psychologically resistant to the existence of a deity but also helpful for theists, who could equally ask whether they are unduly resistant to atheism.

Additionally, looking at divine hiddenness through the lens of depth helps remind us that talk about the mere existence of God is only the first step in a long series of questions. Famously, St. Thomas Aquinas's *Summa Theologica* only spends a tiny fraction of its content asking whether God exists, and once he concludes that he does, there are still over two thousand pages of questions left to be answered. Say we were to establish that there is some kind of God-like being. The questions of how to know him deeply would still remain, and the issue of why God would reveal himself in far more depth to some people than to others would then become very pertinent.

Finally, I think looking at the "there must be an answer, even if I do not know what it is" response to divine hiddenness can help us to recognize some interesting aspects about the nature of belief and challenges to beliefs. It can help theists understand why atheists find this answer so unconvincing, and help atheists understand why, from a theistic perspective, it is not hand-waving at all but an epistemically justified way of resolving a tension between two beliefs by letting go of the less strongly held one.

Ultimately, the problem of divine hiddenness will remain fertile ground for debate in years to come. But then again, if God exists, why leave us debating?

7

Theist Responding to the Debate

God Best Explains a Fine-Tuned Universe

Robin Collins

This essay will argue that many related fine-tunings of the universe's basic structure provide strong support for theism over naturalism. I begin by laying out the fine-tuning for life argument for theism, often called the *anthropic fine-tuning argument.* After doing this, in the second section I address major objections to this argument. In the third section, I look at two other fine-tunings of the fundamental law structure of the universe, that of the beauty and discoverability of the laws of nature. Finally, in the fourth section I show how recent work on the metaphysics of laws of nature clarifies how the fundamental lawlike regularities in the world provide a further powerful argument for theism. The material in the third and fourth sections strengthens the overall fine-tuning argument by showing that the fine-tuning for life is just the tip of an enormous iceberg of designlike features of the universe. Furthermore, it demonstrates the inability of the leading objection to the anthropic fine-tuning argument—that of the possibility of a multiverse—to account for these additional aspects of the universe.[1]

Anthropic Fine-Tuning Argument

In this section, I first present the evidence for the anthropic fine-tuning argument (i.e., the fine-tuning for life) and then present how this evidence supports the existence of God. Finally, I consider some objections to the argument.

Anthropic fine-tuning refers to the fact that the universe must be structured to an enormous degree of precision for life to occur, particularly the

1. Significant portions of this paper were taken from Robin Collins, "The Case for Cosmic Design," in *God or Blind Nature? Philosophers Debate the Evidence (2007–2008)*, ed. Paul Draper (Internet Infidels, 2008).

life of what I call *embodied conscious agents* (ECAs) that can act on what they believe are moral values. Undergirding this argument is the assumption that such life requires stable, reproducible complexity, and so the fine-tuning is primarily about the conditions for the existence of such complexity. This fine-tuning comes in three forms: (1) the fine-tuning of the laws of nature, (2) the fine-tuning of the fundamental parameters of physics, and (3) the fine-tuning of the initial distribution of the mass-energy of the universe.[2]

Fine-Tuning of Natural Laws

To begin, consider the laws of nature, by which I mean the general rules of how nature behaves. To say that the laws are fine-tuned means that if we did not have just the right combination of laws, ECAs would probably be impossible. For example, according to current physics there are four forces in nature: gravity, the weak force, electromagnetism, and the strong nuclear force that binds protons and neutrons together in an atom. Each of these forces is necessary for ECAs. If gravity did not exist, for instance, masses would not clump together to form stars, which provide energy sources for ECAs, or to form planets, which provide a place for them to exist. If the electromagnetic force didn't exist, there would be no chemistry. If the strong force didn't exist, protons and neutrons could not bind together, and hence no atoms with atomic number greater than hydrogen would exist. Other principles of physics also appear necessary for ECAs. For example, as the late Princeton University physicist Freeman Dyson pointed out, if the Pauli exclusion principle did not exist, which is what keeps more than two electrons from occupying the same energy state in an atom, all electrons would occupy the lowest atomic energy state, undercutting the ability of atoms to form complex molecules.[3] Thus, if any of these fundamental laws or principles were missing from the law structure of our universe, the existence of ECAs would be much less likely, if not impossible.

2. For an excellent recent overview of the extensive evidence for anthropic fine-tuning, see Luke Barnes and Geraint Lewis, *A Fortunate Universe: Life in a Finely Tuned Cosmos* (Cambridge University Press, 2016). For an extended and careful treatment of the fine-tuning argument for theism, see Robin Collins, "The Teleological Argument: An Exploration of the Fine-Tuning of the Universe," in *The Blackwell Companion to Natural Theology*, ed. William Lane Craig and J. P. Moreland (Wiley-Blackwell, 2009), 234–52.

3. Freeman Dyson, *Disturbing the Universe* (Harper & Row, 1979), 251. Dyson also showed in 1967 that without this principle solid and liquid matter would become unstable, collapsing to a vastly smaller volume in less than a billionth of a second.

Fine-Tuning of Fundamental Parameters

Next, consider the fine-tuning for life of the fundamental parameters of physics, often called the constants of physics. These are fundamental numbers that, when plugged into the equations expressing the laws of physics, determine the universe's basic structure. For instance, Newton's gravitational constant G helps determine the strength of gravity via Newton's law of gravity: $F = Gm_1m_2/r^2$, where F is the force of gravitational attraction between two bodies of mass m_1 and m_2, and r is the distance between them. If, for example, G were twice as large, then this force of attraction would be twice as large as well. The fine-tuning evidence shows that many of these parameters must fall into extremely narrow ranges for ECAs to exist.

Gravity provides a good illustration. Using a standard measure of force strengths, which turns out to be roughly the relative strength of the various forces between two protons in a nucleus, gravity is the weakest of the forces, and the strong nuclear force is the strongest, being a factor of around 10^{40} (that is, ten thousand billion, billion, billion, billion) times stronger than gravity. If we increased the strength of gravity a billionfold, for instance, the force of gravity on a planet with the mass and size of the Earth would be so great that organisms anywhere near the size of human beings, whether land-based or aquatic, would be crushed. (The strength of materials depends on the electromagnetic force via the fine-structure constant, which would not be affected by a change in gravity.) Even a much smaller planet of only forty feet in diameter, which is not large enough to sustain organisms of our size, would have a gravitational pull of one thousand times that of Earth, which is still too strong for organisms of our brain size, and hence our level of intelligence, to exist. As astrophysicist Martin Rees notes, "In an imaginary strong gravity world, even insects would need thick legs to support them, and no animals could get much larger."[4] Of course, a billionfold increase in the strength of gravity is a lot. Still, compared to the total range of the strengths of the forces in nature (which span a range of 10^{40} as we saw above), it is tiny, being one part in ten thousand billion, billion, billion. Indeed, other calculations show that stars with lifetimes of more than a billion years, as compared to our sun's lifetime of ten billion years, could not exist if gravity were increased by more than a

4. Martin Rees, *Just Six Numbers: The Deep Forces That Shape the Universe* (Basic Books, 2000), 30.

factor of three thousand. This would greatly inhibit their existence by greatly shortening the time for the evolution of ECAs.[5]

The most impressive case of anthropic fine-tuning of the fundamental parameters is that of the cosmological constant. When positive, it acts as a repulsive force, causing space to expand. When negative, it acts as an attractive force, causing space to contract. If it were too large, space would expand so rapidly that galaxies and stars could not form. If it were too small, the universe would collapse before life could evolve. In today's physics, it is taken to correspond to what is called *dark energy* that permeates all of space. The anthropic fine-tuning of the cosmological constant is typically estimated to be around one part in 10^{120}, an enormously small number. To get an idea of how precise this is, it would be like throwing a dart at the earth's surface from outer space and hitting a bullseye one trillionth of a trillionth of an inch in diameter, less than the size of an atom! Even Nobel Prize–winning physicist Steven Weinberg, a critic of fine-tuning, admits that the fine-tuning of the cosmological constant is highly impressive.[6]

Further examples of the fine-tuning for life of the fundamental parameters of physics can also be given, such as that of the mass difference between the neutron and the proton. If, for example, the mass of the neutron were slightly increased by about one part in seven hundred, stable hydrogen-burning stars would cease to exist.[7]

Initial Conditions of the Universe

Two other types of fine-tuning should be mentioned. One is that of the universe's initial conditions, which refers to the fact that the initial distribution of mass-energy, as measured by entropy, must fall within an exceedingly narrow range for (intelligent) life to occur. According to Roger Penrose, one of Britain's leading theoretical physicists, "In order to produce a universe resembling the one in which we live, the Creator would have to aim for an absurdly tiny volume of the phase space of possible universes."[8] How tiny is this volume?

5. See Robin Collins, "Evidence for Fine-Tuning," in *God and Design: The Teleological Argument and Modern Science*, ed. Neil Manson (Routledge, 2003), 178–99.

6. Steven Weinberg, "A Designer Universe?," *Skeptical Inquirer* 25, no. 5 (2001), originally published on October 21, 1999, by *The New York Review of Books* (see p. 67). Also, see discussion in Barnes and Lewis, *Fortunate Universe*; Collins, "Evidence."

7. See Collins, "Evidence"; and John Leslie, *Universes* (Routledge, 1989), 39–40. Also, see the many cases of fine-tuning presented in Barnes, *Fortunate Universe*.

8. Roger Penrose, *The Emperor's New Mind: Concerning Computers, Minds, and the Laws of Physics* (Oxford University Press, 1989), 343.

According to Penrose, if we let $x = 10^{123}$, the phase space volume would be about 1/10x of the entire volume.[9] (Phase space is the space that physicists use to measure a system's various possible configurations of mass-energy.) This precision is far greater than the precision required to hit an individual proton given that the entire visible universe were a dart board! Finally, biochemist Michael Denton extensively discusses various higher-level features of the natural world, such as the many unique properties of carbon, oxygen, water, and the electromagnetic spectrum, which appear optimally adjusted for the existence of complex biochemical systems.[10]

It should be pointed out that some physicists and scientists have been skeptical of some of the prominent cases of fine-tuning in the literature. As others and I have shown in detail, this skepticism is warranted in some cases, but in other cases the arguments based on physics for fine-tuning are solid.[11] Nonetheless, even if none of the cases of purported fine-tuning were established with certainty, the argument would still have significant force. As philosopher John Leslie has pointed out, "clues heaped upon clues can constitute weighty evidence despite doubts about each element in the pile."[12]

Inferring to God

In this subsection, I show how the fine-tuning evidence strongly supports theism over what I call the *naturalistic single-universe hypothesis*, namely, the hypothesis that there is only one universe and that this universe is not the result of a transcendent intelligence or principle. Along the way, I incorporate the problem of evil into the fine-tuning argument by showing that even when combined with the existence of evil in the world, the evidence of fine-tuning strongly confirms theism. To complete the argument against naturalism, in the next section I present why theism is to be preferred over the multiverse hypothesis, which is the leading nontheist explanation of the fine-tuning.

I begin with the so-called *law of likelihood*, according to which an event or state of affairs E counts as evidence in favor of a hypothesis H_1 over H_2 if E is more probable under H_1 than H_2, with the degree of support proportional

9. Penrose, *Emperor's New Mind*, 343.

10. Michael Denton, *Nature's Destiny: How the Laws of Biology Reveal Purpose in the Universe* (Free Press, 1998), 300.

11. . See Collins, "Evidence"; and Barnes and Lewis, *Fortunate Universe*.

12. John Leslie, "How to Draw Conclusions from a Fine-Tuned Cosmos," in *Physics, Philosophy, and Theology: A Common Quest for Understanding*, ed. Robert Russell et al. (Vatican Observatory Press, 1988), 300.

to the ratio of probabilities under the two respective hypotheses.[13] The law of likelihood shows why an ink splotch that looks like the face of Abraham Lincoln would support the hypothesis that the splotch was designed over the hypothesis that it was the result of a random spill, since the existence of such a configuration of ink marks is not improbable under the design hypothesis but is enormously improbable under the random spill hypothesis.

Using the law of likelihood, the anthropic fine-tuning argument can be stated as follows:

Premise 1: Under the naturalistic single-universe hypothesis, it is exceedingly improbable that the initial conditions, laws, and fundamental parameters of physics of our universe would exhibit the enormous fine-tuning required for embodied conscious agents to exist.

Premise 2: This fine-tuning is not exceedingly improbable under theism.

Conclusion: Therefore, the law of likelihood implies that the universe's extreme fine-tuning provides strong evidence for theism over the naturalistic single-universe hypothesis.

This argument only shows that the fine-tuning evidence strongly confirms theism. As shown in the footnote at the end of this sentence, to show that theism is likely true, one would have to use Bayes' theorem and show that the prior probability of theism is not enormously small.[14] I believe my response

13. To deal with certain potential counterexamples, one might also restrict the principle to non–*ad hoc* hypotheses, such as hypotheses that were advocated by people before the discovery of these features of the universe.

14. Bayes' theorem tells us how much a body of evidence E raises the ratio of probabilities of two hypotheses, H_1 and H_2, from what it was before the evidence became known. Mathematically,

$$\frac{P(H_1|E)}{P(H_2|E)} = \frac{P(H_1)}{P(H_2)} \times \frac{P(E|H_1)}{P(E|H_2)}$$

(Here, for any propositions A and B, P(A|B) represents the probability of A given B.) The left-hand ratio is called the ratio of posterior probabilities, which gives us the degree to which we should judge H_1 to be more (or less) likely than H_2 after knowing evidence E. On the other hand, the first right-hand ratio is called the ratio of prior probabilities, which gives the degree to which we judge H_1 to be more (or less) likely than H_2 prior to knowing evidence E. Finally, the last ratio is known as the Bayes' factor. It tells us the degree to which the evidence confirms or disconfirms hypothesis H_1 over H_2 and is given by the ratio of probabilities of evidence E on hypothesis H_1 to that on H_2.

To illustrate, substitute for H_1, H_2, and E, respectively, theism (T), the naturalistic single-universe hypothesis (NSU), and the existence of a life-permitting universe (LPU). The fine-tuning argument claims that LPU is far, far more probable on theism than the NSU, making the Bayes' factor, P(LPU|T)/P(LPU|NSU), extremely large. This means that unless one judges theism to be enormously less likely than the NSU apart from the existence of a life-permitting universe, one should judge the probability of theism to be

to the "Who designed God" objection given in the next section effectively establishes this latter claim.

Next, I will briefly defend each premise of the argument.

Defense of Premise 1

In defending premise 1, I begin by pointing out that the sort of probability used here is not statistical probability, since this would require that the universe be generated by some physical process that churns out life-permitting universes at some relative frequency, contrary to the naturalistic single-universe hypothesis's stipulation that ours is the only universe. Rather, the probability used here is what philosophers call *epistemic* probability, which can be thought of as a measure of rational degrees of expectation. For example, when scientists say that the theory of evolution is *probably* true, they are clearly not talking about statistical probability such as some repeatable trial in which the theory turns out to be true with some relative frequency. Instead, they are saying something to the effect that given the total body of available evidence, a *rational* person should expect that the theory of evolution is true.

One might question this use of epistemic probability by arguing that it is merely subjective. One response is to note that epistemic probability is both used and needed for many widely accepted inferences in everyday life and science. For example, consider evolutionary biologist and geneticist Edward Dodson's summary of the case for evolution, understood as the thesis of common ancestry.[15] Says Dodson: "All [pieces of evidence] concur in *suggesting* evolution with varying degrees of cogency, but most can be explained on other bases, albeit with some damage to the law of parsimony. The strongest evidence for evolution is the concurrence of so many independent probabilities. That such different disciplines as biochemistry and comparative anatomy, genetics and biogeography should all point toward the same conclusion is very difficult to attribute to coincidence."[16] Here, Dodson claims that the primary support

---

much larger than that of the NSU after learning of the fine-tuning evidence. So, for instance, if $P(LPU|T)/P(LPU|NSU)$ were a billion, and $P(T)/P(NSU)$ were one in a million, $P(T|LPU)/P(NSU|LPU)$ would be one thousand, making theism one thousand times as likely as the NSU given the fine-tuning evidence, LPU.

15. According to the thesis of common ancestry, all life arose from one, or at most a few, simple life forms by the process of descent with modification. The evidence cited by Dodson is really evidence for this thesis, not the more general thesis that unguided chance plus natural selection was the mechanism by which this happened.

16. Edward Dodson, *The Phenomena of Man Revisited: A Biological Viewpoint on Teilhard de Chardin* (Columbia University Press, 1984), 68.

for evolution is that a variety of features of the world, such as the structure of the tree of life, would not be improbable if evolution is true but would be very improbable under the other potential nonevolutionary hypotheses, such as special creation. This improbability is not statistical improbability, nor can it be justified by an appeal to statistical improbability, since this inference was not based on statistics regarding the relative frequency of life on a planet having these features under either the evolutionary hypothesis or some nonevolutionary hypothesis. Nor was it based on a theoretical model from which those statistics could be derived. Thus, it would be completely unjustified if it were a statistical probability. Instead, it should be understood as a form of epistemic probability, for example, as claiming that certain features of the world are (rationally) very *unexpected* under the contender nonevolutionary hypotheses but not under the evolutionary hypothesis.

Another example is the use of epistemic probability in the confirmation of atomic theory. According to philosopher Wesley Salmon, what finally convinced virtually all physical scientists by 1912 of the atomic hypothesis was the agreement of at least thirteen independent determinations of Avogadro's number based on the assumption that atomic theory was correct.[17] The scientists reasoned that if atomic theory were false, such an agreement between thirteen different determinations of Avogadro's number would be exceedingly epistemically improbable—in Salmon's words, an "utterly astonishing coincidence."[18] Indeed, if scientists had not judged the agreement to be extraordinarily improbable if atomic theory were false, it is difficult to see why they would consider it strong evidence in favor of atomic theory. On the other hand, the scientists reasoned that such an agreement would be expected if atomic theory were true. Thus, by implicitly using the law of likelihood, they reasoned that these independent determinations of Avogadro's number strongly confirmed atomic theory. Yet, this judgment of improbability is obviously not based on statistical probability, even that given by a theoretical model, since we have no statistics or models of how often we would have gotten this agreement in universes in which atomic theory was false.

These examples show that many scientific inferences are based on informed, intuitive judgments of the epistemic probability of a body of evidence on a

17. Wesley Salmon, *Scientific Explanation and the Causal Structure of the World* (Princeton University Press, 1984), 219–20. Avogadro's number (= 6.02252 × 1023) is defined as the number of atoms in twelve grams of carbon 12 and, by definition, is equal to the number of elementary entities in one mole of any substance.

18. Salmon, *Scientific Explanation*, 220.

hypothesis. For most people, this kind of intuitive judgment underlies their impression that the cosmic fine-tuning is enormously improbable under the naturalistic single-universe hypothesis. And since such intuitive judgments ground our belief in our major scientific theories, it would be arbitrary to reject them in the case of the fine-tuning argument without strong reasons to do so.[19]

Arguably, this judgment regarding the probability of the fine-tuning under the naturalistic single-universe hypothesis can be more objectively grounded than those other scientific probability judgments mentioned above. Specifically, one can ground it in a version of the well-known *principle of indifference*, which says that when we have no reason to prefer one outcome over another, we should assign equal probability to each outcome. As Roy Weatherford notes in his book *Philosophical Foundations of Probability Theory*, "An astonishing number of extremely complex problems in probability theory have been solved, and usefully so, by calculations based entirely on the assumption of equiprobable alternatives [that is, the Principle of Indifference]."[20] As a mundane example, using the principle of indifference we would give a twenty-sided fair die a 1/20 chance of coming up on any given side. In fact, the entire field of statistical mechanics, a cornerstone of modern physics, is based on the principle of indifference.[21]

Despite its broad applicability, those familiar with the philosophical literature on this principle will recognize that it is subject to the so-called Bertrand paradoxes, especially when applied to cases of continuous variables as in the fine-tuning argument. Elsewhere, I show how one can avoid this paradox using what I call the *restricted principle of indifference*, which restricts these probability judgments to cases in which a variable is what I call a *natural variable*, that is, a variable that directly corresponds to a physical quantity or appears in the simplest mathematical formulation of the relevant area of physics. I also show in detail how this restricted principle can be applied to the fine-tuning.[22] In

19. Of course, the skeptic might object that scientific theories are testable, whereas the theistic explanation is not. But why should testability be epistemically relevant? After all, testability is about being able to find evidence for or against a theory in the future. What matters for the likelihood of a hypothesis's (approximate) truth, however, is the current evidence in its favor, not whether it is possible to find evidence for or against it in the future.

20. Roy Weatherford, *Foundations of Probability Theory* (Routledge & Kegan Paul, 1982), 35.

21. For example, quantum statistical mechanics assigns an equal probability to each energy state of a physical system while classical statistical mechanics treats equal volumes of the parameter space of the so-called canonical variables (called the *phase space*) as equally probable.

22. Collins, "Teleological Argument," 234–52.

simple terms, for a parameter that is a natural variable, the probability is given by the ratio of the width of the calculated life-permitting range for its values to that of what I call the epistemically illuminated (EI) range, defined as the range of values for which one can determine whether it is life-permitting. For example, since the cosmological constant is typically taken to correspond to the dark energy density (a physical quantity), it can be considered a natural variable. Further, typical estimates are that its life-permitting range is at most thirty times its current value. Yet, our physical models allow us to determine the effects on life of increasing it up to an enormous value, usually taken to be 10^{120} of its value in our universe. By the restricted principle of indifference, this would make its probability of falling into the life-permitting range $30/10^{120}$ (less than $1/10^{118}$), an enormously small number.[23]

Defense of Premise 2

Next, I turn to premise 2. The reason that a life-permitting universe is not exceedingly improbable under theism, as premise 2 asserts, is that it is plausible to think that the existence of the kind of embodied conscious agents in our universe—specifically those that are highly vulnerable to both moral and natural evil—gives rise to certain unique types of goods. Consequently, we can see a reason why a perfectly good God would create such a universe, thereby rendering its existence not enormously epistemically improbable. As Richard Swinburne has stressed, among other goods this kind of embodiment gives conscious agents extensive opportunity to act in deeply virtuous ways, such as by exercising self-sacrificial love in risking their own temporary well-being for others in a natural disaster.[24] I go further than Swinburne in arguing that such agents helping each other can give rise to certain types of eternal connections of appreciation, contribution, and intimacy between personal beings, particularly human beings, connections that I argue are intrinsically good. I then argue that since they are eternal, the good of these connections can plausibly be thought to outweigh the evils required for their existence.[25]

Thinking in terms of highly vulnerable embodied conscious agents allows

23. If there are multiple comparable good candidates for natural variables, then the probability is to be taken as being somewhere between that given by each of the natural variables.

24. For example, as stressed by Richard Swinburne, embodiment permits persons to be vulnerable to others and their environment, thereby allowing for such moral goods as sacrificially helping others in a natural disaster. See Richard Swinburne, *Providence and the Problem of Evil* (Oxford University Press, 1998).

25. Robin Collins, "The Connection Building Theodicy," in *The Blackwell Companion*

us to combine the leading atheist argument against God, the argument from evil, with the fine-tuning argument and then show that the joint evidence of fine-tuning and evil confirms the existence of God. This is done by noting that the existence of such highly vulnerable agents makes it highly likely that there would be the kind of evils we find in the world. For if such agents are to be highly vulnerable to moral and natural evil, then God can only rarely intervene (apart from persistent prayer) to stop the evils, since otherwise they would not be highly vulnerable. Further, to be highly vulnerable to moral evil means that one is both highly vulnerable to committing great moral evils (in the right circumstances) and being the victim of such evils. To be highly vulnerable to natural evils means that one will be subject to suffering as a result of the operation of the natural world. Thus, insofar as God has a reason to create a universe with such agents, God has a reason to create a world that results in the kinds of evils we find, thereby making it no longer improbable that God would create such a world. However, since such a world requires extreme fine-tuning, it would still be enormously improbable under the naturalistic single-universe hypothesis. Consequently, the law of likelihood implies that the existence of a universe that allows for highly vulnerable embodied conscious agents, and thus much evil, to exist strongly supports theism over the naturalistic single-universe hypothesis.

Some Common Objections

In this section, I go through some of the most common objections to the fine-tuning argument.

Who Designed God Objection

Probably the most common objection to the design argument is what I call the "who designed God objection," which is the claim that the structure of God requires just as much special order (i.e., fine-tuning) as the universe and is thus as much in need of explanation. For example, this is Richard Dawkins's main objection to any version of the design argument.[26] The central premise of this objection is that God's mind must be as well-ordered as the universe. However, little argument is usually given for this premise except statements

to the Problem of Evil, ed. Dan Howard-Snyder and Justin McBrayer (Wiley-Blackwell, 2014), 222–35.

26. See Richard Dawkins, *The Blind Watchmaker* (Norton, 1986), 316.

such as J. J. C. Smart's claim that "the designer of an artefact must be as complex as the artefact," or David Hume's claim that "there is no more difficulty conceiving that the several elements [of nature], from an internal unknown cause, may fall into the most exquisite arrangement, than to conceive that their ideas, in the great universal mind, from a like unknown cause, fall into that arrangement."[27] As far as I can tell, undergirding these statements are two assumptions: (1) the designer's mind must contain the "blueprint" of the thing being designed, and (2) the blueprint of the universe in God's mind must be as complex as the universe itself, since the structure of an artifact must mirror that of the blueprint.

To respond to this objection, we can divide the order in God's mind into two aspects: a necessary order arising from God's awareness of all possible realities and a voluntarily chosen order. Regarding the necessary order, many philosophers, both atheists and theists, have postulated the existence of what they call "possible worlds" to ground *modal logic*, that is, the logic of possibility and necessity. These possible worlds are typically considered complete representations (or, more informally, "blueprints") of possible ways reality could be, and they are typically thought to exist necessarily. Because they exist necessarily, their existence is no more coincidental than mathematical truths, such as the theorem in Euclidean geometry that the circumference of a circle is equal to the number π times the circle's diameter. To illustrate, if we measure several circles, and this relation between the diameter and circumference (approximately) holds, we don't find this a coincidence in need of further explanation because, we reason, this relation is necessary.

Theists have commonly thought of these possible worlds as ideas or blueprints in God's mind, which in turn constitutes the necessarily existing order in God's mind. Or if they existed outside God's mind, God's awareness of them could be thought to induce a corresponding order in God's mind. In either case, since the possible worlds necessarily exist, this order is not coincidental and thus not in need of explanation. The rest of the order in God's mind is also not coincidental, since God voluntarily chooses it.

Although I believe the above adequately answers the "who designed God objection" as it is commonly raised, there remain two places where the God explanation might involve hypothesizing an unexplained coincidence: (1) God's desire to create a life-permitting universe, and (2) the very existence of a being

27. J. J. C. Smart, "Laws of Nature and Cosmic Coincidence," *Philosophical Quarterly* 35, no. 140 (1985): 275–76; David Hume, *Dialogues Concerning Natural Religion*, 2nd ed., ed. Richard Popkin (Hackett, 1980), 17–18.

with the core attributes of God. To address the former, begin by assuming the widely held thesis going back to Plato that goodness and beauty are intrinsically self-motivating or desirable (i.e., a person's perception of a state of affairs as good or beautiful gives them some reason to bring it about). Second, assume, as suggested in the previous section, that God's creation of a universe with highly vulnerable embodied conscious agents allows for unique types of moral goods.[28] Thus, God would have a reason to create such a universe, thereby making God's doing so no longer coincidental.

Finally, I present two routes for addressing the worry that the mere existence of a being like God is coincidental. My first route begins with the intuitive and widely shared idea that consciousness is at the foundation of reality. It goes as follows:

1. Either consciousness, the not-conscious, or a combination of the two is fundamental.[29]
2. Since there are only three possibilities, and consciousness being fundamental seems at least as likely as the two other possibilities, consciousness being fundamental is not coincidental.[30]

28. This is a version of an argument given by Richard Swinburne, *The Existence of God*, 2nd ed. (Oxford University Press, 2004), 103–5. One could also use this argument to explain why God created a universe whose mathematical structure exhibits beauty and elegance, and, if one assumes that certain additional moral goods are realized by the universe being scientifically discoverable, the argument explains why God created a discoverable universe. These features of the universe are discussed more in the third section below.

29. I define a fundamental reality as a reality such that all other realities—except perhaps abstract realities like mathematical truths—depend on it, while it depends on nothing else.

30. To clarify, it would only be coincidental if there were many, many other alternatives that we judged as equally good candidates for being fundamental, or if something about consciousness being fundamental made it intrinsically highly unlikely. To elaborate on the former, one could argue that there are an infinite number of combinations of consciousness and nonconsciousness that could be fundamental. Given that each of these alternatives seems just as good as only consciousness being fundamental, then the latter becomes enormously coincidental. There are several replies to this objection. First, one could invoke the idea that only positive facts need explanation, and hence the more brute positive facts one postulates, the more is left unexplained. Arguably, this is the intuition behind the typical formulation of Ockham's razor that one "must not multiply entities beyond necessity." See Paul Vincent Spade, Claude Panaccio, and Jenny Pelletier, "William of Ockham," *Stanford Encyclopedia of Philosophy*, last modified September 11, 2024, https://tinyurl.com/7dcap73k. In the case of the hypothesis that consciousness is fundamental, there is only one unexplained positive fact, with the other fact being a purely negative fact, that nothing else is fundamental. (Being unlimited is the same as having no limits. Thus it is a strictly negative

3. Assume consciousness and agency go together, implying that consciousness and agency are jointly fundamental. (I define "agency" as the ability to give being [actuality] to a mental representation of a state of affairs.)
4. Since this consciousness/agency is fundamental, it follows that it is not limited by anything external. Assuming it also has no internal limitations, it follows that it has no limitations whatsoever.[31]
5. Unlimited consciousness would contain representations of every possible reality, and unlimited agency would have the power to actualize any such representation.[32] That is, it would be omniscient and omnipotent. Furthermore, God's will having no external or internal constraints means that God is perfectly free.

My second route is based on the common intuition that an infinite mind is needed to ground the existence of mathematical truths, possible worlds, and other abstract objects and truths. For example, the late nontheist mathematician Reuben Hersh indirectly acknowledges this intuition. After recognizing the force of the arguments for mathematical Platonism—the idea that mathematical truths exist independently of human consciousness and the physical universe—he claims that although "Platonism in the full sense . . . is of course *tenable within a religious world-view (belief in a Divine Mind),*"

---

fact and therefore does not add to the number of unexplained positive facts.) In contrast, the combination hypothesis postulates more than one positive fact. Second, one could argue that the idea of consciousness being fundamental is grounded in a deep intuition, since it arises across diverse cultures. For example, most Hindus would state that consciousness being fundamental is part of their view of the foundation of reality being *Saccidananda*, that is, *sat* (essence of existence), *cit* (consciousness), and *ananda* (bliss). (Finally, one could note that even if one were to consider each of the possible combinations of conscious states with unconscious states as equally good alternatives for being fundamental, we seem to have no grounds for thinking that the set of combinations such that the conscious states have sufficient knowledge and power to create our universe is much smaller than the entire set of combinations. Thus, even in this case it is still plausible to think it is not coincidental that an underlying conscious reality with enormous knowledge and power exists.)

31. An example of the kind of internal limitation I have in mind is one in which, as a brute fact or some hidden metaphysical necessity, God cannot create some otherwise seemingly possible state of affairs, such as a world with unicorns. Further, one could justify the claim that the lack of internal limitations is not coincidental by noting it is a strictly negative fact. One could then appeal to a version of Ockham's razor, as done in the previous footnote.

32. To make room for human libertarian free will, we could further hypothesize that God only gives being to part of the blueprint for reality. Then God concurs with our choice to actualize new states of affairs, thereby allowing us to have some free choice in what aspects of the world become actual.

it is not tenable within a "general world view [that] excludes mysticism."[33] Since he rejects such a worldview, he attempts to develop an alternative to mathematical Platonism.

Philosopher Mark Balaguer makes a similar observation for why many reject mathematical Platonism, noting that "Platonism is a very attractive view because it provides an extremely natural and pleasing account of mathematical practice and mathematical discourse. But despite this, many philosophers do not endorse Platonism because they cannot bring themselves to accept its ontology."[34] Balaguer then goes on to argue that most alternatives to Platonism have severe problems. Given that an infinite mind is needed to ground mathematical truths and possible worlds, and given that these necessarily exist, it follows that this infinite mind necessarily exists, and hence that its existence cannot be coincidental. It is important to emphasize that I am not arguing here that we can prove that we need such a mind to ground mathematical truths and possible worlds, only that it is *plausible* to think that such a mind is needed. This in turn helps us intuitively see why such a mind's existence is necessary—because it undergirds all necessary truths.[35] Finally, it should be noted that this second route only gets us partway to God since it does not show that the mind is omniscient or omnipotent.[36]

The above arguments do not *prove* that the God hypothesis avoids positing a reality whose existence is as coincidental as that of a fine-tuned universe. They do, however, make it *plausible* to think that it does. Given how deeply implausible it seems that the universe's extensive fine-tuning is a brute fact, the God hypothesis stands out as the more coherent and compelling explanation.

33. Reuben Hersh, "Some Proposals for Reviving the History of Mathematics," in *New Directions in the Philosophy of Mathematics*, ed. Thomas Tymoczko (Berkhäuser, 1986), 18 (italics mine).

34. Mark Balaguer, "Fictionalism in the Philosophy of Mathematics," in *Stanford Encyclopedia of Philosophy*, last modified July 23, 2018, https://tinyurl.com/5n6auy5w.

35. The initial puzzlement about God's existence being necessary stems from the fact that necessary truths always seem to be hypotheticals based on our grasping necessary relationships between properties or states of affairs. For example, necessarily, if A = B and B = C, then A = C. Yet, asserting God necessarily exists does not seem to be of this form. However, the above argument allows us to put God's necessary existence into a hypothetical form: necessarily, if mathematical truths and possible worlds have reality (a state of affairs), then there must be an infinite mind (another state of affairs) that grounds that reality.

36. Arguments from mathematics to God are explored in more depth in Christopher Menzel, "The Argument from Collections" and Tyron Goldschmidt, "The Argument from (Natural) Numbers," in *Two Dozen (Or So) Arguments for God: The Plantinga Project*, ed. Jerry Walls and Trent Dougherty (Oxford University Press, 2018).

Grand Unified Theory Objection

One common objection is that some grand unified theory might eventually explain the values of the fundamental parameters. Hence, it is argued, we do not need to invoke a designer to explain why these parameters have life-permitting values. As astrophysicists Bernard Carr and Martin Rees note, however, "even if all apparently anthropic coincidences could be explained [in terms of such a unified theory], it would still be remarkable that the relationships dictated by physical theory happened also to be those propitious for life."[37] For the theist, then, the development of a grand unified theory would not undercut the fine-tuning argument but would only serve to deepen our appreciation of the creator's ingenuity. Instead of separately fine-tuning each parameter, under this view God carefully chose those laws that would yield life-permitting values for each of them.[38]

Multiverse Objection

Another objection to considering fine-tuning for life as evidence for God takes us almost into the realm of science fiction: the proposal that there are a vast number of universes, each with different values for the fundamental parameters of physics. If such multiple universes exist, it would be no surprise that the parameters in one of them would have just the right values for the existence of intelligent life, just as if enough lottery tickets were generated, it would be no surprise that one of them would turn out to be the winning number. Further, it is no surprise that we observe *our* universe to have these values, since having them is necessary for our existence.

How did these universes come into existence? Typically, the answer is to postulate some physical process that produces them, what I call a "universe generator." Against the naturalistic version of the universe-generator hypothesis, one could argue that the universe generator itself must be "well designed" to produce even one life-sustaining universe. After all, even a mundane item such as a bread-making machine, which only produces loaves of bread instead of universes, must be well-designed as an appliance *and* have just the

37. B. J. Carr and M. J. Rees, "The Anthropic Cosmological Principle and the Structure of the Physical World," *Nature* 278 (1979): 612.

38. I am, however, skeptical that such a unified theory will be developed: current attempts have been unsuccessful at reducing the number of free parameters—the standard model of particle physics has twenty-four, and it looks like string theory generates its own effective free parameters that have to be set just right for a complex life-permitting universe to exist. See Barton Zwiebach, *A First Course in String Theory* (Cambridge University Press, 2004), 9.

right ingredients (flour, yeast, gluten, and so on) in just the right amounts to produce decent loaves of bread. Indeed, as I have shown in detail elsewhere, if one carefully examines the most popular and most well-developed universe-generator hypothesis, that based on inflationary cosmology, one finds that it contains just the right fields and laws to generate life-permitting universes. Eliminate one of the fields or laws, and no life-sustaining universes would be produced.[39]

Finally, neither the universe-generator hypothesis nor even the hypothesis that all possible universes exist as a brute fact can explain the other design-indicating features of our universe that I elaborate below, such as why *our* universe has an elegant, intelligible, and discoverable underlying mathematical structure.[40] The reason is that in its purported explanation for the fine-tuning for life, it crucially relies on what is known as the *observer-selection principle*, which states that it is not coincidental that we observe that the universe we are in is observer-permitting, since beings like us (understood as generic observers) could not have found ourselves in any other kind of universe. However, suppose the universe is much more elegant or discoverable than we would expect the typical observer-permitting universe to be. In that case, it is still coincidental that we find ourselves in such a universe.

Indeed, because of the limitations of the observer-selection effect, the multiverse hypothesis encounters the often-cited *Boltzmann brain problem*, particularly when it attempts to account for the universe's low initial entropy by claiming it is a random fluctuation. The problem is that it is far, far more likely for observers to exist as random fluctuations with an order corresponding to a brain surrounded by a sea of chaos than to exist within an ordered universe. Thus, considering ourselves as generic observers, we should expect to find ourselves as such Boltzmann brains.

A similar argument applies even if we think that true observers require a much larger region of order, such as the size of the solar system or the galaxy. As often noted, it is far, far more likely by random chance for an ordered region the size of the solar system or galaxy to exist than for the entire universe to

39. See Robin Collins, "The Multiverse Hypothesis: A Theistic Perspective," in *Universe or Multiverse*, ed. Bernard Carr (Cambridge University Press, 2007), 464–66.

40. Despite these objections to the naturalistic version of the universe-generator hypothesis, I am not objecting to the existence of many universes or even a universe generator. For the theist, the existence of many universes would simply support the view that creation reflects the *infinite creativity* of the creator, who is so creative that he or she creates not only a reality with an enormous number of planets and galaxies but one with many universes. (God could create these universes directly or by means of creating a universe generator.)

have the amount of order—corresponding to relatively low entropy—for stars and galaxies to form. Now, some, such as atheist cosmologist Sean Carroll, have used this as an objection to the universe's being fine-tuned for life since, as Carroll notes, all that is necessary for life is a much more localized region of order.[41] However, the claim that the universe is also fine-tuned for scientific discovery can easily explain this, since seeing other galaxies is enormously helpful for astrophysics and cosmology (e.g., it was essential for discovering the big bang theory). Thus, this objection provides a powerful example of what I call *the fine-tuning of the universe for scientific discovery*, a type of fine-tuning that I briefly discuss in the next section below.

Other Life-Permitting Laws Objection

According to what I call the "other life-permitting laws objection," there could be other life-permitting sets of laws or values of the parameters that we know nothing about. The easiest way to address this objection is by a dartboard analogy. Suppose there was a dartboard extending far into the distance but with a large square-meter spot illuminated by a searchlight with a single bullseye of one square millimeter (one-millionth of a square meter) in it. If we saw a dart hit the bullseye, we would take this as extraordinarily strong evidence that the dart was aimed instead of thrown at random despite not knowing whether the unilluminated region had a high density of bullseyes. Why? Because we would reason that it would be exceedingly unlikely for the dart to hit the bullseye instead of somewhere else in the illuminated region if the dart were thrown at random, but not unlikely if it were aimed. In analogy, using our definition of the epistemically illuminated (EI) range for a parameter as the range of values for which we can determine whether they are life-permitting, we can say that the fact that the life-permitting bullseye is exceedingly small compared to the EI range provides strong evidence that its value was chosen by design.

Other Kinds of "Fine-Tuning"

Beauty and Elegance of Laws

The beauty and elegance of the laws of nature also point to divine design. Nobel Prize–winning physicist and convinced atheist Steven Weinberg, for

41. See Sean Carroll, "Does the Universe Need God?," in *The Blackwell Companion to Science and Christianity*, ed. J. B. Stump and Alan Padgett (Wiley-Blackwell, 2012), 192.

instance, devotes a whole chapter of his book *Dreams of a Final Theory* to explaining how the criteria of beauty and elegance are commonly used with great success to guide physicists in formulating laws. As Weinberg points out, "mathematical structures that confessedly are developed by mathematicians because they seek a sort of beauty are often found later to be extraordinarily valuable by the physicist."[42] Later, Weinberg comments that "physicists generally find the ability of mathematicians to anticipate the mathematics needed in the theories of physics quite uncanny," even admitting that "sometimes nature seems more beautiful than strictly necessary."[43] Indeed, one of the most prominent theoretical physicists of this century, Paul Dirac, has gone so far as to claim, as Einstein did, that "it is more important to have beauty in one's equations than to have them fit experiment."[44] The beauty, elegance, and ingenuity of such mathematical equations make sense if the universe was purposefully designed like an artwork, but they appear surprising and inexplicable under the nondesign hypothesis.

Some have claimed that the beauty we see in nature is merely subjective, like seeing the Big Bear or the Big Dipper in the random pattern of stars in the night sky. To say that the beauty of the mathematical structure of nature is merely subjective, however, completely fails to account for the enormous success of the criterion of beauty in producing predictively accurate theories, such as Einstein's general theory of relativity. We would not expect merely subjective impressions to lead to highly successful theories.

Intelligibility and Discoverability

Finally, the laws of nature themselves seem to be carefully arranged so that they are intelligible, and also discoverable, by beings with our level of intelligence. Many prominent physicists have stressed this. Albert Einstein, for example, famously remarked that "the eternal mystery of the world is that it is comprehensible. . . . The fact that it is comprehensible is a miracle."[45] Similarly, in a famous essay Eugene Wigner, one of the principal founders of quantum mechanics, claimed, "The miracle of the appropriateness of the language of

42. Steven Weinberg, *Dreams of a Final Theory: The Scientist's Search for the Ultimate Laws of Nature* (Vintage, 1992), 153.

43. Weinberg, *Final Theory*, 157, 250.

44. P. A. M. Dirac, "The Evolution of the Physicist's Picture of Nature," *Scientific American*, May 1, 1963, 47.

45. Albert Einstein, *The Quotable Einstein*, ed. Alice Calaprice (Princeton University Press, 1996), 197.

mathematics for the formulation of the laws of physics is a wonderful gift which we neither understand nor deserve."[46] As theoretical physicist Paul Davies notes: "A common reaction among physicists to remarkable discoveries of the sort discussed above is a mixture of delight at the subtlety and elegance of nature, and of stupefaction: 'I would never have thought of doing it that way.' If nature is so 'clever' that it can exploit mechanisms that amaze us with their ingenuity, is that not persuasive evidence for the existence of intelligent design behind the physical universe?"[47] Further, Davies notes, "uncovering the laws of physics resembles completing a crossword in a number of ways. . . . In the case of the crossword, it would never occur to us to suppose that the words just happened to fall into a consistent interlocking pattern by accident."[48]

Work on articulating detailed examples of this intelligibility and discoverability has just begun in the last thirty years. For instance, in a recent book devoted to this issue, philosopher Mark Steiner concludes that the world is much more "user-friendly" for the discovery of its fundamental mathematical structure than seems explicable under naturalism.[49]

In 2010, it occurred to me that this claim could actually be tested—the claim that the mathematical form of the laws of nature was providentially chosen so that we could discover them. If that were true, we would reasonably expect the fundamental parameters of physics to take on values that *optimize* the success of science. This implies that changing those values should leave our ability to discover the universe unchanged or worse, never better.

To test this idea, I calculated how changing the values of different parameters affected the usefulness of major instruments—such as telescopes—that probe key areas of physics like cosmology. (I called these instruments *contributors to discoverability*.) I did this by examining how changing a parameter's value affected the major instruments influenced by it, and then judging the overall change in discoverability when all the effects on the instruments were combined.

When I ran the calculations, I found that the results fell within what I call the *plausibility-optimality range* (POR)—the range of parameter values that are plausibly optimal for overall scientific discovery. To estimate the POR, I first identified the major *contributors to discoverability* affected by the parameter.

46. Eugene Wigner, "The Unreasonable Effectiveness of Mathematics in the Natural Sciences," *Communications on Pure and Applied Mathematics* 13, no. 1 (1960): 14.

47. Paul Davies, *Superforce: The Search for a Grand Unified Theory of Nature* (Simon & Schuster, 1984), 235–36.

48. Davies, *Superforce*, 235–36.

49. Mark Steiner, *The Applicability of Mathematics as a Philosophical Problem* (Harvard University Press, 1998), 176.

As I did so, a deeper pattern appeared: the parameter values also tended to fall within a smaller subrange of the POR that maximized a major contributor, or group of major contributors, to scientific discovery. I later referred to these narrower ranges as *contributor-maximality ranges* (CMRs).

In hindsight, I realized that a parameter lying in such a CMR greatly reinforced the appearance of some sort of fine-tuning for discoverability. Why? First, these ranges were usually far narrower than the POR, making coincidence far less plausible. Second, estimating the POR required identifying all the major contributors and then subjectively weighing their importance, since those contributors often changed in opposite directions as the parameter varied. Finding a CMR, by contrast, required examining only one contributor, thereby avoiding both the need for multiple comparisons and the subjectivity of weighing them together.

Before observing this deeper CMR pattern, I realized that *discovering* that the universe was fine-tuned for scientific discoverability might be even more important than scientific discovery itself. From this idea came a natural extension, which I later called the *fine-tuning for the discoverability of discoverability*, or simply the *discoverability-of-discoverability hypothesis* (DDH), which claimed that the fundamental parameters were also fine-tuned to maximize the likelihood that we would recognize some kind of fine-tuning for discovery. I then realized that the DDH *predicts* the CMR pattern I was seeing: by falling within a CMR inside that POR, the value of a parameter's connection with discoverability became harder to dismiss as chance or just a subjective projection, thereby making the fine-tuning related to discoverability even more evident. Hence, both my prior philosophical reasoning and the empirical pattern I found pointed toward the DDH.

To make the DDH's predictions more precise, I had to consider cases where several CMRs might exist within a single POR. The ability of a parameter's value falling into a CMR to signal discoverability fine-tuning grows with three factors: the contributor's connection with discoverability (determined by its significance), the narrowness of the CMR, and how easily the CMR—and the parameter's position within it—can be recognized. The DDH therefore predicts that a parameter's value will lie in the CMR subrange of the POR that best satisfies all three of these conditions.

Because each factor strengthens the CMR's potential to signal discoverability fine-tuning, a simple rule follows: if one CMR scores better on any one of the criteria (for example, recognizability) and is at least as good on the other two (significance and narrowness), then a parameter's value falling into it creates a stronger signal of discoverability fine-tuning.

To test this prediction, I focused on parameters whose life-permitting, POR, and potential CMR ranges could be estimated with reasonable confidence. I also required that each life-permitting range be large enough to make a potential CMR small by comparison. These criteria narrowed the test cases to two parameters in cosmology and ten fundamental parameters in particle physics.

All of them turned out to fall within the ranges predicted by the DDH, implying a degree of fine-tuning tighter than one part in a billion trillion of the life-permitting range. As explained in the previous section, the multiverse hypothesis can at best account for why parameter values fall within the observer-permitting range. Thus, if my analysis is correct, the DDH fine-tuning lies far beyond what any multiverse explanation can cover. That is a major advantage of the fine-tuning argument from discoverability over the one from life. In addition, the DDH also makes *falsifiable* predictions, allowing it to be tested like other scientific theories.

Although I have verified many of the cases with other physicists and have been convinced of the fine-tuning myself, my results and arguments have not been thoroughly vetted in the literature. So, for now, the reader should take the DDH as providing a serious prospect of new, game-changing fine-tuning evidence for God.[50]

Laws of Nature

Before we had extensive evidence for the fine-tuning for life, the very existence of the lawlike regularities—that is, those expressed by the laws of nature—provided an undeveloped but powerful case for the existence of God. Importantly, the common "universe-generator" version of the multiverse hypothesis (discussed earlier in the second section) cannot explain these regularities, since it assumes their existence.

Now, many people are unaware that many nontheistic philosophers hold that these lawlike regularities—such as that masses always attract each other—exist as brute facts without further explanation. This view, often called the *regularity theory*, goes back to the famous Scottish philosopher David Hume (1711–1776) and therefore is also often called the *Humean view*. The other major nontheist account of the laws of nature is called the *necessitarian theory*.

50. For an early version of my argument before I developed the DDH, see Robin Collins, "The Argument from Physical Constants: The Fine-Tuning for Discoverability," in Walls and Dougherty, *Plantinga Project*.

It hypothesizes the existence of underlying necessities that account for these regularities. The intuition that the regularity theory postulates a cosmic coincidence that demands explanation is cited as the major reason for rejecting it by recent necessitarians, such as philosopher David Armstrong. Indeed, Armstrong goes as far as to say, "If you believe that [the regularities are a brute fact], I say, you will believe anything."[51]

I share this sense of absurdity in supposing that the regularities are a brute fact. However, even regularists often share this intuition. For example, Norman Swartz, an advocate of the regularity view, comments that:

> No one would be prepared to allow that a column of cars, a thousandfold in length, all red, could be a coincidence. Large-scale coincidences cry out for explanations that reveal the contrivance, planning, or deliberation behind the phenomenon. . . .
>
> There are probably more than 10^{60} electrons in the universe, and all of them, we may suppose, have precisely the same electrical charge. Now although I am prepared to allow that five red cars in a row might be dismissed as a coincidence, can I allow that 10^{60} items with precisely the same electrical charge is likewise a coincidence?[52]

Swartz then goes on to reject both the God explanation and the necessitarian view, presumably because he thinks they cannot ultimately solve the coincidence problem. He thus concludes that despite this intuition of cosmic coincidence, "At some point, we have our backs to the wall. It seems to me reasonable to think the wall to be at the point where we say, 'Well, these countless particles all have the same properties because that's just the way the world is.'"[53]

Necessitarians also often argue that the regularity theory undercuts any rational justification for our practice of enumerative induction. For, they claim, if we truly believe that there is no reason why observed events follow a certain pattern, then we have no reason to believe that unobserved events will follow the same pattern. For example, if a coin is flipped ten times and each time heads comes up, but no reason can be found for this, we would attribute

51. David Armstrong, "Reply to Van Fraassen," *Australasian Journal of Philosophy* 66, no. 2 (1988): 229.

52. Norman Swartz, *The Concept of Physical Law* (Cambridge University Press, 1985), 203–4.

53. Swartz, *Physical Law*, 204.

the result to chance and, consequently, we should not expect heads instead of tails on the next flip. Yet such inductive inferences are central to science: for instance, from observing that many, many masses in a wide variety of circumstances attract each other, scientists inferred the law of universal gravitational attraction, namely that all masses in the universe attract one another.

The only response I can see the regularist giving is that given by David Hume, namely, that there are no grounds for believing the regularities will continue other than our deep psychological inclination to believe this. This response, however, opens the door to all kinds of beliefs that we, including regularity theorists, would consider irrational. For instance, it is difficult to see how they could object to someone who believed, based on a psychological inclination, that the world just happens to be ordered, as a brute fact, in such a way that they will survive death and experience heavenly states of bliss forever and ever. The normal reason we have for rejecting such beliefs is that they go far beyond what we can observe and involve grand coincidences, but clearly regularists cannot use this as a reason. Further, since regularists believe that psychological inclinations are ultimately brute facts, and the above seemingly irrational belief is compatible with everything we know, they have no rational basis for privileging their psychological inclinations. The end result is that they undercut reason itself.

I now argue that the main nontheist alternative to the regularity view, the necessitarian view, also cannot solve the cosmic coincidence and induction problems, even though at first it might seem to; in contrast, theism can.

Until the late 1970s, necessitarian accounts of laws typically fell under what is called a *substance, powers, and liability view*, which claims that the fundamental regularities in the universe are the result of physical entities with various powers and liabilities. For example, masses always attract each other because each mass has the *power* to attract other masses and the *liability* to be attracted by them. However, this view still involves the cosmic coincidence that entities of a particular type—masses, electrically charged objects, and so forth—all share some set of powers in common. This is analogous to how it would be a vast coincidence that, as a brute fact, all US pennies have the picture of Abraham Lincoln on them. By the late 1970s, a new type of necessitarian account was developed to solve this coincidence (and related induction) problem: the so-called *relations-between-universals* (RBU) *theory*.[54] However,

54. See, for instance, David Armstrong, *What Is a Law of Nature?* (Cambridge University Press, 1983); and Michael Tooley, *Causation: A Realist Approach* (Oxford University Press, 1988).

elsewhere I argue in detail that their new account runs into the same problems they accuse regularists of having, an argument I will now summarize.[55]

I begin by granting that the RBU view can account for strictly *repetitive regularities*, such as that like charges always repel each other. The coincidence in such regularities is their repetitiveness: some property B (being repelled) always occurs when property A (being a pair of like charges) occurs. The coincidence does not concern what these two properties are, just that they are always bound together. They attempt to account for this repetitiveness by claiming that of "law-like" necessity: if the first property of the pair occurs, the second property must appear with it. This would be like a society in which each person is randomly paired with another for marriage. Although it would be by chance that any two people were married, their being married would nonetheless explain the repetitive regularity of them usually being seen together at various gatherings.

As another analogy, it would be like the manager of a grocery store allowing the clerk to set the price for each banana between thirty and forty cents and then directing them to stamp the chosen price on each banana. Now, suppose the clerk randomly picked the price in this range, and it turned out to be thirty-six cents. Other than chance, there would be no explanation for why it was thirty-six cents instead of some other value in the range. However, the repetitive part of the regularity—that each banana had the same number stamped on it—would be explained by the fact that each banana was stamped with the same stamper combined with the fact that some random number was chosen for the stamper.

Next, suppose that the grocery store decided to sell bananas by the pound, and the store wrapped bananas together in bunches of various weights. Further, suppose that the manager had written a million randomly chosen functions relating the price to the weight of the bunch, with each function put on its own slip of paper in a box.[56] Finally, suppose the manager told the clerk to stir the box and pick one of the functions. In this scenario, it would be extremely unlikely for the clerk to pick a simple function, such as that each bunch got the same price *C* or a linear function in which the price was proportionate to the weight.

The last banana example is analogous to the problem RBU necessitarians face for the vast majority of the laws of nature. Few of them are of the simple

55. See Robin Collins, "God and the Laws of Nature," *Philo* 12, no. 2 (2009): 142–71, https://doi.org/10.5840/philo200912211.

56. To make this more realistic, we could stipulate that the function is such as to make the cost per pound for each bunch between some lower and upper limit, such as forty cents per pound to seventy cents per pound.

variety that all *A*s are *B*s, but rather they involve functional relations between various quantities. For example, consider Newton's law of motion, $F = ma$, which gives the amount of force (F) required to cause the acceleration (a) of an object of mass (m). This law states how three quantities vary with each other (e.g., if one doubles the mass, it says that twice the force is required to cause the same acceleration). RBU necessitarians attempt to extend their account to functional regularities by hypothesizing that some properties are bound with the property of following a functional relation. In the case of $F = ma$, for example, Armstrong would say that the property of being a force is bound by a lawlike necessity with the property of *being such that* $F = ma$.

This potentially could explain the repetitiveness of the regularity, just as the clerk's choosing some particular function might explain why the price of every bunch is given via the same function. However, it leaves unexplained why the laws of nature take on such simple functional forms, especially given that simple functions are vastly outnumbered by complex functions. This is analogous to finding that the price on the various bunches of bananas involved the linear relationship of price = weight × 35 cents/pound. In this case, we would *not* think the clerk merely chose the functional relationship at random from the million possibilities in the box but rather had a strong preference for simple functions.

This shows that the simplicity and intelligibility of the equations of physics constitute the real coincidence posed by the lawlike regularities of nature, not the fact that they follow the same functional relationship. To see this more clearly, suppose that one collected a thousand measurements of the relation of force versus acceleration for a given mass and plotted them as data points on a graph. No matter what those data points are, it is a mathematical fact that one can always find an infinite number of functions that go through those points, as can be verified by simply drawing various curves through them. And, for any of the functions one chooses, it is true that every data point has the repetitive regularity of satisfying that function. So, it's not the fact that our observations fall under this type of repetitive regularity that is coincidental, since that occurs by mathematical necessity.

In response, one could postulate a metaphysical principle of simplicity that makes it more likely for the universe to follow simple laws than complex ones. The universe, however, is far, far more complex than one would expect from such a principle, since there is a vast array of possible universes far simpler than ours (e.g., a universe with empty space, a universe with a few particles that move in straight lines, and so forth). To deal with this problem, cosmologist Max Tegmark has proposed that we combine the maximalist multiverse hypothesis—one in which all logically consistent realities exist—with the claim that universes that have simpler laws should be given a higher probabilistic weight.[57] Since life can only occur in a sufficiently complex universe, Tegmark's hypothesis implies that we should expect to find ourselves in a reality whose laws have a complexity at most only slightly greater than that needed for life, arguably something we do find. However, because one could explain any occurrence by arbitrarily postulating some probabilistic measure that gives a high probabilistic weight to the occurrence, in order to have any explanatory force, Tegmark would have to offer some independent basis for this measure, other than that it takes away the coincidental character of the simplicity of the world. This is something he has not done. Moreover, his proposal will fail to explain the discoverability of nature, insofar as it goes beyond what arises from the simplicity of the laws.

Conclusion

I have argued above that even taken alone, the fine-tuning for life offers strong evidence for theism over naturalism. However, as mentioned in the introduction, the fine-tuning for life evidence is only the tip of a large iceberg of the order of the universe that points to design, such as the elegance and discoverability of the laws of nature, and the fact that the laws can be expressed in simple mathematical equations that we can grasp. These additional features not only provide additional evidence for a design-like order, but they also bypass some of the major objections—such as the multiverse objection—to the fine-tuning for life argument.

Additional Response to Dan Barker's Debate Position

It is true that cases of fine-tuning often depend on more than one parameter. However, this is not relevant to most advanced presentations of the fine-tuning evidence.[58] Such presentations show that the life-permitting region of the joint space of the values of multiple parameters is very small compared to the total theoretically allowed region.

As a further response to Dan's claim, consider the following analogy. Imagine you found a water tank with two pipes: one pumping water in and the other

57. Max Tegmark, "Parallel Universes," in *Science and Ultimate Reality*, ed. J. D. Barrow et al. (Cambridge University Press, 2004), 488.

58. For example, as found in Barnes and Lewis, *Fortunate Universe*.

pumping water out. Further, suppose you noticed that the output pump is precisely adjusted to maintain a constant water level. The fact that if the output pump were adjusted differently, one could adjust the input pump to compensate would not take away the need for explanation. All you would have done is shift the fine-tuning from the output pump to the combined fine-tuning of both pumps so that the water input and output perfectly balance each other.

Concerning the other life-permitting laws, I addressed this in a section of my chapter under the corresponding title. The conclusion was that advocates of fine-tuning only need to show that the life-permitting region is very small compared to what I called the epistemically illuminated region—that is, the region of possible values of the parameters for which we can reasonably determine whether they are life-permitting.

As for the multiverse, Dan's response and prisoner-execution analogy fails, since even with the other executions, your survival would be very improbable on the wanted-to-kill-you hypothesis but not improbable on the purposely missed hypothesis. Thus, by the law of likelihood of Bayesian confirmation theory presented earlier, the latter hypothesis is confirmed over the former hypothesis.

The fact that the other people got executed is irrelevant to these probabilities. For example, finding that out does not negate the improbability of missing under the wanted-to-kill-you hypothesis. To me, Dan's response shows the problem with merely relying on intuition apart from well-recognized principles of probabilistic reasoning.

Regarding the multiverse in general, I noted in my chapter that many features of the universe remain highly coincidental under this hypothesis, but arguably not under theism: for example, the beauty and discoverability of the laws, as well as their very existence.

8

Nontheist Responding to the Debate

God or the Multiverse?

Philip Goff

The fine-tuning of physics for life needs to be taken seriously. According to our best current theories, it was incredibly improbable that a universe like ours would be compatible with the existence of life. It required a number of the fundamental constants to have values falling in a very narrow range. And yet, against incredible odds, the right numbers came up. This needs explaining.[1]

There seem to be two possible explanations. Perhaps our universe was created by an all-powerful loving being who made sure the numbers were right for life, because life is a good thing.[2] Alternately, maybe our universe is one of a huge number of universes, each of which has its numbers fixed randomly in such a way that statistically at least one is going to get the right numbers for life. If enough people play the lottery, someone's going to win.[3]

Suppose these are the two possible explanations. How beautiful and fascinating that our universe turned out to be ambiguous in this way, presenting

At the beginning of this project Philip Goff identified himself as an agnostic/nontheist who agreed to write on the fine-tuning argument in favor of atheism. However, at some point during the course of the writing of this book, Goff converted to what he refers to as "a mildly heretical version of Christianity." He now believes in a good God of limited power, and because of this, Goff is now considered a theist by many.

1. Martin Rees, *Just Six Numbers: The Deep Forces That Shape the Universe* (Basic Books, 2000), 4; G. F. Lewis and L. A. Barnes, *A Fortunate Universe* (Cambridge University Press, 2016), 1–32.

2. Robin Collins, "The Teleological Argument: An Exploration of the Fine-Tuning of the Universe," in *The Blackwell Companion to Natural Theology*, ed. William Lane Craig and J. P. Moreland (Wiley-Blackwell, 2009), 208–9; Luke Barnes, "A Reasonable Little Question: A Formulation of the Fine-Tuning Argument," *Ergo* 6, no. 42 (2019): 1220–21, https://doi.org/10.3998/ergo.12405314.0006.042.

3. Scientists defending this position include Leonard Susskind, *The Cosmic Landscape:*

us with powerful evidence, but powerful evidence that could point either to cosmic hope or to random good fortune. Of course, all the atheists who take fine-tuning seriously go for the multiverse explanation, and all the theists go for God. But if both explanations can in principle do the job, then everyone should give a nonnegligible credence to each possibility. And if you think one side is the better explanation, then your view had better be based in some serious argument rather than in just cultural biases supporting your preferred option.

For most of this paper, I will assume that the fine-tuning of physics for life needs explaining, and that either God or the multiverse explains it. From this starting point, we will assess the plausibility of each option. In the final section, we will consider a third alternative.

Why Go for a Multiverse?

When two theories both explain the data, we tend to select on the basis of theoretical virtues such as *parsimony*: the feature a theory has more of when it postulates fewer entities. Why go for a more costly theory when a more parsimonious one is available?

One might initially think the God hypothesis is more parsimonious than the multiverse theory, as the former postulates only one extra thing (God) while the latter postulates a huge number of extra things (universes).

However, there are different kinds of parsimony, and not all are equal. The following distinction is standardly thought to be significant:

> *quantitative parsimony*: committing to few things
> *qualitative parsimony*: committing to few *kinds* of things[4]

To make this distinction clear, consider the following theories:

> *many-particle physicalism*: everything is made up of ten trillion particles
> *few-particle dualism*: everything is made up of a trillion souls and a trillion particles

String Theory and the Illusion of Intelligent Design (Back Bay, 2005); Brian Greene, *The Hidden Reality: Parallel Universes and the Deep Laws of the Cosmos* (Vintage, 2011); Max Tegmark, *Our Mathematical Universe: My Quest for the Ultimate Nature of Reality* (Knopf, 2014). Philosophers include John Leslie, *Universes* (Routledge, 1989); J. J. C. Smart, *Our Place in the Universe: A Metaphysical Discussion* (Blackwell, 1989); Derek Parfit, "Why Anything? Why This?," *London Review of Books* 22, no. 2 (1998): 22–25; Darren J. Bradley, "Multiple Universes and Observation Selection Effects," *American Philosophical Quarterly* 46 (2009): 61–72.

4. David Lewis, *Counterfactuals* (Blackwell, 1973), 87.

In terms of *quantitative* parsimony, few-particle dualism is the cheaper theory, as it postulates only two trillion entities, in contrast to its rival that postulates ten trillion entities. However, many-particle physicalism is the more *qualitatively* parsimonious option, as it postulates only one *kind* of entity (physical particles) while its rival postulates two kinds of entities (physical particles and souls).[5]

It is broadly accepted that qualitative dualism is the more important characteristic, which would seem to give the advantage to the multiverse. The multiverse theorist postulates many more entities of the same kind (i.e., physical universes) whereas the God hypothesis postulates a radically different kind of thing: a nonphysical, timeless, necessary being. If God and the multiverse are equal in all other respects, the multiverse wins.

Another point in favor of the multiverse is that many physicists think there is independent support for the relevant kind of multiverse. At the same time, it's crucial to bear in mind that the case for the multiverse is hotly contested, and many physicists reject it altogether. A recent article casts considerable doubt on the ability of the multiverse hypothesis to account for the fine-tuning of the cosmological constant, which records the strength of the force that powers the accelerating expansion of the universe.[6]

How so? It's somewhat baffling that the cosmological constant is so tiny; you have to put really specific numbers into the relevant equation to get such a small number. To explain this, multiverse theorists hypothesize that only a tiny percentage of universes have such a low number, and that the reason we find ourselves in one is that the value of the cosmological constant in our universe is the highest it can be in order to be compatible with life. The article in question purported to show that the cosmological constants could in fact have been significantly higher and still allow for life, contrary to the assumptions of the multiverse theorist. Of course, this is just one research article, and time will tell the extent to which its conclusions are challenged. Suffice to say there is no established consensus regarding the multiverse. (It's worth noting that the article just discussed does not undermine the fine-tuning argument for God, as the latter doesn't rely on anthropic reasoning and so doesn't require that the values of the constants are life optimal. It merely requires that the values compatible with life are significantly rarer than those that aren't.)

5. I'm assuming in this example that we judge parsimony in terms of what entities we find *at the fundamental level.* See Jonathan Schaffer, "What Not to Multiply Without Necessity," *Australasian Journal of Philosophy* 93, no. 4 (2015): 644–64, https://doi.org/10.1080/00048402.2014.992447.

6. Daniele Sorini, John A. Peacock, and Lucas Lombriser, "The Impact of the Cosmological Constant on Past and Future Star Formation," *Monthly Notices of the Royal Astronomical Society* 535, no. 2 (2024): 1449–74, https://doi.org/10.1093/mnras/stae2236.

The rational way to respond to this consideration will depend on your expertise. Maybe if you have the right kind of physics background, you understand the pros and cons of the debate in enough detail to form a solid judgment, perhaps to accept or reject the entire alleged evidential support for the multiverse. But if you're like me, and you don't have the right kind of physics background, all you can do is recognize that *relevant experts hotly debate this hypothesis*.

If there were a settled scientific consensus that a multiverse, one of the right kind to explain fine-tuning, existed, then the fine-tuning argument for God would be entirely undermined. At the other extreme, if there were no scientists at all (or very few) pushing for this kind of multiverse, then we would have to decide between God and the multiverse on other grounds. The real-world position is in between these two extremes. Assuming we have to choose between God and the multiverse as the best explanation of fine-tuning, the fact that some scientists think there is independent support for the right kind of multiverse is a significant but not decisive point in favor of taking the multiverse option.

I'd say the biggest advantage to the multiverse explanation is that it doesn't face the problem of evil, which is a huge challenge to the God hypothesis. As we have made moral progress, and in particular as we have become more sensitive to the moral significance of animal suffering, the idea that a loving creator who could do *anything* would choose to create a universe like this becomes increasingly improbable.

My formulation of the problem of evil revolves around the following conviction:

> *Cosmic sin intuition*: It would be immoral for an all-powerful being to create a universe like this.[7]

A very common response from theists appeals to free will, a great good that God can only give us at the cost of allowing some people to use their free will to cause suffering.[8] But free will can't help us to explain the suffering of the natural world: earthquakes, illness, old age, and death.

Other responses press how the challenges of this world can deepen us spiritually.[9] There may be some goods to be gained from the horrors of the

7. Philip Goff, *Why? The Purpose of the Universe* (Oxford University Press, 2023), 91.

8. Alvin Plantinga, *The Nature of Necessary* (Oxford University Press 1974); Plantinga, *God, Freedom, and Evil* (Eerdmans, 1977).

9. John Hick, *Evil and the God of Love*, rev. ed. (Harper & Row, 1978).

world. But it is immoral to infringe people's rights, even if doing so increases well-being overall. To take the classic example, it would be immoral for a doctor to murder one healthy person and harvest their organs to save the life of five. Similarly, an all-powerful being who kills and maims, through creating and sustaining a world containing hurricanes and cancer, infringes the fundamental rights of many. This is wrong, whether or not the creator is trying to make the world a better place.

A prominent cutting-edge response to the problem of evil is to give up on these "theodicies" (explanations of why God allows suffering) and argue instead that just because we do not know what reasons God might have for allowing suffering does not give us reason to think that God does not have any reasons for allowing suffering.[10] This position is known as *skeptical theism*.

A skeptical theist is likely to object to the cosmic sin intuition as follows:

- We have no reason to think that the kinds of moral considerations we have access to are representative of the kinds of moral considerations to which God has access.
- Therefore, just because the cosmic sin intuition seems correct from our moral perspective gives us no reason to think it's true from God's superior moral perspective.

The problem is that one could apply this reasoning to *any* moral intuition; for example, consider the following argument:

- We have no reason to think that the kinds of moral considerations we have access to are representative of the kinds of moral considerations to which God has access.
- Therefore, just because slavery seems wrong from our moral perspective gives us no reason to think slavery seems wrong from God's superior moral perspective.[11]

10. Stephen Wykstra, "The Humean Obstacle to Evidential Arguments from Suffering: On Avoiding the Evils of 'Appearance,'" *International Journal for Philosophy of Religion* 16, no. 2 (1984): 73–93, https://doi.org/10.1007/bf00136567; Perry Hendricks, *Skeptical Theism* (Palgrave Macmillan, 2023).

11. Jeff Jordan, "Does Skeptical Theism Lead to Moral Skepticism?," *Philosophy and Phenomenological Research* 72, no. 2 (2006): 409–17, https://doi.org/10.1111/j.1933-1592.2006.tb00567.x; Mark Piper, "Skeptical Theism and the Problem of Moral Aporia," *International Journal for Philosophy of Religion* 62, no. 2 (2007): 68, https://doi.org/10.1007/s11153-007-9128-7; Scott Sehon, "The Problem of Evil: Skeptical Theism Leads to Moral

If the first line of argument undermines any justification for trusting the cosmic sin intuition on the basis of careful moral reflection, then the second line of argument undermines any justification for thinking slavery is wrong on the basis of careful moral reflection. But it is not plausible that we have no justification for believing that slavery is wrong; it follows that we should likewise reject this argument against our justification for accepting the cosmic sin intuition.

The skeptical theist may respond thus:

> My argument against the cosmic sin intuition concerns *God's* reasons (to create/not create a certain kind of world), whereas your parody of it concerns *human* reasons (to have/not have slaves). If I'm right that we don't have good access to God's reasons, it doesn't follow that I don't have good access to *my own* reasons.

I take the point that we should be a little more cautious in forming judgments about what reasons an omnipotent and omniscient creator is likely to have, given this is a very different situation to the one we ourselves occupy. But the skeptical theist makes a much stronger point: careful moral considerations can give us *no* grounds for forming even a tentative judgment concerning the rightness or wrongness of certain actions of such a creator. And the foundational premise of the argument for this strong conclusion doesn't differentiate between whether God is thinking about God's own reasons or whether God is thinking about my reasons. It is simply attempting to cast doubt on my grasp of the outcome of God's moral reasoning regardless of its focus.

Moreover, we surely can make at least some judgments concerning what it would be wrong for an omniscient and omnipotent creator to do. Consider the following:

> *Radical cosmic sin intuition*: It would be immoral for an all-powerful being to create a universe where everybody just suffers intense pain for eternity.

If the skeptical theist's argument works against the cosmic sin intuition, then it ought to work against the radical cosmic sin intuition:

- We have no reason to think that the kinds of moral considerations we have access to are representative of the kinds of moral considerations to which an omnipotent and omniscient being has access.

Paralysis," *International Journal for Philosophy of Religion* 67, no. 2 (2010): 67–80, https://doi.org/10.1007/s11153-009-9213-1.

- Therefore, just because the radical cosmic sin intuition seems correct from our moral perspective gives us no reason to think it's true from God's superior moral perspective.

But we surely do know that the radical cosmic sin intuition is true. Therefore, there must be something wrong with the skeptical theist's argument against the regular cosmic sin intuition.

When discussing this on social media—as I'm afraid I do too often—people often take me to be questioning God's moral judgments, which seems a little arrogant to say the least. But this misunderstands the argument. It is important to note that the cosmic sin intuition doesn't mention God but simply an omniscient, omnipotent being. Now, if God does exist, then God's moral conclusions are correct and mine are incorrect; I do have just about enough humility to accept that. If my starting point was that God exists, I'd look around at the horrific suffering of the world and conclude that God must have some reason for allowing it to which I'm not privy.

However, what we are currently considering is someone starting from a position of uncertainty regarding God's existence. From *that* starting point, one should try as best one can—using one's own moral reasoning and also appealing to the extensive moral reasoning of others on this topic—to evaluate the cosmic sin intuition. This is the approach I've taken, and it's led me to the conclusion that the cosmic sin intuition is very likely to be true. And if the cosmic sin intuition is true, then if there is a creator, that creator is either not omnipotent and omniscient, or that creator is immoral. In other words, God does not exist.

This is a huge problem for the God hypothesis. In contrast, there is no problem of evil for the multiverse hypothesis, as the multiverse hypothesis does not predict that there will be no suffering.

To summarize, I have identified three reasons in favor of choosing the multiverse over God as an explanation of fine-tuning:

1. The multiverse hypothesis is more qualitatively parsimonious than the God hypothesis.
2. A significant number of scientists think there is good independent reason to take the multiverse hypothesis seriously.
3. The God hypothesis faces the problem of evil but the multiverse hypothesis does not.

This is a powerful case for choosing the multiverse option, but we've only looked at one side. It's time to consider the case for choosing God.

Why Go for God?

The starting assumption of this essay is that fine-tuning needs explaining, and that either God or a multiverse explains it (in the final section, we will consider a third alternative). In the last section we considered a powerful case for choosing the multiverse over God. The best hope the theist has for overcoming this case is to bring in other arguments for God, thus building a cumulative case for the existence of God. If there are enough independent sources of support for God's existence, then maybe on balance God will come up trumps.

This is a big project and would require evaluating the other arguments for God, many of which are considered in this volume. A slightly more modest task would be to say that some of the arguments for God work *partially*, but that they are still significant when joined with the evidence of fine-tuning. In what follows I will consider three possible ways of doing this.

Something Rather Than Nothing

Cosmological arguments are a family of arguments that aim to demonstrate that God is the best explanation of why the universe exists. In one form, such arguments press that only a "godish" necessary being—a being that somehow explains its own existence—can provide an ultimate explanation of why there is something rather than nothing.[12] In this form, the argument may be open to the universe stretching back infinitely, while maintaining that this would still leave us questioning why this universe has always existed rather than some other universe or nothing at all.

This form of cosmological argument comes in two stages, and the first stage has always seemed to me more plausible than the second. The first stage tries to establish that there must be a necessary being to explain why the universe exists. The second stage tries to establish that this timeless cause or necessary being has the characteristics we associate with God: a personal being who is all-knowing, all-powerful, and perfectly good.

If the theists can complete both stages, then they have an argument for God. But suppose they can establish only the first stage. While not in itself

12. Robert C. Koons, "A New Look at the Cosmological Argument," *American Philosophical Quarterly* 34, no. 2 (1997): 193–211; for a discussion of a Thomistic version of this argument, see Glenn B. Siniscalchi, "Contemporary Trends in Atheistic Criticism of Thomistic Natural Theology," *Heythrop Journal* 59, no. 4 (2018): 689–706, https://doi.org/10.1111/j.1468-2265.2012.00777.x.

establishing God's existence, this may help the theist in their battle against the multiverse theorist by shifting the parsimony advantage from multiverse theory to theism.

If we're just choosing from God and multiverse without any prior commitments, then the latter is arguably the more parsimonious option, for reasons discussed above. But now suppose prior to considering these options that our engagement with the first stage of a cosmological argument has given us a commitment to a necessary being as the ultimate cause of the universe. Suppose further that we are unconvinced by the second stage of any cosmological argument, and so we are left uncertain about the precise nature of this necessary being. The necessary being may have godish characteristics beyond its necessity, or it may not; the first stage of any cosmological argument leaves that open.

Now we bring in the fine-tuning. If we theorize that the necessary being is God, then we get an explanation of fine-tuning without needing to postulate anything further. If we theorize that the necessary being has some unknown non-godish nature, then we need to add a multiverse in between the necessary cause and us in order to explain fine-tuning. The former option looks to be more parsimonious:

- The necessary being has to have some nature, and it's no more of a cost to suppose it has a godish rather than a non-godish nature.
- Supposing that the necessary being has a godish nature saves us postulating a further entity (i.e., a multiverse).

Taking this strategy accepts that neither the fine-tuning argument nor the first stage of the cosmological argument on its own can establish God's existence, as the former loses to the multiverse and the latter can't make good on its second stage. But the hope is that in combination they can do better.

This may help the theist make some progress. But it only deals with the parsimony objections, which still leaves the two other considerations in favor of the multiverse explored in the last section. In my view, this alone will not be enough to ensure that theism wins the day.

Religious Experience

A similar strategy might be attempted with respect to religious experience. Arguments from religious experience may come in stronger or weaker forms. A stronger form appeals to religious experiences to justify full-blooded theism, that is, belief in an all-knowing, all-powerful, perfectly good creator of the universe.[13] A weaker form will justify merely some less specific transcendental reality, for example, some higher reality underlying all things.[14] Let us use the phrase "the Transcendent" to refer to this more loosely defined spiritual reality that people having these weaker experiences seem to be presented with.

The great variety of religious experiences is a powerful defeater for the stronger kind of argument. Consider a Christian, whose contemplative prayer has yielded a deep sense of an omni-God creator, and a Hindu, whose meditation seems to have revealed impersonal formless consciousness at the root of reality. As the two compare their experiences, by what epistemological right can either of them stubbornly cling to her experience being the correct one? In the absence of some reason to give greater weight to one or the other experience, each should hold that the difference is to be explained in terms of their different cultural assumptions.

However, if we define religious experiences in a coarse-grained enough way—as experiences that purport to reveal the Transcendent without being more specific about its nature—then such experiences seem to be cross-culturally pervasive, and the objection from relativity falls away. Of course, this alone will not allow us to establish theism. But suppose we now approach fine-tuning with a prior commitment to the Transcendent. Theism offers a way of cashing out what the Transcendent is while also explaining fine-tuning. In contrast, a nontheist account of the Transcendent (e.g., one that takes the higher reality to be formless consciousness) will leave one having to make the further postulation of a multiverse. All things being equal, the theistic option now looks to be more parsimonious.

Libertarian Free Will

The above two strategies involve postulating something "godish": a necessary being or a greater reality at the root of things. Alternately, the theist may bring to the table something that is not itself a godish entity but that arguably fits better with theism than atheism. One option might be libertarian free will.

There are three standard positions on free will:

13. William P. Alston, *Perceiving God* (Cornell University Press 1991); Alvin Plantinga, "Is Belief in God Properly Basic?," *Noûs* 15, no. 1 (1981): 41–51, https://doi.org/10.2307/2215239; Plantinga, *Warranted Christian Belief* (Oxford University Press, 2000).

14. See the end of the chapter on mysticism (lectures 16 and 17) from William James, *The Varieties of Religious Experience: A Study in Human Nature* (Longmans, Green, 1902).

- *Hard determinism*: Free will is incompatible with a deterministic universe and doesn't exist.
- *Libertarianism*: Free will is incompatible with a deterministic universe and does exist.
- *Soft Determinism*: Free will is compatible with a deterministic universe and exists.

For proponents of the second option, free choices lack a prior cause. In such choices, the agent decides between multiple courses of action, and in doing so causes the resulting action, but the event of the agent's deciding does not itself have a cause. The intuition is clear, whether or not it ultimately stands up to scrutiny: if my decision was settled prior to the moment of the choice, then it isn't really "up to me."

One common objection to libertarian free will presses that there is no middle ground between a decision determined by the mental states of the agent (e.g., their beliefs and desires) and a so-called decision that is really just a random and meaningless happening (akin to the random decay of a radioactive isotope).[15] However, if the agent is *responding to considerations of value*, this is sufficient to differentiate the act of deciding from a random and meaningless event.[16]

If, for example, I'm deciding whether to cheat on my partner, this may be a matter of choosing whether to act for the sake of my own pleasure or for the sake of my commitment to my partner. In both cases, there is an objective reason for action: the fact that something will bring me great pleasure is an objective reason to do it, and the fact that I've made a commitment not to do something is also an objective reason not to do it. If in making the decision I am genuinely responding to an objective reason for action, then clearly my decision is not meaningless and random. We can thus add to the definition of libertarian free will that it involves a capacity to respond to considerations of value. Without this, events that lack a prior cause would just be random and meaningless happenings rather than genuine decisions.

Note that while free will on a compatibilist view may be explained in more fundamental terms, libertarian free will (if it exists) is by definition part of

15. Peter van Inwagen, *An Essay on Free Will* (Oxford University Press, 1983), 106–52; van Inwagen, "Free Will Remains a Mystery," *Philosophical Perspectives* 14 (2000): 1–19; Ishtiyaque Haji, "Control Conundrums: Modest Libertarianism, Responsibility, and Explanation," *Pacific Philosophical Quarterly* 82, no. 2 (2001): 178–200, https://doi.org/10.1111/1468-0114.00124; Alfred R. Mele, *Free Will and Luck* (Oxford University Press, 2006).

16. Lowe made a similar response; see E. J. Lowe, *Personal Agency: The Metaphysics of Mind and Action* (Oxford University Press, 2010).

the fundamental causal workings of the universe. Prior to Sara freely deciding whether or not to go to the party or to stay in and have a bath, it was genuinely open whether her particles would be located in the car or in the bathroom in the next few minutes. It is because of Sara's free choice that the particles are where they are a few minutes later. Moreover, if Sara's choice being determined by a prior cause is enough to render it unfree, then her choice being determined by a synchronous but more fundamental process in her brain will also render Sara's choice unfree. In other words, the event of Sara's deciding—if it is genuinely free in the libertarian sense—is not constituted of some more fundamental brain event. Rather, Sara's choice is part of the basic causal story of why her particles are located as they are a few minutes later.

In other work, I've explored a "pan-agentialist" view, on which particles have a very basic form of libertarian free will.[17] Let's leave my strange ideas to the side here and adopt the more common assumption that free will only exists in fairly complex organisms. Still, if free will is at the present moment part of the fundamental causal workings of reality, as a libertarian is committed to, then the universe must have been set up from the beginning to accommodate this possibility.

When I say "set up," I'm not assuming a God who set it up that way. My point is just that if the fundamental causal principles that governed our universe from its beginning were simply mathematical laws that determine probabilistic outcomes, independent of considerations of value, then libertarian free will would never have emerged. If libertarian free will emerged, then there must have been something in the fundamental causal principles governing our universe ensuring that if such and such conditions emerge, libertarian free will becomes part of the fundamental causal workings of the universe. Let us call this the "objective potential" for libertarian free will.

Suppose, for the sake of discussion, that our universe began with the objective potential for libertarian free will. This does not logically imply the existence of God. However, the universe having an objective potential for free will fits better with theism than it does with atheism, in the Bayesian sense that it is more expected if theism is true than it is if atheism is true. Suppose

17. Philip Goff, *Galileo's Error: Foundations for a New Science of Consciousness* (Pantheon, 2019); Goff, "Grounding, Analysis and Russellian Monism," in *The Knowledge Argument*, ed. Sam Coleman (Cambridge University Press, 2019); Goff, "Cosmopsychism, Micropsychism, and the Grounding Relation," in *The Routledge Handbook of Panpsychism*, ed. William Seager (Routledge, 2019); Goff, "Panpsychism and Free Will: A Case Study in Liberal Naturalism," *Proceedings of the Aristotelian Society* 120, no. 2 (2020): 123–44, https://doi.org/10.1093/arisoc/aoaa009.

you were informed by a super-intelligent being that there are two universes, Universe A and Universe B, and one of them was brought into existence by a good creator and one of them just exists as a matter of brute fact. Your task is to guess which universe is the created one based only on the information that Universe A has the objective potential for free will but Universe B does not. Would you go for Universe A, or would you just toss a coin?

Free will—the capacity to respond freely on the basis of our understanding of the world and of value—is itself a thing of value. All things being equal, a universe in which there are organisms who can act freely is better than a universe in which there aren't. And if libertarians are right, this requires something like libertarian free will. It is not inevitable that a good creator would give the universe the objective potential for free will, but it is not surprising that a creator who cared about value would choose this. In contrast, although the objective potential for free will *could* exist in a brute-fact universe, there's no particular reason to think it would. In other words, a universe that was brought into existence by a good creator is more likely to have the objective potential for libertarian free will than a universe that was uncaused or brought into existence by impersonal processes.

On its own, this may not be incredibly strong evidence for theism. But in Bayesian reasoning, independent bits of support get multiplied together, which can result in a very strong evidential support. It may not count for much that the suspect was in the vicinity at the time of the murder, and it may not count for much that they were wearing the same clothes as the killer, but these two bits of evidence combined may make a strong case. If the weighing of different considerations has left you torn between God and the multiverse, and you happen to believe in libertarian free will, then the fact that libertarian free will fits better with theism than it does with atheism may tip the balance in favor of God.

Multiverse theorists explain apparent design in anthropic terms: although certain features of our universe (e.g., having the right numbers for life) may be rare in the multiverse as a whole, they are not rare in the set of universes with observers. Could the anthropic strategy be applied to libertarian free will? Perhaps universes with the objective potential for libertarian free will are comparatively rare in the multiverse, but these are the only ones containing observers, and thus it is not surprising that we find ourselves in such a universe.

Unfortunately, universes in which there are observers that lack free will seem conceivable. Terry Horgan has imagined conscious organisms that lack "agentive phenomenology."[18] Horgan's imaginary creations find their bodies

18. Terry Horgan, "The Phenomenology of Agency and Freedom: Lessons from Introspection and Lessons from Its Limits," *Humana.Mente* 15 (2011): 77–97.

being moved by their beliefs and desires without them having a sense that they chose to move them. For example, one may be sitting watching TV, feel like having a beer, and suddenly find themselves standing up, moving to the fridge, and taking a beer out without the experience of *choosing* to stand up to get a beer. Conscious organisms that evolved in universes without the objective potential for free will would similarly be pushed around by their beliefs and desires without ever choosing what to do.[19] And if there could be such observers existing without free will, this removes the option of giving an anthropic explanation of our finding ourselves in a universe with the objective potential for free will.

The Final Verdict

The case we have been considering is whether God or the multiverse is the better explanation of fine-tuning. We have been assuming, for the purposes of this evaluation, (1) that fine-tuning needs explaining, and (2) that the choice of explanation is between God and the multiverse.

Not everything can be settled in a short essay. The case for the God option considered above brought in controversial commitments—the need for a necessary being, the existence of the Transcendent, libertarian free will—that many will want to reject. But if the first two commitments can be justified, then the parsimony consideration swings back in favor of theism. And if a commitment to libertarian free will can be strongly justified (a big "if" of course) this may outweigh the tentative scientific support for the multiverse.

However, in my judgment the problem of evil massively swings things back in the other direction. Let's start by considering potential commitments to a necessary being and the existence of the Transcendent. Crucially, these two commitments are perfectly compatible with an atheist multiverse. Now, what I've just claimed may sound counterintuitive to many, so it's worth spending a moment thinking about what such a universe would look like.

Recall we are not assuming that a necessary being must have the traditional characteristics of God. Perhaps the necessary being is an impersonal force that gives rise to the multiverse. Despite being impersonal, the necessary being may have a wondrous intrinsic nature that we are able to directly experience when the mind is calmed through extensive meditation. We're thinking of something like the Force from Star Wars. Although not an agent, this impersonal force

19. At least choice would not exist in such a universe if libertarians are right about free will.

may be eternally bubbling with unrestrained causal capacity, from which an infinity of universes pours forth.

This hypothesis is less simple and unified than theism, but it seems easy to make sense of it. In contrast, for those of us who find extant theodicies implausible, we cannot even make sense of a world in which theism is true, because doing so would require comprehending the unfathomable reasons God might have for allowing terrible suffering. The judgments that cast doubt on the multiverse explanation of fine-tuning (or rather those judgments that arise from commitments to a necessary being and to the Transcendent) merely lower its probability in contrast to the more simple and unified theistic alternative. But the judgments that cast doubt on theism (i.e., the cosmic sin intuition), if true, entail the logical incompatibility of God and the suffering we find in our universe.

Those who know a little bit about the literature on the problem of evil may be surprised that I'm pressing the logical incompatibility of God and evil, as it is widely thought that the logical argument from evil has been universally rejected by both theists and atheists.[20] In fact, what I'm pressing is a middle way between the logical problem of evil and the more popular evidential problem of evil. If the cosmic sin intuition is true, then it follows that God's existence is incompatible with the horrors we find in our universe, as the cosmic sin intuition entails that the action of creating a universe like ours would be inconsistent with the perfect goodness of God. On the other hand, we do not have logical certainty that the cosmic sin intuition is true.

If we had a strong enough reason to think theism is true, then the rational conclusion to draw may be that the cosmic sin intuition is false, even though we cannot see how it could possibly be false. But merely having some reasons to think the relevant form of atheism is somewhat less simple and unified than theism does not constitute such a reason. We ought to go for slightly less simple and unified views if they fit the data better.

If the theist can equip themselves with a commitment to libertarian free will, then this will to a certain extent strengthen their position, given that this commitment fits better with theism than atheism. In my judgment, however, the clash between suffering and God is greater than the fit between free will and God. Free will is a valuable thing, and thus it is not surprising that a good God would create a universe in which free will can emerge. On the other hand, free will is just *one* valuable thing a good God might choose, and there

20. The basis for this rejection of the problem of evil is standardly attributed to Plantinga, *Nature of Necessary*; Plantinga, *God, Freedom, and Evil.*

is nothing to make us think it is inevitable that a good God would go for creatures with free will.

In contrast, if our moral reasoning leads us to support the cosmic sin intuition, this renders it *logically inevitable* that an all-knowing, all-powerful, perfectly good being would not create a universe with the suffering we find. As I said above, the truth of the cosmic sin intuition is not logically certain. Nonetheless, we have a fairly strong justified value claim that (if true) renders the existence of God and the suffering we find in the world logically incompatible, while we have no strongly justified claim that (if true) ensures that God would create free will.

In conclusion, if the choice is between theism and the multiverse, the multiverse wins.

A Conscious Universe

Thus far we have been considering only two options: God and the multiverse. But are these the only two options? In my book *Why? The Purpose of the Universe*, I consider a range of views in between these two options, with a particular focus on *cosmopsychism*: the view that the universe itself is conscious. Those interested can explore my work elsewhere on this view.[21] Here I will simply lay out the basics and how it connects to the above discussion.

The suggestion that the universe is a conscious mind sounds like an extravagant claim. How on earth does this fit with the modern scientific understanding of the universe we get from cosmology? My niece is currently studying physics at Manchester University, and I don't hear her telling me of her lectures on the mental life of the cosmos.

The new wave of panpsychism in contemporary analytic philosophy is rooted in the insights of Bertrand Russell in his book *The Analysis of Matter*. The core point Russell presses is that physics is purely mathematical, and that because of this physics offers us a metaphysically thin account of reality: "Physics is mathematical not because we know so much about the physical world, but because we know so little; it is only its mathematical properties that we can discover."[22]

Physics doesn't care what's going on at the fundamental level of reality, so long as whatever's going on down there has the right mathematical structure. Provided

21. Philip Goff, "Is the Universe a Conscious Mind?," *Aeon*, February 8, 2018, https://aeon.co/essays/cosmopsychism-explains-why-the-universe-is-fine-tuned-for-life; Philip Goff, "Did the Universe Design Itself?," *International Journal for Philosophy of Religion* 85, no. 1 (2018): 99–122, https://doi.org/10.1007/s11153-018-9692-z; Goff, *Purpose of the Universe*, 129–41.

22. Bertrand Russell, *The Analysis of Matter* (Kegan Paul, Trench, Trubner, 1927).

you can tell some metaphysical story that yields the mathematical structures described by physics, you'll be able to get the facts of physics out of that.

Once this lesson is fully absorbed, it becomes clear that cosmopsychism is perfectly compatible with our modern scientific understanding of the universe. Consider the mathematical description (let's call it M) that you'd get if you completely described the universe in the language of physics going right down to fundamental particles. The Russell-inspired cosmopsychist will postulate a very complex mind whose experience embodies structures perfectly isomorphic with the structures articulated by M. In other words, the mathematical structures of physics are realized by the consciousness of the universe.

Of course, just because this is *compatible* with modern physics, it doesn't mean we have any reason to believe it. For what it's worth, I have argued at length that panpsychism, of which cosmopsychism is one form, offers the best account of how consciousness fits into our scientific understanding of reality.[23] Moreover, if we are looking for an explanation of fine-tuning, then a particular form of cosmopsychism that I call "teleological cosmopsychism" is an attractive option, one that avoids some of the challenges to theism discussed above.

Perhaps the easiest way to convey the core of teleological cosmopsychism is to start with theism and modify it. So I invite the reader to bring to mind the traditional all-knowing, all-powerful, perfectly good source of all existence (in so far as that's possible to imagine). But now, rather than imagining this God creating the universe outside of themselves *ex nihilo*, let us suppose instead that God forms the universe out of their own consciousness. Starting from the singularity of the big bang and expanding into more and more complexity, all of physical reality is simply delightful structures realized in the consciousness of God. Or rather, at this point, we can drop talk of "God" and simply identify the physical universe with the conscious mind that realizes M.

Taking this step slices away the parsimony advantage of the multiverse theorist. For now we are not postulating something outside of, and very different

23. Philip Goff, "Against Constitutive Forms of Russellian Monism," in *Russellian Monism*, ed. T. Alter and Y. Nagasawa (Oxford University Press, 2015); Goff, "The Phenomenal Bonding Solution to the Combination Problem," in *Panpsychism: Contemporary Perspectives*, ed. G. Brüntrup and L. Jaskolla (Oxford University Press, 2016), 283–302; Goff, *Consciousness and Fundamental Reality* (Oxford University Press, 2017); Goff, *Galileo's Error*; Goff, "Grounding, Analysis"; Goff, "Cosmopsychism, Micropsychism"; Goff, "Putting Consciousness First: Putting Consciousness First," *Journal of Consciousness Studies* 28, nos. 9–10 (2021): 289–328; Goff, "How Exactly Does Panpsychism Explain Consciousness?," *Journal of Consciousness Studies* 31, no. 3 (2024): 56–82, https://doi.org/10.53765/20512201.31.3.056.

from, the physical universe. Rather we are postulating a single entity that grounds the physical universe. A simple and elegant proposal!

How do the laws of physics figure in this picture? Here we get to the second modification. The conscious universe, as described by teleological cosmopsychism, has the godish characteristics of being omniscient and perfectly good. But unlike the traditional God, the conscious universe is limited in what it is able to do. To be clear, the claim is not that there's something outside of the universe that is constraining it. All theories have to take something as basic. The basic claim here is that there are certain things the universe can and cannot do. The laws of physics, on this view, are interpreted as capturing the limitations of the universe. The universe is pursuing certain good goals, such as the emergence of life, but under severe limitations.

With this second stroke, we cut away the biggest objection to theism: the problem of evil. Suffering, according to teleological cosmopsychism, exists because of the limitations of the conscious universe. If the conscious universe could have jumped straight to creating intelligent life, in something like the way we see depicted in Genesis, then it would have done so. But the universe is simply unable to shape its consciousness into a complex structure in an instant. The only way the universe can fulfill its goals of creating intelligent life is to evolve toward a position in which evolution can begin, with each step in that lengthy journey in line with the rules of physics, which record the limited powers of the universe.

Here at last we have a decent rival to the multiverse. Having removed the disadvantages of profligacy and the problem of evil, the multiverse is left with only the advantage of being "hotly debated by the relevant experts" (at least for us nonphysicists).[24]

What about the potential advantages of theism, that is, its better fit with commitments to a necessary being, the Transcendent, and libertarian free will? The first two of these posits will not add to the simplicity of cosmopsychism relative to the multiverse. To the extent that they require postulating something beyond the physical universe, the extra cost will be borne by both the cosmopsychist and the multiverse theorist.[25] A commitment to libertarian free

24. There are challenges accounting for how human and animal minds emerge on cosmopsychism. But this challenge rears its ugly head on any theory of consciousness. If the worst comes to the worst and we have to be dualists, then we can combine dualism with the cosmopsychist account of the physical universe, thus ending up with a more unified theory of reality than conventional dualism (as there is only consciousness at the fundamental level).

25. It is worth considering whether the necessary being or the Transcendent could be

will, however, would provide the same support to teleological cosmopsychism as it does to theism: libertarian free will is more expected on the assumption that the universe was designed by a good creator, whether or not that good creator was the universe designing itself.[26]

It's a close race. If we're choosing the best explanation of fine-tuning from these two options, a believer in libertarian free will should have a *significantly* higher credence in teleological cosmopsychism, while (nonphysicist) soft and hard determinists should give a *slightly* higher credence to the multiverse (while we wait for the physicists to give a more settled answer on the matter).

I would like to emphasize again in closing that much of this discussion has been premised on the assumption that both God and the multiverse can explain fine-tuning. In fact, I've argued at length in my other work that we *cannot* explain fine-tuning in terms of a multiverse.[27] If that's right, then the multiverse doesn't even make it to the starting line of this race. However, I am very occasionally wrong about things, and so it's worth exploring the lay of the land on the assumption that I'm wrong in this case. This is what I've attempted to undertake in this essay.

---

identified with the physical universe. I have explored the former possibility in other work (Goff, "'Did the Universe Design Itself?,'" 99–122). Either way, the cosmopsychist does not postulate more entities than the multiverse theorist.

26. Given that the conscious universe is not all-powerful, it's possible that it is not able to ensure the universe has the objective potential for libertarian free will. Still, given that libertarian free will is a thing of value, a universe with the objective potential for free will is more expected if that universe was shaped by something (perhaps the universe itself) that cares about value.

27. Philip Goff, *Purpose of the Universe*, 30–35; Philip Goff, "Is Fine-Tuning Evidence for a Multiverse?," *Synthese* 204, no. 1 (2024): 1–22, https://doi.org/10.1007/s11229-024-04621-z.

9

Theist Responding to the Debate

Does the Immaterial Mind of God Make Sense?

Joshua Rasmussen

How did our universe arise? When reflecting upon this question, the words of the Presocratic philosopher Democritus come to mind: "truth is in the depths." This question invites us to examine the fundamental nature of reality. Broadly, theories of reality fall into two categories: *mind-first* or *mindless-first*. Mind-first theories propose that reality is fundamentally mindlike. According to these views, some form of mind or consciousness exists prior to and gives rise to the material world. Conversely, "mindless-first" theories propose the opposite—that nonmental reality is more fundamental, and all mental phenomena emerge from it.

The differences between these theories have far-reaching implications. Consider three big issues. First, the existence of a personal God is at stake. A personal God, as traditionally conceived, is a mental reality that exists independently and prior to everything else. This view aligns with a mind-first view. For if instead reality is fundamentally mindless, then fundamental reality is *not* conscious or personal, and thus a personal, fundamental reality (God) does not exist.

Second, your future hangs in the balance. While not necessarily impossible, a mindless-first theory suggests a low probability of your continued existence after physical death. For if the basic building blocks of reality are mindless, then your existence depends entirely on a specific arrangement of nonmental components, such as particles forming a functioning brain. When these particles disperse, the structure that sustains your consciousness dissolves, implying that you will cease to exist. Unsurprisingly, then, mindless-first theorists tend to reject the idea of continued consciousness after physical death.

If, on the other hand, mind is fundamental and precedes material forms, then a wider door is open to the possibility of your continued existence. For then your consciousness could, at least in principle, exist independently of any structure of atoms, allowing for the prospect of life beyond death.

A third dividing line cuts across questions about your nature. What are you? Is your nature fully and completely explained in the language of third-person physics? Or can you gain unique insight into your fundamental nature through first-person self-awareness? These questions are tied to the kind of reality that grounds your being, whether it is ultimately mental or mindless.

These issues highlight the significance of a mind-first theory. Is mind more fundamental than mindless matter, or is it the other way around? Much depends on one's answer.

Despite the significance of the stakes, the truth is not defined by the importance of a theory. To see the truth, we must examine the nature of reality. So, what is the nature of reality? What do we find when we peer beneath its "depths"?

In this chapter, I will explore the prospect of a mind-first theory of reality. I will begin by considering the power of introspection to reveal certain non-material aspects of our minds. I will then turn to what is widely thought to be the strongest challenge to immaterialist theories of mind: *the problem of mind-body interaction*. To address this challenge, I will develop a mind-first model that, I argue, provides a deep solution to the interaction problem in its various forms. By the end of this chapter, I aim to show that a mind-first view of reality is both defensible and fruitful, offering insights about the nature of reality and our place in it.

The Light of Introspection

To investigate the mental nature of reality, we can use *introspection*. Unlike external observations of landscapes of shapes and colors "out there," introspection grants us access to the inner landscape of consciousness itself. By introspection, you can discern the joy of recalling a cherished memory, the vivid imagery of a daydream, a chain of reasoning in your mind, the feeling of determination before undertaking a difficult task, and so on. Introspection illuminates these realities that exist in your first-person field of consciousness.

Some have worried, however, that introspection is unreliable. Perhaps introspection does not reveal reality as it is. After all, if our perceptions of the external world can be mistaken—subject to illusion, bias, and cognitive error—why should introspection fare any better?

My answer is that while we need not assume that introspection is perfectly reliable, I believe a complete rejection of introspection is self-defeating. Here is my root reason: any argument you might make against introspection will involve inner awareness of a chain of reasons in your mind. This inner awareness itself utilizes introspection. Similarly, even if you find yourself *doubting* the reliability of introspection, your awareness of your doubt is itself based on introspection. So, a complete skepticism of introspective awareness appears to be self-undermining.[1]

Let us suppose, then, that we can use introspection to collect information about our minds. What do we learn? I will next argue that if we take introspection's illumination realistically, then we can justify not only the coherence of the concept of an immaterial mind but also the existence of nonmaterial aspects of our own consciousness.

First, to clarify, following Papineau, I apply the term "nonmaterial aspect" to any attribute not analyzable in terms of spatial aspects (shape, size, motion, etc.) or other aspects expressible in the vocabulary of physics.[2] For example, if a feeling of pain has a sharp negative quality that differs from a spatial aspect or other characteristic physical properties, then that sharp pain quality counts as nonmaterial. This account leaves to the side the prospect of wider notions of "materiality," such as if certain mental aspects are included as irreducibly mental posits in a future physics.

I propose, then, that you can use introspection to verify that at least certain mental aspects are nonmaterial (i.e., not expressible in the vocabulary of physics). Consider, for example, a sense of sharp pain. You can use introspection to be aware of the sharpness of that pain. You also can directly compare the sharpness of a pain with a shape, motion, location, and any other purely third-person physical aspect of brain states. In this way, you can see that the sharpness of pain differs from these material aspects, just as you can see that an itch on your foot differs from the feeling of stepping on a pine cone. You know this difference *directly*.

Here's an objection. Perhaps you cannot see the differences directly. Instead, you can only see a single material reality *from different perspectives*. After all, it is possible to see something from different perspectives. For example, you can see Venus *as* the morning star or *as* the evening star; these are two perspectives of one reality. In the same way, introspection reveals a material reality from a first-person perspective. Thus, you can see a portion of the material world *as* a mental state or *as* a brain state. There is just one kind of reality, though, that is viewed from different perspectives.

1. For an elaboration of my defense of introspection in response to various objections, see Joshua Rasmussen, *Who Are You, Really?* (InterVarsity, 2023), 6–10.

2. David Papineau, *The Rise of Physicalism* (Cambridge University Press, 2009), 12.

However, this "perspectives" reply only works when the reality in question is outside your direct conscious awareness. For when something is outside your direct conscious awareness, you can then experience it indirectly *in different ways*. The problem is that ways of experiencing something are themselves mental states within your direct, introspective awareness. For example, you can be directly aware of the sharpness of a pain and can thereby compare that felt pain with various material states (scatter, motion, etc.).[3] Direct awareness allows you to *directly compare* the pain sensation with other states. For unlike Venus "out there," your mental states are not hidden behind an opaque context; you can be aware of them directly.[4]

Suppose we are never actually directly aware of material aspects "out there." Instead, we only experience the physical world as it appears in consciousness. Then we can't *directly compare* material states out there with our mental states within our consciousness. Still, in that case we can use logic to deduce that the sharpness of pain, taken realistically, is not itself a material aspect. For by logic that which is *within* your direct awareness cannot be the same as that which is *not* within your direct awareness. It follows, therefore, that if we take mental aspects realistically (as illuminated by introspection), we can deduce that mental aspects are not the same as material aspects, regardless of whether we are ever directly aware of material aspects out there.

However, the proposal that your mind has nonmaterial aspects leads to other challenges. If your mind is not exhaustively physical, how does it interact with your body? How can a material body make changes to an immaterial mind? These questions set the stage for a deeper inquiry into the relationship between minds and bodies, an inquiry that I will pursue in the sections that follow.

3. For a fuller defense of your power to witness mental aspects of reality directly, see Rasmussen, *Who Are You, Really?*, 78–106. There I address the illusionist worry that your awareness of mental states might be an illusion. I argue that to experience an illusion, you must experience *x* as something else, that is, *y*. Yet, while your experience of *x* as *y* implies that you do not have direct awareness of *x*, you must have direct awareness of *y*. Therefore, there are at least some things in a mental experience you are directly aware of, *even if* you are experiencing an illusion.

4. Thus, we avoid the masked man fallacy, where one mistakenly infers that a man behind a mask is not someone whom they do not know. See C. Taliaferro, "Masked Man," in *Bad Arguments: 100 of the Most Important Fallacies in Western Philosophy*, ed. Robert Arp, Steven Barbone, and Michael Bruce (Wiley & Sons, 2018).

The Problem of Mind over Matter

Immaterialist theories of a mind face the problem of mental causation. Philosophers have identified three prongs of the problem: (1) *the category problem* of seeing how material and immaterial entities could interact in principle; (2) *the causal exclusion problem*, which builds on empirical evidence for the causal closure of the physical domain; and (3) *the pairing problem*, which raises difficulties for explaining how nonspatial mental causes could be linked to particular physical effects. Together, these objections form a compelling argument against an immaterialist account of a mind's causal efficacy. How might a mind cause physical events, whether to make an arm move or to produce an entire cosmos?

There are three general types of responses to the general problem of mental causation. First, there is *elimination*. This response denies that mental causation exists, either because mental states are not real (per eliminativist materialism) or because mental states, though real, don't cause anything (per epiphenomenalism). A second strategy is *reduction*. This response seeks to analyze mental causation entirely in terms of physical causation via a reductive analysis of mental states. The strategy here is to bring "mind" into the real, physical world where it can make real physical differences.[5] Third, there is *mental power realism*, which seeks to solve the problem of mental causation without reducing or eliminating mental powers.

Advocates of each perspective typically defend their position by critiquing the other two. After all, each view encounters its own challenges. Thus, one way to justify a position is through a process of eliminating the alternatives.

My aim in this chapter will be to take on the challenge of mental causation head on. Rather than seek to eliminate or reduce mental causation, I aspire to show how mental power realism can make sense. To prepare the way, I will first zoom in on each prong of the problem of mental causation so we can appreciate the full force of the problem.

5. Setting aside arguments against reductionism from introspection, mindless-first versions of reductionism still face a further challenge: how can macro-level mental states avoid being causally excluded by more fundamental micro-level physical states. For a development of this challenge, see Andrew Bailey and Joshua Rasmussen, "A New Puppet Puzzle," *Philosophical Explorations* 23, no. 3 (2020): 202–13, https://doi.org/10.1080/13869795.2020.1799661.

The Category Problem of Causal Interaction

The first difficulty stems from the apparent impossibility of interaction between material and immaterial substances. The problem here is about the wide categorical difference between an immaterial mind and the physical world. If the mind is nonphysical while the body is physical, then how could they causally affect one another? Consider that in standard physical interactions, causation involves energy transfer, force application, or other mechanisms that rely on spatial contact or mediation by physical fields. An immaterial mind, however, lacks spatial extension and physical properties. Through what means, then, could an immaterial mind influence a material body, even in principle? Without a clear mechanism of interaction, mind-body dualism seems to depend on an unintelligible causal connection, rendering mental causation deeply mysterious, if not outright impossible.

The Causal Exclusion Problem

The second prong of the problem of mental causation is the causal exclusion problem. This problem emerges from the principle of the causal closure of the physical domain, which states that every physical event that has a cause has a sufficient physical cause. Empirical research in neuroscience and physics supports this principle: whenever we identify the causes of bodily movements, perceptual experiences, or decision-making processes, we find neural events and physical processes that can account for them. Any present gaps in our ability to identify a physical cause can be explained in terms of our current gaps in knowledge. Our track record of discovery, therefore, suggests that there is always a physical cause, even if we haven't yet identified it. But if every physical effect has a sufficient physical cause, then an immaterial mental cause would be *causally excluded* from making any physical difference. In other words, there is no room in the physical world for immaterial minds to make any difference.

The problem of causal exclusion suggests a dilemma: if mental states are genuinely causal, then they must either overdetermine their physical effects (i.e., causing bodily movements in addition to physical brain states that already suffice for those movements), or they must be causally irrelevant, with physical states doing all the causal work. Overdetermination is widely regarded as implausible, because it would imply that every physical action has two distinct, independent causes, a situation never observed in empirical science. The alternative is epiphenomenalism—the view that mental states are causally inert byproducts of physical processes. Epiphenomenalism, however, contradicts everyday evidence that our thoughts and intentions play a role in our actions. Either way, an immaterial mind appears to be causally impotent.

The Pairing Problem

The final prong of the problem concerns how nonspatial causes could *pair* with spatial effects.[6] To illustrate this problem, suppose you intend to raise your arm. How does your intention to raise your arm "know" which arm to raise? Consider that if your intention is not located in space, then your intention is not located in your brain. Instead, your intention is literally nowhere. But if your intention is nowhere, how can we explain why your intention affects *your* body rather than another body?

The problem would go away, one might argue, if the causes were physical entities in space. For when physical causes interact, their spatial relations can explain why one event affects another. For example, a thrown rock shatters a window because it is spatially connected to the window, not to some other distant object. In physical systems, causation is mediated by fields, forces, or direct contact, all of which are inherently spatial.

However, if minds are *nonspatial*, then we cannot appeal to a spatial explanation of causal pairing. An immaterial mind has no spatial coordinates. Thus, it lacks the properties that could explain the pairing of causes with effects. Without a framework to explain causal pairing, the notion of an immaterial mind influencing a specific physical body remains problematic.

In summary, these three challenges—the problem of causal interaction, the causal exclusion argument, and the pairing problem—present significant obstacles for any theory that posits an immaterial mind. Given the empirical evidence for physical causation and the lack of a coherent explanation for how an immaterial mind could causally interact with a physical body, the problem of mental causation stands as a powerful argument against an immaterialist account of the mind.

6. For a development of this challenge, see Jaegwon Kim, *Physicalism or Something Near Enough* (Princeton University Press, 2005). For a critical analysis, see Andrew Bailey, Joshua Rasmussen, and Luke Van Horn, "No Pairing Problem," *Philosophical Studies* 154, no. 3 (2011): 349–60, https://doi.org/10.1007/s11098-010-9555-7.

A Mind-First Theory

In response, I will argue that the problem of mental causation is rooted not in the concept of an immaterial mind but in a *mindless-first* theory of reality. Therefore, to solve the problem of mental causation, I will offer a *mind-first* solution. To see how this solution works, I will first unpack the mind-first theory and identify some independent motivations for its components. Then, in the next section I will show how I think the mind-first theory can solve each of the three problems of mental causation.

The mind-first theory I propose consists of four parts:

1. *Existence*: Mental reality exists.
2. *Fundamentality*: Some mental reality is fundamental (i.e., not derived from or caused by anything more fundamental).
3. *Causal power*: Some mental reality can cause certain effects.
4. *Material emergence*: Material states originate ultimately from mental causes.

Let us look more closely at each part. First, there is the existence proposition, which says that some mental reality exists. By "mental reality," I mean something that can have some form of consciousness. For example, if *you* can be conscious, then you count as a mental reality. We can leave open the nature and form of consciousness that exists. Perhaps consciousness comes in many forms, states, or natures, or perhaps there is a single unified kind of consciousness that all forms of consciousness share. Whatever the case, the mind-first theory includes the claim that at least some form of consciousness exists.

As we have seen, this first proposition aligns with our ordinary introspective awareness of ourselves as conscious beings. While philosophers debate the existence of minds, I will assume that some form of mentality exists for the purposes of this discussion. My goal is to explore how we might account for the existence of minds, at least in principle. Moreover, a major reason for doubting the existence of a mind is the difficulty of explaining first-person mental states solely in terms of third-person physical states, such as particles or fields. I seek to resolve this challenge by reversing the physical-first perspective and proposing instead a mind-first explanation. If this approach succeeds, then a major reason for skepticism about minds dissolves, transforming instead into another reason in support of a mind-first theory.

The next three propositions in the mind-first theory work together to help me account for the mind's role in the physical world. Consider next the fundamentality proposition, which says that some mental reality is *fundamental*.

Fundamental reality does not arise from anything more basic. One motivation for the claim that mental reality is fundamental is that it avoids the hard problem of explaining consciousness. The hard problem arises because materialist explanations appear to leave out first-person experiences. Just as physics takes certain physical laws as primitive rather than deriving them from something deeper, some philosophers treat certain mental reality as fundamental. I will adopt this proposition as part of my mind-first hypothesis to see how it can help us solve the problem of mental causation.

The third proposition is the causal power proposition, which states that mental reality includes causal power. Our everyday experience strongly suggests that mental states cause certain effects. For instance, if you decide to count to ten in your mind, you can witness a sequence of mental events in your mind as you count through some numbers. Introspection allows us to observe sequences of mental states themselves. These sequences would be mysterious and arbitrary if they involved no causal links at all.

Moreover, the existence of mental causation plays a role in understanding how our minds could have evolved. If mental states had no causal efficacy, then they would confer no adaptive advantage, and it would be mysterious why complex minds emerged through natural selection. The very presence of intricate cognitive capacities in biological organisms suggests that minds play an active causal role. While the precise mechanism of mental causation remains an open question, its existence seems evident from both direct experience and evolutionary considerations.

The final part of the mind-first theory is the material emergence proposition, which holds that material states come ultimately from more fundamental, mental causes. There are different ways this might work. To illustrate one idea, developments in physics motivate a mental analysis of matter itself. The prospect of a mental analysis was anticipated by Nobel Prize–winning physicist Max Planck, who remarked, “I regard matter as derivative from consciousness.”[7] More recently, physicist Richard Conn Henry has concluded his analysis of more recent experiments by announcing that “the universe is mental.”[8] According to this analysis, the fundamental nature of matter is itself specifiable in terms of things we know in consciousness (such as informational and perspectival states).

7. Max Planck, “Interviews with Great Scientists: VI. Max Planck,” *The Observer*, January 25, 1931.

8. Richard Conn Henry, “The Mental Universe,” *Nature* 436, no. 29 (2005), https://doi.org/10.1038/436029a.

While a full defense of material emergence is beyond the scope of this paper, this part of the mind-first theory has independent motivations. I will highlight two. First, some philosophers and physicists propose that a mental foundation of matter helps demystify the problem of fine-tuning. The universe appears precisely calibrated for the emergence of life, with physical constants set in a way that allows for conscious beings to exist. Even multiverse theories, which posit many universes, arguably rely on fine-tuning to increase the likelihood that any given universe is life-permitting.[9] If mental reality plays a fundamental role in shaping material reality, then fine-tuning could be explained as the result of a mental bias toward life.

Another possible motivation comes from the phenomenon of psycho-physical harmony, which refers to the striking alignment between mental states and physical processes. The mind-first theory allows us to account for this harmony by positing that material structures arise in a way inherently coordinated with mental states. This hypothesis is not ruled out by physics, as modern physics allows for nonreductive explanations of physical reality (more on this later). Furthermore, as Crummett and Cutter argue, psycho-physical harmony may itself be *more likely* if there is a deeper mental explanation of psycho-physical coordination.[10]

Taken together, these four propositions provide a coherent and well-motivated framework for a mind-first approach to reality. Each proposition has independent support, whether from introspection, the hard problem of consciousness, the reality of mental causation, or explanatory advantages concerning fine-tuning and psycho-physical harmony. In the next section, I will show how this mind-first framework can help us resolve the three problems of mental causation in a deep and systematic way.

How to Solve the Problem of Mental Causation

Let us now consider how the mind-first theory might help us with the problem of mental causation. My general proposal is this: if mind is fundamental, then we can analyze mind-body relations in terms of more fundamental mental-mental relations. To see how this proposal can help us, let us look again at the three prongs of the problem of mental causation.

9. See Robin Collins, "God, Design, and Fine-Tuning," in *God Matters: Readings in the Philosophy of Religion*, ed. R. M. Bernard (Longman, 2003), 54–65.

10. Dustin Crummett and Brian Cutter, "Psychophysical Harmony: A New Argument for Theism," *Oxford Studies in Philosophy of Religion* (forthcoming).

How Mind-First Theory Resolves the Mind-Body Problem

Let's start with the *category problem*. The problem here is about the categorical divide between materiality and immateriality. Many people find it counterintuitive that causation could bridge across these categories. The categorical gap between the immaterial and material realms is simply too vast, one might think, for causal interactions to cross the chasm separating these categories. So, if minds are immaterial, then mind-body causation is impossible.

I think there is something right about the category problem. In principle, we can see that certain types of things cannot cause certain other types of things. For example, I think we can see that the number four cannot cause a pine cone to fall off a tree. The number four has the wrong kind of nature to be able to move pine cones. Similarly, I think it is possible to see that mere motions of carbon atoms cannot, on their own, cause immaterial beings to snap into existence. Here again the cause seems to be the wrong category to produce the effect. The problem with certain causal interactions is not merely that we don't see *how* they could happen. Rather, we do see—by reason—that certain things cannot cause certain other things.

Certain cases of causal interaction, however, are mysterious but not thereby impossible. For example, when I flip a light switch to make a lamp glow, there is a certain mystery there, but I have evidence that light switches can be causally connected to glowing lamps. There is no impossibility there. In general, we can distinguish the sight of an impossibility from the mere lack of sight of a possibility.

In the case of mental causation, I have evidence that certain causal interactions are possible (even if mysterious), while others are impossible. For example, while it is mysterious to me how I manage to count to ten in my mind, I don't see that counting numbers in my mind is impossible. By contrast, I think it is impossible to cause material objects to move just because you *hope that they move* (where "hope" refers to an irreducibly experiential state that you know directly via first-person, introspective experience). Similarly, I think it is impossible for atoms to cause you to have certain feelings of hope *just because of their motions*. Motions on their own are insufficient to make emotions and vice versa. In both cases, a deeper explanation seems to me required.

Fortunately, a mind-first ontology supplies resources for a deeper explanation not only of mental causation but also of physical causation. Consider the connection between hoping to send a text message and the motions of one's fingers to type the message. While a *direct* connection between hope and motion may not be possible, a more fundamental mental reality could in principle create the links. For mental reality could form *both* mental and material states. On this account, even if certain *direct* links are impossible (e.g., hopes directly causing atomic motions), it remains possible for a more fundamental substance to provide an explanation of the causal interactions between mental and material states.[11]

To see how a deeper explanation might work, consider by analogy the activities of cartoon characters on a pixelated screen. Suppose we observe certain pixel changes that correspond with speech. We recognize that the pixel shifts do not themselves *cause* the speech, yet we can still explain the correlation. The deeper explanation lies in the computer system, which systematically links pixel changes and speech patterns. Likewise, a mind-first theory allows for a more fundamental account of mind-body interactions. Even if certain mental states do not directly cause atomic motions, this does not preclude a deeper explanation of the systematic harmony between mental and material states.

At this point, you might worry that positing a more fundamental substance only pushes the problem back a step. How, you might wonder, could a mental substance form material states in space? If there is a general problem with mind-body interaction, how does it help to suppose that mind is *fundamental*?

I have three connected points to offer in response. First, while I do think certain direct links between mind and body are impossible (and can be seen to be impossible by reason), it does not follow that a deeper, unifying explanation is *itself* impossible. While cartoon characters on a screen may appear to push each other by spatial contact, we understand there is a deeper explanation of their motions. In the same way, while material objects on the screen of the material world may appear to interact via spatial contact, force exchange, and energy transfer, there can be a more fundamental explanation.

Consider, second, that the prospect of a deeper explanation of spatial reality is already part of contemporary physics. Physics provides independent examples of causation that do not rely on direct spatial contact. Quantum entanglement, for instance, suggests that correlations between entities can exist independently of spatial distance. A pioneer in quantum field theory, Carlo Rovelli, argues that our best current theories of the nature of matter posit nonspatial, informational realities as more fundamental than spatial reality. He argues that spatial reality is itself emergent from an underlying informational reality.[12] A rising tide of physicists agrees that space-time reality is probably

11. I develop this mind-first theory of mind-body interaction in Rasmussen, *Who Are You, Really?*, 143–70.

12. Carlo Rovelli, *Reality Is Not What It Seems: The Journey to Quantum Gravity* (Random House, 2014), 244–88.

not fundamental. Whether or not they are right, my point here is that a more fundamental explanation has not been shown to be logically incoherent or impossible. On the contrary, a deeper explanation is suggested by our latest scientific models of physical activity itself.

Third, and most importantly for our purposes, I think it is possible to directly *see* how to provide a deeper, mental explanation. For mind-first theory allows a mental analysis of space itself. Consider that a form of "mental" space already exists in visual imagery. For example, if you form a mental image of a purple dragon, you can discern what we might call "mental-spatial" contents within the image itself. The mental-spatial contents of an image form the basis of our concept of spatial reality: we understand "distance" by experiencing spatial distances immediately with visual experience. For example, you can discern spatial distances between right and left elements in your visual experience. In this case, you don't literally enter your mental imagery to cause changes in mental space. Rather, you can interact with the image directly in your mind (e.g., to rotate the image to the right or left).

This account of spatial reality flips the materialist picture. Instead of supposing that spatial images are generated first by mind-independent, spatial objects, we can shave off *mind-independent* spatial objects from our ontology. Spatial objects still exist, but they can be analyzed in terms of spatial contents of images.[13]

This mind-first perspective also simplifies our theory of reality. Instead of positing an extra kind of spatial reality, there is just one kind of spatial reality—the mental-spatial contents we know right within visual imagery. This kind of spatial reality is not *impossible* for a mind to generate. On the contrary, this is precisely the kind of spatial reality that we witness emerging within our own minds. Given a mind-first ontology, therefore, we can (at least in principle) explain the emergence of spatial reality in the universe in terms of the *same kind* of reality that emerges within our own minds.

While this is certainly not the only possible mind-first account, it illustrates at least that there is nothing *incoherent* about a deeper, mental explanation. For if mentality is fundamental, then physical causation itself can be understood as a subset of a more general mental causation. Just as nonphysical laws structure physical reality without needing to "push" particles around, mental states can structure and constrain physical states. Reason does not rule that out.

13. For a development of this mental analysis of physical space, see. Michael Tze-Sung Longenecker, "A Theory of Creation Ex Deo," *Sophia* 61 (2022): 267–82, https://doi.org/10.1007/s11841-020-00801-9.

Resolving the Causal Exclusion Problem

Let us turn to the problem of causal exclusion. This problem depends not just on reason, but on the empirically motivated premise that the physical domain is causally closed (i.e., that every physical event has a sufficient physical cause). If this premise is true, then it would seem there is no room for nonphysical mental causes to enter the scene to make a physical difference.

I have three responses. First, instead of attempting to fit mentality into an already self-sufficient physical world, we can analyze physical processes as themselves a product of an underlying mental reality. One option is to provide a reductive analysis of physical properties in terms of mental properties. This analysis is possible because physics does not reveal the inner nature of material objects but only tells us their relational, functional properties. Thus, it is possible—at least in principle—that material objects themselves can be analyzed in terms of intrinsically mental aspects.[14] According to this analysis, what we call "physical closure" would itself be an emergent feature of an underlying mental causal order.

Second, the science of consciousness suggests that mental causation does not contradict the laws of physics but instead calls for an expanded understanding of physical reality itself. For example, Hiley and Pylkkänen propose a model in which consciousness influences brain activity while remaining within the boundaries of known physical laws.[15] According to their model, even small mental influences on the brain can accumulate over time, leading to significant effects. Similarly, McFadden's research suggests that consciousness integrates information as an energy field.[16] If this theory is correct, then consciousness can influence energy fields, with changes propagating outward to affect both local and distant systems. Further evidence comes from studies on nonlocal consciousness effects. Research from PEAR and the Global Consciousness Project indicates that consciousness correlates with statistically significant changes in random number generators.[17] Importantly, none of

14. See Donald Hoffman and Chetan Prakash, "Objects of Consciousness," *Frontiers in Psychology* 5 (2014): 1–22, https://doi.org/10.3389/fpsyg.2014.00577.

15. B. J. Hiley and Paavo Pylkkänen, "Can Mind Affect Matter via Active Information?," *Mind and Matter* 3, no. 2 (2005): 8–27.

16. Johnjoe McFadden, "Integrating Information in the Brain's EM Field: The Cemi Field Theory of Consciousness," *Neuroscience of Consciousness* 2020, no. 1 (2020): 1–13, https://doi.org/10.1093/nc/niaa016.

17. Roger Nelson, "Global Consciousness and the Coronavirus—A Snapshot," *The Global Consciousness Project*, May 9, 2020, https://tinyurl.com/3wt8xpus.

these studies reduce or eliminate consciousness; they expand our framework of physical reality to account for its causal role. Thus, instead of excluding mental causation, these findings illustrate how it could be integrated into the physical world—just as a mind-first theory predicts.

Finally, we can convert the problem of causal exclusion into an argument for mind-first theory. The argument is this:

1. Mental causation is real.
2. If reality is fundamentally mindless (nonmental), then mental states are causally excluded from making a difference (i.e., mental causation is not real).
3. Therefore, reality is not fundamentally mindless.
4. If reality is not fundamentally mindless, then it is fundamentally mental.
5. Therefore, reality is fundamentally mental.

The first premise draws support from both mainstream empirical science—such as findings in positive psychology and the neuroscience of consciousness—and from ordinary, everyday experience. The second premise follows from the logic of causal exclusion: *if* the most fundamental causal agents are entirely nonmental, then all effects ultimately stem from fundamentally mindless processes, leaving no room for mental causation to make a genuine difference.[18] By contraposition, if mental causation is real, then the fundamental agents of reality are not entirely nonmental. The salient alternative is that these fundamental agents are, at least in part, mental. Thus, we arrive at a mind-first ontology. (This argument leaves open the possibility that reality is *both* mental and material, provided that our conception of "material" is broad enough to accommodate fundamental mentality.)

While this argument warrants further exploration, it at least highlights that the problem of causal exclusion is not solely a challenge for mind-first theorists to consider. Indeed, if the argument is sound, the problem of causal

18. Notice that this premise does not depend on the irreducibility of mental states. Even if we suppose that mental states *reduce* to material, brain states, there is still a causal exclusion problem arising from microphysics: How can mental states make a difference of their own that isn't already caused by nonmental micro-items (e.g., particles and fields)? After all, fundamental mindless agents would still pull the strings on all your behavior. Thus, reduction to nonfundamental macro-states is not enough. We can solve this remaining problem if we reduce mental states to *fundamental* material states, but then we have a version of mind-first theory, so that's not a way out of my argument for a mind-first theory. For further analysis of this kind of "mereological" exclusion problem, see Bailey and Rasmussen, "New Puppet Puzzle," 202–13.

exclusion poses an even greater challenge for mindless-first theories. Given these considerations, a key takeaway, in my view, is not that immaterial causes are impossible, but rather that there cannot be a fundamentally *mindless* explanation of mind-body interaction.

Addressing the Pairing Problem

Consider, finally, the pairing problem, which invites us to explain how an immaterial mind could be causally linked to a specific body. My solution once again involves providing a deeper explanation in terms of a mind-first ontology. If mental reality is fundamental, then I believe we can explain the pairing between mental and material states in terms of more fundamental causes.

Here's why. According to material emergence, material states can be analyzed as emergent from an underlying mental reality. For example, we can analyze spatial relations as constituents of mental space rather than fundamental properties of a mindless reality. Thus, mental reality can, at least in principle, cause spatial structures. If so, then we can analyze the pairing of a mind with its body in terms of more fundamental causes of *both* mental and corresponding spatial states.

To further illustrate this account, here is a more specific theory of your relationship to your body. Assume your body is composed ultimately of quantum fields. The activities of these fields are in turn explained via informational contents of mental states (per the informational theory of matter). Moving your body therefore involves changing informational contents of mental states. You can do this by *intending* and *thinking*, since intending and thinking play the role of informational states. For example, you can form an intention with an informational content (thought) to move your arm upward. You affect "your" body, on this account, because your body is built ultimately out of informational, quantum states generated in you from the time of your body's conception. While my main proposal does not hang on the details of this theory, it illustrates at least the coherence of a deeper explanation of mind-body pairing.

This mind-first account also enables a unified solution to all three problems of mental causation at once. First, there is no category problem with moving your body with your mind, since your body itself ultimately consists of mental (informational) states. Here mind-body interaction reduces to mind-mind interaction. Second, there is no causal exclusion problem because the mental reality is *explanatorily prior to*—and so not excluded by—the informational forms that constitute material reality. Third, you are paired with the body you formed via more fundamental mental activity in the quantum field. Here the pairing of your mind with your body is like the pairing of the cartoon characters and their speech: there is a deeper explanation of both states from a prior mental reality that unifies them together.

Conclusion

The mind-first theory offers a systematic and unifying framework for understanding reality. By positing mental reality as fundamental, we not only sidestep the certain challenges faced by many dualist and materialist models, but we also have a coherent explanation of both mental causation and material emergence.

Moreover, the mind-first framework resolves the problem of mental causation. Rather than seek to explain how a nonphysical mind could interact with a causally closed physical system, a mind-first theory allows us to analyze material reality as emergent from a more fundamental mental order. Thus, mind-first theory dissolves the category problem, the causal exclusion problem, and the pairing problem by reinterpreting the physical world as a structure within a broader mental framework.

In view of these considerations, not only does an immaterial mind make sense, but it also makes sense of a lot of things. A mind-first ontology can help us explain a range of phenomena, including (1) the fine-tuning of the universe for life; (2) the systematic coordination between mental and physical states; and most centrally (3) the reality of mental causation. For these reasons, I recommend the mind-first theory for serious consideration.

10

Nontheist Responding to the Debate

All Minds Are Material Things

Benjamin Watkins

Does God exist? When pondering big questions in that peculiar philosophical sort of way we are quickly confronted with a myriad of competing explanations for various facts. Comparing these explanations and understanding how all of our experiences and theorizing combine into a coherent and intelligible worldview can seem a daunting task, but it is also one relished by philosophers with nothing better to do. The aim of this chapter is to convince the reader that considerations in the philosophy of mind create an epistemic problem for theism in the philosophy of religion. Facts about our minds give us a good reason to excise immaterial minds from our best explanatory theorizing.

In their debate, Adam Lloyd Johnson and Dan Barker discussed whether or not God exists—whether an immaterial mind created and designed the physical universe. Dan seems content merely to reject Adam's theistic explanations, while other times he seems to endorse a naturalistic alternative, but it is unclear what the substance of that alternative is. Dan argues nonphysical minds are contradictory, like a married bachelor, and that decisively rules out Adam's theistic hypothesis.

Dan's argument strikes me as obviously unsound. How exactly does an entirely immaterial mind, like a god or soul, entail a logical contradiction like a married bachelor does? An unembodied mind seems both a coherent and plausible theoretical postulate. Not only is an immaterial mind at least *prima facie* intelligible in a way a married bachelor is not, we could also imagine evidence for it. For example, there might have been evidence for reincarnation, or scientists could have discovered distinctly mental, disembodied forces. As it stands, Dan's argument that immaterial minds are logically contradictory will need to be revised.

We will need to develop an inductive argument that claims an entirely nonphysical mind is unlikely relative to what we know about our minds. This is the central aim of the present chapter, and it can be divided into two distinct stages. The first stage of the argument from material minds aims to answer the question: What fact about our minds gives us reason to reject theism? The conclusion of the first stage is that our minds are identical with (or at least causally dependent upon) material things rather than immaterial things. This stage is defended with a causal argument in the fourth and fifth sections of this chapter.

The second stage of the argument from material minds aims to answer the question: Do we have any reason to reject theism given the fact our minds are material things? If our minds were immaterial, that fact would have been evidence for theism, but because our minds are material things, that fact disconfirms theism. This stage is defended in the sixth section of this chapter. The upshot of these two stages is that our minds and those of nonhuman animals are either identical with, or causally dependent upon, something physical, which gives us reason to reject theism. Before turning to the arguments for each stage, in the next three sections let us first characterize the two competing hypotheses and survey the mind-body problem.

Theism

The philosophy of religion explores the nature, significance, and implications of religious beliefs and practices, but what is of interest to the argument from material minds are considerations that are both explanatory and of religious significance. A theistic hypothesis might be *a potential explanation* if it makes some observation(s) more intelligible, that is, more to be expected. Additionally, it might be of *religious significance* to our lives if what it posits could respond to our religious concerns. Theism might be a potential explanation of surprising facts about the universe and morality if those facts are a matter of course given theism.[1] Theism might be of religious significance if we would expect the god it posits to answer prayers, offer salvation, defeat evil in the end, or love us unconditionally.

Whether a theistic hypothesis is a potential explanation of religious significance will depend on our *model of god*. So what model of god does Adam use? His model of god secures religious significance by supposing that God is "something than which a greater cannot be thought" or *the greatest conceivable being*.[2] But in what sense is his model of god a potential explanation? One con-

1. Gregory W. Dawes, *Theism and Explanation* (Routledge, 2009), 28.

2. Anselm, *Monologion and Proslogion: With the Replies of Gaunilo and Anselm*, trans. Thomas Williams (Hackett, 1996), 100.

vention in the philosophy of religion is to divide arguments into those which derive their conclusions from experience and those derived from pure reason. Adam endorses the former sort of argument and argues that the universe having both a beginning (apparently fine-tuned cosmic order) and objective morality is expected given an intelligent creator, designer, and lawgiver, so he attributes to God's nature the properties of being spaceless, timeless, immaterial, immensely powerful, and perfectly moral.[3] Positing this model of god, Adam infers that theism is the best explanation for facts about the universe and morality.

A question we can now ask is whether there is any plausible hypothesis—logically incompatible with theism—that explains our experience much better than Adam's theistic hypothesis.[4] Consider the problem of evil: How likely is it that an infinitely powerful and perfectly moral God would allow the evils we observe?[5] We would expect a morally perfect God to prevent evil, insofar as God properly could, and there are no nonlogical limits to what an omnipotent being could do. Therefore, it is very surprising we observe the kinds, amounts, and distributions of evil we do.

However, such facts are a matter of course given a naturalistic alternative, that is, a hypothesis logically incompatible with theism like the hypothesis that our lives are the result of mindless chance and processes indifferent to our suffering. Therefore, facts about evil give us a good reason to believe theism is probably false, other things being equal.[6] One way to sidestep the problem of evil is to suppose that God is either limited in power, moral perfection, or both. However, if God is limited in such ways, then we could conceive of a God with more power or a morally better nature. Therefore, this being would be more perfect than God. But that contradicts Adam's supposition that God is the greatest conceivable being.[7] This move sacrifices religious significance for explanatory power.

Similar remarks will apply to any denial that God is immaterial and mental. Were God a physical mind rather than an immaterial one, and assuming some causal laws are statistical rather than fully deterministic, no physical mind

3. Richard Swinburne, *The Coherence of Theism* (Oxford University Press, 1977), 2.

4. David Hume, *Dialogues Concerning Natural Religion: And Other Writings*, ed. Dorothy Coleman (Cambridge University Press, 2007), 80.

5. Hume, *Natural Religion*, 80.

6. Paul Draper, "Pain and Pleasure: An Evidential Problem for Theists," *Noûs* 23, no. 3 (1989): 331–34, https://doi.org/10.2307/2215486.

7. Immanuel Kant, *Lectures on Philosophical Theology*, trans. Allen W. Wood and Gertrude M. Clark (Cornell University Press, 2005), 137.

could be all-powerful because there would always be the possibility it could fail.[8] Again, any being that is not omnipotent contradicts the supposition that God is the greatest conceivable being. The upshot of this is that if we want a potential explanation of religious significance, then we need the suppositions that God's nature is both immaterial and mental. Any theistic hypothesis that might explain a complex, physical universe or transcendent moral laws will imply a sharp ontological distinction between a created universe on the one hand and a nonphysical creator, designer, and lawgiver on the other. Let's call this sharp ontological distinction

> *Supernaturalism*: Mental states have causal priority over physical things; there would be no universe of material objects unless something immaterial and mental willed it so.

In what sense is God's nature *mental*, though? Persons have minds; they are complex unities of mental states like beliefs, desires, and perceptions. If God's nature is to be a potential explanation of religious significance, then it must be at least analogous to our minds. According to *theistic personalism*, God's mind is a complex unity of distinct and successive states analogous to our minds. It might be objected that theistic personalism is too anthropomorphic.[9]

The doctrine of divine simplicity claims that God is neither a composite thing nor a being among others. Rather, he is being itself. Whatever is intrinsic to God is identical to his essence and existence.[10] Let's call any model of God that accepts the doctrine of divine simplicity *classical theism*. According to classical theism, God's nature is a single, simple, immutable, necessary, and impassable act. God's agency, cognition, and experiences are neither complex, distinct, or successive, nor could they be affected or other than they now are. God's nature stands fixed in a single, simple act across all possible worlds.

The difficulty for classical theism is that its incomprehensibility threatens its status as a potential explanation of religious significance. If God is identical to his intrinsic properties, then God is identical to a property, so his properties are a single property. Hence, God is a single property rather than a mind with distinct beliefs, diverse desires, intentions that could be otherwise, successive perceptions,

8. Alvin Plantinga and Michael Tooley, *Knowledge of God* (Wiley-Blackwell, 2008), 97.

9. Hume, *Natural Religion*, 24.

10. Thomas Aquinas, *Summa Theologica,* trans. Fathers of the English Dominican Province, 5 vols. (Benziger Brothers, 1911–1925), I, q. 4, a. 2; see also I, q. 3, a. 2.

or passable sentiments.[11] God's nature would not be mental in any analogous sense to a human person. Any empirical content or religious significance God's nature might have would be inscrutable and indistinguishable from a naturalistic alternative. The physical universe is no more intelligible given a single, simple mental act than it is given a single, simple physical event! The "anthropomorphism" of theistic personalism is preferable, both in theory and in practice, to the incomprehensible and indifferent "mysticism" of classical theism.[12]

Adam (and his Protestant persuasion) would no doubt concede theistic personalism, the supposition that God is the greatest conceivable being, and that theism entails supernaturalism. So, in what follows I will take it for granted that a theistic hypothesis like Adam's involves a model of god whose nature is at least immaterial and mental in a sense analogous to our minds. It will be the supposition that God is immaterial and mental that will be the target of the argument from material minds. Before we turn to that argument, we need to first consider the substance of a plausible alternative hypothesis logically incompatible with theism.

Naturalism

At least one plausible alternative to theism that is also logically incompatible with it is metaphysical naturalism. Naturalism is the hypothesis that there is no causal stuff over and above the physical universe. The domain of causes is exhausted by bits of matter and their aggregates extended over space-time and behaving in accordance with general laws.

> *Naturalism:* The material world has ontological priority over the mental world; there would be no mental things if there were no material world to realize them.

Given this hypothesis, material states have causal priority over mental ones, so all mental states are at least causally dependent on material things. Atheism is the negation of theism, that is, it is the claim that there is no God. Naturalism entails atheism because it entails that there is no such person as God or anything like an immaterial mind. Hence, naturalism and theism are logically incompatible hypotheses.

What about the plausibility of naturalism compared to theism? Naturalism is a plausible alternative to theism in the sense that theism is not much more

11. Alvin Plantinga, *Does God Have a Nature?* (Marquette University Press, 1980), 47.

12. Hume, *Natural Religion*, 35–37.

probable intrinsically than naturalism. The *intrinsic probability* of a hypothesis is a measure of its probability independent of any evidence in its favor, and it is determined by features entirely intrinsic to it, that is, by modesty, coherence, and nothing else.[13]

Modesty is a measure of how much content a hypothesis asserts. Theism asserts more content than naturalism because it entails ontological dualism rather than ontological monism. Theism claims that God's nature is an entirely immaterial mind that caused the physical universe to exist. All plausible explanations share an ontological commitment to a universe of material objects, so it is a fundamental subset of any plausible explanatory hypothesis. However, the ontological commitments of theism extend well beyond the physical universe.

Theism is not only less modest than naturalism, but it also suffers from problems of coherence. *Coherence* is a measure of how well the parts of a hypothesis logically fit together. To consider all the problems of coherence that theism faces would take us well beyond the scope of this chapter, so let's assume, for the sake of argument, that theism is at least as coherent as naturalism. We can reason like this:

> (1) Theism entails ontological dualism, and ontological dualism is not much more probable intrinsically than naturalism because it is less modest (because naturalism entails ontological monism), and theism is at least as coherent. (2) Naturalism entails atheism, and theism is not much more probable intrinsically than atheism because theism is less modest, and atheism is at least as coherent. (3) Therefore, we can take for granted the premise that theism is not much more probable intrinsically than naturalism.

In what follows, I will take it for granted that naturalism is a plausible alternative to theism, and that theism and naturalism are logically incompatible hypotheses.

The Mind-Body Problem

Is there any knowledge so certain that no reasonable person could doubt it? This question might not seem worth asking. After all, the sight of our own hands and the feel of our own bodies are taken as evident. Yet, for René

13. Paul Draper, "Cumulative Cases," in *A Companion to Philosophy of Religion*, 2nd ed., ed. Charles Taliaferro et al. (Wiley-Blackwell, 2010), 415–18.

Descartes (1596–1650), this question was of the greatest importance. Descartes's method of doubt resolved to accept only those beliefs that were so clear and distinct as to be beyond all possibility of doubt. He imagined an evil, deceitful demon who manipulated his perceptions so convincingly that illusions were indistinguishable from reality. Were such deceptions possible, what we take to be *reality* might instead be merely *appearance*.

Within Descartes's method of radical doubt, even something as simple as the existence of his body was less than certain. He entertained the possibility that the evil demon could be making it appear that he had a body when he really did not. Perhaps all his experiences were mere illusions. As Descartes pushed his skepticism further, he discovered something that he could not doubt: mental appearances. Were he to doubt the reality of his body, there had to be a mind doing that doubting. Indeed, were he to perceive anything at all, there had to be a mind doing that perceiving. From this, he reached his famous conclusion: *Cogito, ergo sum—I think, therefore I am.*

At least one lesson from Descartes's method of doubt is that mental appearances are most certain; they are judgments we cannot "get behind" or "outside of." The reality of our minds has a fundamental certainty that material objects, like our bodies, lack. How the world appears cannot be reasonably doubted, but how the world really is—a universe of external objects inferred from our mental appearances—can be doubted. Even in dreams, illusions, or hallucinations, the appearance of things forms a solid foundation for knowing that our minds exist.

The reality of our bodies, however, remains less than certain. This raises two further questions. First, given that we are certain of our minds and the appearance of our bodies, can we trust these appearances as signs of real, external things? Second, if so, what kind of objects are they? There is no incoherence in the supposition that our bodies are unreal and that the universe consists only of appearances, but this is surely not the best explanatory theorizing regarding our experience.

It is hard to believe other people do not also perceive our bodies, or that when other people speak, what we hear is not the expression of another mind. For there to be a common domain of public things, known by many people who perceive them, something must exist beyond each of our private, subjective experiences. The hypothesis that we lack bodies, or that everyone else's body is an elaborate delusion, lacks the explanatory power and theoretical simplicity of the hypothesis that our bodies really do exist and cause our perceptions. Thus, we can admit, though with less certainty than our minds and with reasoning less demonstrative than we might have liked, that there really is an external universe of objects not entirely dependent on our perceptions of them. But what sort of things are they? What is their nature?

According to Descartes, *material things* are nonmental objects with "a determinable shape and a definable location and can occupy a space in such a way as to exclude any other body . . . and can be moved in various ways, not by itself but by whatever else comes into contact with it."[14] We need not claim, as Descartes did, that the essence of the physical is spatial *extension*. Following Thomas Hobbes instead, spatial *location* is a sufficient condition of material things: "a body is that, which having no dependence on our thought, is coincident or coextended with some part of space."[15]

With the suppositions that our minds and bodies are real and our bodies are physical, what about the nature of minds? Following Descartes again, mental things are not material things. Rather, they are distinctly immaterial: a thinking *substance*, something that could exist of itself independently of physical things. The view that our minds and bodies are ontologically distinct substances is often called *substance dualism*:

1. Our mental states are immaterial things.
2. Our bodily movements (and neural events) are material things.

What distinguishes the mental from the physical is that the latter are *in* space and the former are not. Descartes defends this claim with his *conceivability argument*: "I saw that I could conceive that I had no body . . . but yet that I could not for all that conceive that I was not. . . . From this I knew that I was a substance . . . the soul by which I am what I am, is entirely distinct from body."[16]

Recall that if we are to know there is an external world of material things, then those objects must cause our perceptions, and our mental states must *move* our physical bodies if we are to manipulate the world. The regime describing common life, and in which our human agency and cognition are situated, presupposes the causal efficacy of mental phenomena with material things:

3. Our mental states cause bodily movements, and neural events cause mental effects.

14. John Cottingham, Robert Stoothoff, and Dugald Murdoch, eds., *The Philosophical Writings of Descartes* (Cambridge University Press, 1984), 2:17.

15. Thomas Hobbes, *The Collected Works of Thomas Hobbes*, ed. William Molesworth (Routledge, 1992), 1:102.

16. René Descartes, *Discourse on Method and Meditations*, trans. E. S. Haldane and G. R. T. Ross (Cambridge University Press, 1911), pt. 4.

The problem of mental causation explains how our mental states play a causal role in a physical universe.[17] Any science that invokes mental phenomena as indispensable links in causal chains that bring about material observations will be committed to mental causation because the presence or absence of mental phenomena must make a *causal* difference to the world.[18]

How is it possible that my mental desire caused my physical arm to rise? My mind reached into my body and contracted my muscles to raise my arm. Well, how did my mind "reach into" my arm and move those muscles? It caused electrical signals from my brain that in turn caused them to contract. But how did my *desire* cause those electrical signals? Neurons firing in my brain cause those electrical signals. So where does something distinctly mental, like my desire, enter as a link in this causal chain of neural firings? If two distinct things really are causally related, one psychological and the other neurological, then just *what* relates them such that they *can* causally interact? Such a relation is surely possible, and agency, cognition, and mental sciences presuppose such a relation. It is this problem of mental causation that the next section will seek to answer.

Before we do that, however, consider this question: What is it for an embodied brain, something with a location in space and linear dimensions, to be causally related with an immaterial soul, something wholly lacking either spatial location or extension? If mental states are to move bodies—that is, if the ghost in the machine is to operate the machine—then minds must impact, propel, touch, or otherwise *contact* material things, say at a point on a surface. But to do that, minds must have a spatial location for such interactions to take place at. In that case, minds would be physical by Descartes's own criterion. These reflections raise what is often called *the interaction problem*:

4. Immaterial things do not cause material things, and material things do not cause immaterial things.

17. The problem of mental causation is similar to the problem of evil. There are facts about the world—those of evil and mental causation—that create an evidential problem for theism.

18. Neuroscience reveals that pain is correlated with the firing of C-fibers, injections of sodium pentothal with a loss of consciousness, and neurodegenerative diseases with losses of memory. In fact, all known mental activity is correlated with brain states. The most natural explanation for mind-brain correlations is in causal terms from mental sciences like psychology, cognitive science, and neuroscience. For example, neuroscience explains the correlation between the firing of C-fibers and pain in causal terms: The causes of C-fiber firing (e.g., tissue damage) are one and the same causes of pain.

The interaction problem is not avoided if mass and energy, rather than spatial location or extension, are the defining characteristics of the physical. According to the *conservation of mass and energy*, in a closed system changing over time the net total mass and energy of the system remains constant. So if immaterial things are to causally interact with material things like a brain or body, then they will either have to make use of the mass-energy already present in the system or introduce it from outside. Nonphysical things, lacking both mass and energy, cannot transfer energy to the physical, say by the emission of radiation or the transfer of heat. Immaterial things cannot "reach into" a system and transfer energy any more than they can "reach into" a body and move muscles.

The conjunction of points 1–4 detailed here entails a contradiction. Deciding which proposition we have the most reason to reject is *the mind-body problem*. Substance dualism rejects either 3 or 4, and *substance monism* rejects either 1 or 2. Among the dualist options, *interactionism* rejects 4, and *parallelism* rejects 3. Among the monist options, *idealism* rejects 2, and *materialism* rejects 1. If we suppose both mental causation and the reality of a physical universe, then we can take idealism and parallelism off the table, so our choice comes down to interactionism and materialism.[19]

Whether our minds are immaterial or material will turn on whether we have more reason to accept 1 and reject 4 or reject 1 and accept 4. If the former, then we should be interactionists, but if the latter, then we should be materialists. Interactionists can solve the problem of mental causation by arguing from substance dualism and a solution to the interaction problem. In other words, interactionism must argue that mental states and neural events are ontologically distinct and that nonphysical things do cause physical ones. On the other hand, materialists can sidestep the interaction problem by arguing that our minds are material things rather than immaterial, thus solving the problem of mental causation. Additionally, if we take the reality of a physical universe, mental causation, and the interaction problem (i.e., 2–4) as premises, then the conclusion is materialism. Let's call this a *causal argument for materialism*.

19. By taking for granted mental causation and the reality of matter, we have rejected both idealism and parallelism as actual solutions to the mind-body problem. This is, admittedly, to beg the question against those views in the context of the mind-body problem (indeed to even pose the problem of mental causation is to beg the question against idealism and parallelism, as that problem asks how mental states can *cause material* effects), but all discussions must begin somewhere and limit their scope, and the reality of matter and mental causation is common ground between interactionists and materialists of limited scope.

An In-Principle Objection to Interactionism

Are our minds immaterial things like disembodied souls, or are they material things like embodied brains? Taking the existence of matter for granted, we saw that Descartes's conceivability argument motivated the former view called substance dualism. In addition to a physical universe, we also took mental causation for granted. The conjunctions of substance dualism and mental causation we called interactionism. The coherence of interactionism is threatened by the interaction problem. Recall that materialism was the rejection of substance dualism. The acceptance of a physical universe, mental causation, and the interaction problem constitute the premises of a causal argument for materialism. The question before us is this: Do we have more reason to accept materialism and reject interactionism or more reason to reject interactionism and accept materialism?

The aim of this section is to argue for materialism and against interactionism. If the interaction problem is understood as the claim that immaterial souls do not cause material things because they *cannot* cause them, then the premises of the causal argument for materialism constitute an *in-principle objection to interactionism*. Whether this objection succeeds or not will turn on whether immaterial souls can, in principle, cause material things.

Why think that immaterial souls cannot, in principle, cause material effects? Reasons to think they cannot go back at least to Descartes's contemporaries. Princess Elisabeth of Bohemia put the interaction problem to Descartes like this:

> I beg you to tell me how the human soul can determine the movement of [muscles] in the body so as to perform voluntary acts—being as it is [immaterial]. For the determination of the movement seems always to come about from the moving body's being propelled—to depend on the kind of impulse it gets from what it sets in motion, or again, on the nature and shape of this latter thing's surface. Now the first two conditions involve contact . . . but . . . contact seems to me incompatible with a thing's being immaterial.[20]

In light of the above reflections, Princess Elisabeth raises an in principle objection to interactionism:

20. Elizabeth Anscombe and Peter Geach, trans. and eds., "Princess Elisabeth of Bohemia to Descartes, May 6–16, 1643," in *Descartes: Philosophical Writings* (Nelson, 1969), 274–75.

> I admit it would be easier for me to concede matter and extension to the soul, than the capacity of moving a [material thing], and being moved, to an immaterial being.[21]

According to Princess Elisabeth, it is easier, in principle, to reject substance dualism and admit the interaction problem than it is to accept interactionism and solve the interaction problem. Descartes, surprisingly, seemed unable to even *see* the interaction problem much less appreciate its force:

> The whole problem contained in such questions arises simply from a supposition that is false and cannot in any way be proved, namely that, if the soul and the body are two substances whose nature is different, this prevents them from being able to act on each other.[22]

Adam in his debate with Dan, similarly, does not seem too bothered by the interaction problem and dismisses it almost out of hand: "We might not know exactly *how* the immaterial interacts with the physical, but I don't *see* why it couldn't" (emphasis mine). Unfortunately, neither Adam nor Descartes has anything more than incredulity to offer as a solution to the interaction problem.

As a solution to the interaction problem, incredulity is clearly inadequate. The difficulty is not merely that minds and bodies are different things. Rather, it is that they are different *in such a way* that precludes their interaction *in principle*. Princess Elisabeth saw this more clearly than Descartes did, and Dan may see it more clearly than Adam does: "If I walk across this stage, isn't it weird that my soul is following my cranium . . . what's tethering it there?" As an argument from Dan, this is also clearly inadequate. Dan's own incredulity is not a substitute for an actual argument, but it should prompt us to formulate one. Let us now turn our attention to formulating a causal argument for materialism in the same spirit as Princess Elisabeth's in principle objection to Descartes's interactionism.

According to substance dualism, it is the nature of physical bodies to be in space, and the nature of immaterial minds not to be. For the two to interact, as is supposed by mental causation, what is not in space must act on what is in space. But how can this be? How can the soul evade all our attempts to locate it, yet it moves our bodies and is affected by neural events in our brains at certain

21. Anscombe and Geach, "Elisabeth of Bohemia to Descartes," 68.
22. Cottingham, Stoothoff, and Murdoch, *Philosophical Writings of Descartes*, 2:275.

locations? Action on a body takes place *at* a location *in space* by way of contact with a surface or by way of a transfer of energy through a medium. Hence, a nonphysical mind must stand in *a spatial relation* to a material body, if they are to causally interact. But immaterial minds are not located in space, so their immaterial natures preclude their causal interaction with the physical.

Here is a materially different way of raising the interaction problem. Suppose substance dualism is true, and we are standing next to each other. I then decide to raise my arm. Why doesn't my mental act cause your arm to rise? Why doesn't my mental act cause both of our arms to rise? What relation underlies the correct and incorrect pairings of *cause* and *effect* in this case? We might look for a *pairing relation* that holds only between my mental act (cause) and the movement of my arm (effect). The obvious candidate for such a relation is space. What pairs my mental act with my bodily movement is the spatial location where their interaction takes place. Pairing causes with effects is intelligible if and only if we can *situate* them at locations or *orient* them toward one another within physical space.[23] Notice that using spatial location as a pairing relation is unavailable given substance dualism. Immaterial things, by definition, do not stand in spatial relations to material things. Just because your body is located there and mine is located over here gives us no reason to think my disembodied soul could not be paired with your arm, nor that it could not interact with both of our arms at the same time.[24]

It might be objected that causal interactions between immaterial and material things, and the pairing of immaterial causes with material effects, are simply an unexplainable brute fact or a primitive relation. However, the interaction problem has nothing to do with either the primitiveness or bruteness of causation and everything to do with a nonphysical thing's lack of spatial location. Even if we suppose God divinely ordained the pairings of immaterial causes and their material effects, they must stand in some relation to one another—some relation that God's will wrought. Unless we know just what that relation is, we have no idea if God could will it. The problem is not in answering *how* God related immaterial causes and material effects, nor in answering *why* God related them as he did. Rather, the problem is answering *what* God did when relating the two. To this question, we cannot even gesture toward an answer.

23. Given the state of contemporary physics, we must tolerate the reality of "action at a distance." But this is no counterexample to the current point about spatial location and causation because action at a distance still causally relates objects *at a distance*.

24. Jaegwon Kim, *Physicalism, or Something Near Enough* (Princeton University Press, 2005), chap. 3.

Does mental causation fare any better if we suppose materialism? This mental cause *here* contacts that bodily effect *there*, and this mental experience *here* is paired (or correlated) with that brain state *there*, given materialism, because their locations are spatially related, that is, "here" and "there" are spatially contiguous. Additionally, neurophysiology is in the business of discovering the causal relations between neural states, and if mental states *just are* neurophysiological states, then the causal explanations from neurophysiology will entail the possibility of causal interactions (both mind-to-brain and brain-to-mind). To help us see this, consider the following schema α:

(α) Neurophysiology
A material brain state, N_1, causes a neurophysiological event, N_2
N_1 is a mental thing
N_2 is a material thing
Hence, mental causation is possible

The last line of α is derived from the second line, and the second line is from the first. The third and fourth lines are merely rewrite rules for describing mental causation in material terms.[25] The upshot is that α sidesteps the interaction problem altogether. N_1 can contact, touch, or impulse N_2 (or transfer energy to N_2), because their locations in space are contiguous, and nothing without a spatial location is invoked; hence no interaction problem arises in the first place.

Unlike in α, the possibility of mental causation given interactionism is not a matter of course. Can interactionism guarantee the possibility of mental causation like α can? Our previous considerations suggest it cannot. Consider a comparable schema:

(β) ???
The immaterial state of a soul, N_1, causes a neurophysiological event, N_2
N_1 is a mental thing
N_2 is a material thing
Hence, mental causation is possible

25. Notice that the third and fourth lines do not describe empirical information from a neurophysiological perspective; they relate concepts in a mental language game and a neurophysiological one. Formally, definitions are not premises of a proof, so they come along for free. As rewrite rules, they allow us to take an existing causal explanation and substitute (one for one) our mental language into them.

The second line of β merely assumes there is no interaction problem and then derives the possibility of mental causation from that assumption. If that assumption is not derived from any existing theory analogous to neurophysiology, and we cannot state a pairing relation between N_1 and N_2, then substance dualists have no right to the assumption that mental causation is possible *in principle*, as there is no principle, theory, or metaphysical framework that makes that possibility intelligible. The upshot is that materialism, rather than interactionism, can vindicate mental causation. What materialism affords us is the most modest and coherent explanatory framework to understand mental causation, and we need that to understand the unity of mind and body or correlations between mental states and brain states. Trying to understand mental causation without a spatial framework is like trying to understand relations such as north and south, left or right, without any frame of reference. We have no principled way of making any sense of such suggestions.

We are now in a position to articulate a formal in-principle objection to interactionism in the same spirit that Princess Elisabeth put it to Descartes. Suppose our brains and bodies have spatial location. Either our disembodied souls have spatial location, too, or they do not. If we are substance dualists, then we must accept the latter because the former entails materialism by Descartes's definition of a material thing. Hence, if our minds have spatial location, then they are material things and mental causation is possible. Again, this follows from the definition of a material thing, and we derived the possibility of mental causation from the second line of α. If minds do not have spatial location, then minds are immaterial things and mental causation is impossible. Once again, this follows from the definition of an immaterial thing, and recall we were unable, in principle, to derive the possibility of mental causation from the second line of β. We have no theory analogous to neurophysiology, and we have no idea what relation could pair N_1 and N_2. Finally, if we suppose mental causation is possible, as both interactionists and materialists suppose, it follows that our minds are material things.

A *De Facto* Objection to Interactionism

Recall the question that began the last section: Are our minds immaterial things, like disembodied souls, or material things, like embodied brains? Taking the existence of matter for granted, we saw that Descartes's conceivability argument motivated substance dualism. Also recall that mental causation is entailed by any actual explanation of a physical event involving a mental act by a human person. Our thoughts and desires must make a causal difference to matter if they are to potentially explain any material observations. However, according to the interaction problem, immaterial things make no causal difference to the physical universe.

Of the possible solutions to the mind-body problem, we took idealism and parallelism off the table. Most of us are not prepared to deny the reality of matter or give up mental causation. That leaves us with materialism, interactionism, and the problem of mental causation.

Can mental states make a causal difference to a material world? We saw in the last section that there is an in-principle objection to interactionism: our brains and bodies occupy space. Either our minds do, too, or they do not. If minds are immaterial things, then they do not occupy space. If minds have spatial location, then they are material, and mental causation is possible. If minds do not have spatial location, then they are immaterial, and mental causation is impossible. If mental causation is possible, as interactionists and materialists suppose, then materialism follows.

If the above in-principle objection to interactionism is right, then disembodied souls cannot explain mind-brain unity or mind-brain correlations. The most natural reply is to infer that there is no interaction problem from substance dualism and mental causation. Given substance dualism, if minds *do* causally interact with brains and bodies, as seems evident, then it follows that at least one immaterial thing and one material thing do *in fact* causally interact. Hence, there is no interaction problem. The issue with this reply is that it begs the question at hand. Recall the problem of mental causation: Is it possible for an immaterial thing to cause a physical event? In the case of materialism, we derived an answer to this question from neurophysiology and identified a pairing relation (i.e., spatial relations) between mental causes and material effects. To state that immaterial things simply do in fact cause physical events is to completely ignore the interaction problem, just as Descartes did to Princess Elisabeth and as Adam did to Dan in their debate. Even if this reply did not beg the question in the current context, it is clearly an inadequate reply to that problem.

Let's concede, for the sake of argument, that the in-principle objection to interactionism fails, though it is entirely unclear *why* it fails. Perhaps souls, though still immaterial things, can also be spatially located.[26] Perhaps souls,

26. If minds are immaterial things with a spatial location, then a spatial location is not sufficient to distinguish a material thing from an immaterial one. To make good on this suggestion, we need some other sufficient condition for being a material thing to distinguish them from immaterial things, but I do not think there are any other plausible accounts. Defending that claim is beyond the scope of the present chapter. For such a defense, see Ned

though lacking a definable location in physical space, can causally interact with material things. These possibilities do not entail that such causal interactions *in fact* occur. If the interaction problem is instead understood as the claim that immaterial things do not *actually* interact with material things, then the premises of the causal argument for materialism constitute a *de facto objection to interactionism*.

Let's consider a simple example of mental causation. Suppose my itching actually explains my scratching because it causes a neural event in my brain that, in turn, causes my bodily movement. Much is already known about the physicochemical processes that in fact cause the firing of a bundle of neural fibers. The movement of charged molecules through a nervous system to a motor cortex causes electrical potential to build up in a neuron until it reaches a critical point and then it discharges—sending new electrical signals back through the nervous system, where the electricity causes muscles to contract. Presumably, if my desire to scratch is to move my body, then my desire must causally influence the motions of molecules in the actual causal chain from my nervous system, through my motor cortex, and finally to the movement of my body. Some events, such as quantum events, may be truly random and without a cause, but those physical events that do have a cause—and this seems to include all bodily movements—have an actual explanation in terms of sufficient material causes. This claim can be stated as the general empirical principle of

> *Causal Closure*: Every physical event (that has a cause) has a sufficient material cause.

Materialism offers the only plausible way of securing mental causation given causal closure. The empirical support for this principle comes from physiology, neuroscience, and other sciences of the human body.[27] These sciences have revealed no sign of nonphysical forces operating in the brain and body, which are the places influenced from immaterial things that would be expected to show up. On the contrary, neurophysiology strongly suggests that every physical event in the brain and body is actually explained in terms of sufficient neurological causes, and effective quantum field theory predicts that all brain

---

Markosian, "What Are Physical Objects?," *Philosophy and Phenomenological Research* 61, no. 2 (2000): 375–95, https://doi.org/10.2307/2653656.

27. David Papineau, "The Rise of Physicalism," in *Physicalism and Its Discontents*, ed. Carl Gillett and Barry Loewer (Cambridge University Press, 2001), 8–9.

events reduce to the four fundamental forces: gravitational, electromagnetic, and strong and weak nuclear forces.[28] Any other forces or dynamics acting within the regime of brain events are too weak to influence human behavior. Indeed, if one were to peruse the scientific literature, one would not find ingredients or dynamics beyond those postulated by physics, chemistry, and biology. From the fact that every physical event in the brain and body examined so far has involved a sufficient material cause, and our scientific research has reached an advanced stage, we can conclude that it is likely all physical events involve a sufficient material cause.

Now let's suppose substance dualism is true. In our imagined case, my itch is nonphysical, and the neural event that begins a neurophysiological causal chain in my brain is physical. Hence, the neural event in my brain has two putative causes: an immaterial one and a material one. Let's make one further plausible stipulation about this case: it is not a genuine case of causal overdetermination. That is, it is not the case that if I was not itching, I would in fact still scratch (because my neurons were firing), or that if my neurons were not firing, I would in fact still scratch (because I was itching). This claim can be stated as the general metaphysical principle of

> *Causal Exclusion*: No single event can have more than one sufficient cause occurring at any given time, unless it is a genuine case of causal overdetermination.[29]

If this is right and every neural event actually has a sufficient neurophysiological cause, and neural events are not in fact caused twice over, then we have more reason to reject the putative immaterial cause than we do the known material one. Therefore, it follows that immaterial things do not *actually* explain physical events because they do not *in fact* cause them. This is one way of understanding the interaction problem as a *de facto* objection to interactionism.

Some interactionists may object that the above considerations are question-begging because they merely assume causal closure. This objection is misguided because there are substantial empirical reasons for accepting the causality, explanatory power, and self-sufficiency of the physical. But rather than belaboring this point any further, we can motivate the interaction problem without appealing to causal closure.

28. Sean M. Carroll, "Consciousness and the Laws of Physics," *Journal of Consciousness Studies* 28, no. 9–10 (2021): 18, https://doi.org/10.53765/20512201.28.9.016.

29. Kim, *Physicalism*, 42.

When anyone feels an itch, we know it is correlated with a specific neural state—let's call it *N*. If *N* occurs, you will itch; but if *N* does not, you will not feel any itch. Consider the claim that an itch causes you to scratch, and your itching is also distinct from *N*, that is, the former is immaterial, and the latter is material. Suppose further that neurophysiologists have discovered a causal chain from *N* to your scratching. The existence of such a causal chain is highly likely; as we have already seen, we know a great deal about causal processes underlying many sensory processes like an itch, tickle, and pain. This suggests that your scratching has two putative causes: one immaterial (the itch) and one material (*N*). Given that neurophysiology has discovered a sufficient material cause of your bodily movement, how can the same event be caused twice over by two distinct causes? It would seem the material cause threatens the supposed immaterial one. Assuming this is not a genuine case of causal overdetermination, the immaterial cause does not in fact cause your scratching—*N* does. We have again arrived at the interaction problem. Notice that in developing it we have used some reasonable assumptions about the neurophysiology of sensory experiences and causation but not causal closure.[30]

We are now in a position to articulate a formal *de facto* objection to interactionism. Suppose that all our neural events have spatial locations. It seems apparent that mental states actually explain bodily movements because they in fact cause neural events. What actually explains the fact that this neural event occurs on this occasion? We know that every neural event that causes a bodily movement has a material cause in terms of a prior neural state, whether that follows from causal closure or has been discovered by neuroscience. If substance dualism is true, then the mental cause of the neural event is an immaterial thing, and the neural cause of the neural event is physical. Hence, the neural event that causes the bodily movement has two putative causes: an immaterial mental cause and a material neural cause. But given this is not a genuine case of causal overdetermination, it follows from causal exclusion that a nonphysical mental state does not actually explain my bodily movement, because it does not in fact cause the neural event that in fact causes my bodily movement.

By contrast, if materialism is true, then the mental cause of the neural event that causes a bodily movement and the neural cause of that event are one and the same thing. Hence, the neural event that causes a bodily movement has only one putative cause, a material mental cause, and this is not a genuine case of causal overdetermination. Therefore, it follows that a material mental

30. Jaegwon Kim makes this same point in *Physicalism*, 154–55.

state does actually explain my bodily movement because it in fact causes the neural event that in turn causes my bodily movement. Once again, materialism actually vindicates mental causation, while substance dualism preempts or precludes it. In what follows, I will take for granted that the in-principle objection to interactionism of the previous section and the *de facto* one of this section constitute sound causal arguments for materialism.

From Material Minds to Atheism

Having completed the first stage of the argument from material minds, we are now in a position to complete the second and formally articulate *the argument from material minds* in its entirety. Suppose that theism is neither intrinsically more probable than naturalism nor logically compatible with it, and that materialism is true. The only remaining premise is that materialism is much more likely given naturalism than theism. Therefore, materialism gives us a *prima facie* good reason to reject theism.

What form does the argument from material minds above take? Historically, it has been formulated inductively with an *enumerative induction*. A generalization is made about a whole population based on observations from a representative sample.[31] All known minds (both human and nonhuman) involve embodied brains; therefore, by enumerative induction, all unknown minds probably involve embodied brains too. If God is essentially an unembodied mind, then it is unlikely God exists.[32]

The argument from material minds in this chapter does not take the form of an enumerative induction. Another inductive form, also endorsed by Adam in his debate with Dan, is often called "an inference to the best explanation" or *abduction*. The best explanation is the most probable hypothesis among competing explanations given some fact to be explained. We can model the argument from material minds with an abductive schema:

(γ) Theism and naturalism are logically incompatible.
Theism is not much more probable intrinsically than naturalism.

31. Such arguments date back to at least Epicurus and Lucretius. See Diogenes Laertius, *Lives of Eminent Philosophers*, vol. 2, *Books 6–10*, trans. R. D. Hicks, Loeb Classical Library (Harvard University Press, 1925), see 10.63; E. J. Kenney, ed., *Lucretius: De rerum natura, Book III*, 2nd ed. (Cambridge University Press, 2014).

32. For a similar argument from material minds using an enumerative induction, see Hume, *Natural Religion*, 62; J. L. Mackie, *The Miracle of Theism: Arguments for and Against the Existence of God* (Oxford University Press, 1982), 100; Plantinga and Tooley, *Knowledge of God*, 96.

Materialism is known to be true, that is, we know our minds are material things.
Materialism is much more likely given naturalism than it is given theism.
Hence, other evidence held equal, theism is probably false.

γ is an inductively valid argument, and if by a "*prima facie* good reason" we mean a reason given by a conclusion that is probable, other things being equal, then our considerations so far entail a *prima facie* good reason to reject theism. The question that remains is what support can be given for the premises of γ. Lines 1 and 2 were defended in the second section of this chapter, and line 3 was defended in the fourth and fifth sections.

What support can be given for line 4? First, God had many more options when creating minds than were available on naturalism (e.g., parallelism and interactionism), that is, the ontology of our minds was much more constrained given naturalism. Second, theism entails supernaturalism—an immaterial mind existed prior to the physical universe and was responsible for creating it. There would not be a universe of material objects if a nonphysical mind did not create it. Given theism, it is antecedently likely that our minds are fundamentally immaterial, but on naturalism material things have ontological priority over mental things—there would be no minds if there were no matter to realize them. Thus, theism confers a much greater likelihood on substance dualism than does naturalism.

The conclusion of the causal argument for materialism was that our minds are, in at least some sense, material things. Some philosophers *reduce* conscious mental states to the third-person material things postulated in physics, that is, all known mental states are *identical* to quantitative things. Others argue conscious mental states and brain states must be *distinct*. Why do we experience pain when neurons, like C-fibers, fire rather than under some other neural condition? Why don't we experience an itch or tickle instead? Why do we have any conscious experience at all when neurons like C-fibers fire? Though we can observe correlations between C-fibers firing and pain, these correlations do not explain why such relations exist in the first place. Why should there even be consciousness in a physical universe? Answering these questions has come to be known as *the hard problem of consciousness.*[33] First-person, qualitative things, like itches, tickles, and pains are not identical with the objective, quantitative things postulated by physics and described

33. David J. Chalmers, *The Conscious Mind: In Search of a Fundamental Theory* (Oxford University Press, 1996), 4.

in third-person terms. Rather, they are *irreducibly* qualitative and subjective. It might be objected that materialism is false because irreducibly subjective, conscious mental states cannot be reduced to third-person material things. Rather, they must be distinctly first-person mental *substances*.

Any objection from the hard problem of consciousness does not succeed because material things are, as we saw in the fourth and fifth sections of this chapter, a necessary condition for mental causation. Instead of a dualism of distinct substances, conscious mental states can either be reduced to third-person material things, like brain states, or are irreducible first-person *properties* that our brains can instantiate on certain occasions. Let's call views that identify conscious mental states with material things *reductive materialism*, and we will call views that claim only that consciousness is causally dependent on material things *nonreductive materialism*. Line 3 of γ can be restated as the disjunctive premise that either reductive materialism or nonreductive materialism is known to be true. This amendment to γ concedes there is a hard problem of consciousness while retaining the same conclusion.

Conclusion

We began this chapter with the question whether God exists, and we understood God's nature as both ontologically distinct from the physical universe (immaterial) and analogous to our minds (mental). Dan Barker, in his debate with Adam Lloyd Johnson, argued that an immaterial mind is not a potential explanation of anything much like a married bachelor. The aim of my chapter has been to revise this argument into an inductive argument that I am calling the argument from material minds: facts about the natures of our minds give us a *prima facie* good reason to reject theism.

We compared theism with a plausible and logically incompatible alternative. According to naturalism, all mental states are at least causally dependent on material things, so it is logically incompatible with our supposition that God's mind is entirely immaterial. Naturalism, we saw in the second section, is more modest than theism and is at least as coherent, so theism is not much more intrinsically probable than naturalism. The argument from material minds can be divided into two stages. The second stage claims there is a fact about our minds better explained by naturalism than by theism, so that fact gives us a *prima facie* good reason to reject theism. The first stage aims to establish the fact about the nature of our minds and has to do with the mind-body problem.

Among the possible solutions to the mind-body problem, we rejected idealism and parallelism by admitting mental causation and that our brains and bodies are physical. This narrowed our choice to interactionism and materialism. Whether our minds are immaterial souls or embodied brains turned on the interaction problem. The fourth and fifth sections of this chapter argued that mental causation, the interaction problem, and the physical reality of our brains and bodies constitute a causal argument for materialism. The causal argument can be formulated as either an in-principle objection to interactionism or a *de facto* one.

According to the in-principle objection, our brains and bodies, being material things, occupy space. Either our minds do, too, or they do not. If minds are immaterial things, then they do not occupy space, and if minds have spatial location, they are material things and mental causation is possible because we can, in principle, pair mental and physical causes and effects. If minds do not have spatial location, then they are immaterial and mental causation is impossible because we cannot, in principle, pair mental and physical causes and effects. Given mental causation is possible and the supposition that our brains and bodies are material things, it follows that interactionism is false. According to the *de facto* objection to interactionism, every physical event has a sufficient material cause, and our mental states actually cause bodily movements. Bodily movements are physical events, and they are not in fact caused twice over. Hence, our minds are material things, specifically, material causes. These two causal arguments for materialism complete the first stage.

The second stage takes for granted that naturalism is a plausible and logically incompatible alternative hypothesis to theism, and that materialism is known to be true. It was then argued (in the sixth section of this chapter) that materialism is much more expected given naturalism than given theism. We saw that it might be objected that the hard problem of consciousness gives us reason to doubt this, but this objection fails. We conceded the hard problem of consciousness and admitted that either reductive materialism or nonreductive materialism is true, that is, either our minds are identical to material things or are at least causally dependent on them. This completes the second stage and brings the argument from material minds to this: naturalism is a plausible, logically incompatible alternative to theism. It is known that our minds are either identical to or causally dependent on material things. That fact is much more likely given naturalism than theism. Hence, other evidence held equal, theism is probably false.[34]

34. I am grateful to Zach Tabor and Daniel Linford, who provided me with invaluable comments on earlier drafts of this chapter. I am also grateful to my mentor, William Brenner, for his guidance and encouragement. And as always, I am thankful to my colleagues at Real Atheology: A Philosophy of Religion Podcast: Justin Schieber, Ben Baver, Ryan Downie, and August D.

11

Theist Responding to the Debate

Can We Be Good Without God?

David Baggett

What a privilege to respond to the debate between Dan Barker and Adam Johnson, which had for one of its goals to model what a friendly conversation on the topic of God's existence can look like. There were moments when Dan's passion came through, but he seemed to direct his ire at certain views he disagreed with rather than at Adam. Friendly discourse on vexed questions is, as Adam said a few times, something of a lost art nowadays, so this was a refreshing exercise, and both debaters are to be commended. In the same spirit, although I will launch criticisms of views I think are misguided or arguments I think weak, none of my attacks are directed at those holding or advancing them.

Andrew Drinkard (the editor) has tasked me to discuss the moral argument portion of the debate from my perspective as a theist, so I won't discuss the cosmological or design arguments. What I will do is lay out Adam's case for the moral argument, then give Dan's reply, which I will attempt to flesh out to make it as strong as it can be. Then I'll offer a reply of my own to what Dan had to say, a reply that will share some overlap with Adam's rejoinder. I'll then extend the discussion by offering a more expansive account of morality than Dan's account and explain why I think it evidentially suggests theism.

Adam Lloyd Johnson's Moral Argument

Adam lays out this version of the moral argument:

1. There are objective moral truths independent of our minds.
2. The existence of God is the best explanation for how there could be objective moral truths.

3. Therefore, God exists.[1]

The formal structure of the argument might appear deductive, but the argument is less deductive than abductive, an inference to the best explanation. What makes this clear is the language of the second premise invoking the notion of "best explanation."

So the argument begins by identifying a class of moral phenomena (objective moral truths existing independent of our minds), then inquires as to what best explains them. Adam gives reasons to think that God provides that best explanation, and then infers that God is the true explanation. But even if God does provide the best explanation, the conclusion that God exists is not a guarantee. This is what makes an abductive argument like this different from deductive versions. There is no airtight case presumed between the premises and the conclusion. The conclusion is a bit more tentative than that. We might even say the conclusion implicitly goes something like this: God probably or plausibly exists.

This distinction between deductive and abductive forms of reasoning can be easily misunderstood. Some prefer deductive approaches because they think that deductive arguments provide "certainty" while inferences to the best explanation do not.[2] But rarely do even valid deductive arguments provide certainty outside the realms of logic or mathematics. That a conclusion follows with airtight certainty from the premises does not render the conclusion certain. Deductive validity only shows that the conclusion is entailed by the evidence, but the question of how reliable the evidence is also needs addressing. Unless the premises are known with certainty, the conclusion won't be able to be known with certainty. It's even possible that a deductive argument could feature premises which are more likely true than not, while the conclusion is not (as Tim McGrew demonstrated a few years back). So the reasons why some think deductive approaches are inherently better than abductive approaches are on occasion confused.

1. Again, Adam Lloyd Johnson offers three arguments in the debate, so he's offering a cumulative case argument for God's existence. We're just confining our attention to this one argument here.

2. Dan Barker at one point in the debate seems to express a preference for deduction. Or at least his characterization of deduction seems to imply as much. In a good deductive argument, the evidence logically entails the conclusion. It doesn't merely make the conclusion more likely than it would otherwise be. Personally, I don't think one logical form is better than another; much depends on the nature of the topic under discussion. Each argument form has its strengths and vulnerabilities.

Adam puts forth an inference to the best explanation. This is typically what such an argument involves: it begins with some phenomenon in need of explanation. Often the phenomenon is surprising or a little mysterious, so there's work to be done to figure out its significance and the best account of it. In this case, Adam identifies objective moral truths independent of our minds. Then the inquirer attempts to construct a list of (possible) explanations. Adam thinks there are reasons to believe that God is the best explanation, and on that basis he at least tentatively infers to God's existence as likely true.

The relevant issues, then, are three: (1) Are there such objective moral truths? (2) Does God provide a robust explanation of such truths? And (3) Do naturalistic explanations provide as good, or perhaps an even better, explanation of such objective moral truths? All of these will be discussed below, each in turn.

Another word on the nature of abduction may be in order, and this is one of those cases where we need to dip into another aspect of the debate that will prove germane to our discussion. Dan characterizes abduction as a "best guess," which is unfortunate in a few respects. To the extent that the term "guess" carries with it the connotation of an unprincipled conjecture, the characterization arguably seems tacitly disparaging. Rightly identifying a best explanation involves quite a bit more than a shot in the dark. Again, from a list of potential explanation candidates the process of abduction uses a set of principled criteria to winnow the list down to the best option among the alternatives.[3] Then it involves an inference to that best explanation as the likely true explanation (at best), which remains subject to further examination and inquiry.

Explanation is the key notion here. We might say "explanationism" is the idea that the ability of an account to provide a robust explanation is evidentially significant. Not everyone adheres to explanationism, but many find it compelling. If something is in need of explanation, and an account of it is provided that does real work of explanation, then the idea behind abduction is that such explanatory potential is evidentially significant. There are indeed limitations to abduction (bad lot objections, etc.), but Dan does not invoke those. For those interested in understanding abduction better, including intelligent and substantive critiques and other concerns it invites, one good source to peruse is Kevin McCain and Ted Poston's *Best Explanations: New Essays on Inference to the Best Explanation*.[4]

3. These criteria include explanatory scope (the more the better), explanatory power (the more the better), avoidance of *ad hoc*-ness (the less *ad hoc*-ness the better), plausibility (the more the better), consistency with other known propositions (the more the better), and the like. By such criteria Dan's claim that he'd be as entitled to posit a multiverse as Adam would posit God is not convincing, at least to me.

4. Published by Oxford University Press in 2017. One last word on the way in which to

Dan Barker's Reply

Dan's response to Adam's version of the moral argument seems to call into question both of Adam's premises, one explicitly and the other implicitly. Dan resists the first premise that affirms that there are moral truths that exist independently of our minds by insisting that there are no objective moral values.[5] Instead he wishes to paint moral values in a way that requires no major metaphysical commitments and certainly no appeal to the transcendent.

The main gist of Dan's response to the moral argument seems to be a rejection of the notion that moral values, in particular, need much of an explanation. They certainly don't need God as an explanation of them. Here I will do my best to re-create his argument from the debate.[6] His account of the "moral principle," as he dubs it, involves several components: a naturalistic paradigm, a mind-dependent account of moral values, a certain meaning of morality, a concern to avoid the danger of "reifying" morality, objective verification of moral values, an appeal to a notion of emergentism, and an account of morality that appeals to the notion of harm. So how does all this go together?

As an atheist, Dan understandably attempts to explain the nature of morality by appeal to the natural world. Moral values, he's convinced, depend on our brains, something that is part of the physical world. He seems to take for granted that the purpose of morality, at a minimum anyway, is to avoid harm

---

couch arguments. Adam just as easily could have employed notions of confirmation theory or induction to advance his moral argument. The relevant objective moral truths, for example, could have been argued to be more likely on theism than on atheism. That would have been another way to make the case that morality evidentially points to God. Or he could have argued that the moral truths render theism at least more likely than it would otherwise be, but without making theism more likely true than not. Richard Swinburne calls that a C-inductive argument, and Swinburne himself endorses such an argument. Or Adam could have been more ambitious and offered what Swinburne calls a P-inductive argument, according to which the moral truths render theism more likely true than not. Since Adam gives three separate arguments for God's existence in the debate, he seems to be after constructing a cumulative case. So even a C-inductive moral argument might have sufficed, which could be joined by the other arguments, and their cumulative effect might well have constituted a P-inductive argument rendering theism more likely true than not, or at least more likely true than naturalism. All of this simply to say that there's a variety of ways in which such arguments can go.

5. Whereas Adam spoke of moral truths, Dan seemed to zero in on moral values, which are arguably one set among others of moral truths. Besides values, for example, we can speak of moral duties, moral freedom, or moral rights, to name just a few.

6. I will set aside his observations about moral guidance and the Bible and the moral lives of atheists, since they seem ancillary to the main discussion, although these are eminently worth discussing at considerable length.

(and, more ambitiously, likely promote harmony) among human beings. This leads him to gravitate toward an account of ethics that mainly considers the consequence of actions. Accordingly, we refer to behaviors that are harmful as immoral, whereas moral actions produce good consequences on balance. Efforts to identify moral values as something in need of explanation, he thinks, mistakenly treat such things as real entities when they are instead just shorthand for behaviors that conform to consequentialist constraints and practical benefits. Moreover, although there are no mind-independent (or "objective") moral values, we can "verify" our moral standards: those behaviors that can be empirically demonstrated to do harm are immoral, and those, presumably, that promote well-being or flourishing are moral.[7] So overall he concludes that it's wrong to affirm the existence of, and seek an explanation for, objective moral values. Why? Because there are no such things.

At any rate, that is how I read what Dan is suggesting in the debate for how we should understand morality. One of the strengths of his view, he would suggest, is that it offers a straightforward answer to a question like "Is abusing women immoral?" Of course, he'd say, because morality by its nature prohibits just such a thing. Doing harm like abuse, by definition (or analysis), is immoral. It's a no brainer. We can empirically demonstrate that abuse is deleterious and inflicts harm. This is the objective verification of which Dan speaks. And since by the very meaning of morality such a thing is immoral, we can know that abusing women is immoral. Such an account need make no appeal to the realm of the supernatural or transcendent; it's all this-worldly, a function of human brains, based on a consideration of real-world consequences and pragmatic benefits. Nothing mysterious or obscure about it in the least. We can keep our feet firmly planted on the ground and our heads out of the clouds.

Adam Lloyd Johnson's Rejoinder and More

Dan would affirm that it's immoral to abuse women, but he rejects the notion that there's an objective value that would undergird such a notion. But if he affirms that it's immoral to abuse women, he's affirming its truth, so he seems to be affirming the moral truth that it's wrong to abuse women.

Since Dan pivoted from language of moral truth to the locution of moral values, let's put it this way: in affirming the immorality of abusing women, he seems to affirm that it's morally bad (to use a moral value term) to abuse

7. The sorts of moral values that might be said to exist in at least some sense are rather like emergent properties, but they don't take on any mind-independent reality.

women. This again suggests he's affirming the truth of a moral value. So how does he say we can verify such a value but that such a value isn't objectively true?

On my reading, his point seems to be that the truth isn't objective because it depends on functioning human brains. But recall Adam's thought experiment contrasting two claims: that twice two is four and that, say, blue is my favorite color. If I were administered a drug that made me think instead that twice two is five and that red is my favorite color, the former belief would be false even if the latter has now been rendered true. This is because, in the second instance but not in the first, the belief in question is mind dependent. (Or brain dependent, to use Dan's language.) Twice two being four is not plausibly thought of as mind dependent in that way. So what about a claim like it's wrong to abuse women? Would my believing that it's morally good to abuse women make it true? Surely not. So in what sense is the moral value in question a function of the human brain?

Indeed, as a consequentialist Dan's more consistent position would be to say that since abusing women causes harm, it's morally bad. In fact, he *does* say this. But how is that consistent with his denial of the objective truth that it's morally bad to abuse women? He needs to explain how we can have it both ways; there seems to be an element of confusion here on his part. Plausibly, "It's wrong to abuse women" is true just in case it's wrong to abuse women. If Dan wants to say it's immoral to abuse women but then deny that it's wrong to abuse women, that seems to raise serious questions about the coherence of his position.

Note that Dan doesn't claim to be a moral relativist. The relativist could affirm that it's wrong to abuse women in a subjective sense, perhaps because the majority of people in a particular culture believe it to be wrong. The wrongness wouldn't be objective but rather subjective and dependent on the prevailing view of the society or culture in question. But as a consequentialist, in contrast, Dan presumably wishes to suggest that if the consequences of an action are sufficiently bad, then the action in question is immoral. This aspect of his moral theory just doesn't fit together very well.

What helps conceal the challenge faced by Dan's view is his shift in language from moral truths to moral values. Moral values are just one among other moral truths, and they often can seem more mysterious than other moral categories. So take instead moral duties, for example. Presumably we have a moral duty not to abuse women. To affirm such a thing doesn't require that we transform duties into "things." It's rather tantamount to saying "We morally ought not to abuse women," or something in that vicinity. Admitting this acknowledges that moral facts for most of us, believers and unbelievers alike, are among our strongest convictions.[8]

8. Hyperbolic concerns about reification pose little threat to moral realism. In my own

So there's a significant tension between Dan's consequentialism, on the one hand, and his denial that there are objective moral values, on the other. The latter view is hard to square. What about the former view? Does a consequentialist account sufficiently undermine Adam's moral argument? Let's turn our attention to that question.

Let's switch our example to torturing children. Is such a behavior bad (or wrong)? Dan would say yes. Again, how he reconciles this with a denial of objective moral truth is unclear. Perhaps he thinks that moral discourse is a particular language game.[9] If we are going to play the game and use moral language, we need to use it consistently and assume a consequentialist view. Actions that do harm are wrong, accordingly, so when using the language game of morality, we are within our rights to say that torturing children for fun is immoral. But since it's only a game we're playing, our language need not track any real truth.

Of course, though, if that were Dan's position, it wouldn't so much explain morality as explain it away. And it would be anyone's prerogative simply to choose not to play the game. Or perhaps to encourage people to change the rules of the game. Think Nietzsche, who would strongly resist Dan's sanguine contentment about the supposed implications of morality that, to Nietzsche's thinking, are simply vestiges of a Judeo-Christian influence.

But here we are shifting our focus away from what Dan says morality is to the matter of confirming that certain behaviors do harm. Once more, Dan's analysis seems to go like this:

1. Torturing children for fun does harm.
2. Whatever causes harm is immoral.
3. So, torturing children for fun is immoral.

What is able to be verified here? Premise 2 is taken as an obvious truth, perhaps a definition. So that's less a matter of verification than axiomatic definition or analysis. Where confirmation or verification comes in is with premise 1. It can be readily verified experientially that child torture for fun is horrific and harmful *in excelsis*. Of course, hardly anyone would deny that; it's not really in much dispute.

So several observations are in order. First, a natural way to treat this approach is to see it as evidence for moral realism—that there are objective moral

case, I try making a case for moral realism not just by an appeal to language but more so the language, logic, and phenomenology of morality.

9. Along Wittgensteinian lines, as seen in his *Philosophical Investigations.*

values and duties. Torturing children for fun is immoral, even if everyone in the world tomorrow were administered a drug that made them think otherwise. This seems correct, and in fact it's deeply consonant with Dan's own consequentialism while at odds with his denial of moral objectivity.

Second, either Dan affirms the second premise or he doesn't. When he denies moral objectivity, it seems that he wants to deny premise 2, but when he sounds like a consequentialist, he wishes to affirm premise 2. The former position seems incoherent, so it's the latter position that deserves more serious scrutiny. If he affirms premise 2, then he's affirming that it's true that whatever causes harm is immoral. Let's grant this point.

Third, what makes this truth true? Dan wants to resist such questions, but it's important to ask. Surely it's a legitimate question what makes it wrong to torture children for fun. And again, Dan at other times actually does answer the question. What makes it wrong can be found in what we mean by morality, he says.

So, fourth, is what we mean by morality simply a language game that carries no actual authority, or is it really the case that morality is authoritative? If the former, Dan has not explained morality but explained it away. If the latter, then another question arises.

Fifth, that question is this: Where does the authority of morality come from? I listened to the debate in vain to get any sense of a good answer to such a question from Dan. This leads to a crucial insight: what is able to be verified is not the moral premise of the argument above, but the empirical matter of whether a particular action does harm. What is the evidence that morality, beyond an agreed-upon way in which to use moral language, carries any authoritative force? That's the distinctively moral premise in need of substantive support. It's what Adam attempted to provide by appeal to the role of God in his metaethics. But it's a question that Dan does not address in the debate.

Let's now change the example again in order to make another needed point. Consider the proposition "Slavery is immoral." Most of us would agree. Dan's explanation of the immorality is that slavery does harm. Yes, but harm to whom? Well, the slaves, certainly, and perhaps to slaveholders, too, it could be argued. But suppose that the number enslaved were relatively small and the benefits far outweighed the harm done. Some such situation could be easily enough envisioned where the overall utility was maximized. If the goal of morality is to maximize utility, then slavery wouldn't be ruled out after all in such cases. A particularly moving and graphic literary example of such a picture can be found in Ursula Le Guin's "The Ones Who Walk Away from Omelos."[10]

10. Ursula K. Le Guin, "The Ones Who Walk Away from Omelos," in *The Wind's Twelve Quarters: Short Stories* (Harper & Row, 1975), 275–84.

Some consequentialists could affirm that slavery is always wrong, because a rule categorically precluding slavery over the long term is what best maximizes utility. Yes, but the wrongness in question is not a very strong sense of wrongness. It's rather something like a pragmatic rule of thumb by which to maximize utility. When Dan makes mention of the usefulness of morality to help us navigate life, he sounds a bit like a pragmatist, so this might be close to his view. It's a possible position to take for sure. But note that what hasn't been provided is anything like a rationale for basic human rights that should never be violated because of, say, the inherent dignity and worth and value of human persons. Indeed, Jeremy Bentham, a luminary in the history of utilitarianism, made clear that he thought of such rights as "nonsense on stilts." John Stuart Mill tried to do better but still ended up making the maximization of utility the ultimate arbiter when it comes to such matters.

I point this out to underscore that Dan's appeal to consequentialism is not necessarily the obviously right choice he seems to think it is. The debate between consequentialists and deontologists is a large one, but to my thinking the biggest drawback of consequentialism is that it leaves little room for some actions to be identified as simply and categorically wrong in virtue of the nature of the action. Relatedly, it doesn't seem to provide the necessary ingredients for a robust account of human value and intrinsic worth. Some actions are simply beyond the moral pale—irrespective of whether they ultimately conduce to a higher utility or better balance of good results over bad ones. There seems something objectionably myopic to reducing morality to a consideration of consequences alone.

Fearing Desiccation

This leads to the last few sections of this essay, in which I'm going to take up Dan's challenge to talk about what morality is and why I agree with Adam that it evidentially points to God. When Dan says morality can be reduced to harm, I think his answer betrays a very thin conception of morality. He seems to be pointing out what we might call the lowest common denominator of morality. Adam would agree that we should refrain from inflicting needless, pointless, purposeless, and gratuitous pain and harm. But that's just the first step of many as we try to grasp the import of morality. It's like the anteroom of a great cathedral, its towering spires going well beyond those first fledgling steps.

Morality is about loving our neighbors as ourselves. It's about recognizing the inherent dignity and sacred worth of other persons of whatever color or creed. It demands the requisite moral agency that can undergird holding people responsible for their choices, praiseworthy for good things they do, and blameworthy for morally wretched behaviors. It includes things we can't not know, like inviolable human rights that we possess whether or not our government confers corresponding legal rights on us. It's about the arc of justice in the movement of history that animated the civil rights movement. It's about obtaining moral knowledge. It's about forgiveness for wrongdoing, the mending of broken relationships, and deliverance from the shame that comes from doing shameful things. It's about moral transformation and the hope for such transformation reaching a point of culmination. It's about the correspondence between virtue and happiness that preoccupied so many great ethicists in the history of the moral argument—from Berkeley to Locke, from Butler to Reid, from Sidgwick (an atheist) to Kant.

When I hear Dan say that morality can be reduced to harm, it's hard to know best how to respond. He's perfectly entitled to think this, and I'm happy to respect his mental freedom to do so, but it's just so lamentably at odds with what I consider to be the marvelously splendored, richly evidential reality and beautiful binding authority of the "moral law within." I tend to suspect that Dan's better angles far exceed the narrow parameters and stultifying strictures of his official position and debate game face. In class I have said many times that atheists tend to be so much better than their worldviews, and Christians never nearly as good as theirs.

As a moral theory, consequentialism is concerned with more than mere descriptions. It's about generating prescriptions, ways in which we ought to behave. So it seems that if there's such a principle as this—that it's wrong to incur harm—it needs to be undergirded by more than how we happened to define a term. What explains the truth of such a principle? What makes it true? What features of the world best explain why we should care about eliminating harm and pain? I agree we should care, and failure to comply with such a principle is eminently blameworthy.

In fact, it's for just such reasons that I find myself wanting to know what it is about reality that makes this so. This is exactly why many people think morality is a fruitful direction to look for insights into the nature of the human condition and the world in which we live. Morality moves and warms our hearts, ignites our imagination, and gets our minds to thinking hard. Superficial accounts just don't cut it.

A good example of a deflated analysis, by the way, is Dan's low view of human agency. Moral duties are notoriously hard to square with determinism, and elsewhere in the debate Dan admitted that he's a determinist. He thinks the combination of prior conditions and the laws governing the universe conspire to make all that happens inevitable and unavoidable. How is such a picture remotely compatible with moral discourse that's prescriptive in nature?

Take a simple nonmoral example. I drive up to the corner intersection in my car and have to choose to turn left or right. On a determinist picture, the way I choose is how I invariably *had* to choose. Now take a moral case: I have to choose between a right action and wrong action. On a determinist picture, whatever way I choose is inevitable. I can't do otherwise. Adam is right to assign primacy to self-causation, and Dan is mistaken thinking that determinism satisfies such a constraint. Ultimately it's not the self that chooses within a determinism worldview but rather the prior conditions and laws of the world that together ensure every "decision."[11]

This brings us back once more to something always at the heart of this discussion, namely, the authority of morality. Where would such authority come from on Dan's worldview? There's good reason why George Mavrodes spoke of the odd nature of binding moral obligations in a naturalistic world.[12] It's a bad fit. Before Mavrodes, the great atheist ethicist J. L. Mackie had argued the same.[13] But we only feel the force of this point by studiously attending to the details, cultivating attentiveness to the moral evidence, rather than embracing a simplistic analysis that leaves out from the picture all of the most interesting and important features of morality, including the inherent features of certain actions that render them virtuous or wicked irrespective of a consideration of consequences alone.

Does God Provide a Robust Explanation of Objective Moral Truths?

Let's get underway answering this culminating question by identifying which among the array of important moral facts we'll be discussing. In this section and the next, our task is one of comparing theism and atheism in terms of their explanatory ability in accounting for various moral phenomena. For

11. Dan is also confused, I think, on the matter of God's foreknowledge and freedom. If God in his omniscience knows what choices he will freely make in the future, the issue isn't that he *can't do otherwise* when that time comes, but that he *won't*. It's analogous to my seeing another person sneeze. My seeing her sneeze doesn't make her sneeze; her sneezing is what enables me to see it. If God's omniscience is at least roughly analogous to perception (as one possibility), the same analysis holds, and God's foresight isn't its cause. A person's free choice could be different, but it just happens not to be. Such is the nature of free choices.

12. See George Mavrodes, "Religion and the Queerness of Morality," in *Ethical Theory: Classical and Contemporary Readings*, 2nd ed., ed. Louis P. Pojman (Wadsworth, 1995).

13. See J. L. Mackie, *Ethics: Inventing Right and Wrong* (Penguin, 1977).

space constraints, let's confine our focus to moral duties, human value, moral knowledge, and the alignment of happiness and virtue.

First, what are moral obligations? Actions that are wrong to do we have an obligation not to do. Conversely, actions that are wrong not to do are actions we have an obligation to do. Moral obligations don't cover the whole moral terrain, but they are an important part of it, and notice that we are not talking about a *feeling* of obligation but *obligation itself*; we can have a feeling that's misleading, after all. But if real, binding, and authoritative moral obligations exist, they require a solid explanation.

Moral obligations dictate to us what we ought to do. They are not mere suggestions. There is something inescapable about them. Failing to discharge our obligations results in a condition of objective guilt. Sometimes people are guilty without feeling guilty, and other times people feel guilty without actually being guilty. We're talking about a real and objective condition of guilt. Failing to do our moral duties arguably has that effect. It is also not uncommon that harm is done by our failure to do our duty.

How do we get a sense of what these features of moral obligations are? It's by the way we use the language of guilt, the logic of moral obligations, and our inner experience when we discharge our duties and when we neglect them. So the language, the logic, and the phenomenology of moral obligations all enable us insight into their nature.

Why is it important to explain these features of moral duties? Because moral duties are part of the evidence we are considering, and what we need to do is slow down and examine the evidence carefully. Otherwise we are liable to miss its significance or settle for a superficial answer. We are often in too big of a hurry. We need to slow down and carefully consider the evidence.

Having looked at the evidence for moral duties, we must ask why theism provides a robust explanation of them. But first let's anticipate an objection: skeptics might say, "Despite what you've said, I see no reason to believe there are such things as moral duties or obligations." How might we reply to this challenge? For most of us, moral obligations seem fairly obvious. In fact, our moral beliefs about duties tend to be beliefs that are both deep and have a wide impact on our other beliefs. Be it a parent's duty to care for his child, or absolute prohibitions against a lying promise, or fraud, or showing contempt for the dignity of another, or sawing people in half, we have a deep intuitive sense that these things are categorically the case.

And our sense that this is so is fairly nonnegotiable—it seems to us the case, which gives us excellent reason to make them a starting point. Can we, on occasion, be wrong about what seems to us the case? Surely we can; this is true even of our sense perceptions. But even when a sense perception is corrected—when we find out mirages in the road are an optical illusion, for example—it happens because of other impressions that seem to us even more obviously true. What seems to us obviously true is a good place to start, and few of us think we, as human beings, don't have even one absolutely binding moral obligation, and most of us would be inclined to think we have quite a number of them. Once we have such obligations and a grasp of some of their salient characteristics, we can ask the next question: What is it about the world that can explain these obligations? Most specifically, what accounts for the *authority* of moral obligations?

It's not too difficult to adopt a watered-down version of moral obligations—say, we should perform the action that produces the best results—and rest content with that. What that does, though, is eliminate the most important characteristic of moral obligations, namely, their authority. That is a crucial piece of evidence to which we need to be attentive. And it calls for a robust explanation. Theism can provide that. And what do I mean by theism? The idea that there is more to this world, ultimately, than atoms and molecules. That there is something supernatural about the world, something transcendent, something sacred—that there is a God, who loves us, who created us, and wants the best for us. Proponents of the moral argument advance the idea that such a God provides a robust explanation of binding moral obligations.

Robert Adams, whom Adam mentioned in the debate, is one such proponent, opting for a divine command theory of moral obligations. His theory, one among others on offer from theists, is predicated on a social theory of obligations, which is extended to include a relation with a divine being with the authority required to issue binding commands that constitute our moral obligations.[14] Not every theistic account of moral duties relies on such an account, but it's one among several possibilities. Moral apologists of various stripes, despite their differences, tend to root the authority of moral obligations in the sort of being who has the ability to generate such duties due to his nature, will, desire, commands, or some combination of these.[15]

Second, human value. In *The Weight of Glory*, C. S. Lewis wrote that there are no ordinary people. "You have never talked to a mere mortal. . . . It is

14. See Robert M. Adams, *Finite and Infinite Goods: A Framework for Ethics* (Oxford University Press, 1999), ch. 10.

15. Unanimity of opinion on the fine-grained details isn't needed. What's supremely telling is that, despite their divergence of opinion on the details, their typical principled agreement is that God is the one responsible for imbuing moral duties with real authority.

immortals whom we joke with, work with, marry, snub and exploit—immortal horrors or everlasting splendors."[16] This is simply something we know viscerally in a way too deep for words. There was a book put out some years ago called *What We Can't Not Know*, and among things we "can't not know" is the profound value of people.[17] Among the so-called natural signs that philosopher C. Stephen Evans identifies are human dignity and worth.

Intimately connected to this reality is that we are the legitimate bearers of basic, inviolable human rights. Historically speaking, religious perspectives have proved highly relevant to convictions about basic human rights. Some, like Nicholas Wolterstorff, even argue that they are a product of Judaism and Christianity, both of which claim that human beings are not only creatures of God but made in the image of God. Grounding human rights in capacities like the power of reason isn't workable, since many who have such rights lack such capacities. "Infants, those with Alzheimer's, and those born with severe mental impairments lack any such rational powers," Evans writes, "but they surely still have whatever inherent dignity and worth belongs to humans as humans."[18]

David Bentley Hart adds this:

> To look on the child whom our ancient ancestors would have seen as somehow unwholesome or as a worthless burden, and would have abandoned to fate, and to see in him or her instead a person worthy of all affection—resplendent with divine glory, ominous with an absolute demand upon our consciences, evoking our love and our reverence—is to be set free from mere elemental existence, and from those natural inclinations that pre-Christian persons took to be the very definition of reality.
>
> And only someone profoundly ignorant of history and of native human inclinations could doubt that it is only as a consequence of the revolutionary force of Christianity within our history, within the very heart of our shared nature, that any of us can experience this freedom. We deceive ourselves also, however, if we doubt how very fragile this vision of things truly is: how elusive this truth that only charity can know, how easily forgotten this mystery that only charity can penetrate.[19]

16. C. S. Lewis, *The Weight of Glory and Other Addresses* (HarperOne, 2001), 45–46.

17. J. Budziszewski, *What We Can't Not Know: A Guide* (Ignatius, 2011).

18. C. Stephen Evans, *Natural Signs and Knowledge of God* (Oxford University Press, 2012), 144.

19. David Bentley Hart, *Atheist Delusions* (Yale University Press, 2009), 213–14. To love one's neighbor as oneself is not to conjure artificial warm sentiments toward them. It is rather to recognize their intrinsic worth and dignity and honor that obtain irrespective of

Third, let's talk about moral knowledge. Moral facts are one thing, but moral knowledge is another. There can be moral facts of which we have no knowledge, but presumably we do have moral knowledge. So the question becomes, What can explain our moral knowledge? What reason do we have to believe that our moral convictions correspond to actual moral truths? A theistic account offers a plausible and powerful account of the correspondence between our moral convictions and objective moral truth. Theism can better explain the reliability of our moral cognitive processes and the cosmic coincidence between our moral judgments and moral truth, and it provides an account of moral knowledge based on a deeply teleological explanation of our belief-generating and belief-evaluating capacities that track objective moral truth.

Fourth, consider the alignment of happiness and virtue. This is a Kantian-inspired argument from providence. The matter at issue here is whether or not morality is a fully rational enterprise. Immanuel Kant did not want to locate the source of moral authority in consequences, and certainly not in whether or not actions generate happiness. This makes Kant sound like one who would insist that we should not care about our happiness at all. We should simply do our duty and aim for virtue, whether the result is happiness or not.

But this turns out to be not quite right, because Kant did recognize that fulfillment and happiness are important to us as human beings, since we are not merely spirit or mind—we also have bodies and various needs and cannot help but want to be happy. Again, actions are not right because they produce happiness; the relationship between virtue and joy is subtler than that. As Kant put it, we should become the sorts of persons who deserve to be happy.

If there is an ultimate disconnect between virtue and happiness, then morality might end up pointing in one direction (toward virtue) while rationality might push in a different direction (our happiness). So ultimately Kant believed there has to be an airtight connection between virtue and happiness, if the enterprise of morality is to be a fully rational one. Our highest good—what is best for us, one might say—is the ideal blend of virtue and happiness.

The correspondence principle to which Kant was pointing had been discussed prior to him by various thinkers, including Butler, Berkeley, and Reid, the latter calling it the "coincidence thesis." Reid, too, had been convinced that virtue and happiness need ultimately to coincide to make full rational sense

---

whether there is reciprocation. This recognizes that we have been endowed by our creator with certain inviolable human rights. To have been made in God's image, created for a reason and purpose, and imbued with inalienable rights is to be loved infinitely by him. This, in my thinking, is the deepest source and best explanation on offer of human dignity and value.

of morality, and the solution he thought most obvious was a benevolent deity. As he put it, "While the world is under a wise and benevolent administration, it is impossible, that any man should, in the issue, be a loser by doing his duty. Every man, therefore, who believes in God, while he is careful to do his duty, may safely leave the care of his happiness to Him who made him."[20] God ensures that morality makes full rational sense.

Can Naturalism Explain Objective Moral Facts?

How does naturalism account for these moral phenomena? Regarding moral duties, it really isn't clear how naturalists can adequately account for them. Having defined morality in a particular way—like avoiding harm—they can dub an action wrong for violating such a principle. But there's a bit of sleight of hand going on here. Morality involves not just the (extensional) matter of which actions are ruled in or out, but the (intensional) matter of why such rules are binding and authoritative.

When Dan says rape is wrong because it creates needless harm, he's simply sidestepping the underlying question of what makes inflicting needless harm wrong. That it's obviously wrong means it's self-evident, but self-evidence is not self-explanation. We need an explanation here, and theism provides one. Naturalism is hard pressed to provide one. Utilitarianism raises a few worries, but naturalism is the real culprit, and it's simply a bad fit when it comes to accounting for moral obligations. Leah Libresco was a well-known atheist blogger who, some years ago, finally decided that her moral commitments were simply at odds with her naturalism, and so she left her naturalism behind, becoming convinced that theism provided the better explanation.

Regarding human value and intrinsic human rights, why treat others as ends in themselves? Why think people have intrinsic dignity and value and worth? Mark Linville argues that no secular variant of ethics contains resources sufficient to explain the moral regard for persons we should have. Our having been made in God's image, however, provides a robust explanation of why we are here, why we possess the value we do, and why persons should be treated as ends in themselves and never merely as means.[21]

Regarding moral knowledge, this is a pressing challenge, I think, for naturalists, who lack an account for why there would be this coincidence between

20. Thomas Reid, *Essays on the Active Powers of the Human Mind* (MIT Press, 1969), 256.

21. Mark Linville, "The Moral Argument," in *The Blackwell Companion to Natural Theology*, ed. William Lane Craig and J. P. Moreland (Blackwell, 2009), 391–448.

our moral judgments and objective moral truths, a challenge that many naturalists themselves have come to recognize. Let me offer just a few examples.

The reason why this challenge is especially acute for naturalists is that they tend to believe in both naturalism and evolution. For most of them, evolution is the only game in town, but combining evolution and naturalism proves dicey where something like moral knowledge is concerned. For the idea is that the moral beliefs we form, according to their evolutionary and naturalistic story, come about not because they are true, but because they conduce to reproductive advantage and that sort of thing. They are evolutionarily adaptive. Now, not everyone thinks this is a decisive case against a naturalistic account of moral knowledge, but it's telling that three of the most important naturalists who discuss this specific issue have given up the notion of moral knowledge predicated on anything like objective moral truths.

Michael Ruse came to the conclusion that morality is best thought of as subjective, not objective, in light of such so-called debunking objections.[22] Sharon Street abandoned objective morality for what's called a constructivist account of morality, and Richard Joyce abandoned the notion that there are any true moral claims at all. He adopted what's called an error theory and a fictionalist account, according to which moral language is simply a useful fiction, but it's not actually true.[23]

Seeing the potential problems with an evolutionary account of ethics based on a naturalistic understanding of the world goes all the way back to Charles Darwin himself. In a famous passage he admitted the salient challenge: "If men were reared under precisely the same conditions as hive-bees, there can hardly be a doubt that our unmarried females would, like the worker-bees, think it a sacred duty to kill their brothers, and mothers would strive to kill their fertile daughters, and no one would think of interfering."[24]

We have two possibilities in that sort of scenario Darwin envisioned: either moral truths themselves change radically in light of our different evolutionary history or, less ambitiously, moral truth remains constant and only our moral beliefs change, which calls into question our moral knowledge. By way of analogy, this example has been used: imagine someone trying to get to Bermuda by boat, but does so by simply allowing the winds and the waves to guide the

22. See Michael Ruse, *Taking Darwin Seriously* (Blackwell, 1986).

23. See Sharon Street, "A Darwinian Dilemma for Realist Theories of Value," *Philosophical Studies* 127, no. 1 (2006): 109–66, https://doi.org/10.1007/s11098-005-1726-6, and Richard Joyce, *The Evolution of Morality* (MIT Press, 2007).

24. Charles Darwin, *Descent of Man*, Great Minds Series (Prometheus, 1998), 102.

vessel. Very rarely will the boat end up in Bermuda; perhaps on some rare occasion it will, but most of the time it won't happen. Moral knowledge seems hard to come by in a purely naturalistic world because the reasons that lead to our moral beliefs are not connected to moral truth itself.

Regarding the argument from providence, Henry Sidgwick's post-Kantian "dualism of practical reason" tells a similar tale. Sidgwick recognized a challenge at the heart of ethics—the potential disconnect between what's best for ourselves and what's best for the larger groups of which we are a part. In essence, it's the tension between rational self-interest and altruism. Often these interests dovetail and cohere. An unscrupulous businessman who develops the reputation of ripping people off may do fine in the short term but less likely so in the long term, which is why something like "enlightened egoism" can often provide us useful moral direction.

However, there invariably come times when conflicts occur between self-interest and altruism. In those situations, Sidgwick discerned two competing senses of reasonableness: doing what's in one's own interest and happiness, on the one hand, and doing what is for the greatest happiness of others, on the other hand.[25] He thought these two impulses equally reasonable, which flew in the face of what he considered to be a nonnegotiable feature of ethics, namely, that ultimately there can be no such conflict between the two kinds of reasonableness. He considered the problem so acute he dubbed it the "dualism of practical reason," and he saw that it threatened, once more, the rationality of the whole enterprise of morality.

Interestingly, he could see but one viable solution. If a providential God ensured ultimate correspondence between self-interest and altruism, between joy and virtue, then morality could be fully rationalized. Sadly, he himself did not follow this line of evidence in his own life, but still we can find the ingredients for such an argument from providence in his discussion of the dualism of practical reason.

Conclusion

Moral arguments for God need not be universally persuasive to be good arguments, and I'm inclined to feel their force, especially when combined with various other compelling arguments on offer both internal and external to morality. But more and more the window for such arguments to find a receptive audience may be closing. Ours is a society that is increasingly individualistic

25. Henry Sidgwick, *The Methods of Ethics*, 7th ed. (Hackett, 1981).

and that increasingly assigns primacy to the sovereign will of the individual to define the meaning of life for themselves.[26]

The price is a heavy one—loss of a strong sense of community and our duties to one another, loss of a sense of teleology and larger purpose, loss of what we hold in common as human beings. We are definitely approaching a crossroads as a culture, and it's a good time for us to redouble our efforts to think about morality and what it suggests about the nature of reality and of ourselves. For this reason, and many others, I applaud Adam and Dan for holding this serious conversation.

26. Carl R. Trueman powerfully chronicles this cultural and philosophical tale. See his *The Rise and Triumph of the Modern Self* (Crossway, 2020).

12

Nontheist Responding to the Debate

Objective Morality Doesn't Need God

David Enoch

Typical instances of "the moral argument" for theism start with some purported feature of morality—say, that it is objective, or that moral obligations give people reasons for actions, or perhaps that morality is *both* objective *and* reason-giving.[1] Proponents of this theistic argument then add the claim that the only or best explanation of that feature of morality involves the existence of a deity or perhaps a loving God or a specific religious set of doctrines. And the argument concludes that a God, or a loving God, or perhaps (for some, indeed for all the theist contributors to this volume)[2] a Christian God, exists. From now on I'll focus on the narrower claim that God is needed in this way to explain morality's objectivity.

I will offer reasons to reject this argument. But I want to start by noting my points of agreement with it. First, I accept the inference rule: the argument seems to be using the rule of inference often called "Inference to the Best Explanation,"[3] and I am fine with establishing serious ontological conclusions

1. The literature sometimes distinguishes between theoretical and practical versions of "the" moral argument; see, for instance, Robert M. Adams, "Moral Arguments for Theistic Belief," in *Rationality and Religious Belief*, ed. C. F. Delaney (University of Notre Dame Press, 1979); C. Stephen Evans and David Baggett, "Moral Arguments for the Existence of God," in *Stanford Encyclopedia of Philosophy*, last modified October 4, 2022, https://tinyurl.com/56h3w339. I here constrain myself to theoretical arguments. Practical ones are deeply suspicious in their own way, and a serious discussion of them will presumably require a discussion of transcendental arguments more generally (and probably of Kant).

2. The historical survey in Evans and Baggett, "Moral Arguments" is also entirely Christian.

3. This is very clear, for instance, in the survey of related arguments in Evans and Baggett, "Moral Arguments," and also in the very title of Adam Lloyd Johnson, ed., *A Debate on God and Morality: What Is the Best Account of Objective Moral Values and Duties?* (Routledge, 2021) and in his introduction to that volume. There are other kinds of moral arguments

about what propositions are true and about what kinds of things exist in the world by inference to the best explanation.

Second, I accept the argument's first premise, namely, that morality is objective. Now, this claim can be understood in more than one way, but the initial idea is familiar enough: there are, according to those who believe in morality's objectivity, moral facts. These facts may apply to you independently of your own judgments, preferences, projects, commitments, or opinions. Furthermore, their truth or validity does not constitutively depend on social practices or conventions. When successful in our moral inquiries, we discover these perfectly objective moral facts rather than create or construct them. When less successful, we may be wrong about these moral facts, just as we may be wrong about physical facts in our less successful scientific inquiries or about mathematical facts in our less successful mathematical inquiries. Now, because my main concern in this chapter is to challenge the moral argument for theism, and because I share a commitment to moral objectivity with those putting forward the argument, I can afford to just assume this here (if I'm wrong about this and morality is not after all objective, then the moral argument for theism fails independently of my criticisms below). So I don't need to *argue* for morality's objectivity here (I've done so extensively elsewhere).[4] Nevertheless, because rejecting morality's objectivity is Dan Barker's way of rejecting the moral argument, and because he raises some initial arguments against morality's objectivity, I briefly address them in an appendix at the end of this chapter.

My way of rejecting the moral argument for theism will consist, then, in rejecting its second premise. Morality's objectivity, and indeed, anything else that can sensibly be said of morality or within it, can easily be made sense of without assuming any theist thesis.

A final preliminary point: I neither assume nor argue for atheism here. Here I settle for arguing that one (kind of) argument *for theism* fails. For this reason, I will call my ways of explaining whatever it is that needs explaining

---

for theism, ones that do not seem to match the pattern described in the text and addressed throughout this paper perfectly. For a detailed discussion of Craig's somewhat different arguments, see Erik Wielenberg, *Robust Ethics: The Metaphysics and Epistemology of Godless Normative Realism* (Oxford University Press, 2014), chap. 2.

4. See David Enoch, *Taking Morality Seriously: A Defense of Robust Realism* (Oxford University Press, 2011), and, for a simpler text meant to convince the philosophically uninitiated that they are already committed to something like morality's objectivity, see my "Why I'm an Objectivist About Ethics (And Why You Are Too)," in *The Ethical Life*, 3rd ed., ed. Russ Shafer-Landau (Oxford University Press, 2014).

about morality *nontheistic explanations*. Such nontheistic explanations should be available, I think, to theists and atheists alike.

In the first section, I note that there is something initially surprising about the moral argument for theism, and that there are worries about its philosophical sincerity. In the following three sections I discuss different versions of the argument—one focusing on the metaphysical question of the source of morality, one focusing on the question how moral knowledge can be secured, and one focusing on moral motivation. A brief appendix follows where, to repeat, I briefly discuss Dan's claims against the objectivity of morality.

The Starting Point and Philosophical Sincerity

Let's start, however, elsewhere. So consider faith, or a religious life. It is, I think, a good question to ask whether faith or leading a religious life requires a belief in the existence of God. It is a good discussion to have, and interesting points have been raised on both sides of the debate. But, when it comes to *this* question, the theist response does seem to be the natural starting point. In a fairly commonsensical sense, religious faith *seems* to involve a belief in God, and leading a religious life (at least within the Abrahamic tradition) also *seems* to involve a belief in God. This doesn't settle the issue—as I said, it seems to me like a good discussion to have, and philosophers have been having it.[5] It's just that unless some fairly strong arguments convince us otherwise, we should stick to the appearances here—faith and leading a religious life appear to involve a belief in God.

I think that the contrast with morality, once put in this way, is clear. When I see a person humiliating another and think or say, "This is wrong," nothing about God (a loving deity or otherwise) seems to be involved, and this doesn't change when I insist that this is objectively wrong (in the sense that, say, such humiliation remains wrong regardless of what the relevant agent believes, the norms of the community, or any such thing). When we admire someone's moral character, there is perhaps a glimpse of the sublime, but nothing at all about God appears to be an immediate part of the picture. As before, this doesn't settle things here. The theist is still at liberty to argue that even though there is no sense in which God seems to be a part of the moral picture here (as

5. Such discussions engage issues, for instance, of whether leading a religious life, or some kinds of religious life, is more about participation in some practices than about belief. Perhaps faith is an attitude consistent with suspension of judgment about the existence of God; etc.

he does seem to be a part of faith or religious life), still upon reflection we find out that he is. This is a good discussion to have. But I believe that the difference between the case of morality and the case of (for instance) faith cannot plausibly be denied. Whereas in the case of faith or leading a religious life, those who deny a necessary commitment to the existence of God have their work cut out for them, in the case of morality the situation is reversed. Surely the starting point is that nothing here is about God, unless those supporting the moral argument can offer convincing arguments to the contrary.[6]

The significance of this point is enhanced by the following one. Some philosophical arguments are *sincere*, in the sense that they put in plain view not just a clever argument attempting to establish its conclusion but also the underlying motivations—the reasons not just for believing that the conclusion is true but also for caring whether it's true or not.[7] When an argument is sincere in this sense, if it's shown to fail, the one putting it forward will be happy with taking back their commitment to its conclusion (after all, a main motivation that made them care about the conclusion is no longer there, once the sincere argument has collapsed). With other arguments, this need not be so. If the argument one offers in support of a conclusion is not very closely related to the reasons they have to care about the conclusion and the argument collapses, a natural response is not to give up on the conclusion but rather seek alternative arguments for that conclusion. After all, the now-discarded argument was not why they cared about the conclusion to begin with! Think about how lawyers representing a client argue their case. If a specific argument fails, they can't afford to be convinced and give up on the client's case. Rather, they seek alternative arguments that will benefit their client.

Using this distinction, then, I want to make two points. First, my impression is that for almost all theists offering a version of the moral argument for theism, the argument is not sincere in the above sense. If I manage to show, by the end of this chapter, that no version of the moral argument works, I do not foresee adherents of Robert Adams (say) or Adam Lloyd Johnson becoming

6. Some theists, and some supporting the moral argument for theism, emphasize the significance of love and claim that God is a necessary part of love (or perhaps of some special kind of love). The point in the text here applies in an especially clear way to such a move. While I remain officially open-minded about what a deeper discussion of love will reveal, surely the starting point is that nothing about God seems immediately relevant to any kind of love I can think of (except, perhaps, the love of God).

7. I characterize some, but not all, arguments for moral realism in this way in *Taking Morality Seriously*, 9–10.

agnostics. Instead, they will come to rely on *other* arguments for their theism, ones in this book or yet other ones.[8]

Second, I want to insist that despite the fact that failing to be sincere in this sense does not necessarily make a philosophical argument flawed,[9] there is nevertheless something to be said for this kind of sincerity. At least usually, a philosophical discussion is better facilitated, and progress in understanding and knowledge are better achieved, when the underlying concerns are placed in plain view. Philosophers, after all, are typically not lawyers.[10]

The discussion in this section—of what the starting point is for the moral argument and whether it is sincere—is related also to a common desideratum of arguments: they should be rationally able to convince someone who is, initially, on the fence regarding their conclusion. Forget then, at least for now, committed theists and committed atheists. Do you think the moral argument has the rational force to convince an agnostic? Does the argument genuinely give someone who's on the fence regarding God a reason to convert to some version of theism? It seems to me that the argument much more often serves intellectually to weaponize already-committed theists. But this, though not insignificant, is not enough for a full vindication of the argument.

The points in this section cannot replace a critical discussion of the moral argument itself, and it is to such a discussion that I turn next. But they suffice, I think, to raise serious suspicions about its force.

What's the Source of Morality?

The question is sometimes asked what the *source* of morality is. Where it comes from, as it were. Now, for those who are happy to give up on morality's objectivity, answers come easy. Perhaps morality is best understood as a set of social conventions. If so, the source of morality is presumably society or its conventions. Perhaps morality is entirely in some imprecise sense, subjective, such that when it comes to you, *you* are the source of morality (but when it comes to me, *I* am). If morality is objective, though, such answers are out the window. And so, the thought seems to be that if morality is objective, its

8. It is an interesting question whether Kant's argument for the existence of God (as a postulate of practical reason) is sincere in this sense.

9. After all, if the moral argument works, it establishes or at least supports its theist conclusion. Furthermore, one may believe a conclusion on the combined strength of several independent arguments, none of which is sufficient on its own to carry the weight of conviction.

10. Well, I am, sort of. But I'm not wearing my lawyering hat while philosophizing.

source must be objective as well. It must be a source that in no way depends on or derives from the contingencies of the conscience of specific people, the conventions of a specific society, or the norms of a specific community. It is at this point that God may be helpful. It seems that the only source that is consistent with morality's objectivity and can explain it is the will of a necessary, perhaps loving, perhaps necessarily good being.[11]

The problem with this argument is that it presupposes that morality is the kind of thing that *has* and indeed *must have* a source. When someone asks, "Where does morality come from?" she presupposes that there must be some place such that morality comes from *it*. Perhaps this geographical way of putting things should not be literally understood. Okay then, but it must be understood *somehow*, and in whatever way in which it is understood, I deny it. Morality need not have a source. It doesn't come from anywhere, and so the whole argument rests on a false presupposition.

One at least plausible way of filling in a nontheistic version of moral realism and objectivity is stating that moral truths (or anyway, the most fundamental ones) are necessary. They have always been true, and they will always be true. They may not be *accepted* or *believed* or *popular* or *consensual* across all times and places, but they are nonetheless *true* across all times and places and, indeed, across all possible worlds. Now, you may be worried about such a view of morality, and this is not the place to allay such worries. The point here is just that on this picture (assuming it is at least a live option in metaethics) there's no sense to be made of the thought that morality has a source. The duty not to humiliate people, on this picture, is not more "source apt" than the number eight or the empty set.[12] The fact that, other things being equal, a life that contains close, loving relationships is better than a life that doesn't have such things is not more in need of a source than the fact that there are no

11. Though problems lie in this direction as well. It's not entirely clear how God can be relevant morally, unless there's a God-independent, prior reason (to do as God says, for instance). There may be ways around this problem, but I just want to note that nothing here is simple, not even the claim that God, *if he exists*, can help here. For discussion of this point from Cudworth in our context, see Wielenberg, *Robust Ethics*, 53. For discussion of this problem in a much wider metaethical context, see Mark Schroeder, "Cudworth and Normative Explanations," *Journal of Ethics and Social Philosophy* 1, no. 3 (2005): 1–28, https://doi.org/10.26556/jesp.v1i3.15; Chris Heathwood, "Could Morality Have a Source?," *Journal of Ethics and Social Philosophy* 6, no. 2 (2012): 1–19, https://doi.org/10.26556/jesp.v6i2.62. For doubts about God as an explanation of goodness, see Michael Huemer, "Groundless Morals," in *A Debate on God and Morality: What Is the Best Account of Objective Moral Values and Duties?*, ed. Adam Lloyd Johnson (Routledge, 2021), 150–54.

12. Huemer, "Groundless Morals," 156 uses similar examples.

true contradictions, or that it's irrational to form beliefs by wishful thinking, or that there is no largest prime.[13]

Once this presupposition that morality has a source (even if merely metaphorically) is made explicit and is then explicitly doubted, it becomes entirely unclear, I submit, what seemed plausible about it to begin with. Why is it that many people—including, it seems, some philosophers[14]—find it natural to ask, "Where does morality come from?" or "What is the source of moral obligations?" but not, "Where does logic come from?" or "What is the source of the empty set?"

I conjecture that the explanation has to do with the special role of *obligations* or of *ought judgments* in morality. Perhaps other things, including other moral things (like the value of intimate relationships) need not have a source. But duties, obligations, and facts about what we genuinely ought to do[15]—all of these must have a source. *Laws* have *legislators.*[16] *Duties* originate from *authorities.* Absolute, objective, unqualified "ought judgments" must have a source, someone or something issuing them, the thought seems to be. The number eight, the empty set, the fact that there is no largest prime, even the fact that intimate relationships make a life go better—all these are not about duties, obligations, or absolute oughts. Hence the difference.[17]

13. Note that the point in this paragraph is *not* that necessary propositions and facts do not allow for explanations thereof. Some do. The point is just that the *source* metaphor remains entirely unclear and unsupported when applied to such necessary truths.

14. And not only theists. See, for instance, Christine Marion Korsgaard, *The Sources of Normativity*, ed. Onora O'Neill (Cambridge University Press, 1996); John Bengson, Terence Cuneo, and Russ Shafer-Landau, "The Source of Normativity," *Mind* 132, no. 527 (2023): 706–29, https://doi.org/10.1093/mind/fzac063. But of course, for each such case it's an open question whether the word "source" is used with the same meaning as that invoked by theists. For Bengson and his coauthors, for instance, the initial question seems similar, but by the time they give their answer, it seems clear that they invoke a different source metaphor from the one needed for the moral argument for theism.

15. Not just what we ought to do according to the law, some convention, etiquette, university rules, or the rules of chess—what we genuinely, unqualifiedly ought to do.

16. Or so we are often told in contexts of discussions of the moral argument—in fact, much more often in such contexts than in contexts in the philosophy of law. But I digress. In the history of ethics, an influential employment of this idea (not en route to theist conclusions) is G. E. M. Anscombe's "Modern Moral Philosophy," *Philosophy* 33, no. 124 (1958): 1–19, https://doi.org/10.1017/s0031819100037943.

17. Robert Adams's version of the moral argument is clear and explicit on starting just from moral obligations. He seems perfectly comfortable talking about sourceless reasons and values. See, for instance, Robert M. Adams, "Divine Commands and the Social Nature of Obligation," *Faith and Philosophy* 4, no. 3 (1987): 262–75, https://doi.org/10.5840

Upon reflection, though, it becomes clear that this thought that obligations or duties require a lawgiver or an authority or a source is an unsupported dogma. True, in some normative systems this is clearly the case (say, valid military commands must be issued by authoritative military commanders). In other systems, it may be the case, though things are not that clear (need all law be posited by a legislator?).[18] And in yet others, the thought that obligations require a lawgiver or an authority is clearly false (you ought not to form beliefs in wishful thinking, and this objective ought has no source, and all is well). So no reason has yet been given to think that morality (or the duty-related parts of it) must have a source.[19] And given the plausibility of the thought that morality is objective, the thought that morality has a source becomes less plausible still. Perhaps the theist may insist that there's something special about *morality*, or indeed specifically *moral* obligations, that explains why moral obligations require a lawgiver, even if some other obligations do not. But it's hard to see how the details here can be filled in while maintaining any plausibility to the initial thought that obligations require a lawgiver.

So sure: accepting morality's objectivity requires accepting absolutely objective and unqualified obligations or oughts. But these can be fully accommodated within a sourceless framework. This means that they can be (for anything thus far said) fully accommodated within a nontheistic metaethics.

Knowledge

Perhaps, though, the best version of a moral argument for theism starts not with a metaphysical thesis about morality or some parts of it having a source but with an epistemological one. The commonsensical starting point is not just, say, that we often have all sorts of moral obligations. Rather, it's also that we often *know* that we do. And this knowledge, too, has to be explained.

/faithphil19874343. I am not sure that this discrimination (obligations must have a source, values and reasons need not) can be sufficiently convincingly motivated, but I cannot discuss this further here.

18. I cannot, of course, enter this discussion here. For my own doubts about this debate, see David Enoch, "Is General Jurisprudence Interesting?," in *Dimensions of Normativity: New Essays on Metaethics and Jurisprudence*, ed. David Plunkett, Scott Shapiro, and Kevin Toh (Oxford University Press, 2019).

19. Adams, "Divine Commands," 262–75, gives reasons, in terms of moral duties being necessarily reason-giving and motivating. But this part of his discussion for the most part seems to rest on conflating motivation and normativity. Of course, I do not pretend to do full justice to Adams's work here.

If God plays a crucial role in how it is that we have moral knowledge, that may embarrass the nontheist realist. She can still maintain, under such a scenario, her metaphysical commitment to moral realism, but only at the price of moral skepticism. And perfectly objective yet entirely unknowable (and more generally, epistemically inaccessible) moral facts seem like a small comfort indeed.[20]

Now, in pursuing an epistemic version of the moral argument, what theists write sometimes sounds as if they are siding with moral skeptics or antirealists.[21] But this can't be what they're doing, of course, for they are as far from moral skepticism or antirealism as anyone is. Theist discussions (for instance, of evolutionary debunking arguments, of which more below) must be read as *reductio* arguments of nontheist moral realism: *Assuming* nontheistic realism, the thought seems to be, there is no way of avoiding moral skepticism. The theist herself does have an epistemic way out, she thinks, but it's not one available to the nontheist.

What is, exactly, the epistemic challenge purportedly facing the nontheist realist? As you might expect, there are different answers to this question. And the answer will depend on the *kind* of realism being discussed. For instance, we can expect that there will be important differences here, both in terms of the nature of the relevant epistemic challenges as well as in terms of the ways of coping with them, between naturalist realists—roughly those who think that moral facts are on a par with other natural facts that can, in principle, be studied by the natural sciences—and non-naturalist or *robust* realists. I will focus here on the latter, both because the epistemic challenges facing robust realists seem to be altogether different and more threatening than those facing naturalists, and because, well, I'm a robust metaethical realist.

When theists present the epistemic challenge—the one they think they are better placed to cope with compared to nontheistic robust realists—they sometimes put things in terms of some necessary condition for knowledge (like Linville's "Dependence Thesis") or in terms of the need for some "assurance" that our initial moral intuitions or responses are not too badly offtrack.[22] But these are not the most productive ways of putting the challenge, partly because any purported necessary condition for knowledge (including something about

20. Adams, "Moral Arguments," seems to suggest that the main advantage of divine command theory over (what I'm here calling) nontheist moral realism is epistemic.

21. Most of Mark Linville's relevant discussion, for instance, may be read in this way. See Linville, "The Moral Argument," in *The Blackwell Companion to Natural Theology*, ed. William Lane Craig and J. P. Moreland (Wiley-Blackwell, 2009).

22. See Linville, "Moral Argument," 404, 407.

"assurance") is bound to be controversial on purely epistemological grounds irrespective of metaethics. A more promising way of putting the challenge—one that is more theory neutral and so harder for the moral realist to avoid—is as follows.[23]

Suppose you have one hundred beliefs about some topic. Suppose further that each of these beliefs is independently initially justified. Then you find out from an independent, highly reliable source that about half of those beliefs are false, but they don't give you further information about which beliefs are the false ones. Now, having found that out, it seems clear that you lost whatever justification you may have had for these beliefs. You should now suspend judgment about all of them. The information you received—that there's no correlation between your beliefs on the relevant topic and the relevant truths—undercuts whatever justification you may have had for those beliefs. Similarly, whatever initial justification you may have for your moral beliefs, if new information comes in that shows that there's no correlation between your moral beliefs and the moral truths, this will serve as an undercutting defeater of your justification for holding them. This is the first input needed for the argument.

The second is about how we typically explain correlations. Often, when two factors are correlated, we seek an explanation of one of them in terms of the other. Perhaps the first factor is causally responsible for the second, or perhaps it's the other way around. Or perhaps one of the factors is *constitutively* responsible for the other. But we seem to (justifiably!) frown upon *brute* correlations, that is, ones that are unexplained, and even more so about those that seem in principle unexplain*able*. For instance: if we toss two coins, each ten times, and receive the exact same heads-tails sequence for both coins, we are strongly inclined to believe that *something* explains this correlation. Indeed, if we wonder whether two factors are correlated, and we have reason to believe that if they are this correlation will be unexplainable, we think of this as a reason to think that they are not after all correlated. Thus, if you don't yet know whether the heads-tails sequences of the two coins are identical, but you suspect that if it were there would be no way to explain the correlation, you'd presumably take that as a reason to believe that the two sequences are

23. I argue that this is the best reading of the epistemic challenge to realism—following similar claims by Field regarding mathematical Platonism—in David Enoch, "The Epistemological Challenge to Metanormative Realism: How Best to Understand It, and How to Cope with It," *Philosophical Studies* 148 (2010): 413–38, https://doi.org/10.1007/s11098-009-9333-6 and then in chapter 7 of *Taking Morality Seriously*. The discussion that follows is based on those texts.

not identical. This is the second part needed for the argument. We can now put the two parts together and see how they give rise to a powerful epistemic challenge to robust realism.

On robust realism (at least the version of it I consider here), moral facts are abstract and causally inert. This follows from this kind of realism being robust or nonnaturalist. Moral facts are also radically independent of us; they do not constitutively depend on our responses, attitudes, preferences, or beliefs about them. This follows from the moral facts being objective, which is surely a central tenet of robust realism and, anyway, one that we are assuming throughout this chapter. But this means that if there is a correlation between the moral facts and our moral beliefs, it will not be explainable in the standard ways in which we explain correlations. The moral facts can't be causally or constitutively responsible for our moral beliefs, because the moral facts are (on robust realism) abstract. And our moral beliefs cannot be causally or constitutively responsible for the moral facts, because of the objectivity requirement. If there is a correlation, then, between the moral facts and our moral beliefs, it will be unexplainable. But this, as we've just noticed, is a reason to think that there is no such correlation (as observed in the second part of the argument above). And if we've now come to learn that the moral facts and our moral beliefs are not correlated, this undercuts whatever justification we may have had for our moral beliefs (this was the first part of the argument above). So on robust realism, we lose justification for all our moral beliefs. Robust realism leads to moral skepticism. The challenge for the robust, nontheist moral realist, of course, is to resist this implication.

Notice that this understanding of the challenge does not deny the initial justification of our moral beliefs. Helpfully, it concedes to the robust realist (for the sake of argument, at least) that our moral beliefs can be initially justified without even challenging the realist to say how. So the realist can help himself to talk of reflective equilibrium, perhaps, or of relying on initially justifying moral intuitions or whatever, really. The challenge, rather, attempts to present an *undercutting defeater* of the initial justification of our moral beliefs.[24] Even

24. Linville, "Moral Argument," 397–98, also presents the challenge as primarily about an undercutting defeater. Actually, the question whether the challenge is about an *undercutting* defeater or an *outweighing* defeater is delicate, and it may be a bit of both. Things depend here on a level of details I can't go into in this chapter. If the information about the unexplainability of the relevant (purported) correlation is seen as a reason to believe the negation of the relevant propositions, or even just directly to reduce one's confidence in them, then it's an outweighing defeater. If the story is told in such a way that the unexplainability of the correlation threatens directly not the truth of the relevant propositions but merely the

if those beliefs were perfectly justified initially, once the information comes in about the unexplainability of a (purported) correlation between the moral facts and our moral beliefs, all such justification is lost.

Over the last two decades, *evolutionary debunking arguments* have become the focus of much philosophical attention.[25] Such arguments make essential use of an evolutionary premise, according to which (roughly) our moral faculties were shaped by evolutionary forces. The argument highlights that it's one thing for a moral belief to be *true* (according to the robust realist, as a matter of necessity independently of us), and quite another for it to be survival and reproduction conducive. Indeed, there doesn't seem to be a reason to think that beliefs shaped by evolutionary pressures—pushing in survival- and reproduction-conducive ways—will hit upon the independent moral truths. If so, there's a disconnect between the set of moral beliefs likely to have evolved under the pressures of natural selection and the set of *true* moral beliefs. The argument concludes, yet again, that (nontheistic) moral realism leads to moral skepticism. There are interesting questions to ask specifically about the relevance of the evolutionary considerations here.[26] However, we don't really need to bother with them here. For robust, nonnaturalist realists, the details of whatever does causally explain our moral faculties are really beside the point, as long as it is acknowledged (as I do here) that *there is some* such causal explanation of our moral faculties. The general worry about the need to explain the correlation between the moral facts and our moral beliefs arises irrespectively of the details of that causal story, evolutionary or otherwise.

This, as you can see, is a general challenge to robust realism. How is it supposed, though, to present an argumentative advantage for *theistic* moral realism over nontheistic realism? The thought seems to be that the theist has an easy explanation available to her of the correlation between the moral facts and our moral beliefs. If we can help ourselves to the existence of God—perhaps also to some of his features, like the kind of lives he wants or plans for us, or

support for belief in them (say, in terms of the reliability of our moral intuitions), then it's an undercutting defeater. Nothing in the discussion in the text depends on this distinction.

25. See, for instance, Sharon Street, "A Darwinian Dilemma for Realist Theories of Value," *Philosophical Studies* 127, no. 1 (2006): 109–66, https://doi.org/10.1007/s11098-005-1726-6; Katia Vavova, "Evolutionary Debunking of Moral Realism," *Philosophy Compass* 10, no. 2 (2015): 104–16, https://doi.org/10.1111/phc3.12194.

26. For some scientifically informed discussion of the details of such arguments, see Arnon Levy and Yair Levy, "Evolutionary Debunking Arguments Meet Evolutionary Science," *Philosophy and Phenomenological Research* 100, no. 3 (2020): 491–509, https://doi.org/10.1111/phpr.12554.

the kind of relationship he intends to have with us—then presumably he can make sure that our moral intuitions, initial judgments, or moral faculties (that then play a role in generating and revising our moral beliefs) are sufficiently in line with the moral facts.[27] For the theist, then, a correlation between the moral facts and our moral beliefs is not after all unexplainable. For the nontheist, no such explanatory route is possible, and so the nontheist robust realist is saddled with the skeptical conclusion. This, of course—together with the implausibility of moral skepticism—is a strong reason to prefer theist over nontheist realism. Indeed, it is also, the thought seems to be, a powerful argument for the existence of God: if robust realism is highly plausible, and moral skepticism is highly implausible, and if theism better accommodates this combination of views than any nontheist realism does, this is a reason to believe theism.[28]

All of this changes, though, if the nontheist robust realist *can* explain the correlation between the moral facts and moral beliefs. So the challenge really is a *challenge*, not a *refutation* or any such thing. If the realist can step up to this challenge and offer a plausible explanation of the correlation between the moral facts and our moral beliefs—an explanation simultaneously compatible with the abstractness of the moral facts, their objectivity, and atheism—the theist doesn't get his or her explanatory advantage here, and then the epistemic version of the moral argument for theism fails.

And indeed, robust realists have been suggesting such explanations. The most promising strategy for such an explanation is what has come to be called *third-factor explanations*.[29] True, often we explain correlations between two factors by explanations from one of the factors to the other. But this, many robust realists emphasize, is not *the only* way of explaining such correlations. Another option is to invoke some *third* factor that explains both correlated factors. What explains, for instance, the correlation between my phone indicating that the time is 7:54 and my laptop indicating that the time is 7:54, and similarly for many other time-readings? Presumably, what does this explanatory work is not some causal (or other) relation from the phone to the laptop or from the laptop to the phone, but rather something else entirely that causally regulates both the reading on the phone and the reading on the laptop. Perhaps, then, while those putting forward the epistemic challenge to robust realism

27. See, for instance, Linville, "Moral Argument," 414.

28. It seems clear that at the end of the day—after going through a lot of other stuff—the challenge Linville lands on is the one in the text.

29. See Vavova, "Evolutionary Debunking," 110–11, and the references there. I believe that the term first appears in Enoch, "Epistemological Challenge," 30.

are right that explanations of correlation that go from the moral facts to the moral beliefs or vice versa are unavailable to the realist, still this doesn't show that a third-factor explanation is not available.[30]

It's one thing to insist on the possibility of a third-factor explanation strategy, but quite another to actually make good on this promise by filling in the details. And different robust realists have attempted different ways of filling in the details. Perhaps, for instance, the very same (evolutionarily developed) cognitive abilities that guarantee that we have rights also guarantee that we can recognize that we do, and this is the third factor that ends up explaining the correlation between our moral beliefs and the moral facts.[31] Or perhaps, to take another example, something about pain is crucially tied both to survival and reproductive success (it's not far-fetched to think that creatures who have not been very good at recognizing and responding to pain are no longer with us) and to our moral beliefs (because pain is recognizably bad by those feeling it).[32] Or perhaps the fact that the evolutionary "aim" (survival, reproductive success, something along these lines) is also of value ensures an initial correlation between our moral beliefs (formed by mechanisms at least partly shaped by evolutionary pressures) and the moral facts, an initial correlation that can then be improved upon by the employment of reasoning mechanisms that evolutionary forces have probably selected for their reliability in other, not necessarily moral contexts.[33] And yet other plausible third-factor stories may be told here by the nontheist robust realists.

True, none of this is either obvious or uncontroversial. Objections have been raised both to the details of specific third-factor explanations and to the strategy as a whole.[34] The important lesson, though, and one that is consis-

30. It's an interesting question whether the theist explanation of the correlation itself counts as a third-factor explanation. Whether this is so will depend, I think, on the specific theological details of the suggested explanations. On some such stories, God presumably preestablishes a harmony between the moral facts and our moral beliefs. If so, this would be a third-factor explanation. On other possible stories, God observes the moral truths and proceeds to shape our moral beliefs accordingly. If so, this is not a third-factor explanation, but rather one that proceeds from the moral facts to our moral beliefs.

31. Erik Wielenberg, "On the Evolutionary Debunking of Morality," *Ethics* 120, no. 3 (2010): 441–64, https://doi.org/10.1086/652292.

32. Knut Olav Skarsaune, "Darwin and Moral Realism: Survival of the Iffiest," *Philosophical Studies* 152, no. 2 (2011): 229–43, https://doi.org/10.1007/s11098-009-9473-8.

33. This is my preferred line. Again, see Enoch, "Epistemological Challenge"; Enoch, *Taking Morality Seriously*.

34. See the survey and the references in Vavova, "Evolutionary Debunking." Especially significant is the criticism that there is something question-begging about the robust realist

tent with things being complex here, is that the kind of epistemic challenge presented to the nontheist robust realist is not remotely conclusive. The jury on the plausibility of (some) third-factor explanations as a way of facing up to this challenge is still very much out.

Before concluding the discussion of the epistemic version of the moral argument, let me make the following two points. First, with any third-factor explanation some feeling of contingency lingers. Perhaps, if the explanation succeeds, our moral judgments are not too far from the moral facts. But they *could have been*. The relation between whatever (probably evolutionary) forces causally regulate our moral beliefs, on one side, and the moral facts, on the other, seems contingent. Perhaps in the real world they nicely align, but isn't it sufficiently problematic that they may not have?[35] I see the worry—certainly on such a picture the success of our moral inquiries is on less firm a ground than they may be thought to be on some other pictures (including perhaps a theist one, but see the next paragraph). But I don't think that this is a problem. The thought that had we developed very differently, many of our beliefs, moral and otherwise, would have been false seems to me like a welcome instance of epistemic modesty. In fact, I'd be suspicious of any story that implied we are bound, and have always been bound, to get things roughly right, or even that it has always been guaranteed that we would have the ability to get things right. Getting our moral beliefs right is an *achievement* that requires, like most achievements, both an effort on our part and for the conditions we find ourselves in not to be too hostile.

Second, recall that the theist game here is a *comparative and explanatory* game. The claim is that the correlation between the moral facts and our moral beliefs, which can only be denied at the price of unpalatable moral skepticism, is better explained by a theist story than by all nontheist ones. But then merely

---

relying, in offering a third-factor explanation, on moral premises (e.g., that pain is bad, that we have rights, or that survival is good). I think that this objection raises intricate dialectical issues—about, for instance, how the fallacy of begging the question is best understood—but that at the end of the day the realist has an adequate response to it. But I can't get into the details here.

35. You may think that this alone—that even though our moral beliefs are by and large true, they could have failed to be—suffices to undermine moral knowledge. But this would be too quick. First, it's entirely not obvious that such a condition—often referred to in the literature as a *safety* condition—is necessary for knowledge. Second, the condition is often put in terms not of whether or not a mistake would be possible, but whether or not a mistake would be *easily* possible. And even if the details about the evolutionary forces that causally regulate our moral beliefs are contingent, it's probably false that they could have *easily* been very different than they actually are.

pointing out some shortcoming in nontheist stories cannot suffice. For explanations are evaluated, here as everywhere else, both *holistically* and *comparatively*. The question to ask is whether, overall, the relevant nontheist epistemological story is better or worse than relevant theist alternatives. And while the answer will no doubt depend on the shortcomings of the nontheist stories, it will also depend on their advantages as well as on the relative advantages and disadvantages of the theist alternatives. I like thinking about this in terms of the metaphor of plausibility points: theories gain or lose plausibility points in virtue of their explanatory and theoretical advantages and disadvantages, and at the end of the day we should go for the theory whose plausibility score is highest. So it's quite possible for a theory to lose plausibility points compared to its alternatives locally on some specific issue and yet emerge overall victorious because of its many other advantages. What this means, specifically, for the discussion of the epistemic version of the moral argument is that we need to be careful about evaluating the relevant theist story as well, not just in terms of how well it does in explaining the correlation between the moral facts and our moral beliefs but *overall*. And here, of course, familiar troubles raise their heads as well. If, for instance, invoking a god raises more explanatory puzzles than it solves, and if troubling questions about the relation between such a god and the moral truths resurface, then all of this goes into the comparative evaluation of theist and nontheist epistemological stories. So it's quite possible that the nontheist story sketched above is not ideal, but it's still overall much more plausible than any available theist story.

Let me give two examples that emphasize this point. First, Sharon Street has recently argued, employing a new version of the problem of evil, that the price of *theism* is moral skepticism.[36] Street's basic idea is that if all we see around us in the world is consistent with the existence of an all-powerful and all-good God, then our moral and evaluative intuitions must be widely off (after all, a lot of what's going on sure *seems* to us terrible). Theism, on Street's view, entails a wide-ranging skepticism about our moral faculties and intuitions. Now, Street may be wrong about this (I am not convinced by all the details in her discussion, but I am nonetheless convinced she has an important point

36. See Sharon Street, "If Everything Happens for a Reason, Then We Don't Know What Reasons Are: Why the Price of Theism Is Normative Skepticism," in *Challenges to Religious and Moral Belief: Disagreement and Evolution*, ed. Michael Bergmann and Patrick Kain (Oxford University Press, 2018). There is something ironic about this—Street, after all, is one of the most influential writers developing evolutionary debunking arguments against moral realism, arguments that many theists like to use as a part of their (epistemic) moral argument for theism.

there). But unless her argument there can be shown to fail, clearly theism loses quite a few plausibility points here. In such a case, even if you're not entirely happy with a third-factor explanation of the kind sketched above, it may still be the best explanatory option out there.[37]

Second, some theists rely in telling their moral epistemology story not just on theism, but on a very specific version thereof—indeed, on highly specific theological doctrines, (e.g., of a loving God or even of Trinitarianism).[38] But if your moral epistemology story relies on such a specific religious doctrine, it is even more vulnerable—any reason to doubt *that specific* religious doctrine is simultaneously a reason to reject your moral epistemology story (and to prefer alternative stories, including the robust realist one). Even other theists, those who reject the specific religious doctrines you are relying on, may now have reason to prefer overall the nontheist robust realist story over your (specific) theist one.

To conclude the discussion of the epistemic version of the moral argument for theism, then, the nontheist robust realist has quite a lot to say epistemically, and it's not clear that she is even in initial trouble here. Even if she is in some initial trouble, though, if she loses some plausibility points, once it is noticed that the game being played here is explanatory (and so also holistic and comparative), it is very hard to see the argument as supplying theism with significant support.

Motivation

Sometimes theists seem to argue that God is necessary not only to give morality a metaphysical foundation or to secure our epistemic access to morality but also to secure for morality the right kind of *motivational force*. People, imperfect as we are, will not be motivated by moral considerations unless there

37. A related point—for which I thank Erik Wielenberg—is the following. Nontheist realists are accused of not being able to explain the purported correlation between our moral beliefs and the truths. Theists can presumably do better on this front. But perhaps they can do *too* well? On theism, or at least on some theist stories, shouldn't we expect a *much stronger* correlation between our moral beliefs and the moral truths than the correlation we do seem to see? Shouldn't we expect moral mistakes to be much rarer?

I'm not saying that there's nothing theists can say by way of reply. All I'm saying is that, first, they *must* say something, and second, once they do, the details of their reply should be factored into the holistic comparative plausibility-point evaluation.

38. See Adams, "Moral Arguments"; Adam Lloyd Johnson, *Divine Love Theory: How the Trinity Is the Source and Foundation of Morality* (Kregel Academic, 2023).

is a God, or perhaps unless they believe in God or are in some interaction with such a deity.

Now, I think that there are interesting questions to ask about moral motivation.[39] But I don't think a motivational version of the moral argument for theism has any strength at all. Here's why.

Talk of motivational force should be disambiguated. Is the claim that without a role for God people can't be *guaranteed* to act morally? Or that they can't even be *able* to act morally? Or that they are *unlikely* to? Or that they are unlikely to, *if they're rational*? Such disambiguation is important, because while all of these claims fail, they fail for different reasons.

True, without God people can't be guaranteed to act morally. But nor can they be guaranteed to act morally *with* God's involvement. And this shows that supplying such a guarantee is not a legitimate requirement from a metaethical theory.[40]

True, if it would have been *impossible* for people to be motivated to act morally without a role for God, then this would have been a problem and perhaps even a (initial or defeasible) reason to believe in God. But what reason is there to believe moral motivation would indeed have been impossible in the absence of (belief in) God? Sometimes I help people simply because they need help. I'm sure you do so as well. Is there anything insufficient by way of motivation here, unless we bring God in? It would be a very weird view of human action and motivation (and an extremely depressing one) to think that the mere fact that someone needs help never suffices, indeed *cannot* suffice, for the motivation to help them, unless one also, say, anticipates divine credit for so doing. I don't see what could possibly support such a view. Nor does there seem to be any irrationality involved in helping someone simply because they need help. So the claim that one can't be *rationally* morally motivated without some role for God is also entirely unconvincing.

Is moral motivation *more likely* assuming God? I'm not sure it would matter if the answer were "Yes," but anyway, I don't see a reason to believe that the answer *is* "Yes." Look around you and tell me how impressed you are with the moral motivation of theists compared to that of atheists. And no cheating, please! You don't get to discount a theist simply in virtue of their bad behavior ("Ah, he's not a *true* Jew or Christian, because a true believer doesn't act

39. I address them in chapter 9 of Enoch, *Taking Morality Seriously*.

40. "Whoever thought that philosophy could replace the hangman?" asks David Lewis in "Desire as Belief II," in *Papers in Ethics and Social Philosophy* (Cambridge University Press, 2000), 60.

this way!"),[41] or even in virtue of their being *different* theists than you. The historical record of theists, it seems to me, is complicated, varied, and overall highly problematic (as is the historical record of atheists). I don't see how a claim about moral motivation being likelier on theism can be supported.[42]

But without a God, there is no guarantee (is there?) that moral considerations and self-interested ones will converge, not even in the longest term. A divine reward-and-punishment mechanism guarantees such convergence. Without it, aren't we sometimes left with an unbridgeable gap between what we ought to do and what would be in our best interest to do? And wouldn't this be a problem? Of course it would, but it would be a *political* one, not a metaethical one. Our self-interest and morality do not always converge. Recognizing this fact is a part of growing up. Facing it is often a moral challenge. And designing institutions that deal with it appropriately is a main task for political philosophy. It is not an advantage of a metaethical theory that it makes us ignore these challenges.

As is usual, there's much more to say. Perhaps there are other ways of understanding the claim about motivation. Perhaps, for instance, there's a special kind of moral motivation that, one may argue, doesn't make sense without a role for God.[43] But the overall picture, it seems to me, is clear: we *can*, at least most of the time, respond well with our motivations and actions to morality's demands. We are never guaranteed to do so. Both these claims are as true on atheism as they are on theism. Beyond that, it's *on you* whether you are sufficiently well morally motivated. So get to work.

Appendix: Dan Barker Against Objectivity

My way of rejecting the moral argument for theism, then, is to show how everything that it is sensible to say of and within morality—including, of course, that it is objective—can easily be accommodated by nontheistic explanations. An alternative way of rejecting the moral argument, though (or anyway, its instance that starts from morality's objectivity), is to reject precisely that starting

41. For instance, check out Wikipedia, "No True Scotsman," last modified March 28, 2025, 21:08 (UTC), https://en.wikipedia.org/wiki/No_true_Scotsman.

42. For a much more intricate discussion of the empirical evidence and for many references, see Wielenberg, *Robust Ethics*, 61–66.

43. The example of being motivated to help someone simply because they need help is an example of what is sometimes called *de re* moral motivation. Perhaps the claim is that another *de dicto* moral motivation only makes sense assuming a role for God. I think that this claim, too, is entirely implausible, but let me note that it may need further discussion.

point. If morality is not objective, then, of course, nothing by way of its purported objectivity has to be explained, and the argument collapses.[44]

This is Dan's way of rejecting the moral argument for theism, and in this appendix I briefly explain why I find what he says in this context unconvincing. This appendix also supports the claims made in the rest of this chapter, for as will be apparent, in responding to Dan's claims and defending morality's objectivity, nowhere will I be invoking God. This appendix too, then, is nontheistic.

Dan believes that "objective moral values" is an oxymoron, as values are a function of the brain. I respond: "values" is a multiply ambiguous term. When you value something, this valuing is (arguably) something that goes on in your brain.[45] In this sense, perhaps also *your values* are a function of what goes on in your brain, of what you value. But it in no way follows from these observations that the fact that something—say, compassion or happiness or, negatively, suffering—is *of value* is a function of the brain. To assume that this is so is to assume, of course, that values, in this sense, are not objective. And to make such an assumption in an attempt to *argue* against the objectivity of morality would be a blatant case of the fallacy of begging the question.

This may be ironic, because Dan accuses the defenders of moral objectivity of begging the question. But whether this is so depends on what arguments, if any, they bring forward to defend morality's objectivity. And though I haven't specified such arguments here, the literature does contain such arguments.[46] These arguments may fail, but this will have to be shown piecemeal, and I don't think Dan has even attempted to do so.

At times, Dan insists that morality comes down to just the intention to act with the minimal amount of harm in the real world. That, Dan seems to think, is just what we *mean* by morality. The first thing to note about this suggestion is that according to it, morality is perfectly objective after all. If morality comes down to the intention to act with the minimal amount of harm in the real world, then moral facts are just as objective as facts about harm and the

44. Perhaps it remains to be explained why many claim morality *seems* objective, but presumably this can be explained by doing psychology, sociology, political science, and evolutionary theory and the like. God is arguably not needed for these explanations (and whether he is depends on other arguments for and against theism, not the moral argument).

45. I'm going to leave the psycho-physical problem and related issues for another occasion, obviously.

46. For instance, Michael Huemer, *Ethical Intuitionism* (Palgrave Macmillan, 2005); Russ Shafer-Landau, *Moral Realism*; Enoch, *Taking Morality Seriously*; Enoch, "Why I'm Objectivist."

intentions to cause it. And so, because the latter are perfectly objective, natural facts, so are the former. So it follows from these things that Dan says that there are after all objective facts about which actions are right and which are wrong. Dan, then, contradicts himself here. He has to decide: either morality is not objective, or it comes down to harm-minimizing intentions, but not both. Second, the suggestion that this is just what we mean by morality is highly implausible indeed. As Dan himself recognizes, the centrality of—let alone exclusive centrality of—harm-minimizing intentions to morality is highly controversial, and it is very hard to believe that all those differing with Dan on this just don't use moral words competently. Third, all of this leaves open the possibility that Dan is still right as a matter of first-order normative ethics. That is, when he puts forward the claim about harm-minimizing intentions, Dan is no longer doing metaethics (much less is he denying the objectivity of morality), and he instead steps into the ethics arena and advances his own first-order theory—his own suggested and very general moral principles. I welcome him into this arena, and though I disagree with his specific theory, I note with satisfaction that he seems committed, along with the rest of us, to morality's objectivity (we just differ on what the objective content of morality is).

Even if morality doesn't boil down to just harm-minimizing intentions, Dan is surely right that facts about harm are at the very least morally relevant. And he also insists (again, perfectly sensibly) that harm facts are perfectly natural facts and, indeed, material facts.[47] He seems to think that this supports the claim that morality itself is material. But nothing like this at all follows. Sure, the things that matter morally are often, perhaps always, material (and are always natural). But this doesn't mean that *the fact that they matter morally* is either natural or material. Perhaps it is—though I've argued in detail that it is not[48]—but this has to be shown. Conflating the ontological status of *the things which matter morally* with that of *the fact that they matter morally* supplies no such support.[49]

Last, Dan sometimes insists that it's not even clear what we're talking about when we're talking about morality, and he demands that morality be defined before the discussion of its objectivity can proceed. When such demands come

47. Again, we're going to have to worry about the mind-body problem some other time.

48. Again, see my *Taking Morality Seriously*.

49. And there's a huge body of literature that discusses such questions, further supporting the claim that Dan's quick argument doesn't work. See, for instance, the literature on the supervenience of the moral on the natural and what follows from it. See Tristram McPherson, "Supervenience in Ethics," in *Stanford Encyclopedia of Philosophy*, last modified October 22, 2019, https://tinyurl.com/3tkzme6u.

from my students—"Can you please define 'morality'?"—I sometimes answer with the annoying "Can you define 'definition'?" Often they cannot. But this doesn't show that they didn't even understand what they were asking me to do, at least in outline. Rather, it shows that being able to supply a definition of something is not a necessary condition for understanding it, at least to an extent. This is true of love, happiness, friendship, definition, and "having a Kennedy face."[50] It is also true of morality. Indeed, in philosophy sometimes definitions are reached, if at all, at the end of a discussion, not (as in mathematics) at its beginning.

Still, we know what we're talking about when we're talking about morality. It's the kind of claims we make when we think that someone acted admirably, that some type of action is almost always wrong, or (indeed) that causing unnecessary harm is to be frowned upon and that we ought not to humiliate people. Some such moral claims are true and perfectly objective, and nothing in Dan's arguments challenges this fact.

So I conclude, with Dan, that the moral argument fails. But, against Dan, I believe it fails not because morality is not objective, but because morality's objectivity can rather easily be accommodated by nontheistic explanations.

50. As in Wittgenstein's famous discussion of family-resemblance concepts.

13

Theist Responding to the Debate

Does the Universe Have a Cause?

Robert C. Koons

I will present two principal arguments for the claim that the universe has a cause. In the first section of this chapter, I define some key terms, and in the second section I describe and distinguish the two arguments. I present the first argument in the third and fourth sections, which rely on the impossibility of infinite causal regresses. In the fifth section, I present the second argument, which looks for a collective cause of the entities making up the universe, even if those entities exemplify one or more infinite regresses. I defend a principle of universal causation in the sixth section, a crucial premise of both arguments. In the seventh section, I discuss briefly the characteristics we can expect the cause of the universe to have. Finally, I refer to some facts about the universe uncovered by modern science that provide confirmation of my metaphysical conclusions.

Some Explications and Definitions

Here are some explications and definitions for some key terms that will appear in my arguments. Some of the terms are so fundamental that they cannot be defined. In those cases, I will explicate the terms by contrasting their meanings with others with which they may be confused.

Possibility. Throughout this paper, I will use "possibility" to refer to fundamental, metaphysical possibility. This is a notion that cannot be defined in nonmodal terms. It means possibility in the broadest sense, an unconditional possibility. It is to be contrasted with logical notions like consistency and with epistemological notions like conceivability or imaginability. We can use possibility to define impossibility and necessity: something is impossible if it is not possible, and something is necessary if it is impossible that it not be the case.

Actuality. Like possibility, "actuality" is too fundamental a notion to be defined. I will assume that there is a real and absolute (nonperspectival) distinction between what is actual and what is merely possible. The actual world is unified, complete, and consistent. If two facts F_1 and F_2 are both actual, then so is their conjunction (F_1 & F_2). A proposition *p* is actually true if and only if its negation ~*p* is not actually true.

Existence. When I speak of "existence," I mean actual existence. Only things that are actually existent can act on other actual things. Actual relations of causation must relate actually existing things.

Causation. I will assume that causation is a binary relation between things: between existing entities or between states or conditions of existing things. I have in mind causation as a kind of production: *making* something to be the case. Causation is more fundamental than time and more fundamental than truth of subjunctive conditionals. The order of time depends on the order of causation (earlier times are earlier *because* they contain causes of things occurring later), and the truth of subjunctive conditionals (e.g., if *p* had been the case, *q* would have been the case) depends on causal powers and capacities of things. I assume, therefore, that it makes sense to hypothesize causal relations that involve items that are nontemporal ("outside" of time). Causal explanation is defined in terms of causation and not vice versa: to explain something causally is simply to describe accurately its causal history. I also assume that causation is asymmetric and transitive: if *x* causes *y*, then *y* does not cause *x* (asymmetry). And, if *x* causes *y* and *y* causes *z*, then *x* causes *z* (transitivity).[1] There is therefore no self-causation or circles of causation.

***A priori* knowledge.** We know something *a priori* when we know it in a way that does not depend for its status as knowledge (its warrant) on any reliance on experience (including both sense experience and introspection). When I know something *a priori*, reason itself demands that I believe it, regardless of what I know (or fail to know) by way of experience. *A priori* knowledge encompasses such things as logic, mathematics, and the basic principles of philosophy.

Real essence (kind-essence). To give the real essence of a kind of thing is to state clearly *what it is to be* that kind of thing. Everything belongs to a unique most specific kind, whose kind-essence is also the essence of that

1. If it turns out that causation is not transitive, then we can use the transitive closure of causation instead (i.e., causation*). The transitive closure R* of a relation R is the smallest transitive relation that contains R. The transitive closure is by definition transitive. I will assume that the transitive closure of causation is asymmetric, ruling out any cycles of causation.

thing. Real essences belong to things in and of themselves, independently of how we conceive of them or what we know of them. Nothing can exist except by exhibiting in actuality its own real essence.

Conceivability. By "conceivable," I will mean what David Chalmers defines as ideal, negative, secondary conceivability.[2] Some state of affairs is conceivable if and only if we cannot know *a priori* that it is impossible, even given complete knowledge of the real essences of the things involved. This kind of conceivability is *ideal* because it concerns what we *cannot* in principle know, and not merely what we *do not* know, *a priori*. It is *negative* because it is defined in terms of the impossibility of the knowledge of what is impossible, not in terms of the possible knowledge of what is possible. And it is *secondary*, because we are allowed to consider what we would know, given complete knowledge of the real essences of things. So, for example, if the real essence of water is composed of H_2O molecules, then it is inconceivable that water not be composed of such molecules.

Pluralities. A plurality is not a single entity but a multiplicity of things.[3] To speak of a plurality is to speak of "them" rather than of an "it." Something belongs to a plurality if it is *one of them*. Pluralities exist whenever their members exist, and philosophers can accept talk about a certain plurality, even if the members of the plurality do not collectively compose a single thing or even belong to a single set. A plurality can be jointly caused by a single thing or by another plurality. I will assume that if x causes plurality P, then x does not belong to P, and if plurality P_1 jointly causes plurality P_2, then P_1 and P_2 have no members in common.

Broadly causable. A thing is broadly causable if it is conceivable that it be caused. Similarly, a plurality is broadly causable if it is conceivable that something causes them (collectively).

Strictly uncausable. A thing or plurality of things is strictly uncausable if and only if it is not broadly causable. So, it is inconceivable that a strictly uncausable thing or plurality be caused.

Infinite regress. An infinite regress is a series of actually existing things, each of which is caused by its successor in the series.

The universe. The universe is the plurality of actually existing, broadly causable things. I claim that the universe has a cause, in the sense that the

2. David Chalmers, "Does Conceivability Entail Possibility?," in *Conceivability and Possibility*, ed. Tamar Szabó Gendler and John Hawthorne (Clarendon, 2002), 145–200.

3. George Boolos, "To Be Is to Be a Value of a Variable (Or to Be Some Values of Some Variables)," *Journal of Philosophy* 81, no. 8 (1984): 430–49, https://doi.org/10.2307/2026308.

universe is caused by some thing or a plurality of things. By definition, no strictly uncausable thing belongs to the universe. Since the universe contains, by definition, all the broadly causable things, if it has a cause, it must have a strictly uncausable cause.

My arguments will depend on the following principles of universal causation, which I will defend in the sixth section.

Universal causation (simple). Every actually existing, broadly causable thing has an actual cause.

Universal causation (pluralized). Every actually existing, broadly causable plurality of things has an actual cause (either a single thing or a plurality of things).

Two Arguments

I will present two arguments for my claim.

1. The argument from the inconceivability of an infinite causal regress (i.e., the anti-regress argument). The precursors for this argument include book 10 of Plato's *Laws*, John Philoponus of Alexandria (490–570 CE), and the Kalām tradition in Islamic philosophy. It has been defended in recent years by William Lane Craig.[4]
2. The argument from the inconceivability of an uncaused plurality of causable things (the pluralization argument). The precursors of this argument include the work of Avicenna, Thomas Aquinas, Duns Scotus, Gottfried Leibniz, and Samuel Clarke.[5]

The first argument relies on the simple principle of universal causation, while the second one relies on the stronger pluralized version.

The Anti-Regress Argument

Here is the first argument in a nutshell:

1. Causation is a strict partial order (transitive and asymmetric).
2. The universe exists (i.e., there are some broadly causable things).

4. See, e.g., Plato, *The Laws*, trans. Trevor J. Saunders (Penguin Books, 1975), and William Lane Craig, *The Kalām Cosmological Argument* (Macmillan, 1979).

5. See, among others, John Duns Scotus, *A Treatise on God as First Principle (De primo principio)*, 2nd ed., trans. Allan B. Wolter (Franciscan Herald Press, 1983).

3. Every member of the universe (the class of broadly causable things) has a cause (simple universal causation).
4. There are no infinite regresses.

Therefore, everything in the universe is caused by one or more strictly uncausable things. Consequently, there is a plurality of one or more strictly uncausable things (the first cause) that jointly causes the existence of all the members of the universe. The conclusion of the argument follows from the four premises by a theorem of set theory (including the axiom of dependent choice).[6]

Premise 1 is a plausible assumption about causation, and premise 2 follows from the fact that there are actual cases of causation. I will discuss premise 3 in the sixth section of this chapter. This leaves premise 4 as the crucial assumption.

In arguing for premise 4, the impossibility of infinite regresses, I will draw on a thought experiment invented by José Benardete, known as the grim reaper story.[7] I will tell here a slightly simpler version of the story. Let's suppose that there is an infinite regress of grim reapers, each of which is assigned a particular time on which to perform its duty. Reaper 1 is assigned noon, January 1, 1 BCE, Reaper 2 the same day in 2 BCE, Reaper 3 in 3 BCE, and so on throughout an infinite past. Each Reaper $n + 1$ passes a death warrant on to its successor (Reaper n) at the end of its assigned period (January 1, n BCE). Each Reaper n follows the following script: (1) If the warrant already contains a numeral larger than n, then Reaper n leaves the warrant unchanged and passes it on, in turn, to reaper $n - 1$; (2) otherwise, Reaper n signs the warrant by writing on it the numeral n.

This story obviously involves some kind of impossibility, since we can derive from it a contradiction. We can prove both that the warrant *will* and *will not* contain a numeral on January 1, 1 CE. First, it must have a numeral on it on January 1, 1 CE. The warrant either did or did not have a numeral on it on the morning of January 1, 1 BCE. If it did, then Reaper 1 would have passed it on unchanged, and it would still have that numeral on it on January 1, 1 CE. If it did not have a numeral in 1 BCE, then Reaper 1 would have written the numeral 1 on it. So, in either case, the warrant will contain some numeral in 1 CE.

However, there is no number n such that the corresponding numeral could be on the warrant at that time. Suppose for contradiction that the warrant in

6. See Paul Bernays, "A System of Axiomatic Set Theory: Part III. Infinity and Enumerability. Analysis," *Journal of Symbolic Logic* 7, no. 20 (1942): 84, https://doi.org/10.2307/2266303; Romane Clark, "Vicious Infinite Regress Arguments," *Philosophical Perspectives* 2 (1988): 369–80, https://doi.org/10.2307/2214081.

7. J. A. Benardete, *Infinity: An Essay in Metaphysics* (Oxford University Press, 1964).

1 CE contains the numeral *n*. Then Reaper *n* must have received a blank warrant from Reaper $n + 1$ and then wrote the numeral *n* on the warrant. Now, either the warrant already had a numeral *n* on it at the beginning of $n + 1$ BCE or it did not. If it did, then Reaper $n + 1$ would have passed this warrant unchanged to Reaper *n*, and Reaper *n* would *not* have written his own number on it. If the warrant did not contain a numeral at the beginning of $n + 1$ BCE, then Reaper $n + 1$ would have written his numeral on it, and, again, Reaper *n* would *not* have written his numeral. This argument applies to any natural number, so the warrant cannot have a number on it in 1 CE.

Since we can prove that the reaper story is impossible, it is inconceivable. Here is an argument from the inconceivability of the grim reaper story to the inconceivability of infinite regresses:

1. If infinite regresses were conceivable, then the grim reaper story would be conceivable.
2. The grim reaper story is not conceivable.
3. Therefore, infinite regresses are not conceivable.

Premise 1 is a consequence of a version of David Lewis's patchwork principle, a recombination principle, that is adapted to the property of conceivability.[8]

Patchwork principle for conceivability. If (1) a certain causal structure S is conceivable, (2) a finite process P is conceivable, and (3) scenario A consists of inserting one or more copies of P into slots in S, each of which is large enough to accommodate P, then scenario A is also conceivable. S is the "frame," P is the "patch," and A is the "quilt." If we have a frame and an unlimited supply of copies of a patch, then we can build the quilt by inserting copies of the patch into the frame.

Some form of recombination is relied on by all of us implicitly every day in planning possible programs or scenarios. For example, suppose that I want to schedule soccer games on a series of dates in the coming month. Given the conceivability of the arrival of the coming month and the conceivability of scheduling a soccer game on a particular date, we conclude that any assignment of games to dates in the month is at least conceivable.

In the case of the grim reaper story, the structure S is the infinite regress of dates (1 BCE, 2 BCE, etc.). The "patch" is the behavioral program of an individual grim reaper. The patch is obviously possible, and a copy of the patch will obviously fit into each of S's year-long slots. So, if S itself is conceivable, then

8. David K. Lewis, *On the Plurality of Worlds* (Blackwell, 1986), 86–92.

the whole grim reaper story would be conceivable. But it is not conceivable. In fact, it involves a provable mathematical impossibility.

The Unsatisfiable Pair Diagnosis

Some critics have argued that the patchwork principle is too strong.[9] Perhaps we should add an exception:

Revised patchwork principle. If (1) a certain causal structure S is conceivable, (2) a finite process P is conceivable, and (3) scenario A consists of inserting one or more copies of P into slots in S, each of which is large enough to accommodate P, then scenario A is also conceivable, *unless A is mathematically impossible.* The move to a revised patchwork principle is called the "unsatisfiable pair diagnosis" of the original grim reaper story. There are two conditions that would have to be met in order to verify the grim reaper story (namely, that the grim reapers' actions depend in a certain way on their predecessors' actions, and that the past is infinitely long), and we have seen that it is mathematically impossible for both conditions to be met.

I don't believe that it is necessary to add this exception to the original principle. If A turns out to be mathematically impossible, that shows us that either S or P is not conceivable (or that it is not conceivable that copies of P be fit into all of the slots of P). The mathematical impossibility of A is a feature of my original argument, not a bug. We haven't been given any good reason to weaken this patchwork principle in this way. The revised version arbitrarily picks out *mathematical* impossibility as the exception. What would happen if we excepted all inconceivable scenarios? In that case, the patchwork principle would become a mere tautology: all scenarios of a certain kind are conceivable, unless they're not. Therefore, we have good reason to reject such a sweeping exception. But the defenders of the unsatisfiable pair diagnosis have given us no reason to treat mathematical inconceivability as an exceptional case. Nonetheless, I will not press this response further here. Instead, I will put forward a new version of the grim reaper story: the chancy grim reaper story.

The chancy grim reaper story. We change the program of each grim reaper. For each number *n*, when Reaper *n* receives the warrant on his assigned date of *n* BCE, a fair coin is flipped. If the coin comes up heads on *n* BCE, Reaper *n* erases anything written on the warrant and signs it with his own numeral. If the coin comes up tails, then Reaper *n* writes his number on the warrant only if

9. Joseph C. Schmid and Alex Malpass, "Benardete Paradoxes, Causal Finitism, and the Unsatisfiable Pair Diagnosis," *Mind* 134, no. 534 (2025): 397–421.

the warrant is blank when he receives it. Otherwise, he passes it on unchanged to his successor, Reaper $n - 1$.

There are two versions of the chancy grim reaper story: the lucky story and the unlucky story. In the lucky story, the coin comes up heads an infinite number of times. This means that for every Reaper *n*, the coin has come up heads infinitely often in the past, and there will be a latest year *m* on which the coin had previously come up heads. There is no logical or mathematical impossibility involved in the lucky story. There will be a number on the warrant on January 2, 1 BCE. The number will correspond with the last time that the coin landed heads.

In the unlucky story, the coin turns up tails every time it is tossed. The unlucky story is inconceivable for the same reason that the original grim reaper story was inconceivable.[10] However, the only difference between the lucky and the unlucky story concerns how the members of a set of completely independent events turned out.

The independence principle. If B is a conceivable scenario, X is a class of mutually independent chance events occurring in B, and C is a scenario that is exactly like B except with reference to (1) events that are possible outcomes of members of X, and (2) conceivable events that are causally downstream from these outcomes, then C is also a conceivable scenario.

In this case, it is certainly conceivable that the coin should turn up heads infinitely many times. Since we're supposing that the coin is a fair one, then any combination of heads and tails outcomes should be conceivable. We therefore should be able to conceive of a scenario in which the coin comes up tails every time. This is an extremely unlikely outcome, but it is clearly conceivable. The conceivability of this outcome is a consequence of the concept of *mutually independent* trials. If we have a class of chancy events that are, by hypothesis, mutually independent, then this means that the probability of each event is not affected by the occurrence or nonoccurrence of other events in the class. So, even if every other coin toss besides toss *n* turns up tails, there is still a 50 percent chance that toss *n* will come up tails. So, it is conceivable that all the coin tosses come up tails. For similar reasons, the probability of a chance event cannot be affected by events that are causally posterior to it. So, the scenario in which every coin toss comes up tails should be conceivable, no matter what

10. It is not necessary that the coin come up tails every time. To get the mathematical impossibility, it is enough to assume that the coin comes up heads only finitely. In that case, there will be an earliest year in which the coin comes up heads preceded by an unbroken chain of tails.

the subsequent results of any of the tosses might be (so long as these results don't affect the mutual independence of the coin tosses).

Here is an argument from the independence principle to the inconceivability of infinite regresses:

1. Given the independence principle, if the lucky story is conceivable, so is the unlucky story.
2. The unlucky story is not conceivable because it involves a mathematical impossibility.
3. Therefore, the lucky story is not conceivable. (From 1 and 2)
4. Given the revised patchwork principle, if infinite regresses were conceivable, then the lucky story would also be conceivable, since it doesn't involve any mathematical impossibility.
5. Therefore, infinite regresses are not conceivable. (From 3 and 4)

So, even if we replace the patchwork principle with the revised principle (as the defenders of the unsatisfiable pair diagnosis advocate), we can still show that infinite regresses are inconceivable, so long as we have the independence principle in hand. This means that we can know *a priori* that infinite regresses are impossible. Since we can also know that everything broadly causable has a cause, we can know that everything in the universe is caused by something strictly uncausable.[11]

I have a second refutation of the conceivability of infinite regresses, one based on the idea of an infinite fair lottery. An infinite fair lottery is a lottery that will certainly produce a unique natural number (from 1 to infinity), providing each number with equal probability (hence, a fair lottery). As Alexander Pruss has argued, if an infinite regress is conceivable, then so is an infinite fair lottery.[12] Imagine again an infinite series of coin tosses, stretching infinitely far into the past and numbered (in reverse) 1, 2, 3, and so on.

Using our revised patchwork principle again, we can deduce the conceivability

11. A very similar grim reaper argument can be used to show that causal circles are also inconceivable. Suppose we put twelve grim reapers in a causal circle, labeling them 1 through 12 (as on a clockface), and suppose that each reaper receives a number from his predecessor (moving clockwise) and adds 1 to this number. This would mean that the numbers associated with each grim reaper keep growing larger as we move clockwise around the face, which is obviously mathematically impossible. If the numbers grow as we move from Reapers 1 to 11, they must shrink when we arrive at 12.

12. Alexander R. Pruss, *Infinity, Causation, and Paradox* (Oxford University Press, 2018), 64–92.

of such a series from the conceivability of an infinite causal regress. Using independence, we can deduce that every combination of results from such a series is conceivable. In particular, we have the conceivability of a result in which the tosses all produce tails except for a single head. This result can be treated as an infinite fair lottery, since each of the numbers had an equal chance of being selected as the unique correspondent to the single heads result.[13]

Here, then, is my final argument against the conceivability of an infinite regress:

1. If infinite regresses are conceivable, then infinite fair lotteries are conceivable. (by revised patchwork principle and independence)
2. If one such lottery is conceivable, so are two independent such lotteries.
3. If two such lotteries are conceivable, then it is conceivable that fundamental principles of probability be violated.
4. It is inconceivable that any fundamental principles of probability be violated.
5. Therefore, infinite regresses are inconceivable.

I take it that the fundamental principles of probability are, like the fundamental principles of logic and probability, known *a priori* to be necessary truths, hence premise 4.

Here is my case for the crucial premise 3. Let's label the numbers selected by the two infinite fair lotteries L_1 and L_2. Suppose we are given the result of lottery L_1, namely m. What is the probability that L_2 is greater than L_1, given that $L_1 = m$? It is clear that this conditional probability is 1 or infinitely close to 1. There are only finitely many numbers less than or equal to m, while there are infinitely many numbers greater than m. Since L_2 is an infinite fair lottery, each number greater than n has a chance of being selected equal to that of any number less than n. I appeal here to a principle of enumeration:

Enumeration. If the members of class C are mutually exclusive events of equal probability, and E is a subset of C, then the conditional probability Prob(E/C) is equal to (or infinitely close to) the ratio #(E)/#(C). If #E is finite and #C is infinite, then Prob(E/C) is infinitely close to 0, and Prob(~E/C) is infinitely close to 1. In fact, by parity of reasoning, the conditional probability $\text{Prob}(L_2 > L_1)/(L_1 = x)$ will be infinitely close to 1, no matter what value L_1 takes.

13. Pruss also shows how it is possible to take any result of an infinite series of coin tosses and to extract from that result an infinite fair lottery, by which we can be guaranteed to obtain a single natural number in a way that made all numbers equally likely to be selected; see Pruss, *Infinity, Causation, and Paradox*, 79–86.

Take an arbitrary intelligent agent who knows with certainty that he will discover that $L_1 = n$, for some particular number n. He also knows (by enumeration) that he will conclude, after learning that value, that the probability of $(L2 > L1)$ is infinitely close to 1. He can therefore conclude that the present rational probability of $(L_2 > L_1)$ must *already* be infinitely close to 1. He also knows, however, by a principle of isomorphism that the probability of $(L_2 > L_1)$ cannot be significantly greater than one half, since the two lotteries are isomorphic in causal structure, and so the two inequalities must have approximately the same probability. Again, this means that an infinite fair lottery requires the rational agent to violate a fundamental principle of probability.

Dynamic coherency. If a rational agent knows that he will continue to be rational and already knows that he will, after updating with some unknown piece of evidence, assign a probability π to some proposition p, then he must already assign probability π to p.

Isomorphism. If two situations are known by an agent to be causally isomorphic, and the agent is ignorant of the result of either situation, then the agent's rational probabilities with respect to the two situations must also be isomorphic.

Violations of dynamic coherence produce a situation in which the agent is subject to a dynamic Dutch book: a set of bets, distributed over time, that are guaranteed to result in a net loss. For example, suppose the agent thinks initially that L_1 has a 50 percent chance of being the larger of the two numbers, but the same agent will certainly judge (after learning the actual value of L_1) that that probability is very close to 0. In that case, the agent will accept a fair bet on L_1 initially but, after learning the actual value, will be willing to sell the bet back for a loss.

The Pluralization Argument

The second argument for a first cause relies on the pluralized version of the principle of universal causation. Let's assume again that the universe exists, that is, that there are some broadly causable things.

Is the universe itself broadly causable? Each member of the universe is broadly causable (by definition). So, we can conceive of a scenario I call the two-worlds scenario. In the two-worlds scenario, there are two parallel universes: our universe and a second one, universe-2, where each member of our universe (universe-1) is caused in the two-worlds scenario by a member of universe-2. This scenario is clearly conceivable, and in this scenario our universe is caused by a second plurality. This is true even if the universe contains one or more infinite regresses. If our universe is infinitely regressing, then our imagined universe-2 will also regress infinitely.

This shows us that we can conceive of our universe having a cause. So, by definition, the universe is broadly causable. Now we can apply the pluralized causal principle, which tells us that the universe must have an actual cause. This actual cause will consist of one or more things that do not belong to the universe, that is, it will consist of one or more strictly uncausable things that collectively constitute an uncaused first cause of the universe.

Here is a possible objection. If our universe does regress infinitely, then it might have an infinitely long past. We can assume that each member of the universe is caused by other members of the universe at some point in this infinite past. When, then, can the supposed cause of the universe do its causing? If we say that the first uncausable cause caused the universe in *n* BCE, this seems to be impossible, since we are supposing that many members of the universe were already in existence then. The year *n* BCE seems to be too late for the supposed causing to occur. In addition, the things existing in *n* BCE were caused by the things existing before *n* BCE, and so the supposed first cause seems redundant. We would have to suppose that everything in the universe was caused twice over: first by its predecessors in the universe, and then again by the first cause.

Here is my response to this objection. We could suppose that each thing in the universe is caused *both* by its time-bound predecessors and by the first cause, but *not independently*. The first cause could cause each thing *x* in the universe by causing *x*'s predecessors and by using those predecessors as instruments in the cause of *x* itself. If causal regresses make sense (which I doubt), then such an infinite case of instrumental causation would also make sense. We don't end up with an objectionable form of overdetermination or redundant causation. The first cause's causing of the universe is spread across all of time.

Defending Universal Causation

The principle of universal causation is a fundamental principle of reason. As such, its truth cannot be demonstrated from more fundamental principles. However, I can argue for the principle dialectically, pointing out the unacceptably high price of rejecting the principle.

Reason directs us to expect causes in the widest possible range of cases. My principle of universal causation makes only one exception: that of strictly uncausable things. But this exception is not really an exception at all, since, if there are any strictly uncausable things, it is, by definition, inconceivable that they should be caused.

One might object that a principle of universal causation ought to be a metaphysical principle (a principle about things in the world) and not an epistemological principle (a principle about what we can know). But I have defined broadly causable in terms of what can be *known a priori.*

I would respond that this epistemological principle is adjacent to an equivalent principle that is purely metaphysical. The reason for this equivalence is that I have used secondary conceivability: conceivability given the real essence of a thing. Consequently, "broadly causable," as I have defined it, is equivalent to a purely metaphysical notion: metaphysically broadly causable.

Metaphysically broadly causable. A thing is *metaphysically broadly causable* if and only if the *infima species* to which it belongs has a kind-essence that does not entail that nothing of that kind has a cause.

If an essence entails that things of a certain kind cannot have a cause, then we could know that those things cannot have a cause, if we knew that essence (and vice versa). So, my original notion of broadly causable and this new notion of metaphysically broadly causable are equivalent. For the same reason, *strictly uncausable* and *metaphysically strictly uncausable* are equivalent.[14]

The principle of universal causation excludes the strictly uncausable. Should we exclude anything else from the scope of the principle? There are several reasons for saying "No." Let's say that a thing whose existence is broadly causable but uncaused is a *brute existent.* A plurality of things whose joint existence is broadly causable but uncaused would be a *brute plurality.* Methodologically, we should reduce the number of brute existents and brute pluralities to the smallest set possible. That would be the empty set, since there is no compelling reason to posit any brute existents or brute pluralities at all. In fact, we should treat brute existents and brute pluralities as inconceivable.

If brute existents and brute pluralities are conceivable, is there any limiting principle? Is there a type of thing F of such a kind that we can say that brute pluralities of type F are conceivable, but not brute pluralities that do not belong to F?

14. It is important to distinguish metaphysically broadly causable from a different notion: that of its being metaphysically possible for a particular thing to be caused. Even if it is metaphysically impossible for a particular thing to be caused to exist (perhaps because its individual identity is necessarily tied to its being uncaused), the thing could still be metaphysically broadly causable, so long as it belongs to a specific *kind of thing* whose essence is compatible with being caused. Both notions are metaphysical in nature, but the category of metaphysically broadly causable is broader in scope.

It's hard to see what that limiting principle would be. It makes sense to ask what kinds of thing can be *caused* by things of type A. For example, what sorts of things can human beings cause to exist? What sorts of things can waterfalls or meteor showers cause to exist? And so on.

But it doesn't make sense to ask what sort of causable things can exist *without being caused* by anything. It seems that if any causable thing could exist without being caused, then *every* causable thing could exist without being caused. There doesn't seem to be any limiting principle. If we said that things of some specific type of causable thing could not exist without being caused, what would be the explanation for this impossibility? In the absence of a principle of universal causation, what could prevent *any* causable thing from existing brutely?

If brute pluralities are conceivable, so are brute existents. There's no reason why it would be easier for a numerous collection of entities to exist uncaused than for an individual to do so. So, if we rule out brute existents, we should rule out brute pluralities as well. So, the pluralized version of the principle of universal causation is just as reasonable as the simple version.

If brute existents are conceivable, then it is impossible to say that brute existents are unlikely or exotic (i.e., distant from the actual world or from any actual situation). What is likely or unlikely (with a certain probability) is the production or nonproduction of a certain kind of event by a certain kind of mechanism. There is nothing that could explain why an uncaused event should have one probability rather than another. Hence, we cannot conceive of a situation in which it is *unlikely* that an uncaused event should occur.

For similar reasons, if brute existents are conceivable, it would make no sense to suppose that certain kinds of brute existents are possible in certain kinds of situations, while other kinds of brute existents are impossible. What is uncaused is unregulated and uncontrolled. If anything can exist uncaused, then anything could begin to exist without cause in any possible situation. Consequently, anyone who believes in brute existents can have no explanation for why we don't see uncaused entities of a wide variety of sorts appearing uncaused all the time. The absence of clear counterexamples to the principle is strong empirical evidence for it.[15]

15. Some suppose that the indeterminism of many interpretations of quantum mechanics counts as a counterexample to the principle. However, this confuses indeterminism with the absence of a cause. Quantum events are not determined by their predecessors, but they are caused by them. See Anscombe's inaugural Cambridge lecture on this crucial distinction; G. E. M. Anscombe, "Causality and Determination," in *Causation*, ed. Ernest Sosa and Michael Tooley (Oxford University Press, 1993), 88–104. Similarly, the virtual particles that

Could a law of nature (like a law of conservation of mass or mass-energy) rule out certain kinds of brute entities' appearing in certain circumstances without ruling out all brute entities? This proposal faces a dilemma: either the law is merely descriptive, or it is prescriptive. If descriptive, it merely describes the fact that there have been no brute existents, or at least none since the big bang. It doesn't offer any explanation of this fact or provide any grounds for supposing such brute existents to be impossible. If prescriptive, the law of conservation must presuppose the principle of universal causation. Without the principle of universal causation, the conservation law could tell us that existing things lack the power to *produce* a set of things with a net increase or decrease of energy, but it could not rule out the *uncaused* appearance or disappearance of energy from the world. In the absence of the principle of universal causation, there would be no explanation for the impossibility of such violations of the conservation of energy. If brute existents were possible, there is no possible mechanism by which their existence or nonexistence could be prevented or, indeed, controlled or regulated in any way.

Finally, I will point out that denying the principle of universal causation undermines various categories of knowledge, leading to various forms of radical skepticism.[16] First, if the principle of universal causation were false, we would be unable to have any knowledge of the future, since any current factors on which we might rely to forecast the future could at any time be overwhelmed by unpredictable and uncaused brute existents. Similarly, any statistical knowledge about the propensities of things would be impossible, since any experiments that we have run in the past could have been distorted by uncaused factors.[17]

In fact, I would argue that, in the absence of the principle of universal causation, we would have no empirical knowledge at all. My current sense data and memory impressions ground my knowledge of the world only on the assumption that they have been caused in the right way by entities of the appropriate kind. If my current sense data and memory impressions were instead brute existents, then I would have absolutely no empirical knowledge. I would

appear spontaneously in the vacuum (according to quantum field theory) are not uncaused: they are caused by the quantum field that fills the "vacuum," a field with the causal power to generate pairs of virtual particles.

16. Robert C. Koons and Alexander R. Pruss, "The Principle of Sufficient Reason and Skepticism," *Philosophical Studies* 178 (2021): 1079–99, https://doi.org/10.1007/s11098-020-01482-3.

17. Alexander R. Pruss, "The Principle of Sufficient Reason and Probability," *Oxford Studies in Metaphysics* 10 (2017): 261–78, https://doi.org/10.1093/acprof:oso/9780198791973.003.0011.

be in a condition every bit as bad as the scenario that Descartes imagined in his first meditation, where he supposes that his mind and all its contents were caused by a deceiving demon.[18]

The threat from the possibility of brute existents is actually much worse than was the threat of Descartes's imagined demon. We can plausibly suppose that Descartes's demon, even if possible, is extremely improbable and an extremely extravagant *recherché* hypothesis. But, as I have argued, if the principle of universal causation were false, there would be nothing improbable or extravagant about the hypothesis that all the current contents of my mind are brute existents.

If the principle of universal causation were false, there would be no reliable processes of any kind, and so no empirical knowledge, since empirical knowledge must be the result of a reliable truth-tracking process.

These reflections support the conclusion that not only can the truth of the principle be known, but also the principle can and must be known *a priori*. If we have to take the brute-existent hypothesis seriously, then all my empirical knowledge would be undermined. The only way to exclude that possibility without vicious circularity is to be able to appeal on *a priori* grounds to the principle of universal causation. If I do not know *a priori* that universal causation is true, I cannot exclude the brute-existent hypothesis from serious consideration. And, so, I could not know that I have any empirical knowledge.

In addition, if I don't *know* that I have any empirical knowledge at all, I don't *have* any empirical knowledge in fact. The live (empirically accessible) possibility that I lack all empirical knowledge would serve as a defeater of all my empirical knowledge. There are some central or paradigmatic cases of knowledge (like my knowing my own name, or my knowing that I have a hand) such that, if I have any empirical knowledge at all, these would be clear and obvious of knowledge. If there are clear and obvious cases of my having empirical knowledge, then I can know that I have some empirical knowledge. So, if I cannot know that I have any empirical knowledge, it follows that I cannot have any empirical knowledge in fact.

Here is the argument:

1. If I cannot know the principle of universal causation *a priori*, then the skeptical brute-existent hypothesis (the hypothesis that all the current contents

18. René Descartes, "Meditations on First Philosophy," in *Descartes: Philosophical Writings*, trans. Elizabeth Anscombe and Peter Geach (Bobbs-Merrill, 1971), 63–64.

of my mind, including all sense data and memory impressions, are uncaused) is, for me, a live possibility (a conceivable situation that is neither unlikely nor known by me to be possibly remote from the actual world, given the current contents of my mind).

2. I can know *a priori* that if the skeptical brute-existent hypothesis were true, I would not have any empirical knowledge.
3. Therefore, if I cannot know the principle of universal causation *a priori*, then my lacking all empirical knowledge is, for me, a live possibility. (From 1 and 2)
4. If the falsity of a proposition is for me a live possibility, then I cannot know that proposition.
5. Therefore, if I cannot know the principle of universal causation *a priori*, I cannot know that I have any empirical knowledge. (From 3 and 4)
6. If I have any empirical knowledge, then I know that I have at least some empirical knowledge.
7. I do have some empirical knowledge.
8. Therefore, I can know the principle of universal causation *a priori*. (From 5, 6, and 7)

Strictly Uncausable Beings

There is a good reason for thinking that the existence of a strictly uncausable thing (the sort of thing that composes any first cause of the universe) would have to be atemporal, that is, beyond the limits of time. Any time-bound entity would be the sort of thing that could change and that could even begin or cease to exist. Anything that is subject to change, especially to the kind of change involved in beginning or ceasing to exist, is the sort of thing that we can conceive of as being caused to begin to exist. So, a strictly uncausable thing must be essentially atemporal.

But how can something outside of time cause the things that make up the universe, much (if not all) of which exist within time? Can a nontemporal cause have a temporal effect? I have assumed that time does not enter into the definition of causation, and so there is no bar to a causal relation holding between two nontemporal items or between a nontemporal and a temporal thing.

Intentional relations, like remembering, anticipating, admiring, contemplating, can stand between a mind existing at one time and an object existing at any other time. Intentional relations are intrinsically free from temporal constraints. Consequently, we can conceive of a timeless intellect that stands eternally in an intentional relation to temporal things. We also know from personal experience that intentional relations can be causal: I can *make* something happen by willing it to happen. For example, I can create a mental image of a hippopotamus by willing that I should have such an image, and I can move my hand by willing my hand to move. So, there is no obstacle to a nontemporal mind's causing temporal things to exist by a timeless act of will. We can see an analogy of this in the act of a writer's imagining a new timeline, like Tolkien's imagination of the temporal structure of Middle Earth. Tolkien was able to create that imagined timeline without actually being a part of it.

If the first cause has any quantities associated with it, they would have to be immeasurably great. Any finite entity is broadly causable. So, a strictly uncausable thing must be infinite with respect to every relevant parameter.

The first cause would have to be absolutely simple. Compound things are broadly causable. A first cause would have to exist necessarily and by its own essence, since contingent things are broadly causable. And a necessary being that is caused to exist necessarily is obviously causable.

Thomas Aquinas argues further that a first cause must have an essence or nature that is identical to its own act of existence (*De ente et essentia* 77–80). If the essence of the first cause were distinct from its existence, we could conceive of something causing their juncture. There would be then no distinction between the possible existence of such a being (its essence sans existence) and its actual existence. Since possibilities exist as such in every possible world, if such a being is possible, it will exist necessarily.

Moreover, the first cause will turn out to be identical to its own essence, since it is absolutely simple and has no mere potentialities. So, for each uncausable essence, there can be only one existing entity that belongs to that essence, since if there were another, it would also have to be identical to the shared essence and thus to the first entity. Since the essence of an uncausable thing must be identical to the thing's act of existence, any such essence will be the essence of a being of pure, unadulterated existence. There couldn't be two distinct essences of this kind, since two essences can be two only by one's including something not contained by the other, but the uncausable essences cannot contain anything beyond pure existence. So, there can be only one uncausable first cause, which we can then describe accurately as "the" cause of the universe.

These reflections help to explain why all natural things, including our minds and their contents, our environment, and everything else contained in space and time, are broadly causable. It is obvious that none of them have the kind of essence that would rend them intrinsically uncausable.

In contrast, we cannot know *a priori* that the contents of mind are located in time after the beginning of time. For all I can know *a priori*, the universe and time itself began to exist right now. So, we cannot exclude "first things" from our principle of universal causation. Similarly, we cannot know *a priori* that the contents of my mind do not contain infinite causal regresses (unless I can know *a priori* that such regresses are impossible). For example, for all I know, my present visual experience V_1 was caused by a very similar experience V_2 a nanosecond ago, and V_2 could have been caused by V_3 a half-nanosecond before that, and so on *ad infinitum*. So, we cannot exclude pluralities that contain infinite regresses from our pluralized version of universal causation.

To sum up, we have good reason to believe that there is a single, absolutely simple, necessarily existing, timeless, and infinite first cause. Moreover, we have good reason to think that it acts in an intelligent way, causing the existence of the temporal universe. In the *Summa Theologica* (Part I, questions 4 through 14), Thomas Aquinas uses these facts in deducing further characteristics of the first cause, namely, that it is an all-knowing, all-powerful, and benevolent creator.

Supplementary Scientific Considerations

Let the *cosmos* be that part of the universe of which we have knowledge, either direct or indirect. If we find that the cosmos has a cause, this provides empirical confirmation of the claim that the universe has a cause. This takes the form of a Bayesian argument: if the whole universe has a cause, then certainly the cosmos has a cause. So, if we discover that the cosmos has a cause, this increases the probability that the whole universe does.

Our best cosmological models indicate that the observable cosmos is just over 14 billion years old, beginning with the big bang. On the standard model, all space, time, and matter begin to exist just after the big bang, because the singularity at the big bang would involve infinite density. The viable nonstandard models agree on the "past-completeness" of the universe: the fact that it has only a finite past.[19] It is reasonable to suppose that whatever begins to exist is caused to exist. So, we have good grounds for concluding that the cosmos has a cause.

Physicists have also discovered the so-called fine-tuning of the fundamental constants of physics and of the boundary conditions of the universe.[20] These numbers and parameters have to belong to very special ranges of

19. Steven C. Meyer, *Return of the God Hypothesis: Three Scientific Discoveries That Reveal the Mind Behind the Universe* (HarperOne, 2021), 87–129.

20. Meyer, *Return of God*, 130–63; Geraint F. Lewis and Luke A. Barnes, *A Fortunate Universe: Life in a Fine-Tuned Cosmos* (Cambridge University Press, 2018).

possible values in order for the cosmos to contain stars and heavier elements, especially carbon.

Where there is a coincidence, we should suppose that there is a cause of the coincidence. We can define a *coincidence* as a case where a number of apparently independent factors conspire to produce a simple and interesting result. In the case of fine-tuning, we find such a large number (in the neighborhood of thirty) of apparently independent factors that are necessary for a number of simple and interesting results, including the prevalence of carbon. But any cause of the fine-tuning coincidences would have to be a cause of the cosmos as a whole.

Finally, we observe that the fundamental laws of the universe (the laws of general relativity and quantum mechanics) are remarkably simple in form. In fact, as Steven Weinberg demonstrated,[21] if the laws of nature did not share a learnable form of elegance and simplicity, we would never have been able to discover them.[22] This is another coincidence that calls for a causal explanation, but only something that caused the cosmos to exist could cause it to be the sort of thing that obeys these simple fundamental laws.

21. Steven Weinberg, *Dreams of a Final Theory: The Scientist's Search for the Ultimate Laws of Nature* (Vintage, 1993).

22. Robert C. Koons, "The Incompatibility of Naturalism and Scientific Realism," in *Naturalism: A Critical Appraisal*, ed. William Lane Craig and J. P. Moreland (Routledge, 2000), 49–63; reprinted in *The Nature of Nature*, ed. Bruce L. Gordon and William A. Dembski (ISI Books, 2011).

14

Nontheists Responding to the Debate

Did the Universe Have a Cause?

Daniel Linford and Alex Malpass

The universe is the combination of all the physical things there have ever been, are, and ever will be. The Kalām cosmological argument (KCA) is an argument for God's existence that makes use of the beginning of the universe. The argument can be broken into two stages. In Adam Lloyd Johnson's opening statement, he offered the first stage, wherein he concluded that the universe had a cause:

1. Whatever has a beginning must have a cause.
2. The universe had a beginning. So,
3. The universe had a cause.

The second stage involves an argument that the universe's cause must be God. Adam tells us that because space, time, and matter didn't exist until the universe began, the universe's cause must be spaceless, timeless, and immaterial. The cause must also be powerful enough to bring forth the universe. There is plenty to be said about Adam's second stage. For example, if some recent ideas in theoretical physics are correct, the combination of all physical things may include more than space, time, and matter. But, here, we set aside our misgivings with the second stage. We argue that there is no good reason to accept either premise of the first stage.

The KCA was proposed by John Philoponus, taken up by medieval Islamic thinkers such as Al-Kindi and Al-Ghazali, and discussed by Immanuel Kant. In our era, the KCA's foremost defender is William Lane Craig. For that reason, much of our attention will be given to what Craig has said in defense of the two premises. Though we don't think the argument succeeds, we do think the argument raises two questions that should interest everyone regardless of their religious beliefs. First, it raises questions about the nature of causation, including whether the universe could have had a cause. Second, it raises questions about whether the universe began to exist.

The Causal Principle

Causation is central to the KCA. For example, Adam's first premise—the causal principle—claims that whatever begins to exist must have a cause and concludes that the universe had a cause. In this section, we show that the KCA makes assumptions about causation incompatible with Neo-Russellianism, a view of causation popular among philosophers of physics. As we will show, given Neo-Russellianism one or the other of the KCA's premises is false. While the case for Neo-Russellianism isn't definitive, without strong reasons to reject Neo-Russellianism we have no good reason to accept the KCA.

Many people see science as the hunt for causes. Adam certainly does; he has said that "one of the fundamental principles of science is that things don't begin or happen without a cause" and "science just is a search for causes."[1] Geologists hunt for the causes of various kinds of rock, while medical researchers hunt for the underlying causes of disease. However, in 1912, philosopher Bertrand Russell argued that when we mature to a sophisticated scientific understanding, we leave the hunt for causes behind.[2] Science, Russell claimed, seeks to explain natural phenomena but not in terms of causes.

For Russell, our most sophisticated science (physics) doesn't make use of causes. Instead, physics is written in terms of mathematics. Furthermore, the mathematical relationships physicists discover do not behave like cause-effect relationships. Consider a few of the features that the relationship between causes and their effects is usually understood to have. To start, there's the *asymmetry of causal influence*: causes are not related to their effects in the same way that effects are related to their causes. Historians say that the assassination of Archduke Franz Ferdinand caused World War I. Ferdinand's assassination caused World War I, but World War I did not cause Ferdinand's assassination. Moreover, causes are *specific*. Many things happened before World War I that did not cause World War I. For example, the planet Mars was such-and-such many miles from Earth in 1790, but no historian would say the location of the planet Mars was just as much a cause of World War I as

1. Adam Lloyd Johnson, "The First-Cause Argument for God (Apologetics for Teens Part 1)," Convincing Proof, posted March 11, 2024, YouTube, 59:54, https://tinyurl.com/2fpb3ppx.

2. Bertrand Russell, "On the Notion of Cause," *Proceedings of the Aristotelian Society* 13 (1912): 1–26, https://doi.org/10.1093/aristotelian/13.1.1.

Ferdinand's assassination. Out of all the things that happened before World War I, we single out Ferdinand's assassination as *the* cause. The relationships physicists discover lack the asymmetry and the specificity of causal relations. For Russell, historians phrase their explanations in terms of causes because our knowledge of history is not as technically sophisticated as our knowledge of physics. When history matures, Russell would argue, historians will stop appealing to causes.

Explanations vary in detail. A *macrophysical* description of a gas cloud uses pressure, volume, and temperature. A *microphysical* description focuses on the positions, masses, and velocities of the cloud's constituent particles. Both describe the same cloud at distinct levels of analysis.

Microphysical descriptions lack the asymmetry of causal influence; the laws and the microphysical state determine both past and future states equally. While World War I was caused by Ferdinand's assassination, in microphysical terms the assassination and the war are interdependent, with neither the cause of the other. Moreover, the microphysical description is not specific. Every past event, even Mars's position in 1790, equally influenced whether World War I happened. Microphysically, nothing at all singles out Ferdinand's assassination as *the* cause.

Without a microphysical asymmetry of causal influence, nothing microphysically distinguishes causes from effects. And since, microphysically, nothing at all singles out causes, events are determined by their entire past and future. The microphysical description is so radically unlike the macrophysical description that using words like "cause" and "effect" can only mislead us.

In 1979 another philosopher, Nancy Cartwright, provided a powerful argument that we need causation after all.[3] According to Cartwright, understanding causal relationships helps us identify effective strategies, like good strategies for avoiding cancer. Let's suppose, for the sake of the example, we discover that smokers are less likely to get cancer. Should we start smoking to avoid cancer? No, we might (for example) also find that smokers tend to exercise more often than nonsmokers. When we compare groups carefully—comparing smokers who exercise to nonsmokers who exercise—we find that smoking increases the risk of cancer. The key to understanding why not smoking is a better strategy involves the recognition that smoking *causes* cancer. We need to recognize causal relationships, and not merely the correlations between variables, to identify effective strategies.

3. Nancy Cartwright, "Causal Laws and Effective Strategies," *Noûs* 13, no. 4 (1979): 419–37, https://doi.org/10.2307/2215337.

Neo-Russellians strike a balance between Russell and Cartwright. Neo-Russellians agree with Russell that science includes a microphysical level of description without causation. But Neo-Russellians also agree with Cartwright that we need causation to distinguish effective strategies from ineffective strategies.

Perhaps there is no microphysical causation. However, this doesn't imply events occur randomly or without explanation. An event can have an explanation without having a cause because some explanations do not involve causes. For instance, it's impossible to connect three houses to three utilities (water, gas, and electric) without two lines crossing. (Try it!) Instead of being explained by a cause, the fact that there is no way to connect three houses to three utilities is explained by a geometric principle: on a plane, three points cannot all connect to three other points without crossing lines. Moreover, theologians have long acknowledged that there can be noncausal explanations. Instead of being explained by a cause, God's existence, they say, is explained by God's essence. Perhaps all microphysical explanations are likewise noncausal.

Adam agrees that not everything needs a cause: "only things that have a beginning need a cause."[4] God, for example, wasn't caused but also isn't unexplained. Neo-Russellians can agree that everything has an explanation while denying that all explanations involve causes. Thus, their disagreement isn't about whether things can begin without explanation but instead whether some beginnings can be explained noncausally.

To reconcile Russell's idea that, at the deepest levels, causation is absent from physics with Cartwright's insight that causation is crucial for formulating effective strategies, Neo-Russellians need to explain how causation became part of our everyday, macrophysical perspective. And even if causation doesn't apply microphysically, Neo-Russellians need to explain why they find descriptions in terms of causation useful.

Since the nineteenth century, a branch of physics known as *statistical mechanics* has shown how macrophysical states relate to microphysical states. Many microphysical states result in the same macrophysical state. Consider an analogy. Suppose that you know that, on average, students earned 85 percent in a course. If that's all you know, you wouldn't be able to determine the grade that any individual student earned. Many combinations of grades result in the same average. Likewise, there are many distinct configurations of the atoms in the air filling a room (i.e., many microphysical states) that result in the same volume, mass, pressure, and temperature (i.e., the same macrophysical state).

4. Johnson, "First-Cause Argument."

Some macrophysical states have fewer corresponding microphysical states than others. Suppose that, in one semester, the average was 0 percent. There is only one way for the average to be 0 percent—every student would have to have a 0 percent grade average. Just as there are fewer ways for the average in a course to be 0 percent than there are ways for the average to be 85 percent, so, too, there are fewer ways to arrange atoms in one corner of a room than throughout the entire room. If the class average is 0 percent one semester, most likely, the class average will be different the following semester. Likewise, if a collection of atoms starts bunched into a corner of a room, following physical law, most of the ways that the collection could evolve involve spreading out over the room. So, most likely, the collection will spread out over the room.

The same could be true for causation. Just as we can use statistical mechanics to explain why gases expand to fill a room, so, too, statistical mechanics explains the asymmetry of causal influence. Statistical mechanics explains why we can single out some small set of past events (e.g., Ferdinand's assassination) as mattering more for an event we want to explain (e.g., World War I). Though microphysical changes anywhere to the past of World War I matter for whether World War I happened, there are comparatively few *macrophysical* events to World War I's past that matter. Statistical mechanics also helps to explain why causation is useful for determining effective strategies. There are all sorts of ways we could have described our world. But we are embedded within our world in a way that makes causation useful. Though we don't have the room to explicate it here, much of this story has been worked out in technical detail in the academic literature.[5]

Provided Neo-Russellianism is true, there are two possibilities. On the one hand, just as causation is a useful way to talk given our perspective embedded within the world but is not a feature of our world at the deepest level, that anything *begins to exist* could merely reflect a useful way to talk given our perspective embedded within the world. Crucially, many Neo-Russellians think that

5. E. Adlam, "Laws of Nature as Constraints," *Foundations of Physics* 52, no. 28 (2022); E. Adlam, "Is There Causation in Fundamental Physics? New Insights from Process Matrices and Quantum Causal Modelling," *Synthese* 201, no. 152 (2023); D. Albert, *Time and Chance* (Harvard University Press, 2003); T. Blanchard, "Physics and Causation," *Philosophy Compass* 11 (2016): 256–66; M. Farr and A. Reutlinger. "Relic of a Bygone Age? Causation, Time Symmetry and the Directionality Argument," *Erkenntnis* 78 (2013): 215–35; H. Field, "Causation in a Physical World," in *The Oxford Handbook of Metaphysics*, ed. M. J. Loux and D. W. Zimmerman (Oxford University Press, 2003); J. Ismael, "Reflections on the Asymmetry of Causation," *Interface Focus* 13 (2023): 1–9; C. Rovelli, "How Oriented Causation Is Rooted into Thermodynamics," *Philosophy of Physics* 1, no. 1 (2023): 1–14.

time is fundamentally undirected—our experience of a distinction between the past and the future arises in the macrophysical world but does not apply to the microphysical world. In that case, at the deepest level of analysis the universe didn't begin to exist in any sense that matters for the KCA. Therefore, the second premise of the KCA is false. On the other hand, our notion that anything begins to exist might reflect more than a merely useful way to talk given our perspective embedded within the world. Perhaps, in the deepest description of our world, some things *do* begin to exist. In that case, in the microphysical description nothing that begins has a cause; the causal principle is false. Either way, the KCA makes implicit assumptions incompatible with Neo-Russellianism.

We don't think this argument is completely decisive. After all, despite the view's popularity, not all philosophers are convinced that Neo-Russellianism is correct. We take a modest position. Our position is that, without a good enough reason to reject Neo-Russellianism, we don't have a good enough reason to accept the KCA.

Objection: Maybe some things can begin without causes. That doesn't mean the universe can begin without a cause. On the one hand, this objection confuses the premises of the KCA with its conclusion. The KCA's first premise claims that anything that begins to exist must have a cause. We don't need to refute the idea that the universe has a cause to throw this premise into doubt. On the other hand, if, as many Neo-Russellians argue, causation is explicable in terms of lower-level physical phenomena, then just as there cannot be nonphysical water, so, too, there cannot be nonphysical causes. In that case, nothing, including God, could have caused the universe.

Objection: Neo-Russellians do not actually deny the causal principle because their view is consistent with positing necessary conditions for anything to begin to exist. Some philosophers reject the causal principle because, the claim goes, some quantum events happen without being determined by anything prior. This claim is based on a controversial interpretation of quantum mechanics. Moreover, there is no need for the Neo-Russellian to accept that any events happen without being determined. Nonetheless, Adam might offer a similar response to Neo-Russellianism as the one William Lane Craig has offered to objections based on indeterministic versions of quantum mechanics. Craig argues that indeterministic quantum events "cannot properly be said to be uncaused" because they have "many physically necessary conditions."[6] Craig may reply that just as indeterministic quantum events are not

6. William Lane Craig, "The Caused Beginning of the Universe: A Response to

uncaused because they have physically necessary conditions, Neo-Russellians aren't really claiming that there are uncaused microphysical events because, in their view, all microphysical events have physically necessary conditions.

Craig is wrong that physically necessary conditions are causes. For example, Gillian cannot be the only female child out of three offspring unless she has two brothers. Gillian's two brothers were a necessary condition for, but not the cause of, her being the only female out of three children. Likewise, a condition that necessitates some other occurrence is not generally the cause of that occurrence. A box cannot have a right side without also having a left side, but neither side causes the other. Furthermore, David Lewis, Mark Colyvan, Steven French, and Juha Saatsi have argued that there are examples in physics where, in the complete absence of causes, a system is constrained to evolve in such a way that some other entity—such as a white dwarf star or a molecule—comes to exist.[7]

Objection: If something can begin without a cause, why don't we see this happening all the time? Some philosophers have claimed that without the causal principle, there is no explanation at all for why entities begin at specific places, times, in some specific number, or why only certain kinds of things begin to exist. For example, Craig wonders why, if things can begin without causes, raging tigers and Italian villages do not pop into existence for no reason. Furthermore, the entities that could pop into existence in front of me over the next second seem to vastly outnumber those that do. If things can begin without causes, why isn't our world overrun by vast numbers of entities inexplicably beginning over the next second?[8] This objection confuses something happening for *no reason* and something happening *without a cause*. While Neo-Russellians think that, microphysically, all sorts of events take place without causes, Neo-Russellians do not claim that things happen for no reason at all.

Quentin Smith," *British Journal for the Philosophy of Science* 44, no. 4 (1993): 627, https://doi.org/10.1093/bjps/44.4.623.

7. David Lewis, "Causal Explanation," in *Philosophical Papers*, vol. 2 (Oxford University Press, 1987), 214–40; Mark Colyvan, "Causal Explanation and Ontological Commitment," in *Metaphysics in the Post-Metaphysical Age: Papers of the 22nd International Wittgenstein Symposium*, ed. Uwe Meixner and Peter Simons (Austrian Ludwig Wittgenstein Society, 1999); Steven French and Juha Saatsi, "Symmetries and Explanatory Dependencies in Physics," in *Explanation Beyond Causation: Philosophical Perspectives on Non-Causal Explanations*, ed. Alexander Reutlinger and Juha Saatsi (Oxford University Press, 2018), 185–205.

8. William Lane Craig and James Sinclair, "The Kalam Cosmological Argument," in *The Blackwell Companion to Natural Theology*, ed. William Lane Craig and J. P. Moreland (Wiley-Blackwell, 2009), 186.

We don't need causation to explain why entities do not begin just anywhere, just any when, or in just any number or kind. Recall the three utilities puzzle. Suppose the first two houses are already connected to all three utilities, the third house is already connected to water and gas, and no two connecting lines have crossed. Independent of whether anything can begin without a cause, an uncrossed connecting line cannot begin between the third house and electric. Even if things can begin without causes, whatever already exists constrains what could begin to exist next.

David Hume is sometimes thought to have denied causation, though for reasons distinct from Russell's. Hume was concerned with a puzzle about possibility: Can the existence of any one thing necessitate the existence of some independent thing? For any two things, where both exist together in reality, is it possible for one to exist without the other? Hume argued that events are independent with no necessary connection between them, so that any event could have existed without any other. Since a cause and its effect are independent, Hume thought that a cause (like Ferdinand's assassination) could possibly occur without its effect (World War I) and vice versa. For Hume's followers, even though raging tigers never pop into existence for no reason at arbitrary places and times, it's nonetheless possible for one to do so. For that reason, Hume would say—even if all things that begin to exist in reality have causes—it's false that anything that begins to exist must have a cause.

Other philosophers deny that for any two things, where both exist together in reality, it is possible for one to exist without the other. They believe in necessary connections. For example, some philosophers believe that natural laws are explained by the essences of the entities they govern. The essence of something defines what it is and, according to essentialists, entities like electric and magnetic fields must behave in certain ways because of what they are. Neo-Russellianism is independent of whether there are necessary connections. Hence, Neo-Russellians can accept that while the fields' behavior isn't caused, the fields' essences determine what happens next. In that case, there are necessary connections between independent things, and raging tigers must not spontaneously pop into existence at arbitrary places and times.

Did the Universe Begin to Exist?

Let's turn to the KCA's second premise, namely, that the universe began to exist. KCA proponents defend this premise in two ways: by drawing upon science and by drawing upon purely philosophical arguments. We first consider what it means for the universe to have had a beginning and then consider both cases in turn.

What Does It Mean for the Universe to Begin?

One might think that the phrase "the universe began to exist" merely means it has a finite age. However, philosophers and physicists have good reason to think the idea is more complicated. For example, some propose that, in the deepest description, time doesn't have a direction. Just as statistical mechanics was able to explain why processes tend to happen in only one direction, perhaps statistical mechanics can explain why, in our ordinary experience, time has a direction from the past to the future. Provided the direction of time is not part of the deepest description of our world, beginnings or endings won't be part of the deepest description either. Other philosophers maintain that if time does not objectively pass, nothing really begins.[9] If so, philosophers who think the passage of time is merely a powerful illusion have good reason to reject the KCA. For the sake of argument, we set these issues aside.

Some KCA proponents have views that make it difficult to understand what it would mean for the universe to begin. For example, Craig argues that God is in time and entered time by creating time. Nothing, including God, has existed for more time than there has ever been. If time is finite, then since God entered time some finite number of years ago, God is finitely old. Yet God is beginningless. If Craig is right, some things with a finite age, like God, are beginningless. In that instance, to make a good case for the beginning of the universe Craig needs to show that the universe is not only finitely old but is one of the finitely old things with a beginning. Most arguments for the beginning of the universe (including Craig's) only attempt to show that the universe is finitely old. Hence, if Craig is right that some finitely old things are beginningless, most arguments for the beginning of the universe fail.

The Scientific Case

Setting aside what it may mean for the universe to have a beginning, is there a good case to be made that the universe has a finite past? In our view, science cannot tell us whether the universe has a finite past. You might be perplexed. "Surely," we can imagine you saying, "science has shown that the universe

9. Craig and Sinclair, "Kalam," 183–84; William Lane Craig, "Creation and Divine Action," in *Routledge Companion to Philosophy of Religion*, ed. Chad Meister and Paul Copan (Routledge, 2007), 318–28; William Godfrey-Smith, "Beginning and Ceasing to Exist," *Philosophical Studies* 32, no. 4 (1977): 393–402, https://doi.org/10.1007/BF00368694; David Oderberg, "The Beginning of Existence," *International Philosophical Quarterly* 43, no. 2 (2003): 146, https://doi.org/10.5840/ipq20034325; Ryan Mullins, *The End of the Timeless God* (Oxford University Press, 2016), 135–36, 143, 147.

originated in the big bang!" We agree with the scientific consensus: the largest visible portion of the universe is expanding, and the largest visible portion was once much hotter and denser. But there is no scientific consensus as to whether the big bang was the beginning of everything physical. Cosmologists navigate a sea of conjecture and speculation. For some, the universe has a finite past, but others disagree.

A singularity can be understood as a boundary of space-time, beyond which space-time cannot extend. This isn't a precise definition—it is still up for debate[10]—but it suits our purposes. If we could show that a specific kind of singularity exists in the past of every space-time point, as in some big bang models, we would know the universe's past isn't infinitely long.

Adam claims the Einstein Field Equation (EFE)—the central equation in Einstein's theory of gravity—entails that the universe originated in a singularity and that Einstein introduced the cosmological constant to avoid a beginning.[11] Both science and history are more complex. On the scientific side, while some solutions to the EFE describe the universe expanding out of a singularity, other solutions compatible with all available data do not. In any case, as discussed below, we have good reason for thinking the EFE is only approximately true for contexts less exotic than those near the putative singularity. Hence, even if the EFE did entail an initial singularity, there's no good reason to believe that entailment. On the historical side, Einstein was following previous researchers such as Hugo von Seeliger, who used an analogous method in modifying Newtonian gravitation.[12] Einstein was also motivated by his desire to explain matter.[13] For Einstein, a future theory, one supplanting the EFE, would explain matter and remove singularities.

Adam thinks there is a scientific consensus. Although Adam acknowledges that no specific model with a beginning is uncontroversial, he thinks

10. John Earman, *Bangs, Crunches, Whimpers, and Shrieks* (Oxford University Press, 1995); Erik Curiel, "The Analysis of Singular Spacetimes," *Philosophy of Science* 66 (1999): S119–S145; Erik Curiel, "Singularities and Black Holes," in *Stanford Encyclopedia of Philosophy*, last modified February 27, 2019, https://tinyurl.com/2p8xnrn2; Pankaj Joshi, "Spacetime Singularities," in *Springer Handbook of Spacetime*, ed. Abhay Ashtekar and Vesselin Petkov (Springer, 2014), 409–36.

11. Both claims appear in Johnson, "First-Cause Argument."

12. John Norton, "The Cosmological Woes of Newtonian Gravitation Theory," in *The Expanding Worlds of General Relativity*, vol. 7 of *Einstein Studies*, ed. Hubert Goenner et al. (Birkhauser, 1999), 271–322.

13. John Earman and Jean Eisenstaedt, "Einstein and Singularities," *Studies in History and Philosophy of Science Part B: Studies in History and Philosophy of Modern Physics* 30, no. 2 (1999): 185–235, https://doi.org/10.1016/S1355-2198(99)00005-2.

that almost "everybody agrees that the universe had a beginning."[14] On the contrary, scientific opinion is currently divided with strong claims made on all sides. Alexander Vilenkin writes that the "proof" is "now in place," and "cosmologists can no longer hide behind the possibility of a past-eternal universe."[15] Meanwhile, Sabine Hossenfelder writes, "If you read yet another headline about some physicist who thinks our universe could have begun this way or that way, you should really read this as a creation myth written in the language of mathematics."[16] Our view aligns with Sean Carroll and the majority of physicists, who say that we simply don't know whether the universe is eternal.[17]

Since all cosmological models, whether they have a finite past or not, are speculative, controversial, and subject to criticism, we wouldn't bet on any specific model. Instead, our view aligns with Robert Geroch's perspective: "the mere existence of a [model] having certain global features suggests that there are many models—some perhaps quite reasonable physically—with very similar properties."[18] Even unrealistic models can illustrate features the universe might possess.

This highlights a mistake commonly made in arguments either for the view that the universe began or for the view that the universe was beginningless. The probability that any individual lottery ticket will win may be low, but we shouldn't conclude that, most likely, no ticket will win. Compare this fact about lotteries to one of Craig and Sinclair's arguments.[19] They argue that since individual cosmological models with an infinite past are improbable, probably, the universe doesn't have an infinite past. On the contrary, just as the fact that no individual lottery ticket is likely to win doesn't show that, probably, no ticket will win, so, too, the fact that no individual cosmological model with an infinite past is probable doesn't show that, probably, the universe doesn't have an infinite past. The situation is completely symmetric for models with a

14. Johnson, "First-Cause Argument."

15. Alex Vilenkin, *Many Worlds in One: The Search for Other Universes* (Hill & Wang, 2007), 176.

16. Sabine Hossenfelder, "We Don't Know How the Universe Began, and We Will Never Know," *Backreaction*, August 27, 2022, https://tinyurl.com/2rta6mpc.

17. Sean Carroll, *From Eternity to Here: The Quest for the Ultimate Theory of Time* (Dutton, 2010), 50–51.

18. Robert Geroch, "Space-Time Structure from a Global Viewpoint," in *General Relativity and Cosmology*, ed. B. K. Sachs (Academic Press, 1971), 78.

19. Craig and Sinclair, "Kalam"; William Lane Craig and James Sinclair, "On Non-Singular Space-Times and the Beginning of the Universe," in *Scientific Approaches to the Philosophy of Religion*, ed. Yujin Nagasawa (Palgrave Macmillan, 2012), 95–142.

beginning. No specific cosmological model with a beginning is probable, but this does not entail that a beginning is improbable.

To argue for a beginning, one needs to either show that some specific cosmological model with a beginning is probable or else that the disjunction of all possible beginningless models—even models no one has thought of—is improbable. We don't see a way that one could successfully do either.

Though the situation may change in the future, current physics provides two compelling reasons for thinking we cannot know whether the universe began.

The first reason is the physics horizon. Scientific theories typically apply within some limited domain and break down outside it. Engineers still use Newtonian physics to build bridges because bridges are neither small enough for quantum mechanics to matter nor large enough for general relativity (GR) to matter. But Newtonian physics breaks down when we turn to atoms, where we need quantum mechanics, or black holes, where we need GR. Scientific theories typically don't indicate where they might break down. Typically, we need to look beyond the theory itself for that information.

Present-day physics is different. Our best theories describing particles smaller than atoms (i.e., the standard model of particle physics) and gravity (i.e., GR) both include internal hints about where they might fail. They are said to predict their own demise.

We need both theories to extrapolate the universe backward to the big bang. The standard model likely fails at extremely high energy. GR likely fails at extremely high energy densities and extreme space-time curvatures. When we use these theories to extrapolate the universe backward in time, we encounter increasingly large energies, densities, and curvatures. This marks the conditions where our current theories likely break down, creating a boundary between what we understand and what we don't—the *physics horizon.*[20]

As Ellis and others point out, the physics horizon presents a unique problem.[21] If we can't trust our physical theories beyond the physics horizon, from

20. George Ellis, "Before the Beginning: Emerging Questions and Uncertainties," *Astrophysics and Space Sciences* 269 (1999): 693–720, https://doi.org/10.1023/A:1017277730994; George Ellis, "On the Philosophy of Cosmology," *Studies in History and Philosophy of Science Part B: Studies in History and Philosophy of Modern Physics* 46 (2014): 5–23, https://doi.org/10.1016/j.shpsb.2013.07.006; George Ellis, "The Standard Cosmological Model: Achievements and Issues," *Foundations of Physics* 48 (2018): 1226–45, https://doi.org/10.1007/s10701-018-0176-x; George Ellis, Roy Maartens, and Malcolm MacCullum, *Relativistic Cosmology* (Cambridge University Press, 2012), 530–32.

21. George Ellis, "Before the Beginning," 705–6; Ellis, Maartens, and MacCullum, *Relativistic Cosmology*, 531.

where will a new theory come? The conditions beyond the physics horizon exceed those experimentally available. Cosmological data cannot be used to test new theories while also using those theories to explain the universe's evolution. Thus, the physics horizon represents a limit to our understanding and a boundary to what we can independently verify.

Jacobus Erasmus, one prominent KCA proponent, has replied that while GR may not describe the highly exotic conditions near the big bang, we can trust its prediction of a cosmic beginning.[22] GR and GR's successor—a future theory of quantum gravity—describe the same reality at distinct levels. Hence, Erasmus concludes, if GR predicts a beginning, so, too, must quantum gravity. Erasmus is mistaken for two reasons.

First, Erasmus's reasoning cuts both ways. If it's true that something having a beginning at a higher level implies a beginning at a lower level, then having a beginning at a lower level should imply having a beginning at a higher level. GR supplanted Newtonian gravity. Newtonian gravity includes its own description of the big bang, with many of the same equations but without a beginning. Hence, a beginning described at one level doesn't need to appear at other levels. Second, Erasmus falsely assumes that a successor theory must only make small revisions to the theory it replaces. While the successor must replicate past empirical successes, the successor can introduce unexpected and drastic changes. For example, Newtonian gravity fails dramatically for some large-scale objects (e.g., neutron stars and black holes) described by GR. Likewise, whatever happened at the big bang likely radically differs from GR's predictions.

Let's move on to the second compelling reason for thinking we cannot know whether the universe began with the big bang: the Malament-Manchak theorem. First, some background. Since no signal can travel faster than light, I can only receive signals from a specific region of space-time known as my *past light cone*. This applies to all observers. The full set of observations made by all observers in space-time forms a collection of past light cones. If we were to construct another space-time model that includes all the same past light cones as the original, any observer in the original has a counterpart in the new model who makes all the same observations. As a result, no observation in the universe described by the original model could distinguish between the two.

The global properties of space-time are those that space-time possesses as a whole. To know whether space-time as a whole has a beginning, we need

22. Jacobus Erasmus, *The Kalām Cosmological Argument: A Reassessment* (Springer, 2018), 153.

to know its global properties. We can only glimpse a small part of space-time. Perhaps we have evidence that the small part to our past includes a beginning, the objection from the physics horizon notwithstanding. There are space-time models where there is no universal direction of time, so no objective beginning, but that include regions where, according to the region's direction of time, the region had a beginning. For all we know, we could be in a space-time like that.

As David Malament conjectured and J. B. Manchak proved, given any set of past light cones from almost any space-time model, we can construct another space-time model that includes the same past light cones but with distinct global properties.[23] No observation could favor the first model over the second. Space-time models with an overall direction of time, and so with the possibility of an objective beginning, have an observationally indistinguishable counterpart without an overall direction of time and without the possibility of an objective beginning.

Maybe we've moved too quickly. Couldn't we extrapolate from the largest observable part of our universe to infer that the rest of the universe probably has the same properties? Philosopher Nelson Goodman distinguished lawlike generalizations, which can be projected into new circumstances, from accidental generalizations, which usually cannot.[24] For example, if previously examined bits of copper are electrically conductive, we can infer that unexamined bits of copper will likely be as well. However, if all previously examined coins from my pocket are nickels, this doesn't mean unexamined coins will also be nickels. Lawlike generalizations can be projected because confirming their instances increases the probability that they apply to unexamined cases.

Lawlike generalizations are typically based on local properties. When we use generalizations based on local properties to infer the global properties of space-time, we limit ourselves to space-time models that fit those local properties. However, even with these restrictions, it's possible to construct

23. David Malament, "Observationally Indistinguishable Space-Times," in *Foundations of Space-Time Theories*, ed. John Earman, Clark Glymour, and John Stachel, Minnesota Studies in the Philosophy of Science 8 (University of Minnesota Press, 1977), 61–80; J. B. Manchak, "Can We Know the Global Structure of Spacetime?," *Studies in History and Philosophy of Science Part B: Studies in History and Philosophy of Modern Physics* 40, no. 1 (2009): 53–56, https://doi.org/10.1016/j.shpsb.2008.07.004. For a less technical discussion, see J. B. Manchak, "The Universe Is Unknowable from Within It," *IAI News*, January 24, 2025, https://tinyurl.com/mu88nksh.

24. Nelson Goodman, *Fact, Fiction, and Forecast*, 4th ed. (Harvard University Press, 1983), 73.

different space-time models with the same set of past light cones but a distinct global structure.[25] Some lawlike generalizations, namely, those involving a phenomenon called *quantum entanglement*, are not based on local properties. Quantum entanglement won't allow us to receive signals from outside our past light cones, so it doesn't help us to discover space-time's global structure either. Therefore, we cannot infer from the largest observable part of our universe that the rest of the universe probably has the same properties.

Objection: Don't the singularity theorems show that the universe began to exist? Three theorems—one by Stephen Hawking and Roger Penrose,[26] another by Arvind Borde, Alan Guth, and Alexander Vilenkin,[27] and a third by Aaron Wall[28]—have been claimed to show that space-time is singular. We don't have room to explicate those theorems here. However, no known singularity theorem escapes the physics horizon or Malament-Manchak theorem. Regarding the physics horizon, the predicted singularity lies within the region where known physics likely doesn't apply. Regarding the Malament-Manchak theorem, even if we knew there was a singularity in our past, we couldn't infer that it's to the past of all space-time points. So, the singularity theorems are no help in determining whether the universe began.

Objection: Doesn't the second law of thermodynamics show that the universe is past finite? On the largest observable scales, entropy is on the rise. If the universe has been around forever, shouldn't the universe have reached thermodynamic equilibrium? First, the universe may lack an equilibrium state altogether, forever increasing in entropy.[29] Second, some cosmological models suggest a mechanism for resetting a large region of space-time, like the largest observable region, to a low entropy state.[30] The lesson from the Malament-

25. Manchak, "Can We Know," 55.

26. Stephen Hawking and Roger Penrose, "The Singularities of Gravitational Collapse and Cosmology," *Proceedings of the Royal Society A* 314, no. 1519 (1970): 529–48, https://doi.org/10.1098/rspa.1970.0021.

27. Arvind Borde, Alan Guth, and Alexander Vilenkin, "Inflationary Spacetimes Are Incomplete in Past Directions," *Physical Review Letters* 90, no. 15 (2003): 1–4, https://doi.org/10.1103/PhysRevLett.90.151301.

28. Aaron Wall, "The Generalized Second Law Implies a Quantum Singularity Theorem," *Classical and Quantum Gravity* 30, no. 16 (2013): 1–35, https://doi.org/10.1088/0264-9381/30/16/165003.

29. For example, see Sean Carroll and Jennifer Chen, "Spontaneous Inflation and the Origin of the Arrow of Time," *arXivLabs* (2004): 1–36, https://doi.org/10.48550/arXiv.hep-th/0410270.

30. Nikodem Popławski, "Cosmology with Torsion: An Alternative to Cosmic Inflation," *Physics Letters B* 694, no. 3 (2010): 181–85, https://doi.org/10.1016/j.physletb.2010.09.056;

Manchak theorem still applies: even if the largest region we can observe has a low entropy boundary in its past, it does not follow that the universe, as a whole, has a low entropy boundary.

Again, we do not claim that any specific model is probable; we doubt that any specific model is probable. These examples illustrate features a realistic model might, for all we know, include. A finite age for the universe doesn't follow from the second law of thermodynamics.

The Purely Philosophical Case

There's little hope for a scientific case for premise 2. But premise 2 has also been defended through philosophical arguments. We will consider two such arguments: the *Hilbert hotel argument* and the *successive addition argument.* We find both unconvincing. Moreover, we will draw a general lesson concerning attempts to demonstrate the impossibility of an infinite or beginningless past.

The Hilbert's Hotel Argument

Let's start with the Hilbert's hotel argument:

1. An actual infinite cannot exist.
2. An infinite temporal regress of events is an actual infinite.
3. Therefore, an infinite temporal regress of events cannot exist.

Craig supports the first premise that an actual infinite cannot exist, through thought experiments like Hilbert's hotel. Hilbert's hotel has infinitely many rooms. In an ordinary hotel, if every room is occupied, no additional guests can be accommodated. Not so for the infinite hotel. By shifting guests around—moving the guest in room 1 to room 2, the guest in room 2 to room 3, and so

Nikodem Popławski, "Universe in a Black Hole in Einstein-Cartan Gravity," *The Astrophysical Journal* 832, no. 96 (2016): 1–8, https://doi.org/10.3847/0004-637X/832/2/96; Paul Steinhardt and Neil Turok, "Cosmic Evolution in a Cyclic Universe," *Physical Review D* 65, no. 12 (2002): 1–20, https://doi.org/10.1103/PhysRevD.65.126003; Paul Steinhardt and Neil Turok, *Endless Universe: Beyond the Big Bang—Rewriting Cosmic History* (Broadway, 2007); Anna Ijjas and Paul Steinhardt, "Fully Stable Cosmological Solutions with a Non-Singular Classical Bounce," *Physics Letters B* 764, no. 10 (2017): 289–94, https://doi.org/10.1016/j.physletb.2016.11.047; Anna Ijjas and Paul Steinhardt, "Bouncing Cosmology Made Simple," *Classical and Quantum Gravity* 35, no. 13 (2018): 1–19, https://doi.org/10.1088/1361-6382/aac482.

on—a new guest can be accommodated. Any number of new guests can be accommodated.[31]

Craig exploits a counterintuitive property of infinite sets. In a finite hotel, there are fewer even-numbered rooms than total rooms. Not so for infinite sets. Although not all counting numbers are even, there are as many counting numbers as there are even numbers. Mathematicians say that infinite sets can include a proper subset that has the same size (or cardinality) as the full set.

Absurdity

Metaphysical possibility refers to what is possible in the broadest sense, even if it doesn't exist in the actual world. Craig argues that the "absurdity" of Hilbert's hotel helps to establish that an actual infinite is metaphysically impossible: "Hilbert's Hotel is absurd. But if an actual infinite were metaphysically possible, then such a hotel would be metaphysically possible. It follows that the real existence of an actual infinite is not metaphysically possible."[32] What does Craig mean by "absurd"? Perhaps "absurd" means strange. But something being strange does not entail being metaphysically impossible. As Alexander Pruss notes, the possibility of the strange "is proved by the strangeness of the platypus."[33]

If Craig could prove that the existence of an actual infinite leads to a contradiction, he would demonstrate its impossibility. Craig sometimes appears to argue that Hilbert's hotel leads to contradictions. He claims that when guests check out, absurdities arise because subtraction or division, applied to infinite collections, produces contradictory results. For example, when all the guests with room numbers greater than three check out, we are left with three guests, while, if all the guests with room numbers greater than five check out, we are left with five guests. Nonetheless, "in both cases we subtracted the identical number of numbers from the identical number of numbers and yet did not arrive at an identical result."[34] The idea is clear. Subtracting numbers means mentally removing them from a collection. However, the devil is in the details.

Craig is careful to note that the purely abstract mathematical systems describing the infinite are perfectly consistent: "While such a system may be perfectly consistent in the mathematical realm, given its axioms and conventions, I think that it is intuitively obvious that such a system could not possibly exist

31. William Lane Craig, *The Kalām Cosmological Argument* (Macmillan, 1979), 84–85.
32. Craig and Sinclair, "Kalam," 110.
33. Alexander Pruss, *Infinity, Causation, and Paradox* (Oxford University Press, 2018), 12.
34. Craig and Sinclair, "Kalam," 112.

in reality."[35] In the way mathematicians usually describe the infinite (Cantorian transfinite cardinal arithmetic) there is no such thing as subtraction. Therefore, in the abstract realm, the cases Craig imagines—where subtracting infinity from infinity leads to inconsistencies—do not occur. However, for Craig, this rule is just a convention mathematicians created to ensure consistency and cannot be enforced in the real world. When considering an infinite library, Craig writes: "While we may correct the mathematician who attempts inverse operations with transfinite numbers, we cannot in the real world prevent people from checking out what books they please from our library."[36] Craig mistakenly assumes that removing guests from Hilbert's hotel or withdrawing books from an infinite library only involves "subtraction." Craig is mistaken. Instead, such cases involve *relative complements*. The relative complement of set A in set B is everything in B that isn't in A. For example, if A = {2, 3, 4} and B = {1, 2, 3}, the relative complement of A in B is {1}. Similarly, if A is the numbers greater than 3 and B is the counting numbers, the relative complement of A in B has only three members; if A is the set of numbers greater than 5, the relative complement of A in B has five members. No contradiction results.

We can consistently describe Craig's thought experiments—whether they concern hotels, libraries, or whatever—using relative complements. We can describe the behavior of Hilbert's hotel mathematically, including various numbers of guests checking out, and never arrive at contradictory results.

While an actual infinite may not involve a contradiction, philosophers often argue something is metaphysically impossible without identifying a strict contradiction. Unfortunately, as Craig admits, there are no "clean, decisive markers of what is [metaphysically] possible or impossible." Instead, philosophers rely on "intuitions and conceivability arguments," which are "much more subjective" than strictly logical arguments. Yet, these arguments "cannot be refuted by facile observations" that a strict logical impossibility hasn't been shown.[37]

Two replies. First, if Craig is right and appeals to metaphysical impossibility end up in subjective appeals to intuitions, then Craig's case is quite weak. Even if, before studying the infinite, your intuitions align with Craig's, not everyone's will. And what about our intuitions *after* we study the infinite? As Graham Oppy notes, "these allegedly absurd situations are just what one ought

35. Craig, *Kalām*, 82.

36. William Lane Craig and Quentin Smith, *Theism, Atheism, and Big Bang Cosmology* (Oxford University Press, 1995), 15.

37. Craig and Sinclair, "Kalam," 106.

to expect if there were large and small denumerable physical infinities."[38] Thus, in this context appeals to intuition are unconvincing.

Second, plausibly, our intuitions are reliable for familiar matters but unreliable for exotic scenarios.[39] Appeals to intuition are inherently weak, and there are good reasons not to rely on intuition concerning exotic scenarios. If Craig's premise can only be defended by intuition, we can be perfectly rational in not buying his premise.

Perhaps by "absurd," Craig means that Hilbert's hotel is metaphysically impossible. If so, we'd expect a *reductio* argument in support. In a *reductio* argument, a proposition is shown to imply a contradiction, and we are led to infer that the proposition is impossible. Sometimes, Craig seems to offer a *reductio*. For example, he writes, "it is ontologically absurd that a hotel exists which is completely full and yet can accommodate untold infinities of new guests just by moving people around."[40] The idea seems to be that anything that is full cannot accommodate new guests, Hilbert's hotel is full, yet Hilbert's hotel can accommodate new guests. So, we have a contradiction.

But this argument equivocates between two meanings of the word "full." If "full" means all the rooms are occupied, then while Hilbert's hotel is full, being full does not entail being unable to accommodate new guests. Clearly, Hilbert's hotel can have all its rooms occupied and still make room for new guests. On the other hand, perhaps "full" means no new guests can be accommodated, but then Hilbert's hotel isn't full because it can accommodate new guests.

Perhaps Hilbert's hotel is metaphysically impossible because Hilbert's hotel contradicts a metaphysically necessary principle. Craig proposes Euclid's maxim (EM) as a metaphysically necessary principle. According to EM, the whole is greater than any proper part. Hilbert's hotel violates EM because one of the hotel's proper parts, the even-numbered rooms, has just as many members as the entire hotel. However, whether any principle, including EM, is metaphysically necessary is controversial. Since we know that abstract collections, like counting numbers, violate EM, Craig argues that EM only applies to concrete things. If something is concrete, Craig claims, EM applies. We propose a simpler and less controversial alternative: if something is finite, EM applies. Our proposal has the advantage of being a basic mathematical

38. Graham Oppy, *Philosophical Perspectives on Infinity* (Cambridge University Press, 2006), 48.

39. James Ladyman and Don Ross, *Every Thing Must Go: Metaphysics Naturalized* (Oxford University Press, 2007), 2.

40. Craig and Sinclair, "Kalam," 111.

fact, as for finite collections, proper parts are smaller than the whole, but not necessarily for infinite collections. Absent any argument that EM is metaphysically necessary (and Craig doesn't offer one), we are back to mere appeals to intuition.

The Successive Addition Argument

According to the successive addition argument (SAA), time can't stretch back infinitely because the past is formed through a process called *successive addition*. Events move from the future, to the present, and then into the past, one at a time. As time passes, past events accumulate gradually, like counting numbers one by one. According to the SAA, this step-by-step process could never result in an infinite past.

Here's the SAA:

1. A collection formed by successive addition cannot be an actual infinite.
2. The series of past events is a collection formed by successive addition.
3. Therefore, the series of past events cannot be an actual infinite.

Craig believes that the second premise requires the objective passage of time.[41] Many philosophers would reject the second premise because they think time does not objectively pass. Moreover, even if time does objectively pass, and events are added one by one to the past, proponents of an infinite past may doubt the past *formed* by successive addition. After all, if the past is infinitely long, there never was a time when the past *grew* to be infinitely long. Instead, events were only ever added to an already infinite past. We set both objections aside.

Our objections target premise 1, namely, a collection formed by successive addition cannot be actually infinite. To see things clearly, counting up should be distinguished from counting down. Let's begin with counting up. Craig writes: "The impossibility of the formation of an actual infinite by successive addition seems obvious in the case of beginning at some point and trying to reach infinity."[42] Imagine George is counting numbers, one number per second. Supposing nothing stops George from counting, George will count to any arbitrarily large natural number. But George's counting always remains finite. Successive addition can only yield finite results.

41. Craig and Sinclair, "Kalam," 124.
42. Craig and Sinclair, "Kalam," 117.

One of us (Alex) has recently updated an important objection to this point due to Dretske.[43] If George never stops counting, for every number George will (eventually) count that number. And that means the *number* of numbers George will count is infinite. That is, George will count every member of an actually infinite collection.

Does this constitute a counterexample to premise 1 of the SAA? George's future includes infinitely many counting events, each added one at a time. Thus, the collection of George's future counting events is an actually infinite collection formed by successive addition. If so, premise 1 is false.

Craig could object that there will never come a time when George reaches an infinitieth number; the set of numbers George has counted will never be infinite. If so, isn't the collection of numbers George will count only potentially infinite, that is, a collection that, while always finite, grows toward infinity as a limit? This objection confuses the set of numbers George *will* count with the set of numbers George *will have* counted at various points in the future. Suppose the set of numbers George will have counted will never be infinite. Unlike potential infinities, the numbers George will count do not grow towards infinity as a limit; instead the set of numbers George will count is successively *subtracted from* as each number is successively removed from the future and added to the past. So long as George never stops counting, the numbers George will count form an actually infinite collection.[44]

Craig might object that just because each member of a collection has a certain property, the whole collection need not share that property. For example, every student in a class has a biological parent, but there is no biological parent all the students share—the students aren't siblings. Similarly, Craig could argue that just because George will count each number, it doesn't mean he will count all of them. Craig is mistaken. While we cannot always infer from each to all, in some cases we can. If each child has a mother, no child is motherless. Similarly, if George counts each number, no number is left uncounted. The collection of George's future counting events is actually infinite.

43. Fred Dretske, "Counting to Infinity," *Analysis* 25 (1965): 99–100, https://doi.org/10.1093/analys/25.Suppl-3.99; Alex Malpass, "All the Time in the World," *Mind* 131, no. 523 (2022): 788–806, https://doi.org/10.1093/mind/fzaa086.

44. We have set aside, for example, Malament-Hogarth space-times, which allow, in some sense, someone to have already counted to infinity. See John Earman and John Norton, "Forever Is a Day: Supertasks in Pitowsky and Malament-Hogarth Spacetimes," *Philosophy of Science* 60, no. 1 (1993): 22–42, https://doi.org/10.1086/289716; Oppy, *Infinity*, sec. 4.6; J. B. Manchak, "Malament-Hogarth Machines," *British Journal for Philosophy of Science* 71, no. 3 (2020): 1143–53.

Thus, we think it is debatable whether premise 1 of the SAA is true when we consider counting up.[45] What about counting down? Imagine encountering George, who says, "3, 2, 1 . . . Phew, I've just finished counting down through all the numbers." Such a scenario is certainly strange and not a physically realistic possibility. But is such a scenario metaphysically impossible?

The Mirror Principle

Let's assume, for argument's sake, that counting up toward infinity can never produce an actual infinite. It's tempting to conclude that the opposite process—a beginningless series of additions with an endpoint—is also impossible. Craig asks, "If one cannot traverse the infinite by moving in one direction, how can one traverse it by moving in the opposite direction?"[46]

This idea seems to assume a "mirror principle"—that if an endless series is impossible, so is a beginningless one.[47] However, several philosophers have recently challenged the mirror principle.[48]

The issue with counting to infinity is that there's no "final number" to reach. But an infinite countdown, though beginningless, does have an endpoint. If there's a problem with the countdown, it's not due to a lack of an endpoint.

Craig sometimes puts the argument another way. An infinite counting up is a potential infinite, always growing but never actually infinite. As Craig notes, "a potential infinite cannot be turned into an actual infinite by any amount of successive addition since the result of every addition will always be finite."[49] If the mirror principle held, this would also rule out infinite countdowns.

However, an infinite countdown doesn't involve converting a potential infinite into an actual one. At every point in the past, George has already counted down infinitely. No conversion is needed. Thus, we can dismiss the mirror principle.

45. Although, for an interesting response, see Mohammad Saleh Zarepour, "Counting to Infinity, Successive Addition, and the Length of the Past," *International Journal for Philosophy of Religion* 92, no. 3 (2022): 167–76, https://doi.org/10.1007/s11153-022-09843-0.

46. Craig and Sinclair, "Kalam," 118.

47. This idea is also discussed in J. P. Moreland, "The Kalam Cosmological Argument," in *Philosophy of Religion: Selected Readings*, 2nd ed., ed. Michael Peterson et al. (Oxford University Press, 2001), 196–208.

48. Felipe Leon, "Moreland on the Impossibility of Traversing the Infinite: A Critique," *Philo* 14, no. 1 (2011): 32–42, https://doi.org/10.5840/philo20111413; Wes Morriston, "Infinity, Time, and Successive Addition," *Australasian Journal of Philosophy* 100, no. 1 (2022): 70–85, https://doi.org/10.1080/00048402.2020.1865426; Malpass, "All the Time."

49. Craig and Sinclair, "Kalam," 118.

The Principle of Sufficient Reason.

Instead of appealing to a mirror principle, Craig sometimes appeals to the apparent violation of the principle of sufficient reason: "We could ask, why did he not finish counting yesterday or the day before or the year before? By then an infinite time had already elapsed, so that he has had ample time to finish. Thus, at no point in the infinite past should we ever find the man finishing his countdown, for by that point he should already be done!"[50] Yesterday, George had already spent an infinite amount of time counting down; he should have been done by then. While this has some initial plausibility to it, we think it contains an obvious error. Compare the following:

1. If George is finishing an infinite countdown today, then there have been infinitely many past counting events.
2. If there have been infinitely many past counting events, then George is finishing an infinite countdown today.

To us, statement 1 seems obviously true. Supposing the counting events are regularly spaced out in time, his finishing the task now means he must have been doing it forever.

In contrast, statement 2 is not obvious. Just because an infinite amount of time has passed doesn't mean that anyone is finishing a countdown right now. The fact that there "has been enough time" already doesn't mean that it has happened. The amount of time that has passed is enough for an infinite countdown to be finishing now, but it's not a strict logical requirement.

But surely, there is no *reason* why George is finishing now rather than yesterday or tomorrow. If so, this would violate the principle that all contingent facts have a sufficient reason. A great deal hangs on what's meant by "sufficient reason." Does a sufficient reason have to entail what the reason explains? If not, what is the relationship exactly? This pushes the discussion too far afield for present purposes, but there is a lively debate on this topic in the literature.[51]

However, one thought is that we can provide strong sufficient reasons in the following manner. George finished today rather than yesterday (etc.) for two reasons: (1) yesterday, he was counting the number 2, and (2) George counted one number per day. George's finishing today is logically entailed by these two reasons. Craig needs to tell us why this is not explanation enough.

50. Craig and Sinclair, "Kalam," 121–22.

51. See, e.g., Alexander Pruss, *The Principle of Sufficient Reason: A Reassessment* (Cambridge University Press, 2006); Morriston, "Infinity," 70–85.

Drawing a General Lesson

We can learn a general lesson from thought experiments that aim to show the impossibility of an infinite past, which we'll call finitist thought experiments. These include examples like Hilbert's hotel, counting up to infinity, or converting a finite series into an infinite one as well as others not covered here.[52] Finitist thought experiments typically follow two approaches: one tries to show that an infinite past leads to a contradiction, while the other argues that it violates a metaphysically necessary principle. The success of the latter depends on showing that the principle is indeed metaphysically necessary, but we'll set that point aside for now.

Both strategies face a key objection: they show, at most, that certain combinations of conditions lead to a contradiction. This means the conditions cannot all be true together, but it does not mean any single condition is to blame.[53] You should not conclude that your existence is impossible just because a scenario involving the combination of your existence and nonexistence is impossible. Similarly, the fact that thought experiments involving an infinite past lead to contradictions doesn't show that an infinite past is impossible.

Fans of finitist thought experiments could reply that the fact that various finitist thought experiments entail a contradiction is best explained by the impossibility of an infinite past. We remain unconvinced. A simpler explanation is that contradictions arise because the conditions in the thought experiments cannot all be true at once. Alternatively, friends of finitist thought experiments might reply that had an infinite past been metaphysically possible, various finitist thought experiments would also have been possible. But we are equally unconvinced by this reply. Again, the fact that your existence is possible does not imply that your existence conjoined with your nonexistence is possible.

52. See, for example, the grim reaper thought experiments described in Robert C. Koons, "A New Kalām Argument: Revenge of the Grim Reaper," *Noûs* 48, no. 2 (2014): 256–67, https://doi.org/10.1111/j.1468-0068.2012.00858.x; Robert C. Koons, "The Grim Reaper Kalam Argument: From Temporal and Causal Finitism to God," in *The Kalām Cosmological Argument: Philosophical Arguments for the Finitude of the Past*, ed. Paul Copan and William Lane Craig (Bloomsbury Academic, 2017).

53. Similar points have been made in Nicholas Shackel, "The Form of the Benardete Dichotomy," *British Journal for the Philosophy of Science* 56, no. 2 (2005): 397–417, https://doi.org/10.1093/bjps/axi121; Landon Hedrick, "Once More to the Hotel," *Religious Studies* 58, no. 1 (2022): 18–29, https://doi.org/10.1017/S003441252000013X; Troy Dana and Joseph Schmid, "Grim Reaper Paradoxes and Patchwork Principles: Severing the Case for Finitism," *Journal of Philosophy* (forthcoming); Joseph Schmid and Alex Malpass, "Benardete Paradoxes, Causal Finitism, and the Unsatisfiable Pair Diagnosis," *Mind* 134, no. 534 (2025): 397–421.

Conclusion

Adam's version of the Kalām Cosmological Argument states: (1) whatever has a beginning must have a cause; (2) the universe had a beginning; therefore, (3) the universe had a cause. No good reason has been offered to accept either premise. First, contemporary philosophy of physics casts doubt on the assumptions the argument implicitly makes concerning causation. Second, the scientific and philosophical cases for premise 2 are unconvincing. The scientific case relies on extrapolating far beyond the domain where we can have reasonable confidence. The various philosophical defenses of premise 2 are not persuasive either. We concluded by drawing a general lesson about the limitations of thought experiments in arguments against an infinite past.

For all that we've said, both of the KCA's premises may be true, but no compelling reason has been provided to support them. Until persuasive reasons are offered, we remain humble and withhold our assent. Nonetheless, the KCA introduces two philosophical questions worthy of further investigation: whether the nature of causation allows for the universe to have had a cause, and whether the universe began to exist. Here, we encounter the deepest of cosmic mysteries. As T. H. Huxley wrote in 1887, "The known is finite, the unknown infinite; intellectually we stand on an islet in the midst of an illimitable ocean of inexplicability. Our business in every generation is to reclaim a little more land."[54] We encourage readers, whatever their current beliefs, to join us in pursuing both questions.

54. Thomas Henry Huxley, "On the Reception of the 'Origin of Species,'" in *The Life and Letters of Charles Darwin*, ed. Francis Darwin, vol. 1 (Dodo, 2008), 568.

15

Response to the Contributors

Concluding Remarks for Theism

Adam Lloyd Johnson

First I want to express a heartfelt thank you to David Williamson and the Central Florida Freethought Community for inviting me to the 2022 debate upon which this book is based. I'm thankful for the nontheists who allowed me to attend their conference and treated me with kindness and appreciation. I'll never forget an older atheist couple who told me afterward that they were thinking about not attending the debate but were glad they did because they said they'd never before heard these arguments for God I presented. I also want to thank Dan Barker for being a respectful, friendly debater. To those who wrote chapters for this book, thank you for the time you spent sharing your expertise. Last, I'm especially thankful to Andrew Drinkard for traveling to the debate with me and for all his hard work in spearheading and overseeing this book.

In this initial section of this chapter I'll briefly address several issues that came up throughout this book. Dan suggested I sometimes leaned toward "arguing from authority" when I quoted key thinkers in the debate.[1] I agree it's a mistake to think something is true just because an expert says it is, but that's not why I share such quotes. First, I share them in order to point people to good resources, if they want to learn more. Second, I recognize I'm not an expert in many of these areas, so it's important to see what those who've spent years studying these issues have to say. Third, I want to show that there are contemporary proponents of theistic arguments at the highest level of academia to counter the narrative, which even I used to believe, that only uneducated people believe in God. Fourth, I want to encourage people by letting them know about the many nontheists who have turned to God lately—including one of

1. Dan Barker, "Expanding on the Debate: Additional Points and Arguments for Atheism," 62.

the authors of this book, Philip Goff, and former "New Atheism" leader Ayaan Hirsi Ali. Some are even wondering, with the decline in the New Atheism movement, if possibly we're on the verge of a "New Christian" movement.[2]

I continue to be surprised by what Dan says about abductive reasoning. This form of reasoning is often referred to as "inference to the best explanation" because it directs us to the explanation for the evidence being considered that's the most comprehensive, coherent, and satisfactory. In our debate Dan said, "abductive logic . . . is just a fancy word for your 'best guess.'"[3] In his recent book *Contraduction*, he described having an "epiphany" during the debate when he "suddenly glimpsed what is wrong with the reasoning. It is backward."[4] He claims my use of abductive reasoning is a "fatal flaw"[5] in my approach and coined the term *contraduction* to express what he thinks in my arguments is a "hidden fallacy that inverts reality."[6] He was so inspired by his epiphany that after the debate he wrote the book *Contraduction* to disparage abductive reasoning. In this book he states backward reasoning happens when we "invert reality and flip our interpretation of what we observe," and we all "sometimes fool ourselves, unknowingly reversing reality to fit our preconceptions."[7] I agree people make these mistakes sometimes, but that's not what abductive reasoning is at all. Dan probably should've consulted his philosophical friends before writing a book against abductive logic. Thankfully I don't have to defend my use of abductive reasoning because nontheists Benjamin Watkins and David Enoch have already done so in this book.[8]

As I noted in the debate, there are numerous arguments for God. To whet your appetite, check out *Two Dozen (Or So) Arguments for God* published by Oxford University Press. However, in our short debate I only had time to discuss three main families of such arguments—first cause, design, and moral. I personally find design arguments the most persuasive. Evidently Dan does, too, in light of his remark that the "fine-tuning argument might give us

2. Nathan Guy, "Some of Christianity's Biggest Skeptics Are Becoming Vocal Converts," *Christianity Today* 68, no. 6, September/October 2024, https://tinyurl.com/bdeazdss. See also Justin Brierley, *The Surprising Rebirth of Belief in God: Why New Atheism Grew Old and Secular Thinkers Are Considering Christianity Again* (Tyndale Elevate, 2023).

3. Dan Barker, "Does God Exist? A Debate," 26.

4. Dan Barker, *Contraduction* (Hypatia, 2024), 2.

5. Barker, "Expanding on the Debate," 65.

6. Barker, "Expanding on the Debate," 61.

7. Barker, *Contraduction*, 2, 6.

8. Watkins, "Nontheist Responding to the Debate," 212–13. Enoch, "Nontheist Responding to the Debate," 235–36. Theist David Baggett also affirmed abductive reasoning and suggested a resource for those who want to understand it better on pp. 217–18. See also Peter Lipton, *Inference to the Best Explanation*, 2nd ed. (Routledge, 2004).

a suspect," and "it just gives you permission to consider that there might be some suspect out there."[9] Dan pushed back against the fine-tuning argument by noting that sometimes it's difficult to detect design.[10] In practice, there definitely are situations when it's difficult to know if something is designed or not, such as when an archeologist digs up an item that looks like a circular plate but might just be a flat rock. However, there are other times when we can be extremely confident something was designed, such as if that archeologist discovered sentences written on the plate. Thankfully, we don't have to rely merely on our subjective intuitions to detect design because specified complexity, a common definition of design, can actually be quantified using probability.[11] Dan also pushed back by noting that the vast majority of the universe, except for our planet, seems quite hostile to life and thus not fine-tuned for its flourishing.[12] Elsewhere I've responded to this objection with an analogy of finding a cabin in the woods—even if the rest of the woods was in complete disarray, from the cabin alone we'd conclude a designer had been there.[13]

As for the multiverse objection, the *Oxford Handbook of the History of Modern Cosmology* summarizes well one of the primary concerns about the multiverse theory: "Although multiverse proposals are motivated by trends in fundamental physics, the detailed accounts of how the multiverse arises are typically beyond theoretical control. As long as this is the case, there is a risk that the claimed multiverse explanations are just-so stories, where the mechanism of generating the multiverse is contrived to do the job."[14] In addition, in this book Philip Goff and Robin Collins did a tremendous job explaining why Dan is terribly wrong to claim the "multiverse kills the fine-tuning argument."[15] Though at one point Goff wrote "if God and the multiverse are equal in all other respects, the multiverse wins,"[16] later he clarified "that much of this discussion has been premised on the assumption that both God and the multiverse can explain fine-tuning. In fact, I've argued at length in my other work that we

9. Barker, "Does God Exist?," 30.

10. Barker, "Expanding on the Debate," 73–74.

11. George D. Montanez, "A Unified Model of Complex Specified Information," *BIO-Complexity* 2018, no. 4 (2018): 1–26, https://doi.org/10.5048?BIO-C.2018.4.

12. Barker, "Expanding on the Debate," 76.

13. Adam Lloyd Johnson, "A Cabin in the Woods: A Former Statistician Responds to a Critique of the Bayesian Version of the Fine-Tuning Argument for God's Existence," *Eleutheria* 5, no. 1 (2021): 18–31, https://doi.org/10.70623/FREB6449.

14. Chris Smeenk, "Philosophical Aspects of Cosmology," in *The Oxford Handbook of the History of Modern Cosmology*, ed. Helge Kragh and Malcolm S. Longair (Oxford University Press, 2019), 524.

15. Barker, "Expanding on the Debate," 72.

16. Philip Goff, "Nontheist Responding to the Debate: God or the Multiverse?," 159.

cannot explain fine-tuning in terms of a multiverse. If that's right, then the multiverse doesn't even make it to the starting line of this race."[17] Collins in turn explained that even if there is a multiverse, a strong case could be made that it, too, requires fine-tuning.[18] He also noted that the fine-tuning for life argument is just the tip of the iceberg when it comes to design arguments and presented several design arguments impervious to multiverse objections.

Mind Games

I agree with Benjamin Watkins that Dan's argument that "nonphysical minds are contradictory" is unsound.[19] However, Watkins described a legitimate form of reasoning when he explained an argument against the notion of an immaterial mind: "All known minds (both human and nonhuman) involve embodied brains, therefore, by enumerative induction, all unknown minds probably involve embodied brains too."[20] This is exactly the same reasoning I used in my design argument, where I noted that since we've only ever seen design come from an intelligent mind, if the universe has evidence of design, then it's reasonable to conclude the universe came from an intelligent mind. Dan used this type of reasoning as well: "We have never observed an effect without a natural cause. The universe appears to be an effect. Therefore the universe had a natural cause."[21]

This form of reasoning is appropriate because none of us are arguing that our conclusions are necessarily certain or that other conclusions are impossible, only that our conclusions are reasonable based on past observations. If I've only ever seen my neighbor Bob take his trash can to the curb, and let's say I've seen this thousands of times, then when I wake up and see his trash can at the curb, it would be appropriate for me to conclude, based on past observations, that Bob took it there. However, it would be poor reasoning to conclude it necessarily *must* have been Bob who took it there, especially if I had good reasons to think otherwise. If my wife tells me Bob is out of town and someone is house sitting for him, then I'd have a good reason to reject my initial conclusion.

17. Goff, "Nontheist Responding to the Debate," 175.

18. Collins, "Theist Responding to the Debate," 144–45.

19. Benjamin Watkins, "Nontheist Responding to the Debate: All Minds Are Material Things," 193.

20. Watkins, "Nontheist Responding to the Debate," 212.

21. Barker, "Expanding on the Debate," 73. Dan also used this form of reasoning to argue, similar to Watkins, that "we have never observed a mind without a brain. God has a mind. Therefore, God has a brain" (81).

With that in mind, do we have good reasons to doubt Dan's conclusion that the universe had a natural cause and Watkins's conclusion that all minds have embodied brains? I think we do. If the first-cause argument I presented is correct, then before the universe, which is nature (i.e., space, time, and matter), came into existence, there was no space, time, or matter. As I'll discuss below, this conclusion is supported by modern cosmology. If there wasn't any "nature" before the universe existed, then the cause of the universe couldn't have been "natural," as Dan concluded, but must have been supernatural (i.e., beyond nature). Also, Dan's first premise that "we've never observed an effect without a natural cause" is highly suspect, considering we have a tremendous amount of documented evidence for miracles.[22] As for Watkins's conclusion, if because of the design of the universe we have good reason to think the cause of the universe had an intelligent mind, then it's reasonable to conclude this mind was immaterial, hence not embodied, because before the universe existed, there was no matter. In addition, in their chapters Rasmussen and Goff both make a compelling case that an unembodied mind is the fundamental level of reality. To summarize, though Dan's and Watkin's form of reasoning is legitimate, there are good reasons to reject their conclusions.

As a sidenote, in the debate Dan argued that something can come from nothing by using an example of a vacuum with energy potential from which, he claimed, occasionally, because of quantum potential, particles come into existence.[23] This issue often comes up when nontheists suggest that the universe could have come from nothing.[24] However, as the *Oxford Handbook of the History of Modern Cosmology* points out, "obviously a vacuum state is not nothing: it exists in a spacetime, and has a variety of non-trivial properties."[25] In addition, such a vacuum would be governed by some sort of laws or rules, which would be a form of information, similar to the laws that govern our universe. "True nothing" is what Dan gave me for my birthday last year—literally no thing (i.e., the complete absence of anything whatsoever, even information). Since it seems illogical that something could come from "true nothing," it's reasonable to conclude the universe must have come from some thing. The question then is, What's the most plausible candidate for this "thing" that brought the universe into existence?

22. Craig S. Keener, *Miracles Today* (Baker Academic, 2021); Keener, *Miracles: The Credibility of the New Testament Accounts* (Baker Academic, 2011).

23. Barker, "Does God Exist?," 35.

24. For example, see the following book by nontheist Lawrence M. Krauss, *A Universe from Nothing: Why There Is Something Rather Than Nothing* (Atria, 2013).

25. Smeenk, "Philosophical Aspects of Cosmology," 520.

Last, I want to challenge the primary argument in Watkins's chapter. To set up his argument he asked: "Do we have any reason to reject theism given the fact our minds are material things?" He answered with "because our minds are material things, that fact disconfirms theism."[26] He argued abductively that if our minds are material, then the best explanation for this is that there is no God.[27] That seems like quite a stretch. Whether human minds are material or immaterial seems to have little, if anything, to do with whether or not God exists. While "human minds being immaterial" might "fit" better with some theistic belief systems as opposed to atheism, it surely doesn't seem that the "best" explanation for human minds being material is that God doesn't exist. In fact, though I respectfully disagree with them, there are many theists, including many Christians, who maintain that human beings, including our minds, are 100 percent material.[28]

Moral Arguments

Though I personally find design arguments the most compelling arguments for God, I've focused in my research and writing over the last twelve years on moral arguments. Here's the basic one I presented in the debate:

1. There are objective moral truths independent of our minds.
2. The existence of God is the best explanation for how there could be objective moral truths.
3. Therefore, God exists.

I'm using the term *objective truth* here to refer to facts that are fixed in the sense that they're not dependent on how humans think. This is the opposite of something that's *subjective*, which does change when our thinking about it changes, because it's dependent on how we think. Your favorite color is subjective because it's based on how you, the subject, thinks. If you change your mind about your favorite color, then your favorite color changes. Alternatively, those who affirm morality is objective maintain, for example, there's something fixed about the truth that it's wrong to rape and murder, similar to how there's

26. Watkins, "Nontheist Responding to the Debate," 194.

27. Watkins, "Nontheist Responding to the Debate," 212–13.

28. Peter van Inwagen, "A Materialist Ontology of the Human Person," in *Persons: Human and Divine*, ed. Dean Zimmerman and Peter van Inwagen (Oxford University Press, 2007), 199–215.

something fixed about $2 + 2 = 4$.[29] Such facts don't change even when our beliefs about them change. In addition, we don't create such objective facts; instead we discover them.

There are at least four aspects to objective moral truth we've discovered:

1. Some actions, such as building an orphanage, are morally good, whereas other actions, such as rape and murder, are bad. But this generates a question: What *makes* some actions good and others bad?
2. Humans have moral obligations—certain things we ought to do and other things we shouldn't. But where do these authoritative "oughts" come from?
3. Humans have moral worth. Every person is special and should be treated respectfully. But why are humans more special than other forms of life such as thorn bushes?
4. Humans have moral rights such as the right to life and various freedoms. But how do we have such rights while other forms of life, like roaches, don't?

Most agree that these moral truths are objective, but that's not enough. In order to justify such a position, we need to provide a theory that explains *why* we should think these four aspects of morality are objective. That's what this conversation is about: Who has the better explanation for *how* morality could be objective? Below I'll summarize the theory I've proposed.

First, my explanation of what makes an action morally good has been influenced mostly by philosopher Robert Adams, who served as a professor at numerous places, including Yale and Oxford. He argued God is the ultimate fixed standard of moral goodness, and therefore a human action is morally good when it resembles God.[30] My position is similar, but over the years I've developed a theory that goes beyond the mere theism I argued for in the debate, in that it proposes that ultimate moral goodness is the loving relationships between the members of the Trinity.[31] God as Trinity is the perfect

29. For an example of a nontheistic philosopher who specializes in this area and uses the term *objective* in the way I've described, consider Russ Shafer-Landau's explanation that the purpose of his book is to defend "the theory that moral judgements enjoy a special sort of objectivity: such judgements, when true, are so independently of what any human being, anywhere, in any circumstance whatever, thinks of them." See Russ Shafer-Landau, *Moral Realism: A Defence* (Oxford University Press, 2003), 2.

30. Robert M. Adams, *Finite and Infinite Goods: A Framework for Ethics* (Oxford University Press, 1999).

31. Adam Lloyd Johnson, *Divine Love Theory: How the Trinity Is the Source and Foundation of Morality* (Kregel Academic, 2023).

standard of moral goodness, a fixed and unchanging measuring stick by which our actions can be measured to see if they're good or not. It's morally good to build an orphanage because that resembles the love within the Trinity, the ultimate fixed standard of goodness. But telling hurtful lies about someone is morally bad because that doesn't resemble the love within the Trinity.

Second, my explanation for moral obligations, why we *ought* to do good things, begins by noting God created us to extend the loving fellowship of the Trinity. Our obligations *originate* from this purpose God created us for—to enjoy loving relationships with him and others. Our obligations are *generated* when God makes us aware of what's good and bad and that we should do what's good. He makes us aware of this indirectly through our conscience and directly through his commands. It's important to note God's commands are merely instructions on how to best achieve the purpose we're created for—to love God and love others. We should follow God's instructions because of our loving relationship with him; obeying God is one of the ways we express our love for him. In that sense the *basis* of our obligations is our relationship with God, similar to a parent-child relationship.[32] It's important to keep in mind that these reasons for why we should obey God are not out there floating independently from God but are grounded in God's very being.

Third, my explanation for why every human has moral worth is that we're created in God's image to resemble God in enjoying loving relationships.

Fourth, my explanation for moral rights is similar to that given by America's founding fathers—we're all endowed by our creator with certain unalienable rights. And these rights flow from being created in God's image to enjoy loving relationships. My work over the last twelve years has primarily focused on making the case that this Trinitarian explanation of morality, which I call divine love theory, is better (i.e., more plausible) than nontheistic explanations.

Dan Barker's Objections to the Moral Argument

Dan pushed back against the first premise of the moral argument I presented by trying to argue that morality is subjective, not objective. This puts him out of step with many nontheist philosophers who have come to affirm objective morality over the last few decades. David Enoch is a prime example of this

32. Note my explanation of obligation is quite different from Dan's mischaracterization that "with God the reason [an action is something we ought not to do] is behind a curtain: 'Because I said so.'" Barker, "Expanding on the Debate," 80.

shift, and in his chapter he mentioned many other such nontheist philosophers who hold this position.[33] Note that Enoch's explanation of objective morality is similar to mine in that he wrote moral facts "apply to you independently of your own judgments" and "we discover [them] . . . rather than create or construct them."[34] I agree with Enoch that nothing in Dan's arguments challenges the fact that some moral claims are true and perfectly objective.[35] For example, Dan implied that morality must be subjective because people disagree about various moral issues.[36] But that doesn't seem right. When people disagree about a mathematical principle or scientific fact, does that mean those things are subjective? When people disagree about a moral issue, they're actually assuming there's an objectively correct answer—the one for which they're advocating! If they thought morality was merely subjective, like their favorite ice-cream flavor, then they wouldn't bother arguing about it.

One of Dan's strategies for arguing that morality is subjective spun a circle of confusion. This is most clearly seen where he wrote, "2 + 2 = 4 . . . is not an objective entity,"[37] but then in the very next paragraph wrote, "2 + 2 = 4 . . . is true independent of humanity."[38] What's going on here? Isn't that exactly what people like David Enoch and I are saying: that something is objectively true if it'd still be true independent of human minds (i.e., if no humans existed to be aware of it)? If Dan's correct that "2 + 2 = 4 . . . is true independent of humanity," then doesn't that mean it is an objective truth? So why does he say, "2 + 2 = 4 . . . is not an objective entity"?

This confusion comes about because Dan, in his strategy to argue *moral* truth is subjective, claimed there's a sense in which *all* truths are subjective. As part of this strategy, Dan argued that truth is merely the mental awareness of facts (i.e., a function of our brains). He wrote that if "all life in the universe were to disappear" then "the 'truth' . . . of . . . statements would no longer exist because there would be no minds to decipher and interpret them."[39] That's how he can say that even "2 + 2 = 4 . . . is not an objective entity"—his point is that since all truths are merely things minds are aware of, if there weren't any minds, then there wouldn't be any truth. His position is that truth is subjective, including moral truth, in the sense that it's a function of our minds. That's

33. Enoch, "Nontheist Responding to the Debate," 249.
34. Enoch, "Nontheist Responding to the Debate," 236.
35. Enoch, "Nontheist Responding to the Debate," 256.
36. Barker, "Expanding on the Debate," 78–80.
37. Barker, "Expanding on the Debate," 78n27.
38. Barker, "Expanding on the Debate," 79.
39. Barker, "Expanding on the Debate," 78.

how he can rhetorically conclude that "since a moral . . . truth is a concept understood by a functioning mind, and since to be objective means to exist independently of the mind, how can there be an objective moral truth?"[40] Obviously, if there weren't any minds, then there wouldn't be any "mental awareness of facts." But why define truth as just our "mental awareness of facts" in the first place? Dan defined it that way because part of his strategy of trying to argue that moral truth is subjective is to claim all truth is subjective (i.e., that truth is merely a function of our brains).

Clearly this strategy doesn't work, as Dan himself should realize, considering that in the very next paragraph, he wrote, "2 + 2 = 4 . . . is true independent of humanity."[41] Obviously, as even Dan affirms here, there's an important distinction between "our subjective mental awareness of a fact" and the "objective fact" itself. Dan's mistake is that in his attempt to argue moral truth is subjective by claiming all truth is subjective, he equated "our subjective mental awareness of a fact" with "the fact itself." Just because we have an "awareness of a fact" in our minds, such as 2 + 2 = 4, doesn't mean the "fact itself" is *only* a subjective function of our brain and thus not objective.[42] To summarize, Dan's strategy of arguing that moral truth is subjective by claiming all truth is merely a subjective function of our brain collapses in on itself within his very own argument.

As for premise 2, that God is the best explanation for objective morality, it's important to keep in mind what I'm *not* arguing. I'm *not* arguing nontheists can't live good lives, and I'm *not* arguing they can't know moral truth.[43] Nontheists can do both of those things. I'm arguing that God is a better, more plausible explanation for the *existence* of objective morality than nontheistic explanations.

Dan suggested I abandoned this second premise during the debate when I affirmed his "harm principle" is helpful for knowing moral truth.[44] Dan is mistaken here; I was merely acknowledging that "seeing what causes people

40. Barker, "Expanding on the Debate," 78.

41. Barker, "Expanding on the Debate," 79.

42. Enoch made a similar point concerning Dan's suggestion; he noted that to assume when something "is of value" and "that fact is a function of the brain" is to assume "that values . . . are not objective. And to make such an assumption in an attempt to argue against the objectivity of morality would be a blatant case of the fallacy of begging the question." Enoch, "Nontheist Responding to the Debate," 254 (emphasis removed).

43. I'm using the term *good* here in a simple comparative way. It's an important part of Christian theology that all humans, including all theists and nontheists, are morally imperfect to one degree or another and thus require God's forgiveness in order to be reconciled back to a right relationship with him.

44. Barker, "Response to the Contributors," 346–47.

harm" is a good way for all of us to *discover* what's morally true (i.e., it's helpful epistemologically). Our conscience informs us that harming others is wrong, and then through life experiences we learn what causes harm and what doesn't. However, as I'll argue below, this "harm principle" is not a plausible explanation for the *existence* (ontology) of objective moral truth. Dan explained that his theory is that morality just *is* this "harm principle," namely, that "if you are acting with the intention of minimizing overall harm, you are acting morally."[45] David Enoch is correct that Dan here isn't "doing metaethics" (the branch of philosophy that tries to explain the nature and foundation of morality itself) but is only stepping "into the ethics arena" (the branch that merely tries to explain what's right or wrong in practice) by suggesting "very general moral principles."[46]

Dan went on to argue that "since Adam knows that there exists at least one natural moral philosophy with objectively justified values [Dan's harm theory], he can't maintain that a hypothetical supernatural supreme being is the best explanation."[47] But that's not how this works; just *knowing* there's a proposed nontheistic moral theory doesn't mean I can't argue a theistic theory is the better explanation. All it means is that I can't claim a theistic theory is the *only* theory! I agree with David Enoch that considering the plausibility of different theories is the right approach in trying to figure out which is the better explanation.[48] With that in mind, let's consider the plausibility of Dan's theory.

Evaluating Dan Barker's Moral Theory

To begin with, as both David Enoch and David Baggett point out, Dan seems to contradict himself by maintaining morality is subjective but then claiming his "morality is the avoidance of harm" theory is somehow objective.[49] However, because there are nontheists who try to build a theory of objective

45.Barker, "Expanding on the Debate," 80. In the debate Dan said "morality simply boils down to the intention to act with the minimal amount of harm in the real world. That's what we mean by morality. . . . I think you can boil down morality to one word, and that's the word *harm*." Barker, "Does God Exist?," 29–30.

46. Enoch, "Nontheist Responding to the Debate," 255.

47. Barker, "Expanding on the Debate," 80.

48. Enoch, "Nontheist Responding to the Debate," 249–50.

49. After explaining Dan's inconsistency Baggett wrote: "he needs to explain how we can have it both ways; there seems to be an element of confusion here on his part." Baggett, "Theist Responding to the Debate," 221. Enoch wrote: "Dan . . . contradicts himself here. He has to decide: either morality is not objective, or it comes down to harm-minimizing intentions, but not both. . . . The suggestion that this is just what we mean by morality is highly implausible indeed." Enoch, "Nontheist Responding to the Debate," 255.

morality based on this harm principle, and because Dan claims this principle is objective in some confusing sense, I'll show how such a theory fails as an explanation of *objective* morality. In addition, since Dan also seems to reject objective morality, I'll also point out the problems faced by a theory of *subjective* morality based on this harm principle.

First, Dan's explanation of what *makes* an action morally good or bad has numerous problems. What makes, for example, building an orphanage good and rape and murder bad? Sure, if you redefine good to mean "that which avoids harm," then obviously there are objective facts about what best avoids harm. But why assume in the first place it's morally good to avoid harm? Dan hasn't given us good reasons to accept that huge assumption at the foundation of his theory. Of course, most of us *think* avoiding harm is good, but that's the very definition of being subjective, not objective. If there's no God, then it's hard to see how nontheist Richard Dawkins was wrong when he wrote, "There is at the bottom, no design, no purpose, no evil and no good; nothing but blind pitiless indifference."[50]

Second, Dan's theory doesn't provide a convincing explanation of where our moral obligations or duties come from. In fact, Dan proposed "ought" "comes from nowhere. Ought is simply half of a conditional statement: *if* we want less harm, *then* we ought to act in ways to minimize it."[51] At a minimum this would make obligations subjective because it's based on what we subjectively want. But his proposal is actually much worse, even absurd. To see why, consider that when it comes to providing an explanation for moral obligations, philosophers want to explain why *everyone* has certain obligations, for example, to refrain from rape and murder. If Dan's theory is correct, then *only* those who *want less* harm ought to refrain from rape and murder. We could never tell people who *want more* harm that they shouldn't rape and murder because, according to Dan's theory, they wouldn't *have* such moral oughts.[52] Overall, if there's no God, then it's hard to see how nontheist scientist Jacques Monod was incorrect when he wrote that "man at last knows that he is alone in the unfeeling immensity of the universe, out of which he emerged only by chance. His destiny is nowhere spelled out, nor is his duty."[53]

50. Richard Dawkins, *River Out of Eden: A Darwinian View of Life* (Basic, 1996), 133.

51. Barker, "Expanding on the Debate," 80.

52. Adam Lloyd Johnson, "Is It Morally Permissible for Some People to Rape and Murder? Responding to Erik Wielenberg's Argument That Divine Command Theory Fails to Explain How Psychopaths Have Moral Obligations," *Religions* 14, no. 4 (2023): 507, https://doi.org/10.3390/rel14040507.

53. Jacques Monod, *Chance and Necessity: An Essay on the Natural Philosophy of Modern Biology* (Knopf, 1971), 180.

Third, Dan's theory struggles to explain why humans have objective moral worth. According to Dan's naturalism, we just happen to be a few steps further down the evolutionary path, cobbled together accidentally through a haphazard process of random mutation and natural selection. If we ever encounter higher forms of life in the universe, why should they consider us any more valuable than we consider sewer rats? Of course, *we think* we're special, but that's subjective. If there's no God, then it's difficult to see why nontheist Bertrand Russell was wrong when he wrote that "man is the product of causes which had no prevision of the end they were achieving . . . his origin, his growth, his hopes and fears, his loves and his beliefs, are but the outcome of accidental collocations of atoms."[54]

Fourth, Dan's theory doesn't provide a plausible explanation of where our moral rights come from. If there's no God, then nontheist Friedrich Nietzsche was correct that moral rights were invented by the weak to try to make the strong feel guilty for oppressing them. If there's no God, then it's hard to see why nontheist Peter Singer was wrong when he said that our insistence of human moral rights is an unwarranted speciesist type of chauvinism.[55]

The First Good Argument

G. E. Moore's "open question" argument helps explain why Dan's theory of moral goodness, whether it's subjective or objective, is unsuccessful. Moore, one of the founders of analytic philosophy, said that people commit a naturalistic fallacy when they try to define moral goodness by identifying it with a nonevaluative property such as the avoidance of harm. Whatever nonevaluative property someone claims is identical with moral goodness, it will always be an open question whether that property itself is morally good. For example, if someone claims moral goodness is not harming others, the open question becomes, Why is not harming others morally good? Dan hasn't provided good reasons to accept that major assumption at the foundation of his theory. Moore argued the only way to avoid this "open question" argument is to conclude, as he did, that moral goodness is a separate nonreductive property. Aquinas argued similarly that "each good thing that is not its goodness is . . . good by participation. But that which is [good] . . . by participation has something prior to it from which it receives . . . goodness. This cannot proceed to infinity. . . . We must therefore reach some first good, that is not by participation good

54. Bertrand Russell, "The Free Man's Worship," *The Independent Review* 1 (1903): 416.

55. Peter Singer, *Animal Rights and Human Obligations* (Prentice Hall, 1976), 1.

. . . but is good through its own essence."[56] I've developed a moral argument for God based on these ideas that I call the "first good argument," because it parallels the first-cause argument. In order to set this up, let me step back for a moment to summarize the first-cause argument.

The first-cause argument begins by noting that when we evaluate an effect, we naturally ask, "What caused this?" Once we figure out what caused it we may ask, "Well, what caused *that*?" And then "What caused *that*?" And so on. To avoid this going on forever there must be something ultimate that just *is*; something that doesn't have a cause. Those are the only two options—either there's an infinite number of causes going backward forever, or there was a first cause. As discussed throughout this book, philosophers and mathematicians have illustrated numerous problems with the idea that there have been an actual infinite number of causes. Therefore, it seems most plausible that there's a first cause, something that wasn't caused by anything else but just exists on its own as the ultimate fundamental reality. Since it seems there must be a first cause, eventually we reach a point where when you ask, "Well, then what caused *that*?" you'd just have to stop because you've arrived at something that doesn't have a cause. Many scientists used to think the universe was the ultimate uncaused reality, but over the last hundred years scientific discoveries have provided strong evidence that the universe had a beginning. Therefore, we can reasonably conclude the universe isn't the uncaused cause. Of course, theists argue God is the best candidate for this first cause, that he is the ultimate fundamental reality.

To see how my first good argument parallels this first-cause argument, consider that the conversation often goes like this: Why is refraining from rape and murder morally good? Dan would say it's good because it avoids harm. But why is avoiding harm morally good? To avoid this going on forever, there must be something ultimate that just is the good itself. Eventually we reach a point in every moral theory where when you ask, "Well, why is *that* good?" you'd just have to stop because, to avoid an infinite series, there must be something that just *is* goodness itself. When the question is asked, the answer is similar to the end of the first-cause argument—because it just is. There's nothing before it that caused it, and there's nothing behind it that makes it good—it just *is* the good. Moral theories cannot avoid this—every moral theory has to include some sort of ultimate moral good, as many nontheist philosophers recognize. For example, nontheist Wes Morriston, in describing his moral theory, wrote:

56. Thomas Aquinas, *Summa contra Gentiles*, trans. Anton C. Pegis, 3 vols. (Hanover House, 1955–1957), 138.

"Why are love and justice and generosity and kindness and faithfulness good? What is there in the depths of reality to make them good? My own preferred answer is: Nothing further. If you like, you may say that they are the ultimate standard of goodness. What makes them the standard? Nothing further. Possessing these characteristics just is good-making. Full stop. . . . No matter what story you tell about the ontological ground for moral value, you must at some point come to your own full stop."[57] These two arguments are similar in that the first-cause argument concludes there's nothing causally before the first cause that caused it and the first good argument concludes there's nothing behind the first good that makes it good—it just *is* the good.

In summary, to avoid an infinite series every moral theory must include an ultimate good that just is goodness itself. Dan proposed avoiding harm is the ultimate good, whereas I'm proposing God is the ultimate good. Here's the key question: Which proposed ultimate good, avoiding harm or God, is the better, more plausible explanation for objective morality? Elsewhere I've provided multiple reasons to conclude that God as Trinity is the best candidate for this first good.[58] God is the end (or beginning, depending on how you're thinking of it) of the explanatory chain of causes and of moral good. Even the reasons why we should obey God are grounded in God himself because he is the ultimate fundamental reality.

Evaluating David Enoch's Moral Theory

David Enoch provided a more sophisticated nontheistic explanation of objective morality often called robust realism or non-naturalism. I don't have room here to address all the aspects of his theory, but, for interested readers, I wrote an entire book arguing that my divine love theory is a better explanation for morality than robust realism.[59] Enoch claimed my Trinitarian theory is more vulnerable to being refuted than a standard theistic theory, because any reason to doubt the specific theological idea that God is a Trinity would also be a reason to reject the overall theory.[60] But this fails to consider all the additional advantages a Trinitarian theory has over a mere theistic theory when it comes to explaining numerous aspects of morality such as, just to mention one, the

57. Wes Morriston, "God and the Ontological Foundation of Morality," *Religious Studies* 48, no. 1 (2012): 29, https://doi.org/10.1017/s0034412510000740.

58. Johnson, *Divine Love Theory*.

59. Johnson, *Divine Love Theory*.

60. Enoch, "Nontheist Responding to the Debate," 250–51.

social basis of morality.[61] As with scientific theories, a more detailed theory that explains more aspects of reality is superior, all else equal, to a simple theory that doesn't explain as much.

I'm glad Enoch agrees, contra Dan, that moral theories should be evaluated abductively (i.e., by inference to the best explanation).[62] As he noted, we should go with the theory that has the highest overall plausibility score.[63] Though he encouraged this approach, unfortunately he often didn't follow it but instead merely argued that his theory is just a viable possibility. At the beginning of his chapter he wrote, "morality's objectivity . . . can easily be made sense of without assuming any theist thesis."[64] Then throughout he used language such as morality "can easily be accommodated by nontheistic explanations," and "it is at least a live option."[65]

In addition, he claimed that if he could "offer a plausible explanation of the correlation between the moral facts and our moral beliefs . . . the theist doesn't get his or her explanatory advantage here, and then the epistemic version of the moral argument for theism fails."[66] Then he noted, "the most promising strategy for such an explanation is . . . *third-factor explanations*."[67] But he also clarified that "it's one thing to insist on the possibility of a third-factor explanation strategy, quite another to actually make good on this promise by filling in the details."[68] He also admitted that "the jury on the plausibility of (some) third-factor explanations as a way of facing up to this challenge is still very much out."[69] As a sidenote, elsewhere I've argued these third-factor explanations don't solve the robust realist's "lucky coincidence" problem, namely, that our moral beliefs just luckily happen to match up with their proposed objective moral facts.[70] My point here is that if we should go with the theory that has the highest overall plausibility, then Enoch has to do more than merely offer a live, possible, or even plausible nontheistic alternative. Instead, he has to show his alternative is *more* plausible than theistic theories.

The suggestion that Enoch's explanation for morality is superior to theistic

61. Johnson, *Divine Love Theory*, 41–64.
62. Enoch, "Nontheist Responding to the Debate," 235–36.
63. Enoch, "Nontheist Responding to the Debate," 250.
64. Enoch, "Nontheist Responding to the Debate," 236.
65. Enoch, "Nontheist Responding to the Debate," 253, 240.
66. Enoch, "Nontheist Responding to the Debate," 247.
67. Enoch, "Nontheist Responding to the Debate," 247.
68. Enoch, "Nontheist Responding to the Debate," 248.
69. Enoch, "Nontheist Responding to the Debate," 249.
70. Johnson, *Divine Love Theory*, 165–224.

ones comes across a bit hollow considering his theory is simply that objective morality just doesn't have an explanation! The basic tenet of robust realism is that objective moral truth has no explanation; it just is. For instance, Enoch wrote morality "doesn't come from anywhere" and the most fundamental "moral truths . . . are necessary. They have always been true, and they will always be true." [71] Ironically, by describing moral truth as necessary, timeless, and unchanging, it almost sounds like he's describing God. In fact, fellow nontheist and robust realist Erik Wielenberg even used what theists say about God being ultimate to explain these necessary brute facts when he wrote these truths "are the foundation of (the rest of) objective morality and rest on no foundation themselves. To ask of such facts, 'where do they come from?' or 'on what foundation do they rest?' is misguided in much the way that, according to many theists, it is misguided to ask of God, 'where does He come from?' or 'on what foundation does He rest?' The answer is the same in both cases: they come from nowhere, and nothing external to themselves grounds their existence; rather, they are fundamental features of the universe that ground other truths."[72] While it's certainly possible that necessary, timeless, and unchanging truths exist on their own without an explanation, source, or foundation, I argue such truths are best explained by being grounded in a necessary, timeless, and unchanging being—God.

Enoch claimed I haven't provided reasons to think morality has a source, that I'm just presupposing that it does as an unsupported dogma.[73] Has he provided reasons to think morality doesn't have a source, or is he just presupposing it doesn't as an unsupported dogma? Of course, neither proposition should be presupposed but instead should be backed up with good argumentation. At the end of the day, what's more plausible: that morality has a source, or that it exists on its own without a source?

To weigh the plausibility of these two options, it's important to recognize that Enoch's theory of objective morality is based on the idea that there are necessary, brute moral facts that exist on their own without a foundation as Platonic abstract objects. Though he prefers to describe his theory as a form of "robust realism," he noted, "I will not be offended if you call me a Platonist."[74] Later he wrote that "according to robust realism . . . the normative truths

71. Enoch, "Nontheist Responding to the Debate," 240.

72. Erik J. Wielenberg, *Robust Ethics: The Metaphysics and Epistemology of Godless Normative Realism* (Oxford University Press, 2014), 38.

73. Enoch, "Nontheist Responding to the Debate," 242.

74. David Enoch, *Taking Morality Seriously: A Defense of Robust Realism* (Oxford University Press, 2011), 8.

are out there, as it were, in Plato's heaven, utterly independent of us and our motivations."[75] Fellow robust realist Erik Wielenberg also admitted his view is Platonic when he stated that "if we want to situate my view in the history of philosophy, I think it is very Moorean and it's also Platonic. People sometimes use Platonic like as a type of criticism but I embrace the label."[76]

As I explained above with my first good argument, nearly everyone agrees there must be an ultimate ontological stopping point, if for no other reason than to avoid an infinite regress. Thus, it boils down to the following question: What is a more plausible ontological ultimate—God or ungrounded moral facts that exist as Platonic abstract objects? While considering the proposal that abstract objects are the ultimate fundamental reality, philosopher Stephen Evans argued that it "is far from obviously true" that moral truths are brute in the sense of being without explanation because the "fact that so many naturalists, including philosophers such as Mackie and Nietzsche, find the idea of non-natural moral facts odd or queer, shows that they are indeed the kind of thing one would like to have an explanation for."[77] Evans pointed out that it "seems almost irresistible for a Platonist to ask what the fact that moral truths are deep truths about the universe says about the nature of ultimate reality. Platonism itself in some ways makes the world mysterious and posits features of the world that cry out for explanation."[78]

Even from the very beginning, when abstract objects were proposed by Plato, which he called forms, he proposed they had a source which he called the Good, an idea which clearly had strong theistic overtones. Since then, many throughout history have argued that God is the best explanation for the existence of abstract objects. Evans explained that "many theists in fact have thought that Platonism itself makes far more sense in a theistic universe than it does otherwise, since in a theistic world the Forms do not have to be seen as independent realities but can be understood as Ideas in the divine mind."[79] That's why he noted it "is no accident that there is a long tradition of theistic (and even Christian) Platonism."[80]

Platonists not only believe that moral truths are abstract objects; they also

75. Enoch, *Taking Morality Seriously*, 217.

76. Erik Wielenberg, "Armchair Atheism, Ep. 4—Morality Without God? With Erik Wielenberg," Armchair Atheism, posted March 2, 2015, YouTube, 34:23, https://tinyurl.com/2yyk627s.

77. C. Stephen Evans, *God and Moral Obligation* (Oxford University Press, 2014), 152.

78. Evans, *God and Moral Obligation*, 153–54.

79. Evans, *God and Moral Obligation*, 154.

80. Evans, *God and Moral Obligation*, 153.

maintain logical truths and mathematical truths, including numbers themselves, are abstract objects. For this reason I was surprised that both David Enoch and Dan claimed that it was inconsistent for philosophers to argue moral truths need a source but don't argue that numbers, mathematical truths, and logical truths need a source.[81] Evidently neither of them is aware of all the arguments that argue God is the best explanation for abstract objects such as numbers, mathematical truths, and logical truths.[82] Those who have made such arguments thought it was more plausible that God, as opposed to abstract objects, is the fundamental reality. Even in this book, Robin Collins discussed Platonism and argued it's plausible to think an infinite mind is needed to ground necessary truths such as mathematical truths.[83]

One reason God is a better candidate than abstract objects for the ultimate ontological stopping point is that he, as commonly understood by theists, is an infinite, necessary, and, most importantly, a *concrete* causal being. The key distinction between abstract objects and concrete objects is that the former are noncausal, that is, they can't enter into the causal chain of events. Concrete objects on the other hand—which include both material things such as cucumbers, planets, or electrons and immaterial things, if they exist, such as angels, God, and souls—can enter into the causal chain of events. Since abstract objects, if they exist, are noncausal entities, it's difficult to fathom how they could be the ultimate ontological stopping point that caused everything else. It's more plausible to think that God is the ultimate fundamental reality because he, as a concrete causal agent, could have caused everything else to come into existence.

While it's true theists believe there are certain necessary facts about God (that he exists, has a certain moral nature, is Triune, etc.), these are facts *about* an ultimate concrete being that theists believe exists necessarily. Whereas Enoch's brute ethical facts are supposed to be stand-alone, ungrounded abstract facts that exist on their own without a foundation. Enoch suggested that

81. Enoch wrote: "why is it that many people—including, it seems, some philosophers—find it natural to ask 'Where does morality come from?' but not 'Where does logic come from?'" Enoch, "Nontheist Responding to the Debate," 241. Dan wrote something similar concerning C. S. Lewis in his responding chapter. Barker, "Expanding on the Debate," 79–80.

82. In Collins's chapter, he noted philosophers who have made arguments for God from mathematics (143n36). In addition, consider Greg Welty, "Theistic Conceptual Realism," in *Beyond the Control of God? Six Views on the Problem of God and Abstract Objects*, ed. Paul M. Gould (Bloomsbury Academic, 2014), 94. While Welty's entire dissertation focuses on his argument for God from abstract objects, here he merely summarizes it by referring to Robert Adams's work.

83. Collins, "Theist Responding to the Debate," 142–43.

theistic theories of morality also include ungrounded moral facts when he wrote, "it's not entirely clear how God can be relevant morally, unless there's a God-independent, prior reason (to do as God says for instance)."[84] This objection to theistic moral theories is often called the "prior obligations objection." However, when I explained above my Trinitarian theory of moral obligations, I noted that the "reasons we should obey God" themselves are grounded in God. There's a vast difference between positing facts *about* a proposed concrete being, facts that are grounded in that being, and mere facts that supposedly exist abstractly on their own without any grounding or foundation.

To summarize, there are strong reasons why it doesn't seem plausible to many theists and nontheists that moral facts could just exist on their own without any explanation or foundation. In addition, there are good reasons to conclude that God is a more plausible candidate for the ultimate fundamental reality than Enoch's proposed Platonic abstract objects.

First-Cause Arguments

In the debate I presented a first-cause argument based on the premise that the universe had a beginning, often referred to as the Kalām cosmological argument. But what if the universe didn't have a beginning? Would that mean God doesn't exist? It'd certainly mean the Kalām argument would fail. However, there are many first-cause arguments for God (often called cosmological arguments) that don't assume nor require that the universe had a beginning.[85] For example, there are first-cause arguments based on the premise that since the universe is contingent (it could have been otherwise or even not existed at all), it requires something necessary (noncontingent) to ground it and concludes God is the best explanation for this necessary being. Some of the most well-known versions of this type of first-cause argument include those formulated by Thomas Aquinas and Gottfried Leibniz, with contemporary proponents including Alexander Pruss and Joshua Rasmussen.[86] However, since I used a Kalām argument in the debate I'll defend that type here.

There are numerous strong philosophical reasons and scientific evidence to conclude the universe had a beginning. While this scientific evidence isn't

84. Enoch, "Nontheist Responding to the Debate," 240n11.

85. See Bruce Reichenbach, "Cosmological Arguments," in *Stanford Encyclopedia of Philosophy*, last modified June 30, 2022, https://tinyurl.com/bddrc8cs.

86. Alexander Pruss and Joshua Rasmussen, *Necessary Existence* (Oxford University Press, 2018).

absolutely conclusive (empirical evidence never is), many find it quite convincing.[87] Physicist Alexander Vilenkin, widely recognized for his work in cosmology, writes: "It is said that an argument is what convinces reasonable men and a proof is what it takes to convince even an unreasonable man. With the proof now in place, cosmologists can no longer hide behind the possibility of a past-eternal universe. There is no escape, they have to face the problem of a cosmic beginning."[88] The most celebrated cosmologist of our time, Stephen Hawking, states: "Almost everyone now believes that the universe, and time itself, had a beginning at the Big Bang."[89]

Certainly, we need to be careful not to overstate the strength of the evidence indicating the universe had a beginning. But we also shouldn't understate it, as Daniel Linford and Alex Malpass did in their chapter. Astonishingly they concluded that "there is no good reason to accept either premise," premise 1 being that whatever has a beginning must have a cause, and premise 2 being that the universe had a beginning.[90] Obviously they're not convinced by the evidence, but it's quite extreme to claim there are no good reasons at all to think the universe had a beginning. Though in their conclusion they boldly proclaimed there are no good reasons to accept the Kalām argument's premises, throughout their chapter they merely pointed out that these premises aren't absolutely conclusive, something that everyone acknowledges. In other words, their arguments simply don't support their extreme conclusion.

They tried to cast doubt on the premise that the universe had a beginning by discussing the many speculative cosmological models that include an eternal universe. Of course, as with all scientific theories, many people are working hard to continually develop, test, and improve the standard Lambda-CDM model of the big bang, a process that involves challenging it, questioning its assumptions, and proposing possible changes or even alternative models. Some of these models are quite speculative, but that's a normal part of scientific investigation and development. In the *Oxford Handbook of the History of Modern Cosmology*, Helge Kragh explains that

> alternative cosmological views are many and confusingly diverse not only today but have also been so in the past. They cover a broad spectrum, both

87. For a historical overview of the discovery of this scientific evidence, see Stephen C. Meyer, *The Return of the God Hypothesis* (HarperCollins, 2021), 69–129, 239–59, 326–408.

88. Alexander Vilenkin, *Many Worlds in One: The Search for Other Universes* (Hill & Wang, 2006), 176.

89. Stephen Hawking and Roger Penrose, *The Nature of Space and Time*, The Isaac Newton Institute Series of Lectures (Princeton University Press, 1996), 20.

90. Linford and Malpass, "Nontheists Responding to the Debate," 277, 301.

> as regards of how general and fundamental they are and as regards of how seriously they are taken and intended to be. While some theories are put forward by scientists who think their theories are candidates for the real structure of the universe, others are suggestions of a much less committed nature. They may be toy models or just loose ideas thrown up to see if they work or not. And then there is a large number of alternative cosmological theories which belong to the fringe of science and typically (but not always) are suggested by amateurs outside the scientific community.[91]

The problem is that Linford and Malpass overstate the viability of these speculative models, many of which face insurmountable problems. All sorts of possibilities have been, and continue to be, proposed that would entail an eternal universe. But it's not prudent to build an argument on speculative possibilities or dismiss a well-established theory by merely noting other models are possible. Instead, we should base our positions on what's supported by the best evidence we currently have.

Similarly, philosophical arguments like the ones Robert Koons provided in his chapter provide a strong, but not conclusive, case that an actual infinite can't exist in reality. As with the empirical evidence for the beginning of the universe, it's not enough to simply point out that the case against an actual infinite isn't absolutely conclusive. It comes down to whether it's more plausible that there can be an actual infinite in reality or if it's more plausible that there can't be an actual infinite in reality.

It's quite ironic that Linford and Malpass attempted to show the premises of the Kalām argument aren't conclusive by using a view of causation, Neo-Russellianism, that's much less conclusive than premise 2, namely, the idea that the universe had a beginning.[92] They wrote that "while the case for Neo-Russellianism isn't definitive, without strong reasons to reject Neo-Russellianism we have no good reason to accept the [Kalām argument]."[93] Suggesting that defenders of the Kalām have to provide strong reasons to reject something more controversial than the premises of the Kalām itself is a bizarre, poor attempt to shift the burden of proof. As for causation, in his

91. Helge Kragh, "Alternative Cosmological Theories," in *The Oxford Handbook of the History of Modern Cosmology*, ed. Helge Kragh and Malcolm S. Longair (Oxford University Press, 2019), 122.

92. See Mathias Frisch, "Causation in Physics," in *Stanford Encyclopedia of Philosophy*, published August 24, 2020, https://tinyurl.com/3prk4xx2. In section eight it notes that while Neo-Russellian arguments have attracted attention again lately, causal theories of explanation are the default view.

93. Linford and Malpass, "Nontheists Responding to the Debate," 278.

chapter Robert Koons presented a strong case for why we should affirm the principle of universal causation.[94]

Everybody agrees the Kalām's premises are not absolutely certain; there's hardly anything that can be proven with such certainty. To defeat an argument you must do more than merely point out that the premises are "debatable" and "subject to criticism." Arguments should be judged on the plausibility of their premises. An argument is compelling if its premises are more plausible than not, and the more plausible the premises are, the more compelling the argument is. In the case of the Kalām argument, is it more plausible based on the best current evidence that the universe had a beginning, or more plausible that the universe didn't have a beginning?

I appreciate the fair, balanced position of Stephen Barr, the physics professor at the University of Delaware whose book I recommended in the debate. He has noted that "one of the most dramatic discoveries in the history of science is that the universe began in an explosion that took place about 15 billion years ago. The evidence for this 'Big Bang Theory' has become so strong in the last thirty years that it is no longer seriously questioned."[95] He explains that "most physicists tend to think of the Big Bang as really being the beginning of the physical universe, and with it, the beginning of time itself."[96]

After pointing out the objections that have been raised concerning bouncing universe theories, which is one class of models that include an eternal universe, Barr writes that "beyond all of these objections, which are very cogent, the bouncing universe idea simply has not helped physicists to solve any theoretical problems, and consequently it no longer receives a great deal of attention. (However, there has been a very interesting recent attempt to revive it.)"[97] This "interesting recent attempt" he refers to is the Steinhardt-Turok cyclic model, one of the alternative theories Linford and Malpass suggested.[98] However, according to the *Oxford Handbook of the History of Modern Cosmology*, this "theory has been developed in a series of papers, but its impact on mainstream cosmology remains limited."[99]

94. Koons, "Theist Responding to the Debate," 268–73.

95. Stephen M. Barr, *Modern Physics and Ancient Faith* (University of Notre Dame Press, 2003), 33.

96. Barr, *Modern Physics*, 47.

97. Barr, *Modern Physics*, 54.

98. Linford and Malpass, "Nontheists Responding to the Debate," 291–92.

99. Kragh, "Alternative Cosmological Theories," 152. On p. 121 Kragh also writes that cyclic models have "always been considered heterodox or of little plausibility. Although declared dead several times they continue to attract attention, in part because they combine

After Barr explains that three older theories that attempted to avoid a cosmic beginning "are either discredited now or strongly disfavored," he notes, "more recent ideas like baby universes and eternal inflation are still *possibilities*."[100] Keep in mind that *possible* doesn't mean *probable* or even *plausible*. After discussing these possibilities, he explained that these

> are very serious ideas, and one of them may *someday* be shown to be right. . . . Nevertheless, suppose that it could be shown somehow, indirectly, that the Big Bang was not the beginning of time. That would still not resolve the issue of where there *was* a beginning of time; it would only show that the Big Bang itself was not that beginning. The Big Bang may have been just a bounce, but that does not tell us whether there was a first bounce. The Big Bang may have been the time when our universe started forming as a blister on a pre-existing space, but that does not tell us whether that pre-existing space itself had a beginning. . . . However, . . . [it's] not about what we will know *someday*; it is about what we know now, and what trends we can discern in discoveries up to this point. . . . Will it turn out that the "universe" that began with the Big Bang is actually part of some larger universe? Quite *possibly*. Will that larger universe prove to be something eternal? The entire history of discovery would lead one to doubt it.[101]

He then reiterates that "the facts that science has taught us give strong reason to doubt that the universe is eternal."[102] Later he clarifies that

> the Second Law of Thermodynamics and the Borde-Guth-Vilenkin theorem raise formidable obstacles to constructing realistic and consistent models of a past-infinite universe. The speculative models that try to get around these obstacles are unconvincing and indeed rather far-fetched. . . . Most cosmologists and particle theorists would agree that a past-infinite universe seems disfavored at present and that all attempts so far to construct a consistent, realistic, and plausible model of one have not had success, and people have been trying for a long time. . . . [T]his does not prove that the universe is past finite, but on the other hand it is not without significance.[103]

---

elements of big-bang theory with a universe existing eternally." He notes on p. xi that such models are still discussed but "mainly outside mainstream cosmology."

100. Barr, *Modern Physics*, 54 (emphasis added).

101. Barr, *Modern Physics*, 58–59 (emphasis added).

102. Barr, *Modern Physics*, 60.

103. Personal correspondence used with permission dated January 1, 2025.

Using an abductive approach once again, we can confidently say that the theory the universe had a beginning, while not the only *possible* explanation, is by far the best explanation of the evidence we currently have.

The So-Called Problem of God's Hiddenness

In response to Joseph Folley's chapter, I should say upfront that I reject the notion God is hidden because, it seems to me and numerous others, there are many strong reasons and evidence to believe God exists. As I'll explain below, the main problem at the root of this issue isn't that God is hiding from us but that we are hiding from God.

No matter how much evidence we had for God, I suppose the question could always be asked, "Well, why not a bit more?" But that doesn't mean God is somehow hidden. Eventually we just run into the epistemological brick wall we always do when we try to achieve any type of knowledge that's absolutely certain.[104] Since I don't believe we can achieve that level of certainty in any area, including science, it doesn't surprise me that we can't be absolutely certain about God either. But couldn't God give us the evidence we'd need to be (if not absolutely) strongly certain he exists? I believe there's a sense in which he has. Obviously Dan disagrees but just because some people don't think there's good evidence for God doesn't mean there isn't. By the way, contra Dan, God doesn't need philosophers to come up with arguments for his existence[105]—all philosophers are doing is articulating the objective reasons and evidence that lead many of us to conclude there is a God.

As for experiencing God subjectively, many claim to experience his presence, but there are also many who say they don't. Couldn't God make his presence known in such a way that we'd all be directly aware of him all the time? I don't see why he couldn't. Therefore, it's worth exploring why some *think* there's little to no good evidence for God and why God doesn't make everyone directly aware of his presence all the time. However, I refer to this topic as the argument of divine hiddenness, because calling it the problem of divine hiddenness gives the incorrect impression that there's little evidence for God.

Various plausible reasons have been proposed for why God doesn't provide

104. For a further discussion of this epistemological issue, see my discussion of scientists Michael Polanyi and John Polkinghorne that affirm critical realism on pp. 45–47 where I begin discussing the relationship between faith and reason in my previous chapter.

105. Barker, "Does God Exist?," 25.

even more evidence of himself or give us a constant direct awareness of his presence all the time. For example, as Andrew Drinkard suggested, it might be the case that God knows people who don't believe in him would reject having a relationship with him even if they came to believe he existed.[106] Since God cares about having a relationship with people more than merely having them believe he exists, there'd be little purpose in giving such individuals more evidence or making them directly aware of his presence. Doing so might even drive them further away from wanting to have a relationship with him. This is the point I was trying to make in the debate in response to Dan's comment that he wouldn't worship God if he became convinced God exists because he thinks God is a terrible being.[107] I didn't mean this as an *ad hominem* attack, and I apologize to Dan that it came across that way.[108]

As Joe Folley pointed out, the divine hiddenness argument is based on a hypothetical group of people who never choose to have a relationship with God before their death, but would have if only they had more evidence of him.[109] The basic idea is that if God exists, then we wouldn't expect this to happen, and therefore we have good reason to conclude God doesn't exist. However, as Folley noted, this argument hinges on the hopelessly difficult task of verifying empirically whether or not such people actually exist.[110] I suppose we could call this the problem of nonresistant nonbeliever hiddenness!

There are at least three reasons it's difficult for the atheist to show empirically there are such people and for the theist to show there aren't. First, it's not only that these folks don't have a relationship with God now, but it must be the case they never enter into such a relationship, and it's impossible for us to know the future. Second, as I discussed above, it's not merely whether these hypothetical people would believe God exists or not if only they had more evidence, but if they would choose to enter into a relationship with God or not, which adds another layer of empirical difficulty. Third, because the psychology of our motivations is tremendously complex, it's difficult to understand fully our own possible resistance toward some beliefs and choices, much less the possible resistance of others. At a minimum, as Folley mentioned, we

106. Drinkard, "Theist Responding to the Debate," 89.

107. Barker, "Does God Exist?," 34–35.

108. Barker, "Expanding on the Debate," 81.

109. Folley, "Nontheist Responding to the Debate," 117.

110. Folley wrote "this is a contingent empirical claim that would ultimately require verification" (118) and "such a claim would require substantial empirical evidence" (119).

all struggle with resistance toward beliefs we dislike.[111] Since this argument against the existence of God hinges on whether or not there are such nonresistant nonbelievers, and since it's difficult to know empirically one way or the other, there's a sense in which this argument runs into a stalemate between those who claim there are such people and those who claim there aren't.

As for Folley's concern about people who've never heard about Christianity, I encourage folks to check out how Molinists address this issue in the resources Drinkard recommended.[112] In brief, a Molinist would say, contra Folley, it's not an enormous coincidence that, to use his example, everyone in ancient China happened to be resistant but instead that God knew beforehand who would resist and who wouldn't, if someday they'd hear of Christianity. As a result of this "middle knowledge," [113] God then placed many of those he knew would resist in times and places where they wouldn't hear of Christianity and placed those he knew wouldn't resist in times and places they would hear of Christianity (Acts 17:26–27). In other words, God orchestrates circumstances such that everybody who *would* trust in Christ if they heard of Christianity *will* hear of Christianity. In addition, a strong case can be made from Acts 10 that if someone, even in ancient China, responds well to the light they have (the general revelation of creation discussed in Rom. 1:19–20; 2:14–15), then God somehow gives them more light (special revelation, i.e., Scripture or direct revelation) so that they know how to have a relationship with him.

Last, Folley's point should be well taken that even if you think the argument of divine hiddenness scores some points against believing God exists, it's quite reasonable to still believe in God if you think the arguments for God score more points.[114] I'd also add that this same rationale applies toward the problem of evil argument against God as well. In other words, overall I'd say the arguments for God are much more compelling than the arguments against God.

111. "The whole discussion about resistance to beliefs is not only helpful for atheists to consider whether they truly are psychologically resistant to the existence of a deity but also helpful for theists, who could equally ask whether they are unduly resistant to atheism." Folley, "Nontheist Responding to the Debate," 128.

112. Drinkard, "Theist Responding to the Debate," 92n18. Especially Kenneth Keathley, *Salvation and Sovereignty* (B&H Academic, 2010).

113. According to Molinism, God's middle knowledge refers to his knowledge of what every person would freely choose in all possible circumstances. This type of knowledge enables God to orchestrate outcomes by placing people in various circumstances without predetermining the choices they will make in those circumstances, thus preserving both divine sovereignty and human free will.

114. Folley, "Nontheist Responding to the Debate," 126–27.

The Problem of Hiding from God

If Christianity is true, and there are good reasons and evidence to believe it is, then God himself through the Bible has given us an explanation for why we often don't experience his presence more directly.[115] Don't get me wrong, I strongly believe that "since the creation of the world His invisible attributes, His eternal power and divine nature, have been clearly seen, being understood through what has been made, so that they are without excuse" (Rom. 1:20, NASB), which explains why so many people around the world and throughout history have believed there is a God. However, in Genesis we're told Adam and Eve enjoyed the direct presence of God in the garden of Eden, and in Revelation it says humanity will someday enjoy this presence again when "He will dwell among them" and "God Himself will be among them" (Rev. 21:3, NASB). So why don't we always experience God's presence like this now?

According to Christianity the main problem isn't that God is hiding from us but that we are hiding from him. Whether the story of Adam and Eve should be taken literally, and thus they were the federal heads of all humanity, or more allegorically, and thus they figuratively represent humanity as a whole, it's clear from Genesis that God created us to enjoy loving relationships with him and with each other—Adam and Eve are described communing with God and experiencing his presence directly. However, they rebelled against him because they wanted to be the ones, instead of God, who decided for themselves what is good and evil. Afterwards it says they "hid from God" because they were ashamed of what they did (Gen. 3:8–10). The primary consequence of this rebellion of ours was that humanity's relationship with God was ruined, and we were banished from Eden and sent out, so to speak, from the presence of God. There's a sense in which God gave us over to what we wanted—to be away from God, hidden from him, having independence from him so we could choose for

115. Though I don't have the space available here, elsewhere I've made the case that Christianity is true and the Bible is from God. In my previous chapter (41–44) I laid out the basic structure of my approach for making this case but much more can be found at www.convincingproof.org. If we can successfully make the case that we do have an unmistakable, or nearly so, divine message, then this addresses the "divergent religious views" aspect of Folley's depth argument of divine hiddenness (124–26). As with the evidence for God, just because some people don't think there's good evidence the Bible is from God doesn't mean there isn't. I would say that especially the teachings of Jesus are about as unmistakably a divine message as one could ask for. As for Folley's "lack of religious experience" aspect of his depth argument of divine hiddenness, I'd say that an argument against the existence of God based on a lack of subjective religious experience is even worse than the poor argument for God based merely on subjective religious experience (121–23).

ourselves what is good and evil. Thus, according to Christianity, humanity is currently in a state of rebellion, running from God, hiding from God, wanting to do things our own way. The reason he often feels distant from us is that we've alienated ourselves from the God who created us and loves us.

The point I'm trying to make is that a lack of evidence isn't the only issue at play here—there's also a spiritual dimension to this that should be accounted for. Don't get me wrong, I think we should base our beliefs on good reasons and evidence; that's why I spend my time providing people good reasons and evidence that Christianity is true. Sometimes that's all people need—as soon as they discover the strong reasons and evidence for Christianity they choose to trust in Christ. But I also believe, because I'm convinced Christianity is true, that according to God there's also a spiritual aspect to this that needs to be considered.

The rest of the Bible lays out God's strategy to reconcile us back to himself. Paul explained to the Greek philosophers in Athens that

> From one man He has made every nationality to live over the whole earth and has determined their appointed times and the boundaries of where they live. He did this so that they might seek God, and perhaps they might reach out and find Him, though He is not far from each one of us. For in Him we live and move and have our being, as even some of your own poets have said,[116] "For we are also His offspring." . . . Therefore, having overlooked the times of ignorance, God now commands all people everywhere to repent, because he has set a day when he is going to judge the world in righteousness by the man he has appointed. He has provided proof of this to everyone by raising him from the dead" (Acts 17:26–31, HCSB).

As Paul noted, God wants us to seek him but the problem is, if left to ourselves, none of us do. Paul explains elsewhere that "there is none who seeks for God," and "there is none who does good" (Rom. 3:11–12). That's why God is seeking us through his plan to restore humanity back to a right relationship with himself. This plan culminated with God the Son becoming human, dying on the cross to pay the penalty we deserve for our evil choices, and promising that whoever trusts in him will be forgiven, reconciled back to God, and spend eternity enjoying loving relationships with him and with each other.

116. Paul's quote "in him we live and move and have our being" derives from *Cretica* by the Greek philosopher-poet Epimenides, and his statement "For we are also his offspring" comes from *Phenomena* by the Greek poet Aratus.

As I noted above, God cares more about having a relationship with us than merely having us believe he exists. If his goal was just to have more people believe he exists, then yes, it *might* be the case more people would believe this, if he provided additional evidence of himself. However, since his goal is to woo us back to a relationship with himself, it's reasonable to conclude it was a superior strategy, as opposed to overwhelming us with his direct presence, to accomplish this subtly through Christ becoming one of us (i.e., taking on human nature, walking among us, and gently pointing the way back to God). Consider an analogy where a father has a son who rebels against him, cuts off his relationship with him, and joins a band of evildoers, causing ruin to himself and others. Wouldn't it be more effective for the father to try and overcome the child's waywardness through gentle encouragement and explanation instead of direct confrontation, which could easily drive the child away more? Folley used a similar analogy when he talked about how a loving father would try to overcome the resistance of his son not by force but by gentle encouragement and explanation.[117] Similarly, it seems reasonable that God's strategy of reaching us through the incarnation of Christ is the most optimal approach of wooing people back to himself. God didn't overbearingly confront us with his direct presence or boom declarations down at us from heaven. Instead, he lovingly revealed himself to us through Christ, as he became one of us, and gently explained how our loving relationship with God can be restored.

117. Folley, "Nontheist Responding to the Debate," 113.

16

Response to the Contributors

Concluding Remarks for Atheism

Dan Barker

In her gracious introduction, Dolores Morris decries *refutation mode* and celebrates civil dialogue. Of course, this was a debate, so Adam and I had to engage in rebuttal. We disagree about much, but I'm sure that in our hearts, we want the same thing. We want truth, meaning, morality, kindness, fairness, justice, and love. In that regard, we are indeed friends. And who made the rule that friends can't argue? True friendship welcomes honest disagreement. Instead of *refutation mode*, I like to think we are in *learning mode*. What follows is in the spirit of friendly rebuttal.

Miracles

Arguing only for "mere theism," Adam presented no real evidence during the debate, but he did hint at miracles when he objected that the multiverse hypothesis "proves too much," suggesting that *if* God gave us direct evidence, some of us might dismiss it as randomness. I responded to that argument.

Now, finally, in his additional points, Adam offers testable evidence: "Because we have so many early, independent, corroborating, and extensive historical sources that describe Jesus's miracles and resurrection, I and many others are convinced Jesus' message is from God. . . . I'm most impressed by the prophecy in Daniel 9 that predicted several hundred years in advance when the Messiah would arrive." *This* is what we should have been debating. Confirmed miracles would be impossible to ignore. Adam says many are convinced by the miracle reports, but why is not everyone? Perhaps because that is just what they are: reports.

Even if the reports were reliable, does it follow that miracles are evidence for God? Supernatural events might be compatible with the existence of a supreme being, but a supreme being may not be the only explanation.

Are the miracles confirmed? Adam says only, "I'm most impressed," so I could simply respond with "I'm not impressed." But in the spirit of amicable debate, I'll offer some brief reasons for skepticism.

The Resurrection

Paul wrote that if Jesus did not rise from the dead, faith is useless (1 Cor. 15:14). But I wonder exactly what it is Adam expects us to believe. When you look closely at the resurrection stories, they don't hang together.

Take Mark, Matthew, Luke and John from Easter morning to the end of each book. Also take Acts 1:3–12 and Paul's creedal passage in 1 Corinthians 15:3–8. Leaving nothing out, try writing a coherent narrative of the resurrection story. I tried it. It can't be done. In the chapter "Leave No Stone Unturned" in my book *Godless*, I describe at least seventeen irreconcilable differences in the accounts.[1] These include the identity of the women who visited the tomb, the time and purpose of their visit, whether the tomb was open or closed when they arrived, the location of Jesus's first appearance and ascension, and so on. The reports do not agree. This doesn't mean the authors were all liars, but it does mean some of those corroborating sources Adam mentions were not always truthful.

Thomas Paine noted these problems as well. "I lay it down as a position which cannot be controverted," he wrote, "first, that the agreement of all the parts of a story does not prove that story to be true, because the parts may agree and the whole may be false; secondly, that the disagreement of the parts of a story proves the whole cannot be true."[2] Of course, this by itself doesn't disprove the resurrection. It just means that the sources Adam mentions are not entirely reliable.

Adam also says they are independent, but we know that is not true. The author of Mark borrowed from another source, and the writers of Matthew and Luke copied from Mark (also borrowing from another source). They were most likely not eyewitnesses, since their stories were composed decades after the alleged event.[3] Many believe that the resurrection must have occurred because the early Christians were reportedly persecuted and killed for their faith, and who would die for a lie? But if that is true, how did any of them live long

1. Dan Barker, *Godless: How an Evangelical Preacher Became One of America's Leading Atheists* (Ulysses, 2008).

See also freethoughtnow.org/easter-challenge.

2. Thomas Paine, *The Age of Reason* (Citadel, 1974).

3. The author of Matthew writes about Matthew in the third person, for example, which shows that someone pretending to be Matthew wrote the book. See Matt. 9:9, 10 and 10:3.

enough to write those tales? Life expectancy then was about forty years. Mark composed his account more than three decades after the event. Matthew and Luke followed at least a decade after that. The author of John wrote his gospel at least sixty years (!) after the supposed resurrection. We know that human memory is fallible. Why should the allegedly most pivotal event in history rely on the decades-old recollections of elderly preachers or on secondhand testimony?

The story is unique in some ways, but that can be said of all miracle reports. The accounts of the resurrection of the Mesopotamian Tammuz, the Egyptian Osiris, the Greek Dionysus, the Indian Krishna, and the Mesoamerican Quetzalcóatl were believed by millions. The biblical narrative is indeed arresting, but it's just another story. A tale that can't be tested can't seriously count as evidence for miracles.

Paine went on to ask: "Is it more probable that nature should go out of her course or that a man should tell a lie? We have never seen, in our time, nature go out of her course. But we have good reason to believe that millions of lies have been told in the same time. It is therefore at least millions to one that the reporter of a miracle tells a lie."[4] David Hume said: "No testimony is sufficient to establish a miracle unless that testimony be of such a kind that its falsehood would be more miraculous than the fact which it endeavors to establish."[5]

Daniel

Adam casually drops the prophecy of Daniel like a bombshell out of the blue. He then says nothing else about it. What? A confirmed six-hundred-year prophecy would be earth-shattering. Everything we think we know about physics, causality, and the dimension of time—not to mention our ideas of free will—would have to be radically restructured. Maybe it does, but then Adam should have led with *that* instead of tucking it into this book that many in the debate audience may never read. I think he chose abduction over evidence because he knows there is wide disagreement about the dating, authorship, and interpretation of the book of Daniel.

Adam probably believes Daniel 9 was written during the Babylonian captivity, but he certainly knows that most critical scholars are convinced it was written hundreds of years later. The so-called prophecies of Daniel were backdated. It is easy to predict the "future" when you already know what happened.

4. Thomas Paine, *The Age of Reason: Being an Investigation of True and Fabulous Theology* (J. S. Jordan, 1795), part 1, chapter 17.

5. David Hume, "Of Miracles," in *David Hume: Writings on Religion* (Open Court, 1993).

Look at this prophecy: "I am Edwin Seer, writing in December, 1975. Jimmy Carter will become president next year. A decade later a challenging spacecraft will be destroyed and soon after that, so will the Soviet Union. The year after the millennium turns, the tallest buildings will fall. Everyone will have pocket telephones to talk with anyone in the world. America will inaugurate its first female president in 2017. Two decades later, Russia will be destroyed when Krishna returns to punish evildoers." You probably don't believe that prophecy although, like Daniel, it is written in a book. You might ask, "Who is this guy Edwin Seer?" We can also ask, "Who is this guy Daniel?" It's easy to see that Edwin's "prophecy," with accurate predictions *to a point*, was written in 2016 when Hilary Clinton was running for office. After that, he got it wrong.

We can do the same with Daniel. The "prophecies" are indeed mostly accurate to a point.[6] But noticing when they start failing, we see that they were composed not in the sixth century BCE, as the author pretends, but four centuries later during the Maccabean revolt after Antiochus IV Epiphanes defiled the temple, as "prophesied" by "Daniel." The messianic reign was to occur a few years later. It did not. Ptolemy VI did not attack Antiochus, and Antiochus did not retaliate by conquering Egypt. Antiochus did not die in Palestine, as Daniel predicted—he died fighting in the East. After his death, a general resurrection was supposed to follow: "Many of those who sleep in the dust of the earth shall awake . . . Those who are wise shall shine like the brightness of the sky" (12:2–3, ESV). We all know that never happened.

By this reckoning, the "prophecies" Adam refers to were written between 167 and 163 BCE. According to Deuteronomy 18:22, God told his people (through Moses) how to identify a fraud: "If a prophet speaks in the name of the Lord but the thing does not take place or prove true, it is a word that the Lord has not spoken" (NRSV). According to Moses, Daniel was a false prophet. Jeremiah railed against prophets who "speak visions from their own minds, not from the mouth of the Lord" (Jer. 23:16, NIV)

None of this is surprising. There have been many forged prophecies, gospels, and epistles in history. The Book of Mormon, purportedly written in the fourth century CE, follows a similar pattern. After making some amazing predictions (including the voyage of Christopher Columbus), it claims that all the "gentiles" who do not convert to Mormonism—which would be most of the planet—will be destroyed by the Native Americans.[7] That never hap-

6. Although there never was a Darius the Mede, and the ordering of some of the kingdoms is jumbled.

7. The "House of Jacob" in 3 Nephi 20:15–16.

pened. By this measure, the book can be dated to the early nineteenth century, coincidentally about the time Joseph Smith says he discovered it in 1830.

The book of Daniel is cut from the same fantastic fabric. Adam (like Jeremiah) knows there have been many religious forgeries, so why does he think the author of Daniel was immune from the temptation to create one himself? We have to consider the author's state of mind. The "troubled" Daniel said some of his revelations came in dreams: "My spirit was troubled within me . . . my face turned pale; but I kept the matter in my mind" (Dan. 7:15, NRSV). Is this trustworthy testimony? He claimed angelic visitations, which means we have to assume the existence of celestial beings. Maybe Adam can do that, but in my mind it just raises more questions. It also seems to beg the question. How do we know that a supernatural god exists? Because an unknown writer tells us that supernatural creatures told him in a dream that there is a supernatural realm.

If Daniel 9 was truly a prophecy about Jesus, why didn't he tell us his name or the names of his parents? Why didn't he say, "Three dozen years after the death of King Herod, Jesus of Nazareth will be crucified between thieves on a hill outside Jerusalem"? Would that have been too hard for God? Instead, we read weird metaphoric descriptions of psychedelic beasts with splitting horns rising from the sea and a disembodied handwriting on a wall.

There is more to be said, but we can at least admit that Daniel is not entirely reliable. We can't address all the issues here—especially regarding the "seventy weeks" that supposedly preceded the "anointed one" (who Adam pretends was Jesus)—but for the purpose of this book, since Adam did not offer any details, I can leave it at that.

Infanticide

Adam is right that the bible is not directly relevant to "mere theism."[8] But it *is* relevant to a capital-G "Does God Exist?" debate, which he now admits by bringing Christian scripture into his additional points. It is also relevant to morality, which Adam raised during the debate. I could have listed immoral

8. I don't capitalize "bible" unless it appears in a quote or refers to an actual book, such as the New American Bible, which is what we do with "dictionary," "thesaurus," and "lexicon." We don't capitalize "biblical," which we would do if it were referring to a proper noun, like "Dickensian" or "Victorian." The collection of writings some call "The Holy Bible" is a cultural construct without a concrete referent. There are different bibles in various languages, translations, and canons, so we cannot assume we are talking about one particular book.

actions of many gods, so pointing to a horrifying passage from a book Adam believes was inspired by the God he worships is certainly warranted.

During the debate, I brought up the infanticidal Psalm 137:9: "Happy shall they be who take your little ones and dash them against the rock!" (NRSV).[9] Adam tried to soften this atrocity: "It should be noted that the Israelite author here is being held captive in Babylon after the Babylonians had enslaved, raped, and killed his family." How does he know that? Nobody knows who wrote that psalm. The Septuagint translation says it was written by Jeremiah, not by an Israelite refugee. (Jeremiah was not exiled to Babylon.) And why does it matter that the author was suffering in captivity? Is this God's word or not? The writer may have had psychological motivations, but so did all the psalmists. Should they all be ignored? Adam seems to agree with me that the bible is not the word of God but the word of ancient believers.

Adam wrote, "Some of these situations in the Old Testament are merely descriptive; it's not approving what happened but merely describing what took place." That is true in some cases, but not here. "Happy shall they be" is exhortatory. The book of Psalms was sung during worship. If we can gloss over verses that were psychologically motivated, should we ignore "The Lord is my shepherd" or "Make a joyful noise unto the Lord"? Adam brushes aside what *he* doesn't like. When I was an evangelist, I used to sing, "I've taken my harp down from the willow tree, my heart is singing the victory." Those lyrics are based on the same Psalm 137, lamenting the fact that while captive, the Israelites had hung their harps on trees. "How could we sing the Lord's song in a foreign land?"[10] But as Christians, I preached, we can take the harps down and celebrate the end of captivity. If part of that psalm is relevant to modern believers, it is *all* relevant, including smashing babies. "All scripture is inspired by God," Paul wrote, "and is useful for teaching, for reproof, for correction, and for training in righteousness" (2 Tim. 3:16. NRSV). Notice that word "all."

The writer of Psalm 137:9 wasn't simply describing regrettable collateral damage during war time. He said the person who dashes babies against rocks should be *happy* to do it. Could *you* do that? Who but a psychopath would ever form such a thought? That word *happy*—sometimes translated *blessed*—is the same word in Psalm 144:15 ("Happy is the people whose God is the Lord") and Proverbs 3:13 ("Happy are those who find wisdom"). Should we ignore *those*

9. Twenty-four English translations say "little ones," seventeen (such as NASB) say "children," thirteen (such as NLT) say "babies," and three (including NIV) say "infants."

10. Why not? Does worship depend on geography?

verses? Today we are shocked and outraged at infanticide, but in those days it was meant to be a joyous event.

Psalm 137:9 is consistent with the rest of the bible. Here are a few passages where God himself (not the writer) commands, condones or commits infanticide:

> I will punish the world for its evil. . . . *Their infants will be dashed to pieces before their eyes*; their houses will be plundered, and their wives ravished. . . . *their eyes will not pity children.* (Isa. 13:11–18, ESV)

> Samaria shall bear her guilt, because she has rebelled against her God; they shall fall by the sword, *their little ones shall be dashed in pieces*, and their pregnant women ripped open. (Hosea 13:16, ESV)

> Thus says the Lord of hosts, . . . "go and attack Amalek, and utterly destroy all that they have; do not spare them, but *kill both man and woman, child and infant.*" (1 Sam. 15:3, NRSV)

> Now therefore *kill every male among the little ones.* (Num. 31:17, KJV; later in the passage they are instructed to keep the virgin girls alive for themselves)

> And I will dash them one against another, *parents and children together*, says the Lord. I will not pity or spare or have compassion when I destroy them. (Jer. 13:14, NRSV)

> Therefore thus says the Lord God: I, I myself, am coming against you; I will execute judgments among you. . . . Surely, *parents shall eat their children* in your midst. (Ezek. 5:8–10, NRSV)

> Thus says the Lord of hosts, the God of Israel: . . . *I will make them eat the flesh of their sons and the flesh of their daughters.* (Jer. 19:3–9, NRSV)

> So the Lord our God also handed over to us King Og of Bashan and all his people. We struck him down until not a single survivor was left . . . *utterly destroying men, women, and children.*" (Deut. 3:3–6, NRSV)

> At midnight *the Lord struck down all the firstborn* in the land of Egypt. (Exod. 12:29, NRSV)

> Even if they bring up children, I will bereave them until no one is left. . . . *Ephraim must lead out his children for slaughter*. . . . Even though they give birth, *I will kill the cherished offspring of their womb.* (Hosea 9:12–16, NRSV)

> The Lord called to the man . . . "Pass through the city after him, and kill; your eye shall not spare, and you shall show no pity. Cut down old men, young men and young women, *little children* and women." (Ezek. 9:3–6, NRSV)

> I will continue to plague you sevenfold for your sins. I will let loose wild animals against you, and they shall *bereave you of your children*. (Lev. 26:21–22, NRSV)

> Nathan said to David, "Now the Lord has put away your sin; you shall not die. Nevertheless, because by this deed you have utterly scorned the Lord, *the child that is born to you shall die.*" (2 Sam. 12:13–14, NRSV)

Are you happy reading those verses? That is a small sample of the many passages showing God commanding and committing violence that I list in my book *God: The Most Unpleasant Character in All Fiction.*[11] And let's not forget the gruesome story of Jephthah, who, after burning his virgin daughter as a sacrifice to Yahweh, was rewarded with a prestigious judgeship. (Judg. 11 and 12)

Adam questions my ability to interpret scripture. He can do that. But so can I question his ability. According to the Christianity I used to preach, the Word of God was written to all of us, not just to sectarian authorities. If the bible can be properly understood only by a handful of properly trained scholars, then God was inept at revealing his message. Hotel-room bibles are not accompanied by experts to tell us what it *really* means. If I am not free to interpret it as it speaks to me, neither is Adam. And if we disagree about the meaning, doesn't that make God a sloppy communicator?

During the debate, Adam asked, "If we all changed our mind and thought it was okay to rape women tomorrow, would that make rape right?" I countered with Jeremiah 13:22–26, where God boasted that *he* raped women. If God is the source of morals, rape is indeed right. Adam did not rebut this, so I won't elaborate, except to emphasize that God bellowed, "I myself will lift up your skirts" (Jer. 13:26, ESV). How can any moral or loving person pretend to admire such a violent and misogynistic deity?

11. You can also find a list of the passages online at unpleasant.ffrf.org.

Hiddenness

Andrew Drinkard's chapter on divine hiddenness is very creative and sometimes eloquent, but at the end of the day it's just a sermon. Admitting that "God seems hidden," he responds only with speculation. He uses the words "may" (and "maybe") twenty-one times, "could be" nine times, "perhaps" nine times, "might" (such as "might be the case") seven times, and "I believe" six times. For example: "These nonhuman free creatures could be harming humans by somehow frustrating their ability to believe in God. Room doesn't afford me the ability to speculate how this might be the case." Speculation can be useful in creating hypotheses, but hypotheses must be testable to be meaningful in an argument. You can't just say, "It could be like this," and demand that the skeptic prove you wrong. That is a reversal of the burden of proof.

I could also speculate on God's hiddenness:

- After creating the universe, God might have died in childbirth.
- Maybe creation was so strenuous that God was too weak to reveal himself for perhaps billions of years.
- God could have overreached in creation, and the barrier between us may now be too great for him to penetrate.
- Perhaps God exhausted his quota of miracles.
- I believe God might be malicious, like an abusive parent, dangling a bit of suggestive evidence, perhaps deliberately holding back to laugh (see Job 9:23; Prov. 1:26) at our confused reactions, dishonestly promising to answer prayers.[12]
- God could be merely a literary figure. Asking God to reveal himself might be like asking Voldemort to reveal himself. Maybe.

I could go on with these speculations (and so could you) but this is silly. Anybody can concoct maybes. Even if something *may* or *could* be the case, there is work to do before solving the case. If Andrew dismisses my speculations on the basis that God is understood to be all-powerful, I could dismiss his on the basis that God is understood to be all-fictional. Perhaps.

12. "If you believe, you will receive whatever you ask for in prayer" (Matt. 21:22, NIV). "So I tell you, whatever you ask for in prayer, believe that you have received it, and it will be yours" (Mark 11:24, NRSV). See also Matt. 7:7–8, 11; 18:19; Mark 11:22–23; John 14:12–14; 15:7, 16; 16:23–24. See also 1 John 3:22: "And whatsoever we ask, we receive of him, because we keep his commandments, and do those things that are pleasing in his sight" KJV, see also 1 John 5:14–15).

Adam limited the debate to "mere theism," but Andrew dives right into the bible, as if our debate were not about mere philosophy but about his evangelical interpretation of Christian theism. He claims to have a personal relationship with this God, so instead of speculating, why doesn't he ask God to tell *me* why he is hiding?

Andrew disagrees with philosopher J. L. Schellenberg, a "leading proponent" of the hiddenness argument.[13] Let me repeat it here:

1. If a perfectly loving God exists, then there exists a God who is always open to a personal relationship with any finite person.
2. If there exists a God who is always open to a personal relationship with any finite person, then no finite person is ever nonresistantly in a state of nonbelief in relation to the proposition that God exists.
3. If a perfectly loving God exists, then no finite person is ever nonresistantly in a state of nonbelief in relation to the proposition that God exists (from 1 and 2).
4. Some finite persons are or have been nonresistantly in a state of nonbelief in relation to the proposition that God exists.
5. No perfectly loving God exists (from 3 and 4).
6. If no perfectly loving God exists, then God does not exist.
7. God does not exist (from 5 and 6).[14]

It is good that Andrew recognizes I am nonresistant. Schellenberg, like me, was a believer in God at one time. We did not resist belief and still would not, if it were justified. We changed our minds reluctantly after carefully examining the proffered evidence and arguments. Like me, Schellenberg is open to the possibility of an "ultimate reality." We are not close-minded. Many in the world are not resistant, so why is God hiding from people like us?

My Native American ancestors lived on the continent millennia before a territorial deity named Yahweh allegedly used his finger to inscribe commandments on stone tablets for a desert tribe living on the other side of the world.[15] Some of my Lenape ancestors believed in local deities, but none of them believed in the universal God of the bible. How could they? There is no reason to

13. Schellenberg is the creator of the argument.

14. J. L. Schellenberg, *The Hiddenness Argument: Philosophy's New Challenge to Belief in God* (Oxford University Press, 2015), 103. Schellenberg has given me explicit permission to reprint his argument here.

15. I am an enrolled member of the Delaware (Lenape) Tribe of American Indians.

think they would have been resistant to such belief. In fact, after colonization many did adopt Christian theism (though we have to ask how much of that was voluntary). My full-blooded great-grandmother's favorite song was "Rock of Ages." If a perfectly loving God exists, why didn't he pursue a relationship with my ancestors twelve thousand years ago? The modern human species goes back about two hundred thousand years. Was God hiding all those millennia, waiting for the invention of writing?

As I said in the debate, if there is a God, I sincerely want to know it. It would be stupid to deny such a fact of reality, if it is a fact. I also said, "If I met God, I would have to accept it, but it doesn't mean I have to worship him." Belief is not the same as admiration. "Nonresistant nonbelievers," Andrew imagines, "claim they are truly ready to enter a relationship with God," but that is not true. If a God exists, I may be willing, but before I might be *ready* to enter into a relationship with anyone, they have to earn my respect. I don't think a person who demands to be worshiped is worthy of worship. If you are truly worthy, you don't have to demand it. Adam and Andrew appear to be interpreting my cautious attitude as a close-minded rejection, but it is in their minds, not mine, that belief equals submission.

I like how Joe Folley put it in his divine hiddenness chapter: "The whole discussion about resistance to beliefs is not only helpful for atheists to consider whether they truly are psychologically resistant to the existence of a deity, but also to theists, who could equally ask whether they are unduly resistant to atheism." I have sometimes been accused of having a bias against the supernatural, but couldn't some theists equally be accused of having a bias against the natural? Why are so many finite persons in a state of resistant nonbelief regarding naturalism? Folley asks: "Why is it that God not only does not show himself in such a way as to convince nonbelievers, but often does not even show himself to believers?" I suspect Andrew has asked himself this very question.

I do wonder about step 6 of Schellenberg's argument. Does it follow that if no perfectly loving God exists, then God does not exist? God might be unloving.[16] Who made the rule that ultimate perfection must include ultimate love? We all value love, but love seems to be a human projection onto the deity. Why can't ultimate perfection include ultimate hatred?[17] When I look at the

16. Schellenberg does have a chapter in *Hiddenness Argument* called "Must a God Be Loving?" But he never explains why he must. He assumes that God, by definition, must be worthy of worship and that the "ultimistic" quality of love must be included under "personal perfection" (*The Hiddenness Argument: Philosophy's New Challenge to Belief in God* [Oxford University Press, 2015], 89–103). I think this argument needs further development.

17. "I hate them with perfect hatred" (Ps. 139:22).

collection of ancient writings on which Andrew bases his epistemology, that seems to be a more apt description.

I quoted some unloving verses above, but in spite of this evidence Andrew insists that "God is love" (cherry-picking from 1 John 4:16). In *God: The Most Unpleasant Character in All Fiction*, I ask: "How can a handful of sycophantic praises mitigate hundreds of cruel commands and bloodcurdling barbarities? Actions speak louder than words. If Yahweh behaves like a thug, his reputation can't be redeemed by one of his minions simply parroting 'God is love.'" The so-called love of the biblical God is nothing you or I would recognize. It is top-down, controlling, conditional, and punitive, like how a patriarchal husband loves his wife. It offers blessings if you obey and curses if you don't. Read God's covenant with the Israelites in Deuteronomy 28. There are three times as many curses as blessings in that chapter. What if wedding vows included horrific threats for infidelity? How loving is that?

Since Andrew cannot admire the capricious pagan gods, he will understand that neither can I admire the biblical deity. In *God: The Most Unpleasant Character in All Fiction*, I quote almost fifteen hundred biblical passages showing that the biblical deity is no better, and often worse, than the pagan gods.[18] I also show that these verses are not taken out of context, misinterpreted, merely metaphorical, or "morally justified," as some apologists insist. There is no question that the bible glorifies violence. Not all Christians are violent, of course. They are nicer than their God. Most good Christians and Jews today have risen above the brutality of their ancestors. Renowned Christian biblical scholar John J. Collins ends his book *Does the Bible Justify Violence?* with these words: "There is much in the Bible that is not 'worthy' of the God of the philosophers. There is also much that is not worthy of humanity, certainly much that is not worthy to serve as a model for imitation. . . . The Bible has contributed to violence in the world precisely because it has been taken to confer a degree of certitude that transcends human discussion and argumentation. Perhaps the most constructive thing a biblical critic can do toward lessening the contribution of violence in the world is to show that such certitude is an illusion."[19]

It looks like Andrew has a good heart. I also used to preach that the loving God only seems hidden—he is gently revealing himself because love should be freely given without coercion. But that is not what the bible says. If Andrew could learn to read the scripture free of sectarian bias, with a "humble and

18. See unpleasant.ffrf.org.

19. See also biblical scholar Hector Avalos's *Fighting Words: The Origins of Religious Violence* (Prometheus, 2005).

open mindset" (as he exhorts me), he might see that the God he worships is not love. If he wants love, he will find it here on earth, just as we atheists do.

Immaterial Mind

I discussed the concept of immaterial minds in my additional points, but after reading Benjamin Watkins's excellent chapter, I have to defend myself a little. While Watkins and I agree that a mind cannot be immaterial, he disagrees with my claim that the very concept of immaterial minds is an oxymoron. "How exactly does an entirely immaterial mind, like a god or soul, entail a logical contradiction like a married bachelor does?" he asks. "An unembodied mind seems both a coherent and plausible theoretical postulate." Really? If it is true, as Watkins's title claims, that *all* minds are material things, how exactly can a material thing be immaterial?

A bachelor is single. To be married is not to be single, so a married bachelor is an oxymoron. A mind is a physical expression. To be immaterial is not to be physical, so an immaterial mind is an oxymoron.

Watkins claims that minds are *things*, but how can that be? A mind is a function *of* a thing, that is, of a brain in a highly evolved living body. Right after a person dies, their bodily organs are still there, but the heart no longer beats and brain activity has ceased. You can touch the dead heart and brain, but you can't touch the circulation or the thinking. Those are not organs. They are processes *of* organs. When a machine breaks down, it no longer works. The parts are there, but they stop functioning. Death is cessation.

I agree that just because something is contradictory in fact doesn't mean it is contradictory in principle. Watkins's point might be valid, if he could offer a description of mind that does not require physicality. What is functioning in an immaterial mind? Unembodied brain cells? Immaterial computer circuits? Ghostly synapses? Biology is the reason we have the word *mind* in the first place, and biology is physical. Watkins admits: "Our minds and those of nonhuman animals are either identical with, or causally dependent upon, something physical, which gives us reason to reject theism." If he believes, like theists, that there could *theoretically* be unembodied minds (ultimately to rule out, as we both do), he needs to explain how those "minds" might work outside the natural world. Doesn't it follow that if God has a mind, he also has a body? If so, he can't be said to be unembodied.

Joshua Rasmussen's chapter is an ambitious and creative end run around the mind-body problems. I admire his attempt to invert mind and matter, as I do in my book *Contraduction* with time, morality, and free will. But nowhere does he define the word "mind." We all know that minds are expressions of physical brains, yet he seems to presume that the mind is a thing or substance that escapes physical matter. That begs the question, assuming that mind is immaterial from the outset. By his reasoning, the sound of a bell produces the striking of the bell. His intuitive "mind-first" theory of the brain would be like a "digestion-first" theory of the stomach. The simplest way to answer mind-body "problems" is not by needlessly multiplying assumptions but by acknowledging that the natural world is all there is and that the emergent mind is a function of the brain.

Morality

In his chapter, David Enoch states it nicely: "When I see a person humiliating another and think or say 'This is wrong', nothing about God (a loving deity or otherwise) seems to be involved." Morality is natural. It is bottom-up, not top-down. It is based on testable consequences, not untestable supernatural edicts.

I also agree with Enoch that theists are wrong to ask for the source of morality. However, although we agree that the moral argument is unsound, Enoch claims to disagree with me about whether moral values are objective.[20] He admits that objective morality "can be understood in more than one way," but seems to think I don't know that. He (like David Baggett in this book) must have missed what I said in the debate itself: "I will say, and I think most atheists in this room will say, that although objective moral values do not exist, most of our moral values can be objectively verified." As I elaborated in my additional points, I do think moral values are objective in the sense that they can be objectively justified (which is how I think most philosophers see it), but not in the sense that moral values are objective *things* that metaphysically transcend our natural minds (which is how many theists see it). Adam suggests that the objectivity of morality proves there is a transcendent realm that explains the origin of such values. Let me repeat what C. S. Lewis said: "This Rule of Right and Wrong, or Law of Human Nature . . . must somehow or other be *a real thing* . . . there is *more than one kind of reality* . . . something above and beyond the ordinary facts of men's behaviour, and yet *quite definitely*

20. I use "moral value" instead of "moral fact," because I don't think there are "moral facts." There are just facts. The valuing of certain facts or actions is what we mean by morality. Adam tends to use the phrase "moral truth," but a moral truth is just a statement of a value.

real."[21] That is the objectivity I deny. Let me repeat: Since value is a product of a mind, and since to be objective means to exist independently of the mind, an "objective moral value" is an oxymoron. This does *not* mean moral values cannot be objectively explained by reference to real-world consequences. It just means they exist nowhere outside of physical brains.

As an analogy, let's take taste. (Please don't think I am equating morality with taste.) Taste can be considered objective. Since we can demonstrate that musically discordant passages or stinking food or clashing colors are displeasing, does this mean that taste is an *entity* that exists outside of our bodies in a transcendent "taste realm"? If so-called moral truths need a source, then wouldn't also "taste truths"? Of course not. The source is not "out there"—it is within us. Enoch's claim that moral values do not need a source supports my claim that they are not *things*. We don't need an explanation outside of the natural world.

David Baggett is right that morality is richer than the mere lessening of harm. I say exactly that in my book *Mere Morality*, in which I point out that the minimization of harm is the floor, the "mere" basis of morality.[22] Adam, who was good enough to read the book (and acknowledge the nuance), specifically agreed with that underlying principle. But instead of picking at what they think I may or may not understand, why don't they make a positive case that an immaterial God is the best explanation? Baggett says, "Theism can better explain the reliability of our moral cognitive processes and the cosmic coincidence between our moral judgments and moral truth," but he does not say *how*. (His statement may be contraductory.[23] It only seems to be a "cosmic coincidence" from the human point of view, like wondering how our noses became so exquisitely fine-tuned to support eyeglasses.) Besides some God-of-the-gaps suggestions, his only (tentative) answer is the divine command theory, but he certainly knows that this runs into the Euthyphro dilemma: "Is it moral because God wills it, or does God will it because it is moral?" And, as I point out above, it also runs into the iniquitous scriptures, assuming he imagines the bible might be a moral guidebook.

Agreeing that the harm principle provides at least one viable natural basis for morality, Adam is acknowledging that you can be good without God. He

21. C. S. Lewis, "Mere Christianity," in *The C. S. Lewis Signature Classics* (HarperOne, 2017), 27 (emphasis added).

22. Dan Barker, *Mere Morality* (Pitchstone, 2018), 17.

23. I explain contraduction in my additional points and also in my book *Contraduction* (Hypatia, 2024).

is charitable enough to disagree with the bible when it says atheists are all corrupt: "They do abominable deeds; there is no one who does good" and "They have all gone astray; they are all alike perverse" (Ps. 14:1–3, NRSV). We all know the psalmist was perversely wrong about that. Atheists can indeed do good things, like anyone else.

What is the point here? Why do theists raise the moral argument in the first place? It's not because morality is a huge mystery. I think it's because they are grasping for an argument for belief in God. When they suggest that human morality comes not from within but from beyond, they are trying to manufacture a bridge to an imaginary supernatural world. Morality is not the point: God is the point of the moral argument.

Morality is no big mystery. My mother, with only a high-school education, saw it clearly. "If you want to be a good person," she said, "then be a good person."

First Cause

I responded to the Kalām cosmological argument in my additional points. Although Robert Koons doesn't directly address our debate, his chapter attempts to salvage the argument with some novel thinking. But his case is built on such an elaborate tower of assumptions and qualifications that it looks to me like a tottering house of cards. Remove one, and the whole thing tumbles.

Every book of cosmology I have ever read considers the universe to be part of the cosmos, yet he has it the other way around. However, I admire Koons's attempt to invert perspective, making time secondary to causation. In chapter 2, "Time," in my book *Contraduction*, I suggest that the appearance of the passage of time may be an illusion produced by our observation of the change of entropy, much like how we think the sun is rising when it is *we* who are rising. Time is not flowing; we are flowing. The clock ticking, the planet revolving, and our bodies aging are not happening *in* time. They are what we *mean* by time. Koons seems to be using this creative reversal of perspective to get God off the hook, suggesting that since causation does not require time, there is no contradiction in imagining a timeless cause to the universe (or cosmos).

But how does that work? How can a being act outside of time? *Act* is a temporal word. If there is no time, how can thoughts flow? Maybe I'm missing something, so let's look at what Koons discovers at the top of his tower of reasoning. He finds a timeless cause that is utterly *simple*. "Compound things are broadly causable," he asserts. The first cause cannot have any parts, otherwise it would not be first. That might make sense within the framework of physics, but does it make sense within theism? Do most believers think God is simple?

Adam's God is a personal being. A personal being is not simple. It has thoughts—plural. It has intentions. It has principles, desires, dislikes, and memories. It makes decisions and takes action. Before it created (or caused) the universe, it had to contemplate and then initiate the process. The biblical God has emotions. He pronounces judgments. Emotions and judgments are not simple.

If God is simple, like a singularity, subatomic particle, or string, then he is a brute fact of physics. That would mean a Trinitarian God does not exist. Whatever the Trinity is, it is compound. A simple God cannot be three in one.

I think Koons is right to describe causation as a relation, which is certainly true within our universe. But then God could not have caused anything. Before the universe that he supposedly created came into existence, there was nothing to relate to; Koons appears to think creation is the same as causation. A creation *ex nihilo* is not a relationship. It is a miracle. In that case, the causation argument is inapt and irrelevant.

Like Adam, Koons describes God as a super-great being. How are we supposed to imagine that? Presumably there was a time, or a state logically antecedent to creation, in which nothing existed except God. How could he think he was great if there was nothing with which to compare himself? With nothing to measure, size and power would be meaningless. He could just as well think he was puny and weak. Outside of space-time (if such a state is conceivable), there is no framework within which comparative adjectives make any sense.

In our current state of scientific knowledge about the big bang, it seems premature to make any definitive or grandiose claims about the "cause" of the universe. The Stoic philosopher Cicero, praising Aristotle, was convinced by the circular paths of planets and stars that there had to be divine movers. "Anyone who sees this truth and denies it is not only ignorant but guilty of impiety if he says that the gods do not exist," he declared. But if Cicero had known about gravity and spinning planets, he might not have jumped to the conclusion that "the existence of the gods is so abundantly clear that I regard anyone who denies it as out of his mind" (*On the Nature of the Gods* 2.44).[24] I'm sure Robert and Adam do not think I am out of my mind, nor do I think that of them. I simply think they are in the same situation the good-hearted Cicero was in, struggling to answer one mystery with another mystery.

If I had read Daniel Linford and Alex Malpass's chapter before writing my additional points, I wouldn't have needed to say so much about the Kalām

24. Translation from Peter Freeman, trans. and ed., *How to Think About God: An Ancient Guide for Believers and Nonbelievers* (Princeton University Press, 2019).

argument. They agree with me that the premises are questionable, but their argument is more rigorous, especially when they write about infinity.

When my daughters Kristi and Andrea were little girls, I overheard them talking about their ages, wondering how old they might become someday.

"I think the biggest number is a million," Andrea said.

"Uh-uh," Kristi rebutted. "What about a million and one?"

Andrea thought for a few seconds and then said, "Maybe it's a hundred million."

"Then what about a hundred million and one?" Kristi asked.

"Hey Dad!" Andrea yelled. "What's the biggest number?"

"There is no biggest number," I said. "The counting never ends. It's called infinity."

"Well, what about infinity and one?" Kristi asked smugly.

Before I could reply that infinity plus one is still infinity, Andrea said, "I know what the biggest number is! It's dead!"

"Yeah?" Kristi shot back. "What about dead and one?"

Kristi was probably not thinking this, but "dead and one" would be the afterlife. If it is true, as I discuss in my additional points, that the Kalām argument shows the impossibility of an actual infinite series of preceding events—hence, even God, if he actually exists, must have had a beginning (and therefore a cause)—then the same would be true with succeeding events. Since at any time in the future it must be possible to think *backward* to now, that distance must also be finite.[25] God, if he actually exists, will also have an ending. If there is life after death, it can't be eternal.

Free Will

The real debate is not atheism versus theism. It's naturalism versus supernaturalism. The arguments from "immaterial minds" and "moral facts" and "first cause," if sound, would point only to a transcendent realm. It would be premature to jump to the conclusion that, for that reason, God must exist. A supernatural realm might indeed provide a suitable environment for a supernatural deity, which is why I think many theists are eager to argue for metaphysical transcendence. But that would be only a first step toward proving a deity.

It would be like failing to find a blue mouse in my house when my brother says, "Look, there are windows. There's a world beyond!" Did he prove that the mouse exists?

25. This conundrum disappears when we realize that time is not infinite. It is a dimension that arose at the big bang and will end at the death of the universe.

I think the same is true with free will. Many think the existence of libertarian free will would point to something outside the window, beyond natural cause and effect. Free will, in their minds, is supernatural. It was not a major topic of the debate, but I did mention free will briefly (counterfactually) in my FANG approach (the freewill argument for the nonexistence of God). It also came up during questions, and Adam spent some time responding to FANG in his additional points.

In his astute chapter, which argues more strenuously for a multiverse than I do, Philip Goff says there are three standard positions on free will: hard determinism, libertarianism, and soft determinism. That's true, but I think there is also a nonstandard position: *acompatibilism*. In my book *Free Will Explained*, I question whether determinism and free will can be contrasted as linear opposites, like two sides of a tug-of-war with compatibilists perched on the rope.[26] I think it is meaningless to ask if determinism and free will are compatible *or* incompatible because they are not on the same axis. They are *acompatible*. Determinism is horizontal, dealing with linear cause and effect across time. But free will is vertical, dealing with how we judge moral accountability. Free will is not a scientific truth; it is a social truth.[27] I call it "harmonic free will," noting that there is a difference between horizontal melody (one note at a time) and vertical harmony (chords of many notes). Harmony, above and "beyond" temporal melody, produces an illusion of transcendence, like free will does. It's beautiful, but it's not supernatural.

In my reading, the most common philosophical definition of free will is "the ability to choose otherwise." Others, especially some compatibilists, define it differently, more like the ability to make choices according to your desires and nature, even though your nature is itself determined. Compatibilists are determinists who think we can continue to use the phrase "free will" in a meaningful natural sense. It's like the word "sunrise." We all know the sun does not rise, but come on, that's how it looks, so that's what we say. We act "as if" we are free.

Philosophers, scientists, and theologians do not all agree on the definition of free will.[28] It's as if the phrase "free will" has taken on a life of its own, and now we all scramble to attach a definition to it. That may be contraductory. We should turn it around. It seems to me that each of the definitions should have its own terminology instead of trying to cram them all into the same phrase.

26. Dan Barker, *Free Will Explained* (Sterling, 2018), 19–20.
27. See John Searle's *The Construction of Social Reality* (Free Press, 1997).
28. John Calvin and Martin Luther disagreed on whether we even have free will.

What do you think free will means? Isn't the definition contained in the phrase itself? What does *free* mean? It means unrestricted. Unrestricted by what? There are many things that restrict: prisons, chains, locks, fences, rules, physical limitations, and so on. But to theologians (and I think most philosophers), *free* means unrestricted by the laws of nature. Your brain is a product of natural laws, but you feel you are above that, able to choose other than what your evolved nature, personality, preferences, desires, and synapses dictate. If *free* means anything else, it is not interesting or relevant to our debate.

Adam's "sourcehood" definition looks a lot like compatibilism: "Free will is best understood in terms of sourcehood, a position sometimes called causal agent libertarian free will. This position maintains that, for example, I, the person Adam Lloyd Johnson, am the ultimate cause of my choices." Of course, he can't really mean "ultimate" if he believes God is the ultimate cause of everything. That would contradict his causality argument. I think he means "proximate cause." I agree that when we are judging moral accountability—like when a person is on trial for committing a crime—we don't assign blame to a creator or the big bang or distant ancestors who passed on a genetic trait or a company that polluted their childhood drinking water. We look at that one individual—"I, the person Adam Lloyd Johnson"—as the proximate causal agent who committed the deed.[29] Whether their "free will" was libertarian or not is irrelevant.

Libertarian free will is still deterministic, if not by the known laws of nature, then by as yet unknown supernatural or theistic laws. I don't know any proponents of libertarian free will who think it is all chaotic or random.

The reason free will came up during our debate was that I mentioned FANG as one example of incoherence in the traditional definition of God. No matter what any of us thinks about human free will, traditional theists believe God has it. But if you have free will, you cannot know the future. If God knows what he will do tomorrow at noon, then he is powerless to decide to do otherwise before then. He is not free.

Adam disagrees: "It's *possible* that God's foreknowledge of his own choices wouldn't negate his free will because his foreknowledge of his future choices would be caused by his future choices. . . . All that's required to defeat a claim of impossibility is a possibility, not an actuality." What does Adam mean by "caused by future choices"? Is it possible for a person to cause something to happen in the past? Can you have a memory of something that has not

29. Of course, during sentencing, we might take previous causes into consideration, such as childhood abuse or a brain tumor.

happened yet? The absurdity of such an idea would render all debate meaningless. (To deflect a possible objection, I described the incoherency of living "outside of time" above.) Adam says, "Whatever has a beginning must have a cause," but if the cause can be in the *future*, we can't conclude there was an earlier "first cause." And if "all that's required to defeat a claim of impossibility is a possibility," then he can't say that the appearance of "fine-tuning" cannot be explained by chance. (The probability of chance is plausible and known. The probability of backward causation, even if not incoherent, is unknown.) Somebody could just as well blurt out the words, "We don't know that it is impossible for God to violate the law of excluded middle; therefore, true could be false."[30]

Augustine said, "If you could understand it, it would not be God" (*Sermon* 117.5).[31] Then let's throw up our hands and stop trying to understand anything at all. Can we just say "God" and claim victory? That is hardly convincing proof.

Fine-Tuning

In his chapter, Robin Collins claims that if more than one cosmic constant can be adjusted, this would increase the likelihood of a life-permitting universe by very little. That may be true. All I am saying is that the universe is *not quite as fine-tuned* for life as some theists might think it is. No matter the exact probability, Collins has to admit that chance is not an impossible explanation. The evolution of our species, after all, was dependent on a myriad of chance events. And yet, here we are. As I wrote in my additional points, *that* is the real answer to the so-called fine-tuning question. The universe was not fine-tuned for us; we were fine-tuned for the universe.

Why Believe?

Since there is no good evidence or argument, why do so many people believe in God? There are a number of hypotheses that can explain the evolutionary origin of religion.[32] But even if we all agreed on that, it would be committing

30. Yes, I know that a logical possibility is not the same as a physical possibility. But I can't see how reverse causation is logically possible.

31. Quoted in Garry Wills, *Saint Augustine* (Penguin, 1999), xii.

32. See, for example, J. Anderson Thomson Jr., *Why We Believe in God(s): A Concise Guide to the Science of Faith* (Pitchstone, 2011); Pascal Boyer, *Religion Explained: The Evolutionary Origins of Religious Thought* (Basic, 2001); Augustin Fuentes, *Why We Believe:*

the genetic fallacy to conclude that this disproves the existence of the object of that belief. So for the purpose of this book, let's set aside the evolutionary "Why?" and ask a psychological "Why?"

After a debate about God's existence at the University of Wisconsin, I met for a post-debate dinner with some of the Christian organizers. I could sense their eagerness to bring me back into God's love. When the meal was over and it was obvious that I was still unmoved—I told them I had plenty of love in my life, thank you—one of them asked me a parting question: "Aren't you worried about judgment?"

Bingo. Beneath the veneer of their arguments is something deeper. They are afraid. God is not mere theism to them. He is a sovereign judge with eternal consequences.[33] They say "God is love," but for most Christians faith is really about the desire to live forever and avoid punishment. Their arguments are prompted not by dispassionate reasoning but by the desire to save their lives.

The fear of judgment can cloud judgment.

If you are a believer, did you first come to your faith after contemplating fine-tuning, causality or other philosophical arguments? You probably believed *initially* through family, religion, and culture.[34] People you respect told you it is true. When you teach your children about God, do you start with deductive syllogisms, Aristotelian metaphysics, or abductive reasoning? I don't think you believe because you have arguments; you have arguments because you believe.

During my 2012 debate in Oxford, Peter Hitchens, the Anglican brother of Christopher Hitchens, offered no rebuttal. He claimed that arguments and evidence are irrelevant. Pointing to us atheists (Richard Dawkins, Michael Shermer, Peter Millican, and me), he appealed to desire:

> The real question before us is why we choose what we choose. . . . Why would you want to live in a purposeless chaos, in which none of your actions had any significance, in which there was no hope of justice, in which the lives of all those whom you loved ended abruptly at death and had no

---

Evolution and the Human Way of Being (Yale University Press, 2019); E. Fuller Torrey, *Evolving Brains, Emerging Gods: Early Humans and the Origins of Religion* (Columbia University Press, 2017); Jesse Bering, *The Belief Instinct: The Psychology of Souls, Destiny, and the Meaning of Life* (Norton, 2011); Robin Dunbar, *How Religion Evolved: And Why It Endures* (Penguin Random House, 2022).

33. "It is appointed for mortals to die once and after that the judgment" (Heb. 9:27).

34. The greatest single predictor of a person's religion is geography.

> further significance? Why would you want, desire, actively wish to live in a universe as disgusting as that? . . . I think these gentlemen do have a very good reason. . . . They *don't* want justice. They *do* want the dead to be dead. They *do* want the universe to be purposeless. They do *not* want their individual actions to have any other significance than their immediate effect.[35]

I get it. It can be unsettling to think we are merely fragile mortals in an uncaring universe with no point, no ultimate moral guidance, no permanence. It is hard to confess we are not special in the cosmos and daunting to realize that if there is to be any meaning, we have to make it ourselves. Do we trust ourselves to do that? Not if we are taught we are bad little children and broken, depraved sinners. This debate is not really about theology, morality, or philosophy. It's about being afraid to face the reality that we are simply biological organisms in a natural environment. We are animals. (But that is no insult.) We all yearn for meaning that rises above the mundane, but most of us find it in the love of family and community. In the joy of art, music, and literature. In the purpose of charity, exploration, and science. In the fellowship of activism, sports, and other shared social activities. In the hope for justice, fairness, equality, and peace. We won't find it pretending to be more than who we really are.

Peter Hitchens can't imagine a meaningful existence outside of his theological worldview. I reply to him in my book *Life Driven Purpose*.[36] But notice that he thinks we can *choose* for God to exist. Is truth something we choose? We can make choices, of course. We can choose to interpret reality according to fear, desire, religious upbringing, or culture, or we can choose to embrace reality for what it is, even if it doesn't fit our personal opinions. We can choose to rise above the mundane by pretending that a supreme being dispenses purpose, or we can choose to create our own.

In *Heretic: Jesus Christ and the Other Sons of God*, Catherine Nixey points out that the word *heresy* means "choice." Before Christianity, heresy was a good word, but then it became evil.[37] Those who chose to disagree with orthodoxy were persecuted, shunned, expelled, or killed. However, many of us are happy to be called heretics. It's a compliment. There is no greater freedom than the freedom to choose to think for yourself. Theists who believe in free will should

35. You can watch that debate at "The God Debate," OxfordUnion, posted December 21, 2012, YouTube, https://tinyurl.com/4urrpx7r.

36. Dan Barker, *Life Driven Purpose: How an Atheist Finds Meaning* (Pitchstone, 2015).

37. Catherine Nixey, *Heretic: Jesus Christ and the Other Sons of God* (HarperCollins, 2024), 11–12.

be thanking us skeptics, because our freedom to say "No" underscores their freedom to say "Yes."

Maybe, like Peter Hitchens, you admit that your faith has little to do with arguments. Perhaps you've had a "spiritual encounter with God," sensing a presence of joy and love (like I often felt) that causes you to imagine there is something "beyond." But inner experiences, as real and powerful as they may be for some, point to nothing outside our imaginative minds. Not all believers have them. Adam did not raise personal experience during the debate, probably knowing that if it counts for anything, it counts in all faiths, which means it is revealing something about human nature, not about the truth of any religious claim.

On January 1, 2023, I was in Mumbai, India with Amitabh Pal, the Freedom from Religion Foundation's Director of Communications. We were being driven to a festival honoring two of India's centenarian freedom fighters. We arrived a bit late because worshipers were hindering traffic. Thousands of people were standing in long lines, waiting to enter the Shri Siddhivinayak Ganapati Mandir Temple to seek blessings from Lord Ganesha for a prosperous new year. Looking at their faces, I was struck by the devotion that would move hundreds of millions of good and intelligent people to worship a god with the head of an elephant.

While culture and myths can be beautiful, I think you agree with me that our species displays an immense propensity to believe things that are not true. So what makes you exempt from that proclivity? How are you guarding against the delusion that you admit is part of our human nature?

Andrew Drinkard writes, "It's not contentious to admit that humans are notorious for being extremely selfish, prideful, and comfort driven." Really? Can't we also admit that humans are notorious for intelligence, love, empathy, altruism, humility, selflessness, creativity, and charity? If you paint us all with the pessimistic brush of original sin, it can become a self-fulfilling prophecy. You will not only disparage our wonderful species, but you will also force yourself to grovel for redemption from a higher power.

What Difference Does It Make?

During the debate, I mentioned that atheism is not a belief but an absence of belief. For me, it is the cumulative lack of a coherent definition, good evidence, good argument, agreement among believers, a good reply to the problem of evil, and a need to believe. I could have added the lack of reliability and relevance of holy books like the Bible, but our debate was not about Christianity.

The lack of a need to believe explains why so many atheists and agnostics seem unconcerned with God or religion. Some of my atheist friends wonder why I bother debating theists. They feel absolutely no need for faith, worship, or salvation.

Suppose you were serving a life sentence after being convicted of a horrible crime. After a few years, you learn you are suddenly being released from prison. That is good news! But what would make you happier: learning you have been pardoned by the mercy and grace of the governor, or that you were found to be innocent of the crime?

Not long after leaving the ministry, I wrote the song "Life Is Good!" Here is the first verse:

> They used to tell me that I was condemned
> to be punished for eternity,
> But not to be sad. I should be glad
> because Jesus has set me free.
> Then I started thinking, "Pardon me,
> but something here is terribly wrong.
> It makes me happier to know that I don't need to be forgiven—
> I was innocent all along."[38]

Jesus said, "It is not the healthy who need a doctor, but the sick" (Mark 2:17, NIV). In order to need salvation, you have to believe there is something wrong with you. You are sick, broken, rotten, depraved, or condemned. Many of us simply don't feel that way. We are not perfect, but we know we are not damned. We don't need the doctor.

My wife Annie Laurie is a third-generation freethinker. She and her brothers were raised with no religion. They were not indoctrinated with atheism, nor were they prohibited from reading the bible or going to church or synagogue with their friends. They were allowed to think for themselves. When their father Paul was a boy, one Sunday he was sitting in church with his family in southern Missouri, looking at the congregation, listening to the sermon and hymns, when it suddenly dawned on him: "My parents are nuts!" He was shocked that they actually believed those things. Religion never made sense to him. Neither he nor his wife Anne (a lifelong feminist) felt any need for

38. You can hear "Life Is Good!" performed by the Godless Gospel group starting at 21:00 at https://tinyurl.com/4tpkmswf on the Freedom from Religion Foundation YouTube channel.

faith.[39] They raised a happy family with strong moral values and commitment to equality and social justice. They are good people. I married one of them.

Some people believe and some people don't. What difference does it make? We all have to pay the rent, change diapers, go shopping, clean house, wash dishes, educate our children, pay taxes, and take care of our health. We spend our free time in different ways—going to church, hiking, praying, reading—but that is a distinction without a difference. Believers are not happier or healthier than nonbelievers.[40] They don't commit fewer crimes. They don't have longer lasting marriages. They might claim the advantage that *they* are going to heaven, but we don't all believe in heaven. Annie Laurie often says: "The only afterlife that ought to concern us is leaving our descendants and our planet a secure and pleasant future."[41]

Many believers don't realize that our lack of faith—our freedom to think for ourselves—can be just as precious and meaningful to us as their faith is to them. We are not floundering in darkness. We have the light of science, reason, and optimistic humanistic morality. We have friends and family—real love that needs no philosophical arguments to experience. We are *happy* being nonbelievers. We don't condemn those who disagree with us to eternal torture. We can live and let live, but we do wish there was less divisiveness in the world. We have the same feelings of amazement and astonishment—even reverence—for the profound beauty of existence.

Andrew Drinkard puts it eloquently: "Those moments of awe and grandeur that nonbelievers experience when looking at the night sky strewn with diamond-like stars, walking along a beach with a glowing sunset over the water, gazing down from a mountain top over a valley, holding one's newborn, and so on are all beautiful goods that resemble God's nature, which is the Ultimate Good."

Those moments do enrich our lives, but why do they require something "beyond" to give them value? Thinking about the wonder of natural selection, Darwin said, "There is grandeur in this view of life."[42] When I look at the stars,

39. See Anne Gaylor's obituary in *The New York Times*, June 17, 2015, https://tinyurl.com/42d3h9vs.

40. See Ryan T. Cragun and Jesse M. Smith, *Goodbye Religion: The Causes and Consequences of Secularization* (New York University Press, 2024); Phil Zuckerman, *Society Without God: What the Least Religious Nations Can Tell Us About Contentment* (New York University Press, 2008).

41. See Annie Laurie Gaylor, "Belief in Afterlife Is Corrupting, Unhealthy," *Freethought Today* 40, no. 9, November 2023, https://tinyurl.com/mkzkex8y.

42. This is the final sentence of Charles Darwin's *On the Origin of Species*, with an Introduction by Julian Huxley, 150th Anniversary ed. (Signet, 2003).

I see . . . the stars. They are amazing in themselves. Douglas Adams wrote: "Isn't it enough to see that a garden is beautiful without having to believe that there are fairies at the bottom of it too?"[43]

Those fairies may never be found. God may never be found. In the meantime, let's do our best to get along, judging each other by our actions, not by our beliefs.

43. Douglas Adams, *The Hitchhiker's Guide to the Universe* (Del Ray Publishing, 1995).

Afterword

Your Philosophical Journey

Joseph C. Schmid

Philosophy is difficult. *Extremely* difficult. It deals with highly abstract matters and often ventures into unfamiliar terrain. The arguments are complex and face objections from many sides. These objections, in turn, face replies, and those replies face rejoinders, and those rejoinders face retorts, and those retorts . . . well, you get the point. To make matters worse, we're prone to cognitive biases, fallacious reasoning, emotional investment in our favored conclusions, and tribalistic impulses.

And we aren't merely doing philosophy—we're doing *philosophy of religion*. Nearly every area of philosophy intersects with religious questions, and religious questions, in turn, influence almost every area of philosophy. Moreover, there are hundreds—yes, *hundreds*—of arguments for and against God's existence, each defended by incredibly talented professional philosophers.[1] Many such arguments have literally *thousands* of books and papers dedicated to them. Philosophy of religion is also deeply personal. Is there a God? Is there life after death? Should I go to church this Sunday? How should I respond to religious disagreement? How should religion relate to public policy? Given its connections with other fields, its extensive literature and stock of arguments, and its unique susceptibility to personal investments, philosophy of religion is *philosophy on steroids*.

1. For a helpful list of arguments for God's existence, see Chad McIntosh's "Theistic Arguments," available here: https://www.camcintosh.com/theistic/index.html. For a helpful list of arguments against God's existence, see Felipe Leon's "200 (or So) Arguments for Atheism," available here: https://exapologist.blogspot.com/2023/03/200-or-so-arguments-for-atheism.html.

So, we're faced with a choice. We could give up the task of philosophy and despair of ever discovering truths about philosophical and religious matters. Or we could embrace its challenges with open arms, recognizing their tremendous importance and doing our best to navigate them with care, humility, love, and rigor. I, for one, am up for the challenge. Are you?

This book might be the first step of your philosophical journey. Or it might be the thousandth. Either way, every journey needs tools. My aim is to equip you with tools to excel in your philosophical journey. I'll begin with the intellectual virtues you'll need, after which I'll provide thirteen tips for having productive philosophical exchanges. Finally, I'll suggest some places you might visit next.

Getting Virtuous

Philosophical argumentation shouldn't be seen as a game—something to be won or lost. Rather, it should be seen as a mutual endeavor among fellow seekers striving to uncover truth. To excel in this endeavor, we need to cultivate certain intellectual virtues. Without them, we are like sailors lost at sea with nothing to orient us toward the destinations of truth and greater understanding. Here are some of the most important virtues for your journey:

- *Intellectual curiosity* is a deep desire to know, learn, and understand. Intellectually curious individuals reject intellectual laziness, opting instead to research, read, and explore. They don't settle for believing something merely because they've always believed it or because it's comfortable or reassuring. Instead, they strive for well-supported beliefs. Ask questions. Dare to discover more.
- *Intellectual humility* involves recognizing one's limitations. This includes limitations in one's knowledge, analytical abilities, and awareness of the range of reasons bearing on one's beliefs. Acknowledge that there may be further considerations relevant to your beliefs of which you aren't aware. Also recognize the possibility of reasonable disagreement.
- *Intellectual responsibility* demands diligence in characterizing views accurately, seeking out objections, and engaging in fair, honest discourse. Responsible thinkers research issues before making confident claims, seek out the best objections to their views, and take ownership of their intellectual journey.
- *Open-mindedness* is the willingness to revise, reconsider, and question one's beliefs. This requires exploring alternative viewpoints in depth and

entertaining the possibility of being mistaken. Such openness is impossible without *intellectual courage*—the commitment to question deeply held beliefs, challenge assumptions, and follow the evidence wherever it leads.

Thirteen Tips

Knowing about intellectual virtues is one thing; practicing them is another. Here are thirteen tips to help you put them into action:

1. Approach discussions as a collaborative search for truth, not as a battle to be won. This approach *humanizes* others, as you won't see them as members of an opposing team needing to be crushed or defeated. They are, instead, fellow travelers on a journey to discover the treasure of truth. We are all on the same team.
2. Don't enter conversations and arguments with the sole aim of convincing the other person or showing them to be irrational. Instead, be willing to *learn* from them and be genuinely open to the possibility that you're mistaken. Otherwise, you'll become entrenched in your ways and resistant to deepening your understanding of the issues.
3. Say "I don't know" when you genuinely don't know. Become comfortable with uncertainty and not knowing how to respond to certain points. Saying "I don't know" is an exercise in humility and an opportunity to grow. Don't save face by pretending to have all the answers.
4. Put truth and love center stage. Orient yourself toward *these* instead of "winning" a debate, crushing an opponent, proving your rationality, or any other ego-gratifying aim that reveals only pride and insecurity.
5. Engage with a variety of viewpoints and seek out the strongest arguments for positions that differ from your own. Diversify your information sources. If you listen only to theists (or nontheists), you're invariably getting a skewed picture of the issues. You won't hear the best arguments from the other side or the best responses to the arguments of your own side. In short, ditch the echo chambers. Make friends with people of different backgrounds, worldviews, and life experiences.
6. Approach arguments and discussions as an *explorer* rather than an *exposer*. You shouldn't aim to expose others as ignorant, stupid, or badly mistaken. You should instead aim to *explore* the philosophical terrain with your dialectical partners.
7. You are not your ideas. If you identify too closely with your beliefs, any challenge to them will feel like a personal attack, making you defensive

and resistant to revising your beliefs to better reflect reality. Maintain some distance between yourself and your beliefs. Always remember that your value isn't tied to the ideas you have or the beliefs you hold.

8. Avoid stereotypes and caricatures. No one fits neatly into ideological boxes—each person brings unique perspectives, experiences, and skills to a discussion.
9. Go slowly! Philosophy (and truth-seeking in general) requires careful, methodical, and systematic reflection. Take your time when engaging with others. So-called clever, gotcha-type remarks only alienate your interlocutors. It's best to avoid them.
10. Steelman, don't strawman. When you steelman someone's argument, you *strengthen* the argument for them. Improving your interlocutor's argument *significantly* reduces tension and tribalism within discussions. Doing so also reflects an authentic pursuit of truth rather than a desire to "win" an exchange.
11. Don't psychologize. Avoid assuming that others hold certain beliefs simply due to psychological biases. Instead, engage with the reasons and arguments they present. Also important is recognizing psychological influences on *your own* beliefs.
12. Arguments are not weapons; they are tools for understanding. They should illuminate rather than coerce and invite mutual exploration.
13. Recognize room for rational disagreement. Whether someone is rational in believing something is a function of a huge concoction of individual-specific factors, including their particular background web of beliefs, the books and papers they've read, the videos they've watched, the podcasts they've listened to, the *order* in which they've read and listened to these things, the experiences they've had, their precise body of testimonial evidence, what strikes them as plausible, and countless other factors. This individual-specific mixture of factors situates each of us in a unique position on the grand epistemic landscape, equipping each of us with unique and sometimes incommunicable reasons for our beliefs. This is how disagreeing parties can each be rational—the parties are coming equipped with different lenses through which they see the issue, different background reasons, and more. It is also why *intellectual empathy* is so important. It helps you approximately see things from another person's perspective and appreciate their rationality. This, in turn, facilitates the productive, love-oriented exchange of ideas.

These thirteen tips can be condensed into a single sentence: do philosophy with caution, care, humility, and love of both neighbor and truth.

Next Stops on Your Journey

Your journey with this book may be ending, but your philosophical journey is far from over. Here are some valuable resources for exploring the topics of this book in greater depth. This is not an exhaustive or impartial list; these are simply works I have found especially insightful, convincing, or enriching.

- To explore issues in philosophy of religion from both theistic and atheistic perspectives, I *strongly* recommend:
  - Joshua Rasmussen and Felipe Leon, *Is God the Best Explanation of Things? A Dialogue* (Palgrave Macmillan, 2019).
  - Michael L. Peterson and Raymond J. VanArragon, eds., *Contemporary Debates in Philosophy of Religion*. 2nd ed. (Wiley-Blackwell, 2020).
  - Louis Pojman and Michael Rea, eds., *Philosophy of Religion: An Anthology*, 7th ed. (Cengage, 2015).
  - Graham Oppy and Joseph W. Koterski, *Theism and Atheism: Opposing Arguments in Philosophy* (Macmillan, 2019).
  - Richard Swinburne, *Is There a God?* Rev. ed. (Oxford University Press, 2010).
  - Graham Oppy, *Arguing About Gods* (Cambridge University Press, 2006).
  - Jordan Howard Sobel, ed., *Logic and Theism: Arguments for and Against Beliefs in Gods* (Cambridge University Press, 2004).
- On the Kalām cosmological argument:
  - For an excellent appraisal of the scientific case for the beginning of the universe, see Daniel Linford's "Cosmic Skepticism and the Beginning of Physical Reality" (PhD diss., Purdue University, 2022).
  - Wes Morriston, "Infinity, Time, and Successive Addition," *Australasian Journal of Philosophy* 100, no. 1 (2022): 70–85.
  - Alex Malpass and Wes Morriston, "Endless and Infinite," *The Philosophical Quarterly* 70 (2020): 830–49.
  - Felipe Leon, "Causation and Sufficient Reason: Atheism," in *Theism and Atheism: Opposing Arguments in Philosophy*, ed. Graham Oppy and Joseph W. Koterski (Macmillan, 2019).
  - Louis J. Swingover, "Difficulties with William Lane Craig's Arguments for Finitism" (Unpublished paper, 2014), https://tinyurl.com/5ef7cfrm.
  - Finally, see my "Responses to the Grim Reaper Kalam," *Majesty of Reason* (blog), posted May 28, 2024, https://tinyurl.com/32frn82x.
- On the problem of evil:
  - My favorite works on the problem of evil are Paul Draper's "Pain and

Pleasure: An Evidential Problem for Theists," *Noûs* 23, no. 3 (1989): 331–50; and Draper, "Darwin's Argument from Evil," in *Scientific Approaches to the Philosophy of Religion*, ed. Yujin Nagasawa (Palgrave Macmillan, 2012).

- Also see Justin Mooney's comprehensive bibliography on the problem of evil, available on his website: https://www.justinmooney.net/published-work.

- My favorite books on philosophy of mind:
  - John B. Searle, *Mind: A Brief Introduction* (Oxford University Press, 2004).
  - David Chalmers, *The Conscious Mind: In Search of a Fundamental Theory* (Oxford University Press, 1996).
- On the fine-tuning argument:
  - One of the best books on the subject is Geraint F. Lewis and Luke A. Barnes, *A Fortunate Universe: Life in a Finely-Tuned Cosmos* (Cambridge University Press, 2016).
  - One of the most fun papers on the topic is Neil Sinhababu, "Divine Fine-Tuning vs. Electrons in Love," *American Philosophical Quarterly* 53, no. 4 (2017): 423–32.
- On divine hiddenness:
  - Stephen Maitzen, "Divine Hiddenness and the Demographics of Theism," *Religious Studies* 42, no. 2 (2006): 177–91.
  - Andrew Cullison, "Two Solutions to the Problem of Divine Hiddenness," *American Philosophical Quarterly* 47, no. 2 (2010): 119–34.
  - Dustin Crummett, "'We Are Here to Help Each Other': Religious Community, Divine Hiddenness, and the Responsibility Argument," *Faith and Philosophy* 32, no. 1 (2015): 45–62.
- On the moral argument:
  - I've benefited a lot from William Lane Craig and Erik J. Wielenberg, *A Debate on God and Morality: What Is the Best Account of Objective Moral Values and Duties?* ed. Adam Lloyd Johnson (Routledge, 2020).
  - See also Erik Wielenberg's *Value and Virtue in a Godless Universe* (Cambridge University Press, 2012) and his *Robust Ethics: Metaphysics and Epistemology of Godless Normative Realism* (Oxford University Press, 2014).
  - For a recent and formidable nontheist account of objective morality, see John Benson, Terence Cuneo, and Russ Shafer-Landau, *The Moral Universe* (Oxford University Press, 2024).

- On Christianity specifically:
  - Dale C. Allison Jr., *The Resurrection of Jesus: Apologetics, Polemics, History* (T&T Clark, 2021).
  - For a well-argued critique of the (minimal facts) case for the resurrection, see chapter 5 of James Fodor, *Unreasonable Faith: How William Lane Craig Overstates the Case for Christianity* (Hypatia, 2018).
  - I reiterate Adam's recommendation of Paul Copan's work on Old Testament violence, including Copan and Matt Flannagan, *Did God Really Command Genocide? Coming to Terms with the Justice of God* (Baker, 2014); Copan, *Is God a Moral Monster? Making Sense of the Old Testament God* (Baker, 2011); and Copan, *Is God a Vindictive Bully?* (Baker Academic, 2022).
  - I also recommend the following criticisms of Copan's work (which, in my estimation, are quite cogent): Thom Stark, *Is God a Moral Compromiser? A Critical Review of Paul Copan's "Is God a Moral Monster?"* 2nd ed. (self-published, 2011); and Randal Rauser, *Jesus Loves Canaanites: Biblical Genocide in the Light of Moral Intuition* (2 Cup Press, 2021).
- For *any* philosophical topic, you should consult articles in the *Stanford Encyclopedia of Philosophy* and *Philosophy Compass.*

Finally, explore the work of the contributors to this volume. Many have a strong online presence, so look up their debates, discussions, websites and blogs, and social media channels. I challenge you to start reading or listening to a contributor who doesn't share your view about God. You might be surprised by what you discover. Treasures of truth await.

Contributors

David Baggett (theist) is professor of philosophy and director of the Center for Moral Apologetics at Houston Baptist University. He received a PhD in philosophy at Wayne State University. He has authored or edited over a dozen books, including (with Jerry Walls) *Good God* (Oxford), *God and Cosmos* (Oxford), and *The Moral Argument* (Oxford). He is currently working on the fourth book of this tetralogy (also with Jerry Walls) on the topic of moral realism (Oxford). *Good God* received *Christianity Today*'s 2012 Best Book in Evangelism/Apologetics. He has also published nearly forty encyclopedia articles, chapters, and journal articles in publications such as the *Harvard Theological Review*, *Philosophia Christi*, and the *Journal of Religious Ethics*.

Dan Barker (nontheist) is copresident of the Freedom from Religion Foundation (FFRF), cohost of Freethought Radio, and cofounder of The Clergy Project. He is the author of several published works including *Free Will Explained* (Sterling), *Mere Morality* (Pitchstone), *Life Driven Purpose* (Pitchstone), and *Godless* (Ulysses). After nineteen years as an evangelical minister, he became an atheist. His first public appearance as an atheist was on Oprah Winfrey's *AM Chicago*. He travels extensively, lecturing and performing on college campuses, and has participated in more than 140 public debates. He belongs to a number of high-IQ associations, including The Prometheus Society.

Robin Collins (theist), PhD, is Distinguished Professor of Philosophy and chair of the Department of Philosophy at Messiah University. He specializes in philosophy of science, philosophy of religion, metaphysics, and philosophical theology. He has written nearly forty substantial articles and book chapters in these areas with some of the leading academic presses, such as Oxford,

Cambridge, Blackwell, and Routledge. He has appeared in the popular Christian and secular media, including *Christianity Today* and Robert Kuhn's PBS series *Closer to the Truth*. He is well versed in issues relating to science and religion, with graduate-level training in theoretical physics. Professor Collins is widely regarded as the foremost expert on the fine-tuning argument, an argument for the existence of God based on the extraordinarily precise structure that the universe must have for life to exist.

Paul Copan (theist) (PhD in philosophy, Marquette University) is a Christian theologian, analytic philosopher, apologist, and author. He is currently a professor at the Palm Beach Atlantic University (Florida) and holds the endowed Pledger Family Chair of Philosophy and Ethics. He is author or editor of nearly fifty books, including the very popular *Is God a Moral Monster?* as well as its companion volume, the award-winning *Is God a Vindictive Bully?* (both with Baker). He is coeditor of *The Routledge Companion to Philosophy of Religion*, *The Naturalness of Theistic Belief*, *Philosophy of Religion: Classic and Contemporary Issues* (Lexington), and the two-volume anthology *The Kalām Cosmological Argument* (Bloomsbury). He is coauthor of *Creation Out of Nothing* (Baker) and *Biblical Ethics: Walking in the Way of Wisdom* (IVP Academic). He has also contributed essays to over sixty books, both scholarly and popular, and he has authored a number of articles in professional journals. In 2017 and 2024, he has been a visiting scholar at the University of Oxford (Wycliffe Hall and Oriel College). For six years, he served as president of the Evangelical Philosophical Society. He also helped establish the Palm Beach Atlantic University's master's program in philosophy of religion and bachelor of the arts in apologetics. He is cochair of Tyndale Fellowship's Philosophy of Religion Study Group, which meets every summer in England.

Andrew Drinkard (theist) is the cofounder and director of Inspiring Christianity ministries and regularly speaks at churches and conferences about the existence of God. He received a master's in theological studies/apologetics from Liberty University and is currently completing a master's in philosophy from Palm Beach Atlantic University. His work has been published in the *Journal of Classical Theology*. He also assisted in editing *Eternal in Love: A Little Book About a Big God* authored by R. T. Mullins (Cascade).

David Enoch (nontheist) is professor of the philosophy of law at Oxford University. David also holds the Rodney Blackman Chair in the Philosophy of Law in the philosophy department and the faculty of law at the Hebrew University in Jerusalem. He earned his PhD in philosophy from New York University. David works primarily in moral, political, and legal philosophy. His book *Taking Morality Seriously: A Defense of Robust Realism* (Oxford University Press) is a (nontheistic) detailed defense of the objectivity of morality.

Joe Folley (nontheist) completed his undergraduate and master's degree in philosophy at Cambridge University. He now runs the highly successful YouTube Channel *Unsolicited Advice*, where he examines various topics on religion, philosophy, and logic.

Philip Goff (atheist) is a professor of philosophy at Durham University. Goff's main research focus is consciousness, but he is interested in many questions about the nature of reality. Goff is most known for defending panpsychism, the view that consciousness is a fundamental and ubiquitous feature of the physical world. Goff has authored the academic book *Consciousness and Fundamental Reality* (Oxford University Press) and the general-audience book *Galileo's Error: Foundations for a New Science of Consciousness* (Pantheon). His new book *Why? The Purpose of the Universe* (Oxford University Press) argues that the universe has a purpose. Goff has published nearly fifty academic articles and has written extensively for newspapers and magazines, including *Scientific American*, *The Guardian*, *Aeon*, and the *Times Literary Supplement*. The interview with Goff by Pulitzer Prize–winning author Gareth Cook was one of the most viewed articles in *Scientific American* of 2020.

Adam Lloyd Johnson (theist) earned his PhD with a concentration in philosophy of religion at Southeastern Baptist Theological Seminary. He teaches for the Rhineland School of Theology in Wölmersen, Germany and Midwestern Baptist Theological Seminary in Kansas City, MO. He is the author or editor of several published works including *Divine Love Theory* (Kregel Academic) and *A Debate on God and Morality*, coauthored with William Lane Craig, J. P. Moreland, Erik Wielenberg, and others (Routledge). He has published articles in the *Journal of the International Society of Christian Apologetics*, *Philosophia Christi*, *Westminster Theological Journal*, and the *Canadian Journal for Scholarship and the Christian Faith*. He has spoken at numerous churches and conferences in America and around the world.

Robert C. ("Rob") Koons (theist) is a professor of philosophy at the University of Texas at Austin. He has a master's from Oxford University and earned his PhD from UCLA. He is the author or coauthor of five books, including *The*

Atlas of Reality with Timothy H. Pickavance (Wiley-Blackwell) and *Is Thomas's Aristotelian Philosophy of Nature Obsolete?* (St. Augustine Press). He is the coeditor of four anthologies, including *The Waning of Materialism* (Oxford University Press) and *Classical Theism* (Routledge). He has been working recently on an Aristotelian interpretation of quantum theory and on defending and articulating hylomorphism in contemporary terms.

Daniel Linford (nontheist) is a philosopher specializing in philosophy of physics and philosophy of religion. Currently, his research focuses on the philosophical foundations of cosmology. Linford earned his PhD in philosophy from Purdue University, his master's degree in philosophy from Virginia Tech, and a bachelor of science degree in physics from the University of Rochester. He coauthored the book *Existential Inertia and Classical Theistic Proofs* (Springer) with Joseph C. Schmid. He has previously contributed to top philosophy of science journals (*The British Journal for Philosophy of Science*, *Erkenntnis*, and *European Journal for Philosophy of Science*) and top philosophy of religion journals (*Religious Studies*, *International Journal for Philosophy of Religion*, and *Sophia*).

Alex Malpass (nontheist) is a philosopher with research interests in philosophy of religion, metaphysics, logic and philosophy of mathematics. Malpass earned a PhD in philosophy in 2011 at the University of Bristol. He has subsequently published papers in journals including *Mind*, *Philosophical Studies*, *Philosophical Quarterly*, *Synthese*, and *Sophia*.

Dolores G. Morris (theist) is the author of *Believing Philosophy: A Guide to Becoming a Christian Philosopher* (Zondervan Academic). She is an associate fellow at the Kirby Laing Centre for Public Theology in Cambridge and serves on the executive committees for the Society of Christian Philosophers and the Evangelical Philosophical Society. She earned her PhD in philosophy at the University of Notre Dame, where she worked with Alvin Plantinga. Her current areas of focus are philosophy of mind, philosophy of religion, and philosophy of science. Most recently, she is interested in the intersection of these topics as they pertain to the questions about human flourishing.

Joshua Rasmussen (theist) is a professor of philosophy at Baylor University. His research focuses on the nature of fundamental reality. He is the author or coauthor of six books, including *How Reason Can Lead to God* (IVP Academic) and *Who Are You, Really? A Philosopher's Inquiry into the Nature and Origin of*

Persons (IVP Academic). Rasmussen is also the founder of worldview-design.com, a place devoted to helping you build the best worldview possible. You can find out more about his work at joshualrasmussen.com.

Joseph C. Schmid (nontheist) is a PhD student in philosophy at Princeton University. He graduated with a bachelor of the arts in philosophy from Purdue University in 2022. He has authored (with Daniel Linford) *Existential Inertia and Classical Theistic Proofs* (Springer) and *The Majesty of Reason: A Short Guide to Critical Thinking in Philosophy* (Kindle Direct Publishing). He has also published articles in venues such as *Mind*, *The Journal of Philosophy*, *Analysis*, and *Philosophical Studies*. Schmid also creates philosophy videos on his YouTube channel *Majesty of Reason*.

Benjamin Watkins (nontheist) received a bachelor of science degree in mechanical engineering at the University of South Carolina. He works as a civilian nuclear engineer for the United States Navy. He is a host of *Real Atheology: A Philosophy of Religion Podcast*. Watkins has spoken at conferences and participated in numerous public debates on topics within philosophy of religion, philosophy of science, moral philosophy, and the philosophy of mind.

Bibliography

Adams, Douglas. *The Hitchhiker's Guide to the Universe*. Del Ray, 1995.

Adams, Robert M. "Divine Command Metaethics Modified Again." *Journal of Religious Ethics* 7, no. 1 (1979): 66–79.

———. "Divine Commands and the Social Nature of Obligation." *Faith and Philosophy* 4, no. 3 (1987): 262–75. https://doi.org/10.5840/faithphil19874343.

———. *Finite and Infinite Goods: A Framework for Ethics*. Oxford University Press, 2002.

———. "Moral Arguments for Theistic Belief." In *Rationality and Religious Belief*, edited by C. F. Delaney. University of Notre Dame Press, 1979.

Adlam, E. "Is There Causation in Fundamental Physics? New Insights from Process Matrices and Quantum Causal Modelling." *Synthese* 201, no. 152 (2023).

———. "Laws of Nature as Constraints." *Foundations of Physics* 52, no. 28 (2022).

Albert, D. *Time and Chance*. Harvard University Press, 2003.

Alston, William P. *Perceiving God*. Cornell University Press, 1991.

Anderson, Charity. "Divine Hiddenness: An Evidential Argument." *Philosophical Perspectives* 35, no. 1 (2021): 5–22. https://doi.org/10.1111/phpe.12149.

———. "Divine Hiddenness: Defeated Evidence." *Royal Institute of Philosophy Supplement* 81 (2017): 119–32. https://doi.org/10.1017/s1358246117000212.

Anscombe, G. E. M. "Causality and Determination." In *Causation*, edited by Ernest Sosa and Michael Tooley. Oxford University Press, 1993.

———. "Modern Moral Philosophy." *Philosophy* 33, no. 124 (1958): 1–19. https://doi.org/10.1017/s0031819100037943.

Anselm. *Monologion and Proslogion: With the Replies of Gaunilo and Anselm*. Translated by Thomas Williams. Hackett, 1996.

Aquinas, Thomas. *Summa contra Gentiles*. Translated by Anton C. Pegis. 3 vols. Hanover House, 1955–1957.

———. *Summa Theologica*. Translated by Fathers of the English Dominican Province. 5 vols. Benziger Brothers, 1911–1925.

Armstrong, David. "Reply to Van Fraassen." *Australasian Journal of Philosophy* 66, no. 2 (1988): 224–29. https://doi.org/10.1080/00048408812343311.

———. *What Is a Law of Nature?* Cambridge University Press, 1983.

Augustine. *Confessions*. Translated by Garry Wills. Penguin Classics, 2008.

Avalos, Hector. *Fighting Words: The Origins of Religious Violence*. Prometheus, 2005.

Azadegan, Ebrahim. "Divine Hiddenness and Human Sin: The Noetic Effect of Sin." *Journal of Reformed Theology* 7 (2013): 69–90. https://doi.org/10.1163/15697312-12341274.

Bailey, Andrew, and Joshua Rasmussen. "A New Puppet Puzzle." *Philosophical Explorations* 23, no. 3 (2020): 202–13. https://doi.org/10.1080/13869795.2020.1799661.

Bailey, Andrew, Joshua Rasmussen, and Luke Van Horn. "No Pairing Problem." *Philosophical Studies* 154, no. 3 (2011): 349–60. https://doi.org/10.1007/s11098-010-9555-7.

Baker-Hytch, Max. "On Sin-Based Responses to Divine Hiddenness." *Religious Studies* 61, no. 3 (2025): 650–64.

Balaguer, Mark. "Fictionalism in the Philosophy of Mathematics." In *Stanford Encyclopedia of Philosophy*. Last modified July 23, 2018. https://plato.stanford.edu/entries/fictionalism-mathematics/.

Barker, Dan. *Contraduction*. Hypatia, 2024.

———. *Free Will Explained*. Sterling, 2018.

———. *Godless: How an Evangelical Preacher Became One of America's Leading Atheists*. Ulysses, 2008.

———. *God: The Most Unpleasant Character in All Fiction*. Prometheus, 2023.

———. *Life Driven Purpose: How an Atheist Finds Meaning*. Pitchstone, 2015.

———. *Mere Morality*. Pitchstone, 2018.

———. "Supernatural Evil." In *God and Horrendous Suffering*, edited by John Loftus. GCRR, 2021.

Barnes, Luke. "A Reasonable Little Question: A Formulation of the Fine-Tuning Argument." *Ergo* 6, no. 42 (2019): 1220–1. https://doi.org/10.3998/ergo.12405314.0006.042.

Barnes, Luke, and Geraint Lewis. *A Fortunate Universe: Life in a Finely Tuned Cosmos*. Cambridge University Press, 2016.

Barr, Stephen M. *Modern Physics and Ancient Faith*. University of Notre Dame Press, 2003.

Bateman, Herbert W., IV, Darrell L. Bock, and Gordon H. Johnston. *Jesus the Messiah: Tracing the Promises, Expectations, and Coming of Israel's King*. Kregel Academic, 2012.

Benardete, J. A. *Infinity: An Essay in Metaphysics*. Oxford University Press, 1964.

Benson, John, Terence Cuneo, and Russ Shafer-Landau. "The Source of Normativity." *Mind* 132, no. 527 (2023): 706–29. https://doi.org/10.1093/mind/fzac063.

Bering, Jesse. *The Belief Instinct: The Psychology of Souls, Destiny, and the Meaning of Life*. Norton, 2011.

Bernays, Paul. "A System of Axiomatic Set Theory: Part III. Infinity and Enumerability. Analysis." *Journal of Symbolic Logic* 7, no. 2 (1942): 65–89. https://doi.org/10.2307/2266303.

Blanchard, T. "Physics and Causation." *Philosophy Compass* 11 (2016): 256–66.

Boethius. *The Consolation of Philosophy*. Translated by Victor Watts. Penguin Classics, 2000.

Boolos, George. "To Be Is to Be a Value of a Variable (Or to Be Some Values of Some Variables)." *Journal of Philosophy* 81, no. 8 (1984): 430–49. https://doi.org/10.2307/2026308.

Borde, Arvind, Alan Guth, and Alexander Vilenkin. "Inflationary Spacetimes Are Incomplete in Past Directions." *Physical Review Letters* 90, no. 15 (2003): 1–4. https://doi.org/10.1103/PhysRevLett.90.151301.

Boyer, Pascal. *Religion Explained: The Evolutionary Origins of Religious Thought*. Basic, 2001.

Bradley, Darren J. "Multiple Universes and Observation Selection Effects." *American Philosophical Quarterly* 46, no. 1 (2009): 61–72.

Brierley, Justin. *The Surprising Rebirth of Belief in God: Why New Atheism Grew Old and Secular Thinkers Are Considering Christianity Again*. Tyndale Elevate, 2023.

Broad, Jacqueline. *Women Philosophers of the Seventeenth Century*. Cambridge University Press, 2003.

Budziszewski, J. *What We Can't Not Know: A Guide*. Ignatius, 2011.

Calaprice, Alice, ed. *The Quotable Einstein*. Princeton University Press, 1996.

Carr, B. J., and M. J. Rees. "The Anthropic Cosmological Principle and the Structure of the Physical World." *Nature* 278 (1979): 605–12.

Carroll, Sean. "Consciousness and the Laws of Physics." *Journal of Consciousness Studies* 28, no. 9–10 (2021): 16–31. https://doi.org/10.53765/20512201.28.9.016.

———. "Does the Universe Need God." In *The Blackwell Companion to Natural Theology*, edited by J. B. Stump and Alan Padgett. Wiley-Blackwell, 2012.

———. *From Eternity to Here: The Quest for the Ultimate Theory of Time*. Dutton, 2010.

Carroll, Sean, and Jennifer Chen. "Spontaneous Inflation and the Origin of the Arrow of Time." *arXivLabs* (2004): 1–36. https://arxiv.org/abs/hep-th/0410270.

Cartwright, Nancy. "Causal Laws and Effective Strategies." *Noûs* 13, no. 4 (1979): 419–37. https://doi.org/10.2307/2215337.

Chalmers, David J. *The Conscious Mind: In Search of a Fundamental Theory.* Oxford University Press, 1996.

———. "Does Conceivability Entail Possibility?" In *Conceivability and Possibility*, edited by Tamar Szabó Gendler and John Hawthorne. Clarendon, 2002.

Cicero, Marcus Tullius. *How to Think About God: An Ancient Guide for Believers and Nonbelievers.* Translated and edited by Peter Freeman. Princeton University Press, 2019.

Clark, Romane. "Vicious Infinite Regress Arguments." *Philosophical Perspectives* 2 (1988): 369–80. https://doi.org/10.2307/2214081.

Collins, Francis S. *The Language of God: A Scientist Presents Evidence for Belief.* Free Press, 2006.

Collins, John J. *Does the Bible Justify Violence?* Fortress, 2004.

Collins, Robin. "The Argument from Physical Constants: The Fine-Tuning for Discoverability." In *Two Dozen (Or So) Arguments for God: The Plantinga Project*, edited by Jerry L. Walls and Trent Dougherty. Oxford University Press, 2018.

———. "The Case for Cosmic Design." In *God or Blind Nature? Philosophers Debate the Evidence (2007–2008).* Edited by Paul Draper. Internet Infidels, 2008.

———. "The Connection Building Theodicy." In *The Blackwell Companion to the Problem of Evil*, edited by Dan Howard-Snyder and Justin McBrayer. Wiley-Blackwell, 2014.

———. "Evidence for Fine-Tuning." In *God and Design: The Teleological Argument and Modern Science*, edited by Neil Manson. Routledge, 2003.

———. "God and the Laws of Nature." *Philo* 12, no. 2 (2009): 142–71. https://doi.org/10.5840/philo200912211.

———. "God, Design, and Fine-Tuning." In *God Matters: Readings in the Philosophy of Religion*, edited by R. M. Bernard. Longman, 2003.

———. "The Multiverse Hypothesis: A Theistic Perspective." In *Universe or Multiverse*, edited by Bernard Carr. Cambridge University Press, 2007.

———. "The Teleological Argument: An Exploration of the Fine-Tuning of the Universe." In *The Blackwell Companion to Natural Theology*, edited by William Lane Craig and J. P. Moreland. Wiley-Blackwell, 2009.

Colyvan, Mark. "Causal Explanation and Ontological Commitment." In *Metaphysics in the Post-Metaphysical Age: Papers of the 22nd International Wittgenstein Symposium*, edited by Uwe Meixner and Peter Simons. Austrian Ludwig Wittgenstein Society, 1999.

Copan, Paul. *Is God a Moral Monster? Making Sense of the Old Testament God.* Baker, 2011.

———. *Is God a Vindictive Bully?* Baker Academic, 2022.

Copan, Paul, and Matt Flannagan. *Did God Really Command Genocide? Coming to Terms with the Justice of God*. Baker, 2014.

Cotter, Christopher R., Philip Andrew Quadrio, and Jonathan Tuckett. *New Atheism: Critical Perspectives and Contemporary Debates*. Sophia Studies in Cross-Cultural Philosophy of Traditions and Cultures 21. Springer, 2017.

Cottingham, John, Robert Stoothoff, and Dugald Murdoch, eds. *The Philosophical Writings of Descartes*. Vol. 2. Cambridge University Press, 1984.

Cragun, Ryan T., and Jesse M. Smith. *Goodbye Religion: The Causes and Consequences of Secularization*. New York University Press, 2024.

Craig, William Lane. "The Caused Beginning of the Universe: A Response to Quentin Smith." *British Journal for the Philosophy of Science* 44, no. 4 (1993): 623–39. https://doi.org/10.1093/bjps/44.4.623.

———. "Creation and Divine Action." In *Routledge Companion to Philosophy of Religion*, edited by Chad Meister and Paul Copan. Routledge, 2007.

———. *The Kalām Cosmological Argument*. Macmillan, 1979.

———. *The Only Wise God*. Wipf & Stock, 1999.

Craig, William Lane, and James Sinclair. "The Kalam Cosmological Argument." In *The Blackwell Companion to Natural Theology*, edited by William Lane Craig and J. P. Moreland. Wiley-Blackwell, 2009.

———. "On Non-Singular Space-Times and the Beginning of the Universe." In *Scientific Approaches to the Philosophy of Religion*, edited by Yujin Nagasawa. Palgrave Macmillan, 2012.

Craig, William Lane, and Quentin Smith. *Theism, Atheism, and Big Bang Cosmology*. Oxford University Press, 1995.

Crummett, Dustin, and Brian Cutter. "Psychophysical Harmony: A New Argument for Theism." *Oxford Studies in Philosophy of Religion*, forthcoming.

Curiel, Erik. "The Analysis of Singular Spacetimes." *Philosophy of Science* 66 (1999): S119–S145.

———. "Singularities and Black Holes." In *Stanford Encyclopedia of Philosophy*. Last modified February 27, 2019. https://plato.stanford.edu/archives/spr2021/entries/spacetime-singularities/.

Dana, Troy, and Joseph Schmid. "Grim Reaper Paradoxes and Patchwork Principles: Severing the Case for Finitism." *Journal of Philosophy* (forthcoming).

Darwin, Charles. *Descent of Man*. Great Minds Series. Prometheus, 1998.

———. *The Origin of Species*. With an Introduction by Julian Huxley. 150th Anniversary ed. Signet, 2003.

Davies, Paul. *Superforce: The Search for a Grand Unified Theory of Nature*. Simon & Schuster, 1984.

Dawes, Gregory W. *Theism and Explanation*. Routledge, 2009.

Dawkins, Richard. *The Blind Watchmaker*. Norton, 1986.

———. *The God Delusion*. Bantam, 2006.

———. *River Out of Eden: A Darwinian View of Life*. Basic, 1996.

De Cruz, Helen. "Divine Hiddenness and the Cognitive Science of Religion." In *Hidden Divinity and Religious Belief: New Perspectives*, edited by Adam Green and Eleonore Stump. Cambridge University Press, 2016.

———. "Evidential Objections to Atheism." In *A Companion to Atheism and Philosophy*, edited by Graham Oppy. Wiley & Sons, 2019.

Denton, Michael. *Nature's Destiny: How the Laws of Biology Reveal Purpose in the Universe*. Free Press, 1998.

Descartes, René. *The Correspondence Between Princess Elisabeth of Bohemia and René Descartes*. Edited by Lisa Shapiro. University of Chicago Press, 2007.

———. *Discourse on Method and Meditations*. Translated by E. S. Haldane and G. R. T. Ross. Cambridge University Press, 1911.

———. "Meditations on First Philosophy." In *Descartes: Philosophical Writings*. Translated by Elizabeth Anscombe and Peter Geach. Bobbs-Merrill, 1971.

———. "Princess Elisabeth of Bohemia to Descartes, May 6–16, 1643." In *Descartes: Philosophical Writings*, edited and translated by Elizabeth Anscombe and Peter Geach. Nelson, 1969.

Diogenes Laertius. *Lives of Eminent Philosophers, Volume II: Books 6–10*. Translated by R. D. Hicks. Loeb Classical Library. Harvard University Press, 1925.

Dirac, P. A. M. "The Evolution of the Physicist's Picture of Nature." *Scientific American*, May 1, 1963, 45–53.

Dodson, Edward. *The Phenomena of Man Revisited: A Biological Viewpoint on Teilhard de Chardin*. Columbia University Press, 1984.

Draper, Paul. "Cumulative Cases." In *A Companion to Philosophy of Religion*, 2nd ed., edited by Charles Taliaferro, Paul Draper, and Philip L. Quinn. Wiley-Blackwell, 2010.

———. "Pain and Pleasure: An Evidential Problem for Theists." *Noûs* 23, no. 3 (1989): 331–50. https://doi.org/10.2307/2215486.

Dretske, Fred. "Counting to Infinity." *Analysis* 25 (1965): 99–101. https://doi.org/10.1093/analys/25.Suppl-3.99.

Duffy, Stephen J. "Experience of Grace." In *The Cambridge Companion to Karl Rahner*, edited by Declan Marmion and Mary E. Hines. Cambridge University Press, 2005.

Dumsday, Travis. "Divine Hiddenness as Deserved." *Faith and Philosophy* 31, no. 3 (2014): 286–302. https://doi.org/10.5840/faithphil20149217.

Dunbar, Robin. *How Religion Evolved: And Why It Endures*. Penguin Random House, 2022.

Dyson, Freeman. *Disturbing the Universe*. Harper & Row, 1979.

Earman, John. *Bangs, Crunches, Whimpers, and Shrieks*. Oxford University Press, 1995.

Earman, John, and Jean Eisenstaedt. "Einstein and Singularities." *Studies in History and Philosophy of Science Part B: Studies in History and Philosophy of Modern Physics* 30, no. 2 (1999): 185–235. https://doi.org/10.1016/S1355-2198(99)00005-2.

Earman, John, and John Norton. "Forever Is a Day: Supertasks in Pitowsky and Malament-Hogarth Spacetimes." *Philosophy of Science* 60, no. 1 (1993): 22–42. https://doi.org/10.1086/289716.

Ellis, George. "Before the Beginning: Emerging Questions and Uncertainties." *Astrophysics and Space Sciences* 269 (1999): 693–720. https://doi.org/10.1023/A:1017277730994.

———. "On the Philosophy of Cosmology." *Studies in History and Philosophy of Science Part B: Studies in History and Philosophy of Modern Physics* 46, no. 1 (2014): 5–23. https://doi.org/10.1016/j.shpsb.2013.07.006.

———. "The Standard Cosmological Model: Achievements and Issues." *Foundations of Physics* 48 (2018): 1226–45. https://doi.org/10.1007/s10701-018-0176-x.

Ellis, George, Roy Maartens, and Malcolm MacCullum. *Relativistic Cosmology*. Cambridge University Press, 2012.

Enoch, David. "The Epistemological Challenge to Metanormative Realism: How Best to Understand It, and How to Cope with It." *Philosophical Studies* 148 (2010): 413–38. https://doi.org/10.1007/s11098-009-9333-6.

———. "Is General Jurisprudence Interesting?" In *Dimensions of Normativity: New Essays on Metaethics and Jurisprudence*, edited by David Plunkett, Scott Shapiro, and Kevin Toh. Oxford University Press, 2019.

———. *Taking Morality Seriously: A Defense of Robust Realism*. Oxford University Press, 2011.

———. "Why I'm an Objectivist About Ethics (And Why You Are Too)." In *The Ethical Life*, 3rd ed., edited by Russ Shafer-Landau. Oxford University Press, 2014.

Epictetus. *Discourses and Selected Writings*. Translated and edited by Robert Dobbin. Penguin Classics, 2008.

Erasmus, Jacobus. *The Kalām Cosmological Argument: A Reassessment*. Springer, 2018.

Evans, C. Stephen. *God and Moral Obligation*. Oxford University Press, 2014.

———. *Natural Signs and Knowledge of God*. Oxford University Press, 2012.

Evans, C. Stephen, and David Baggett. "Moral Arguments for the Existence of God." In *Stanford Encyclopedia of Philosophy*. Last modified October 4, 2022. https://plato.stanford.edu/entries/moral-arguments-god/.

Farr, M., and A. Reutlinger. "Relic of a Bygone Age? Causation, Time Symmetry and the Directionality Argument." *Erkenntnis* 78 (2013): 215–35.

Feser, Edward. *Aquinas: A Beginner's Guide*. Oneworld, 2009.

———. *Five Proofs of the Existence of God*. Ignatius, 2017.

Field, H. "Causation in a Physical World." In M. J. Loux and D. W. Zimmerman, eds., *The Oxford Handbook of Metaphysics*. Oxford University Press, 2003.

Finlay, Stephen. "Normativity, Necessity, and Tense: A Recipe for Homebaked Normativity." In *Oxford Studies in Metaethics*, edited by Russ Shafer-Landau. Oxford University Press, 2010.

Fischer, John Martin, Robert Kane, Derk Perebom, and Manuel Vargas. *Four Views on Free Will*. Edited by Ernest Sosa. Great Debates in Philosophy. Blackwell, 2007.

Fitzpatrick, Kathleen. *Generous Thinking: A Radical Approach to Saving the University*. Johns Hopkins University Press, 2021.

Flew, Antony, and Gary Habermas. *Did the Resurrection Happen? A Conversation with Gary Habermas and Antony Flew*. Edited by David Baggett. InterVarsity, 2009.

Flint, Thomas P. *Divine Providence: The Molinist Account*. Cornell University Press, 1998.

French, Steven, and Juha Saatsi. "Symmetries and Explanatory Dependencies in Physics." In *Explanation Beyond Causation: Philosophical Perspectives on Non-Causal Explanations*, edited by Alexander Reutlinger and Juha Saatsi. Oxford University Press, 2018.

Frisch, Mathias. "Causation in Physics." In *Stanford Encyclopedia of Philosophy*. Published August 24, 2020. https://plato.stanford.edu/entries/causation-physics/.

Fuentes, Augustin. *Why We Believe: Evolution and the Human Way of Being*. Yale University Press, 2019.

Gamow, George. *One, Two, Three . . . Infinity: Facts and Speculations of Science*. Viking, 1947.

Geroch, Robert. "Space-Time Structure from a Global Viewpoint." In *General Relativity and Cosmology*, edited by B. K. Sachs. Academic Press, 1971.

Godfrey-Smith, William. "Beginning and Ceasing to Exist." *Philosophical Studies* 32, no. 4 (1977): 393–402. https://doi.org/10.1007/BF00368694.

Goff, Philip. "Against Constitutive Forms of Russellian Monism." In *Russellian Monism*, edited by T. Alter and Y. Nagasawa. Oxford University Press, 2015.

———. "Christianity and a God of Limited Power." *Philip Goff* (website). Accessed November 3, 2025. https://tinyurl.com/e5pbu2r5.

———. *Consciousness and Fundamental Reality*. Oxford University Press, 2017.

———. "Cosmopsychism, Micropsychism, and the Grounding Relation." In *The Routledge Handbook of Panpsychism*, edited by William Seager. Routledge, 2019.

———. "Did the Universe Design Itself?" *International Journal for Philosophy of Religion* 85, no. 1 (2018): 99–122. https://doi.org/10.1007/s11153-018-9692-z.

———. *Galileo's Error: Foundations for a New Science of Consciousness*. Pantheon, 2019.

———. "Grounding, Analysis and Russellian Monism." In *The Knowledge Argument Then and Now*, edited by Sam Coleman. Cambridge University Press, 2019.

———. "How Exactly Does Panpsychism Explain Consciousness?" *Journal of Consciousness Studies* 31, no. 3 (2024): 56–82. https://doi.org/10.53765/20512201.31.3.056.

———. "Is Fine-Tuning Evidence for a Multiverse?" *Synthese* 204, no. 1 (2024): 1–22. https://doi.org/10.1007/s11229-024-04621-z.

———. "Is the Universe a Conscious Mind?" *Aeon*, February 8, 2018. https://tinyurl.com/bdzdh2sm.

———. "Panpsychism and Free Will: A Case Study in Liberal Naturalism." *Proceedings of the Aristotelian Society* 120, no. 2 (2020): 123–44. https://doi.org/10.1093/arisoc/aoaa009.

———. "The Phenomenal Bonding Solution to the Combination Problem." In *Panpsychism: Contemporary Perspectives*, edited by G. Brüntrup and L. Jaskolla. Oxford University Press, 2016.

———. "Putting Consciousness First: Replies to Critics." *Journal of Consciousness Studies* 28, no. 9–10 (2021): 289–328.

———. *Why? The Purpose of the Universe*. Oxford University Press, 2023.

Goldschmidt, Tyron. "The Argument from (Natural) Numbers." In *Two Dozen (or So) Arguments for God: The Plantinga Project*, edited by Jerry Walls and Trent Dougherty. Oxford University Press, 2018.

Goodman, Nelson. *Fact, Fiction, and Forecast*. 4th ed. Harvard University Press, 1983.

Greene, Brian. *The Hidden Reality: Parallel Universes and the Deep Laws of the Cosmos*. Vintage, 2011.

Guy, Nathan. "Some of Christianity's Biggest Skeptics Are Becoming Vocal Converts." *Christianity Today* 68, no. 6. September/October 2024. https://tinyurl.com/bdeazdss.

Haji, Ishtiyaque. "Control Conundrums: Modest Libertarianism, Responsibility, and Explanation." *Pacific Philosophical Quarterly* 82, no. 2 (2001): 178–200. https://doi.org/10.1111/1468-0114.00124.

Hart, David Bentley. *Atheist Delusions*. Yale University Press, 2009.

Hawking, Stephen, and Roger Penrose. *The Nature of Space and Time*. The Isaac Newton Institute Series of Lectures. Princeton University Press, 1996.

———. "The Singularities of Gravitational Collapse and Cosmology." *Proceedings of the Royal Society A* 314, no. 1519 (1970): 529–48. https://doi.org/10.1098/rspa.1970.0021.

Hawthorne, John, and Yoaav Isaacs. "Fine-Tuning Fine-Tuning." In *Knowledge, Belief, and God*, edited by Matthew Benton, John Hawthorne, and Dani Rabinowitz. Oxford University Press, 2018.

Heathwood, Chris. "Could Morality Have a Source?" *Journal of Ethics and Social Philosophy* 6, no. 2 (2012): 1–19. https://doi.org/10.26556/jesp.v6i2.62.

Hedrick, Landon. "Once More to the Hotel." *Religious Studies* 58, no. 1 (2022): 18–29. https://doi.org/10.1017/S003441252000013X.

Hendricks, Perry. *Skeptical Theism*. Palgrave Macmillan, 2023.

Henry, Robert. "The Mental Universe." *Nature* 436, no. 29 (2005). https://doi.org/10.1038/436029a.

Hersh, Reuben. "Some Proposals for Reviving the History of Mathematics." In *New Directions in the Philosophy of Mathematics*, edited by Thomas Tymoczko. Berkhäuser, 1986.

Hick, John H. *Evil and the God of Love*. Rev. ed. Harper & Row, 1978.

———. *Philosophy of Religion*. 4th ed. Foundations of Philosophy Series. Pearson, 1990.

Hiley, B. J., and Paavo Pylkkänen. "Can Mind Affect Matter via Active Information?" *Mind and Matter* 3, no. 2 (2005): 8–27.

Hobbes, Thomas. *The Collected Works of Thomas Hobbes*. Edited by William Molesworth. Vol. 1. Routledge, 1992.

Hoffman, Donald. *The Case Against Reality: How Evolution Hid the Truth from Our Eyes*. Norton, 2019.

Hoffman, Donald, and Chetan Prakash. "Objects of Consciousness." *Frontiers in Psychology* 5 (2004): 1–22. https://doi.org/10.3389/fpsyg.2014.00577.

Horgan, Terry. "The Phenomenology of Agency and Freedom: Lessons from Introspection and Lessons from Its Limits." *Humana.Mente* 15 (2011): 77–97.

Hossenfelder, Sabine. "We Don't Know How the Universe Began, and We Will Never Know." *Backreaction*. August 27, 2022. https://backreaction.blogspot.com/2022/08/we-dont-know-how-universe-began-and-we.html.

Howard-Snyder, Daniel. "Divine Openness and Creaturely Non-Resistant Non-Belief." In *Hidden Divinity and Religious Belief: New Perspectives*, edited by Adam Green and Eleonore Stump. Cambridge University Press, 2015.

Howard-Snyder, Daniel, and Paul Moser, eds. *Divine Hiddenness: New Essays*. Cambridge University Press, 2001.

Huemer, Michael. *Ethical Intuitionism*. Palgrave Macmillan, 2005.

———. "Groundless Morals." In *A Debate on God and Morality: What Is the Best*

Account of Objective Moral Values and Duties?, edited by Adam Lloyd Johnson. Routledge, 2021.

Hume, David. *Dialogues Concerning Natural Religion*. 2nd ed. Edited by Richard Popkin. Hackett, 1980.

———. *Dialogues Concerning Natural Religion: And Other Writings*. Edited by Dorothy Coleman. Cambridge University Press, 2007.

———. "Of Miracles." In *David Hume: Writings on Religion*. Open Court, 1993.

Huxley, Thomas Henry. "On the Reception of the 'Origin of Species.'" In *The Life and Letters of Charles Darwin*, edited by Francis Darwin. Vol. 1. Dodo, 2008.

Ijjas, Anna, and Paul Steinhardt. "Bouncing Cosmology Made Simple." *Classical and Quantum Gravity* 35, no. 13 (2018): 1–19. https://doi.org/10.1088/1361-6382/aac482.

———. "Fully Stable Cosmological Solutions with a Non-Singular Classical Bounce." *Physics Letters B* 764, no. 10 (2017): 289–94. https://doi.org/10.1016/j.physletb.2016.11.047.

Inwagan, Peter van. *An Essay on Free Will*. Oxford University Press, 1983.

———. "Free Will Remains a Mystery." *Philosophical Perspectives* 14 (2000): 1–19.

———. "A Materialist Ontology of the Human Person." In *Persons: Human and Divine*, edited by Dean Zimmerman and Peter van Inwagen. Oxford University Press, 2007.

Ismael, J. "Reflections on the Asymmetry of Causation." *Interface Focus* 13 (2023): 1–9.

Jacobs, Alan. *Breaking Bread with the Dead: A Reader's Guide to a More Tranquil Mind*. Penguin, 2020.

———. *How to Think: A Guide for the Perplexed*. Profile, 2017.

James, William. *The Varieties of Religious Experience: A Study in Human Nature*. Longmans, Green, 1902.

Johnson, Adam Lloyd. "A Cabin in the Woods: A Former Statistician Responds to a Critique of the Bayesian Version of the Fine-Tuning Argument for God's Existence." *Eleutheria* 5, no. 1 (2021): 18–31. https://doi.org/10.70623/FREB6449.

———, ed. *A Debate on God and Morality: What Is the Best Account of Objective Moral Values and Duties?* Routledge, 2021.

———. *Divine Love Theory: How the Trinity Is the Source and Foundation of Morality*. Kregel Academic, 2023.

———. "Is It Morally Permissible for Some People to Rape and Murder? Responding to Erik Wielenberg's Argument That Divine Command Theory Fails to Explain How Psychopaths Have Moral Obligations." *Religions* 14, no. 4 (2023): 507. https://doi.org/10.3390/rel14040507.

Johnson, Kelsey. *Into the Unknown: The Quest to Understand the Mysteries of the Cosmos*. Basic Books, 2024.

Jordan, Jeff. "Does Skeptical Theism Lead to Moral Skepticism?" *Philosophy and Phenomenological Research* 72, no. 2 (2006): 403–17. https://doi.org/10.1111/j.1933-1592.2006.tb00567.x.

Joshi, Pankaj. "Spacetime Singularities." In *Springer Handbook of Spacetime*, edited by Abhay Ashtekar and Vesselin Petkov. Springer, 2014.

Joyce, Richard. *The Evolution of Morality*. MIT Press, 2007.

Julian of Norwich. *Revelations of Divine Love*. Translated by Elizabeth Spearing. Edited by A. C. Spearing. Penguin Classics, 1998.

Kant, Immanuel. *Lectures on Philosophical Theology*. Translated by Allen W. Wood and Gertrude M. Clark. Cornell University Press, 2005.

Keathley, Kenneth. *Salvation and Sovereignty: A Molinist Approach*. B&H Academic, 2010.

Keener, Craig S. *Miracles: The Credibility of the New Testament Accounts*. Baker Academic, 2011.

———. *Miracles Today*. Baker Academic, 2021.

Kenney, E. J., ed. *Lucretius: De rerum natura, Book III*. 2nd ed. Cambridge University Press, 2014.

Kidd, Ian James. "Epistemic Vices in Public Debate: The Case of 'New Atheism.'" In *New Atheism: Critical Perspectives and Contemporary Debates*, edited by Christopher R. Cotter, Philip Andrew Quadrio, and Jonathan Tuckett. Sophia Studies in Cross-Cultural Philosophy of Traditions and Cultures 21. Springer, 2017.

Kim, Jaegwon. *Physicalism or Something Near Enough*. Princeton University Press, 2005.

King, Nathan L. *The Excellent Mind: Intellectual Virtues for Everyday Life*. Oxford University Press, 2021.

Koons, Robert C. "Defeasible Reasoning, Special Pleading, and the Cosmological Argument: A Reply to Oppy." *Faith and Philosophy* 18, no. 2 (2001): 192–203. https://doi.org/10.5840/faithphil20011823.

———. "The Grim Reaper Kalam Argument: From Temporal and Causal Finitism to God." In *The Kalām Cosmological Argument: Philosophical Arguments for the Finitude of the Past*, edited by Paul Copan and William Lane Craig. Bloomsbury Academic, 2017.

———. "The Incompatibility of Naturalism and Scientific Realism." In *Naturalism: A Critical Appraisal*, edited by William Lane Craig and J. P. Moreland. Routledge, 2000.

———. "A New Kalām Argument: Revenge of the Grim Reaper." *Noûs* 48, no. 2 (2014): 256–67. https://doi.org/10.1111/j.1468-0068.2012.00858.x.

———. "A New Look at the Cosmological Argument." *American Philosophical Quarterly* 34 (1997): 171–92.

Koons, Robert C., and Alexander R. Pruss. "The Principle of Sufficient Reason and Skepticism." *Philosophical Studies* 178 (2021): 1079–99. https://doi.org/10.1007/s11098-020-01482-3.

Korsgaard, Christine Marion. *The Sources of Normativity*. Edited by Onora O'Neill. Cambridge University Press, 1996.

Kragh, Helge. "Alternative Cosmological Theories." In *The Oxford Handbook of the History of Modern Cosmology*, edited by Helge Kragh and Malcolm S. Longair. Oxford University Press, 2019.

Krauss, Lawrence M. "Cosmology Without Design." *Inference* 5, no. 3 (2020): https://doi.org/10.37282/991819.20.34.

———. *A Universe from Nothing: Why There Is Something Rather Than Nothing*. Atria, 2013.

Ladyman, James, and Don Ross. *Every Thing Must Go: Metaphysics Naturalized*. Oxford University Press, 2007.

Laing, John D. *Middle Knowledge: Human Freedom in Divine Sovereignty*. Kregel, 2018.

Le Guin, Ursula K. "The Ones Who Walk Away from Omelas." In *The Wind's Twelve Quarters: Short Stories*. Harper & Row, 1975.

Leon, Felipe. "Moreland on the Impossibility of Traversing the Infinite: A Critique." *Philo* 14, no. 1 (2011): 32–42. https://doi.org/10.5840/philo20111413.

Leslie, John. "How to Draw Conclusions from a Fine-Tuned Cosmos." In *Physics, Philosophy and Theology: A Common Quest for Understanding*, edited by Robert J. Russell, William R. Stoeger, and George V. Coyne. Vatican Observatory Press, 1988.

———. *Universes*. Routledge, 1989.

Levy, Arnon, and Yair Levy. "Evolutionary Debunking Arguments Meet Evolutionary Science." *Philosophy and Phenomenological Research* 100, no. 3 (2020): 491–509. https://doi.org/10.1111/phpr.12554.

Lewis, C. S. *The Great Divorce*. HarperCollins, 2002.

———. "Mere Christianity." In *The C. S. Lewis Signature Classics*. HarperOne, 2017.

———. "The Problem of Pain." In *The C. S. Lewis Signature Classics*. HarperOne, 2017.

———. *The Weight of Glory and Other Addresses*. HarperOne, 2001.

Lewis, David K. "Causal Explanation." In *Philosophical Papers*. Vol. 2. Oxford University Press, 1987.

———. *Counterfactuals*. Blackwell, 1973.

———. "Desire as Belief II." *Mind* 105, no. 418 (1996): 303–13. https://doi.org/10.1093/mind/105.418.303.

———. *On the Plurality of Worlds*. Blackwell, 1986.

Lewis, Geraint F., and Luke A. Barnes. *A Fortunate Universe*. Cambridge University Press, 2016.

Linville, Mark D. "The Moral Argument." In *The Blackwell Companion to Natural Theology*, edited by William Lane Craig and J. P. Moreland. Wiley-Blackwell, 2009.

Lipton, Peter. *Inference to the Best Explanation*. 2nd ed. Routledge, 2004.

Loftus, John, ed. *God and Horrendous Suffering*. GCRR, 2021.

Longenecker, Michael Tze-Sung. "A Theory of Creation Ex Deo." *Sophia* 61 (2022): 267–82. https://doi.org/10.1007/s11841-020-00801-9.

Lowe, E. J. *Personal Agency: The Metaphysics of Mind and Action*. Oxford University Press, 2010.

Macdonald, Paul A., Jr. "Schellenberg's Noseeum Assumption About Nonresistant Nonbelief." *European Journal for Philosophy of Religion* 13, no. 3 (2021): 139–56.

MacGregor, Kirk. *Luis de Molina*. Zondervan, 2015.

Mackie, J. L. *Ethics: Inventing Right and Wrong*. Penguin, 1977.

———. *The Miracle of Theism: Arguments for and Against the Existence of God*. Oxford University Press, 1982.

Maitzen, Stephen. "Divine Hiddenness and the Demographics of Theism." *Religious Studies* 42 (2006): 177–91. https://doi.org/10.1017/S0034412506008274.

Malament, David. "Observationally Indistinguishable Space-Times." In *Foundations of Space-Time Theories*, edited by John Earman, Clark Glymour, and John Stachel. Minnesota Studies in the Philosophy of Science 8. University of Minnesota Press, 1977.

Malpass, Alex. "All the Time in the World." *Mind* 131, no. 523 (2022): 786–804. https://doi.org/10.1093/mind/fzaa086.

Manchak, J. B. "Can We Know the Global Structure of Spacetime?" *Studies in History and Philosophy of Science Part B: Studies in History and Philosophy of Modern Physics* 40, no. 1 (2009): 53–56. https://doi.org/10.1016/j.shpsb.2008.07.004.

———. "The Universe Is Unknowable from Within It." *IAI News*. January 24, 2025. https://iai.tv/articles/the-universe-is-unknowable-from-within-it-auid-3057.

Markosian, Ned. "What Are Physical Objects?" *Philosophy and Phenomenological Research* 61, no. 2 (2000): 375–95. https://doi.org/10.2307/2653656.

Marsh, Jason. "Darwin and the Problem of Natural Nonbelief." *The Monist* 96, no. 3 (2013): 349–76. https://doi.org/10.5840/monist201396316.

Mavrodes, George. "Religion and the Queerness of Morality." In *Ethical Theory: Classical and Contemporary Readings*, 2nd ed., edited by Louis P. Pojman. Wadsworth, 1995.

McBrayer, Justin P., and Philip Swenson. "Scepticism About the Argument from

Divine Hiddenness." *Religious Studies* 48, no. 2 (2012): 129–50. https://doi.org/10.1017/s003441251100014x.

McFadden, Johnjoe. "Integrating Information in the Brain's EM Field: The Cemi Field Theory of Consciousness." *Neuroscience of Consciousness* 2020, no. 1 (2020): 1–13. https://doi.org/10.1093/nc/niaa016.

McKown, Delos. *The Mythmaker's Magic.* Prometheus, 1993.

McPherson, Tristram. "Supervenience in Ethics." In *Stanford Encyclopedia of Philosophy.* Last modified October 22, 2019. https://plato.stanford.edu/entries/supervenience-ethics/.

Meek, Esther L. *Longing to Know*. Brazos, 2003.

Mele, Alfred R. *Free Will and Luck*. Oxford University Press, 2006.

Menzel, Christopher. "The Argument from Collections." In *Two Dozen (Or So) Arguments for God: The Plantinga Project*, edited by Jerry Walls and Trent Dougherty. Oxford University Press, 2018.

Meyer, Steven C. *Return of the God Hypothesis: Three Scientific Discoveries That Reveal the Mind Behind the Universe*. HarperOne, 2021.

Milton, John. *Paradise Lost.* Edited by John Leonard. Penguin Classics, 2003.

Monod, Jacques. *Chance and Necessity: An Essay on the Natural Philosophy of Modern Biology*. Knopf, 1971.

Montanez, George D. "A Unified Model of Complex Specified Information." *BIO-Complexity* 2018, no. 4 (2018): 1–26. https://doi.org/10.5048?BIO-C.2018.4.

Moreland, J. P. "The Kalam Cosmological Argument." In *Philosophy of Religion: Selected Readings*, 2nd ed., edited by Michael Peterson, William Hasker, Bruce Reichenbach, and David Rasinger. Oxford University Press, 2001.

Morris, Dolores G. *Believing Philosophy: A Guide to Becoming a Christian Philosopher*. Zondervan Academic, 2021.

———. "Sleep Training, Day Care, and Swim Lessons: Skeptical Theism and the Parent-Child Analogy." *Faith and Philosophy* 40, no. 1 (2023): 24–42. https://doi.org/10.37977/faithphil.2023.40.1.2.

———. "Toward a Theology of Tension: A Response to Dru Johnson." *Philosophia Christi* 26, no. 2 (2024): 247–65. https://doi.org/10.5840/pc202426220.

Morriston, Wes. "God and the Ontological Foundation of Morality." *Religious Studies* 48, no. 1 (2012): 15–34. https://doi.org/10.1017/s0034412510000740.

———. "Infinity, Time, and Successive Addition." *Australasian Journal of Philosophy* 100, no. 1 (2022): 70–85. https://doi.org/10.1080/00048402.2020.1865426.

Moser, Paul. "Divine Hiding." In *Divine Hiddenness: New Essays*, edited by Daniel Howard-Snyder and Paul Moser. Cambridge University Press, 2001.

———. *The Elusive God: Reorienting Religious Epistemology*. Cambridge University Press, 2008.

Mullins, Ryan. *The End of the Timeless God.* Oxford University Press, 2016.

Murray, Michael J. "Coercion and the Hiddenness of God." *American Philosophical Quarterly* 30, no. 1 (1993): 27–38.

———. "Deus Absconditus." In *Divine Hiddenness: New Essays*, edited by Daniel Howard-Snyder and Paul Moser. Cambridge University Press, 2001.

Nagasawa, Yujin. "Silence, Evil and Shusaku Endo." In *Hidden Divinity and Religious Belief: New Perspectives*, edited by Adam Green and Eleonore Stump. Cambridge University Press, 2016.

Nagel, Thomas. *The Last Word.* Oxford University Press, 1997.

———. *Mind and Cosmos: Why the Materialist Neo-Darwinian Conception of Nature Is Almost Certainly False.* Oxford University Press, 2012.

Nelson, Roger. "Global Consciousness and the Coronavirus—A Snapshot." *The Global Consciousness Project.* May 9, 2020. https://global-mind.org/papers/pdf/GCP.Corona.edgescience.fin.pdf.

Nixey, Catherine. *Heretic: Jesus Christ and the Other Sons of God.* HarperCollins, 2024.

Norton, John. "The Cosmological Woes of Newtonian Gravitation Theory." In *The Expanding Worlds of General Relativity.* Vol. 7 of *Einstein Studies*, edited by Hubert Goenner, Jürgen Renn, Jim Ritter, and Tilman Sauer. Birkhauser, 1999.

Oderberg, David. "The Beginning of Existence." *International Philosophical Quarterly* 43, no. 2 (2003): 145–57. https://doi.org/10.5840/ipq20034325.

Oppy, Graham. *Philosophical Perspectives on Infinity.* Cambridge University Press, 2006.

Paine, Thomas. *The Age of Reason.* Citadel, 1974.

———. *The Age of Reason: Being an Investigation of True and Fabulous Theology.* J. S. Jordan, 1795.

Papineau, David. "The Rise of Physicalism." In *Physicalism and Its Discontents*, edited by Carl Gillett and Barry Loewer. Cambridge University Press, 2001.

———. *The Rise of Physicalism.* Cambridge University Press, 2009.

Parfit, Derek. "Why Anything? Why This?" *London Review of Books* 20, no. 3 (1998): 22–25.

Pascal, Blaise. *Pensées.* Translated by A. J. Krailsheimer. Penguin, 1995.

Paul VI. "Nostra Aetate: Declaration on the Relation of the Church to Non-Christian Religions." Accessed April 27, 2025. https://www.vatican.va/archive/hist_councils/ii_vatican_council/documents/vat-ii_decl_19651028_nostra-aetate_en.html.

Penrose, Roger. *The Emperor's New Mind: Concerning Computers, Minds, and the Laws of Physics.* Oxford University Press, 1989.

Pew Research Center. "The Global Religious Landscape." December 18, 2012. https://www.pewresearch.org/religion/2012/12/18/global-religious-landscape-exec/.

———. "Religion and Science in the United States." November 5, 2009. https://www.pewresearch.org/religion/2009/11/05/scientists-and-belief/.

———. "Spirituality Among Americans." December 7, 2023. https://www.pewresearch.org/religion/2023/12/07/spirituality-among-americans/.

Piper, Mark. "Skeptical Theism and the Problem of Moral Aporia." *International Journal for Philosophy of Religion* 62, no. 2 (2007): 65–79. https://doi.org/10.1007/s11153-007-9128-7.

Plantinga, Alvin. *Does God Have a Nature?* Marquette University Press, 1980.

———. *God, Freedom, and Evil.* Eerdmans, 1977.

———. "Is Belief in God Properly Basic?" *Noûs* 15, no. 1 (1981): 41–51. https://doi.org/10.2307/2215239.

———. *The Nature of Necessary.* Oxford University Press, 1974.

———. *Warranted Christian Belief.* Oxford University Press, 2000.

Plantinga, Alvin, and Michael Tooley. *Knowledge of God.* Wiley-Blackwell, 2008.

Plato. *The Laws.* Translated by Trevor J. Saunders. Penguin, 1975.

Polanyi, Michael. *Personal Knowledge: Towards a Post-Critical Philosophy.* University of Chicago Press, 1958.

Polkinghorne, John C. *The Polkinghorne Reader: Science, Faith, and the Search for Meaning.* Edited by Thomas Jay Oord. Templeton, 2010.

Popławski, Nikodem. "Cosmology with Torsion: An Alternative to Cosmic Inflation." *Physics Letters B* 694, no. 3 (2010): 181–85. https://doi.org/10.1016/j.physletb.2010.09.056.

———. "Universe in a Black Hole in Einstein-Cartan Gravity." *The Astrophysical Journal* 832, no. 96 (2016): 1–8. https://doi.org/10.3847/0004-637X/832/2/96.

Poston, Ted, and Trent Dougherty. "Divine Hiddenness and the Nature of Belief." *Religious Studies* 43, no. 2 (2007): 183–98. https://doi.org/10.1017/s0034412507008943.

Pruss, Alexander R. *Infinity, Causation, and Paradox.* Oxford University Press, 2018.

———. "The Principle of Sufficient Reason and Probability." *Oxford Studies in Metaphysics* 10 (2017): 261–78. https://doi.org/10.1093/acprof:oso/9780198791973.003.0011.

———. *The Principle of Sufficient Reason: A Reassessment.* Cambridge University Press, 2006.

Pruss, Alexander, and Joshua Rasmussen. *Necessary Existence.* Oxford University Press, 2018.

Quine, W. V. O. "Two Dogmas of Empiricism." *Philosophical Review* 60, no. 1 (1951): 20–43. https://doi.org/10.2307/2266637.

Rahner, Karl. "Anonymous Christianity and the Missionary Task of the Church." In *Theological Investigations*. Translated by D. Bourke. Vol. 12. Darton, Longman & Todd, 1974.

Rasmussen, Joshua. *Who Are You, Really?* InterVarsity, 2023.

Rea, Michael C. "Divine Hiddenness, Divine Silence." In *Philosophy of Religion*, edited by Louis P. Pojman. Mayfield, 1987.

———. *The Hiddenness of God*. Oxford University Press, 2018.

Rees, Martin. *Just Six Numbers: The Deep Forces That Shape the Universe*. Basic Books, 2000.

Reichenbach, Bruce. "Cosmological Arguments." In *Stanford Encyclopedia of Philosophy*. Last modified June 30, 2022. https://plato.stanford.edu/entries/cosmological-argument/.

Reid, Thomas. *Essays on the Active Powers of the Human Mind*. MIT Press, 1969.

Rice University. "First Worldwide Survey of Religion and Science: No, Not All Scientists Are Atheists." *Phys.Org*. December 3, 2015. https://tinyurl.com/bk4ysup6.

Rooney, James Dominic. "We Deserve It: An Augustinian Response to Divine Hiddenness Arguments." *New Blackfriars* 105, no. 6 (2024): 636–50. https://doi.org/10.1017/nbf.2024.52.

Rovelli, Carlo. "How Oriented Causation Is Rooted into Thermodynamics." *Philosophy of Physics* 1, no. 1 (2023): 1–14.

———. *Reality Is Not What It Seems: The Journey to Quantum Gravity*. Random House, 2014.

Ruse, Michael. *Taking Darwin Seriously*. Blackwell, 1986.

Russell, Bertrand. *The Analysis of Matter*. Kegan Paul, Trench, Trubner, 1927.

———. "The Free Man's Worship." *The Independent Review* 1 (1903): 415–24.

———. "On the Notion of Cause." *Proceedings of the Aristotelian Society* 13, no. 1 (1912): 1–26. https://doi.org/10.1093/aristotelian/13.1.1.

Salmon, Wesley. *Scientific Explanation and the Causal Structure of the World*. Princeton University Press, 1984.

Sartre, Jean-Paul. *Existentialism Is a Humanism*. Translated by Carol Macomber. Yale University Press, 2007.

Schaffer, Jonathan. "What Not to Multiply Without Necessity." *Australasian Journal of Philosophy* 93, no. 4 (2015): 644–64. https://doi.org/10.1080/00048402.2014.992447.

Schellenberg, J. L. *Divine Hiddenness and Human Reason*. Cornell University Press, 1993.

———. "Divine Hiddenness: Part 1 (Recent Work on the Hiddenness Argument)." *Philosophy Compass* 12, no. 4 (2017): e12355. https://doi.org/10.1111/phc3.12355.

———. "Divine Hiddenness: Part 2 (Recent Enlargements of the Discussion)." *Philosophy Compass* 12, no. 4 (2017): e12413. https://doi.org/10.1111/phc3.12413.

———. "The Hiddenness Argument." *Annals of Philosophy* 69, no. 3 (2021): 63–66. https://doi.org/10.18290/rf21693-4.

———. *The Hiddenness Argument: Philosophy's New Challenge to Belief in God.* Oxford University Press, 2015.

———. "The Hiddenness Problem and the Problem of Evil." *Faith and Philosophy* 27, no. 1 (2010): 45–60. https://doi.org/10.5840/faithphil20102713.

Schmid, Joseph C., and Alex Malpass. "Benardete Paradoxes, Causal Finitism, and the Unsatisfiable Pair Diagnosis." *Mind* 134, no. 534 (2025): 397–421.

Schroeder, Mark. "Cudworth and Normative Explanations." *Journal of Ethics and Social Philosophy* 1, no. 3 (2005): 1–28. https://doi.org/10.26556/jesp.v1i3.15.

Scotus, John Duns. *A Treatise on God as First Principle (De primo principio).* 2nd ed. Translated by Allan B. Wolter. Franciscan Herald, 1983.

Searle, John R. *The Construction of Social Reality.* Free Press, 1997.

Sehon, Scott. "The Problem of Evil: Skeptical Theism Leads to Moral Paralysis." *International Journal for Philosophy of Religion* 67, no. 2 (2010): 67–80. https://doi.org/10.1007/s11153-009-9213-1.

Shackel, Nicholas. "The Form of the Benardete Dichotomy." *British Journal for the Philosophy of Science* 56, no. 2 (2005): 397–417. https://doi.org/10.1093/bjps/axi121.

Shafer-Landau, Russ. *Moral Realism: A Defence.* Oxford University Press, 2003.

Shermer, Michael. *The Believing Brain: From Ghosts and Gods to Politics and Conspiracies—How We Construct Beliefs and Reinforce Them as Truths.* Times, 2011.

Sidgwick, Henry. *The Methods of Ethics.* 7th ed. Hackett, 1981.

Singer, Peter. *Animal Rights and Human Obligations.* Prentice Hall, 1976.

Siniscalchi, Glenn B. "Contemporary Trends in Atheistic Criticism of Thomistic Natural Theology." *Heythrop Journal* 59, no. 4 (2018): 689–706. https://doi.org/10.1111/j.1468-2265.2012.00777.x.

Skarsaune, Knut Olav. "Darwin and Moral Realism: Survival of the Iffiest." *Philosophical Studies* 152, no. 2 (2011): 229–43. https://doi.org/10.1007/s11098-009-9473-8.

Smart, J. J. C. "Laws of Nature and Cosmic Coincidence." *Philosophical Quarterly* 35, no. 140 (1985): 272–80.

———. *Our Place in the Universe: A Metaphysical Discussion.* Blackwell, 1989.

Smeenk, Chris. "Philosophical Aspects of Cosmology." In *The Oxford Handbook of the History of Modern Cosmology*, edited by Helge Kragh and Malcolm S. Longair. Oxford University Press, 2019.

Smith, James K. A. *You Are What You Love: The Spiritual Power of Habit*. Baker Publishing Group, 2016.

Sorini, Daniele, John A. Peacock, and Lucas Lombriser. "The Impact of the Cosmological Constant on Past and Future Star Formation." *Monthly Notices of the Royal Astronomical Society* 535, no. 2 (2024): 1449–74. https://doi.org/10.1093/mnras/stae2236.

Spade, Paul, Claude Panaccio, and Jenny Pelletier. "William of Ockham." In *Stanford Encyclopedia of Philosophy*. Last modified September 11, 2024. https://plato.stanford.edu/entries/ockham/#OckhRazo.

Stavrakopoulou, Francesca. *God: An Anatomy*. Knopf, 2022.

Steiner, Mark. *The Applicability of Mathematics as a Philosophical Problem*. Harvard University Press, 1998.

Steinhardt, Paul, and Neil Turok. "Cosmic Evolution in a Cyclic Universe." *Physical Review D* 65, no. 12 (2002): 1–53. https://doi.org/10.1103/PhysRevD.65.126003.

———. *Endless Universe: Beyond the Big Bang—Rewriting Cosmic History*. Broadway, 2007.

Stenger, Victor. *The Fallacy of Fine-Tuning: Why the Universe Is Not Designed for Us*. Prometheus, 2011.

Street, Sharon. "A Darwinian Dilemma for Realist Theories of Value." *Philosophical Studies* 127, no. 1 (2006): 109–66. https://doi.org/10.1007/s11098-005-1726-6.

———. "If Everything Happens for a Reason, Then We Don't Know What Reasons Are: Why the Price of Theism Is Normative Skepticism." In *Challenges to Religious and Moral Belief: Disagreement and Evolution*, edited by Michael Bergmann and Patrick Kain. Oxford University Press, 2018.

Stump, Eleonore. "Moral Responsibility Without Alternative Possibilities." In *Moral Responsibility and Alternative Possibilities: Essays on the Importance of Alternative Possibilities*, edited by David Widerker and Michael McKenna. Ashgate, 2006.

———. "Theology and the Knowledge of Persons." *Roczniki Filozoficzne (Annals of Philosophy)* 69, no. 3 (2021): 9–27. https://tinyurl.com/2s3f7fvx.

Susskind, Leonard. *The Cosmic Landscape: String Theory and the Illusion of Intelligent Design*. Back Bay Books, 2005.

Swartz, Norman. *The Concept of Physical Law*. Cambridge University Press, 1985.

Swinburne, Richard. *The Coherence of Theism*. Oxford University Press, 1977.

———. *The Existence of God*. Oxford University Press, 1991.

Taliaferro, Charles. "Masked Man." In *Bad Arguments: 100 of the Most Important*

Fallacies in Western Philosophy, edited by Robert Arp, Steven Barbone, and Michael Bruce. Wiley & Sons, 2018.

Tegmark, Max. "Parallel Universes." In *Science and Ultimate Reality*, ed. J. D. Barrow, P. C. W. Davies, and C. L. Harper. Cambridge University Press, 2004.

———. *Our Mathematical Universe: My Quest for the Ultimate Nature of Reality*. Knopf, 2014.

Thomson, J. Anderson, Jr. *Why We Believe in God(s): A Concise Guide to the Science of Faith*. Pitchstone, 2011.

Tolstoy, Leo. *A Confession*. Translated by Jane Kentish. Penguin, 2008.

Torrey, E. Fuller. *Evolving Brains, Emerging Gods: Early Humans and the Origins of Religion*. Columbia University Press, 2017.

Trisel, Brooke Alan. "God's Silence as an Epistemological Concern." *Philosophical Forum* 43, no. 4 (2012): 383–93. https://doi.org/10.1111/j.1467-9191.2012.00433.x.

Trueman, Carl R. *The Rise and Triumph of the Modern Self*. Crossway, 2020.

Vavova, Katia. "Evolutionary Debunking of Moral Realism." *Philosophy Compass* 10, no. 2 (2015): 104–16. https://doi.org/10.1111/phc3.12194.

Vilenkin, Alexander. *Many Worlds in One: The Search for Other Universes*. Hill & Wang, 2006.

Wall, Aaron. "The Generalized Second Law Implies a Quantum Singularity Theorem." *Classical and Quantum Gravity* 30, no. 16 (2013): 1–35. https://doi.org/10.1088/0264-9381/30/16/165003.

Ward, Keith. *The Evidence for God: The Case for the Existence of the Spiritual Dimension*. Darton, Longman & Todd, 2014.

Weatherford, Roy. *Foundations of Probability Theory*. Routledge & Kegan Paul, 1982.

Webb, William J., and Gordan K. Oeste. "Bloody, Brutal, and Barbaric? Online Appendixes," IVP Press, 2019, https://tinyurl.com/5ccfu3da.

———. *Bloody, Brutal, and Barbaric? Wrestling with Troubling War Texts*. IVP Academic, 2019.

Weinberg, Steven. "A Designer Universe?" *Skeptical Inquirer* 25, no. 5 (2001): 64–68.

———. *Dreams of a Final Theory: The Scientist's Search for the Ultimate Laws of Nature*. Vintage, 1993.

———. "Life in the Universe." *Scientific American Magazine* 271, no. 4 (1994): 44–49. https://doi.org/10.1038/scientificamerican1094-44.

Welty, Greg. "Theistic Conceptual Realism." In *Beyond the Control of God? Six Views on the Problem of God and Abstract Objects*, edited by Paul M. Gould. Bloomsbury Academic, 2014.

Wielenberg, Erik. "On the Evolutionary Debunking of Morality." *Ethics* 120, no. 3 (2010): 441–64. https://doi.org/10.1086/652292.

———. "The Parent–Child Analogy and the Limits of Skeptical Theism." *International Journal for Philosophy of Religion* 78, no. 3 (2015): 301–14. https://doi.org/10.1007/s11153-015-9533-2.

———. *Robust Ethics: The Metaphysics and Epistemology of Godless Normative Realism*. Oxford University Press, 2014.

Wigner, Eugene. "The Unreasonable Effectiveness of Mathematics in the Natural Sciences." *Communications on Pure and Applied Mathematics* 13, no. 1 (1960): 1–14.

Wills, Gary. *Saint Augustine*. Penguin, 1999.

Wray, K. Brad. *Resisting Scientific Realism*. Cambridge University Press, 2007.

Wright, N. T. *The Resurrection of the Son of God*. Vol. 3 of *Christian Origins and the Question of God*. Fortress, 2003.

Wykstra, Stephen. "The Humean Obstacle to Evidential Arguments from Suffering: On Avoiding the Evils of 'Appearance.'" *International Journal for Philosophy of Religion* 16, no. 2 (1984): 73–93.

Zagzebski, Linda T. *Divine Motivation Theory*. Cambridge University Press, 2004.

Zarepour, Mohammad Saleh. "Counting to Infinity, Successive Addition, and the Length of the Past." *International Journal for Philosophy of Religion* 92, no. 3 (2022): 167–76. https://doi.org/10.1007/s11153-022-09843-0.

Zuckerman, Phil. "Atheism: Contemporary Numbers and Patterns." In *The Cambridge Companion to Atheism*, edited by Michael Martin. Cambridge University Press, 2007.

———. *Society Without God: What the Least Religious Nations Can Tell Us About Contentment*. New York University Press, 2008.

Zwiebach, Barton. *A First Course in String Theory*. Cambridge University Press, 2004.

Index of Authors

Index of Subjects